Memory in Autism

Many people with autism spectrum disorders (ASDs) are remarkably proficient at remembering how things look and sound, even years after an event. They are also good at rote learning and establishing habits and routines. Some even have encyclopedic memories. However, all individuals with ASD have difficulty in recalling personal memories and reliving experiences, and less able people may have additional difficulty in memorising facts. This book assembles new research on memory in autism to examine why this happens and the effects it has on people's lives. The contributors utilise recent advances in the understanding of normal memory systems and their breakdown as frameworks for analysing the neuropsychology and neurobiology of memory in autism. The unique patterning of memory functions across the spectrum illuminates difficulties with sense of self, emotion processing, mental time travel, language and learning, providing a window into the nature and causes of autism itself.

Jill Boucher is Professor of Psychology and member of the Autism Research Group in the Department of Psychology at City University, London.

Dermot Bowler is Professor of Psychology and Director of the Autism Research Group in the Department of Psychology at City University, London.

Memory in Autism

Edited by
Jill Boucher
and
Dermot Bowler

CAMBRIDGE
UNIVERSITY PRESS

CAMBRIDGE UNIVERSITY PRESS
Cambridge, New York, Melbourne, Madrid, Cape Town, Singapore, São Paulo,
Delhi

Cambridge University Press
The Edinburgh Building, Cambridge CB2 8RU, UK

Published in the United States of America by Cambridge University Press,
New York

www.cambridge.org
Information on this title: www.cambridge.org/9780521862882

First published 2008

Printed in the United Kingdom at the University Press, Cambridge

A catalogue record for this publication is available from the British Library

Library of Congress Cataloguing in Publication data
Memory in autism/edited by Jill Boucher and Dermot Bowler.
   p.   cm.
Includes bibliographical references.
ISBN 978-0-521-86288-2
1. Autism – Psychological aspects.   2. Memory – Physiological aspects.
3. Memory disorders – Pathophysiology.   I. Boucher, Jill.   II. Bowler,
Dermot M.   [DNLM: 1. Autistic Disorder – psychology.   2. Cognition.
3. Memory – physiology.   4. Memory Disorders – physiopathology.
WM 203.5 M533   2008]
RC 553.A88M42   2008
616.85′882–dc22
                                                              2007050025

ISBN 978-0-521-86288-2

We would like to dedicate this book to the memory of Beate Hermelin, a pioneer in the experimental psychology of autism.

Contents

Tables

Figures

Contributors

ANNA-LYNNE ADLAM, Institute of Child Health, University College London

JOCELYNE BACHEVALIER, Department of Neurobiology and Anatomy, University of Texas Medical School

DORIT BEN SHALOM, Zlotowski Center for Neuroscience, Ben-Gurion University of the Negev

SALLY BIGHAM, Department of Psychology, Thames Valley University, London

JILL BOUCHER, Autism Research Group, Department of Psychology, City University, London

DERMOT BOWLER, Autism Research Group, Department of Psychology, City University, London

MICHELLE DAWSON, Hôpital Rivière-des-Prairies, Université de Montréal

ROBERT DELONG, Department of Pediatrics, Duke University Medical Center

YIFAT FARAN, Zlotowski Center for Neuroscience, Ben-Gurion University of the Negev

DAVID GADIAN, Institute of Child Health, University College London

SEBASTIAN GAIGG, Autism Research Group, Department of Psychology, City University, London

JOHN GARDINER, Department of Psychology, University of Sussex

GERALD GOLDSTEIN, Pittsburgh VA Health Care System

BEATE HERMELIN, Department of Psychology, Goldsmiths University of London

PETER HOBSON, Institute of Child Health, University College London

RITA JORDAN, School of Education, University of Birmingham

SOPHIE LIND, Autism Research Group, Department of Psychology, City University, London

JONATHAN S. MARTIN, Memory Research Unit, Department of Psychology, City University, London

ANDREW MAYES, School of Psychological Sciences, University of Manchester

NANCY MINSHEW, Center for the Neural Basis of Cognition, University of Pittsburgh School of Medicine

LAURENT MOTTRON, Hôpital Rivière-des-Prairies, Université de Montréal

MARIE POIRIER, Memory Research Unit, Department of Psychology, City University, London

LINDA PRING, Department of Psychology, Goldsmiths University of London

CLAIRE SALMOND, Institute of Child Health, University College London

BRENDA SMITH, Department of Psychology, University of Sussex

ISABELLE SOULIÈRES, Hôpital Rivière-des-Prairies, Université de Montréal

MOTOMI TOICHI, School of Medicine, Kyoto University

FARANEH VARGHA-KHADEM, Institute of Child Health, University College London

SARA WEBB, Center on Human Development and Disability, University of Washington

DIANNE WILLIAMS, University of Pittsburgh School of Medicine

Foreword

Despite the fact that memory in people with autism spectrum disorders (ASD) has been researched for over fifty years, there has been very little in the way of attempts to synthesize or codify the findings. The two most notable such attempts are the seminal monographs *Psychological Experiments with Autistic Children* (Hermelin & O'Connor, 1970) and *Seeing and Hearing and Space and Time* (O'Connor & Hermelin, 1978), now over thirty years old. The period since the publication of these two books has seen considerable changes in the landscape of autism research, the most important of which have been an enlargement of the concept of 'autism' to encompass a spectrum of conditions that includes but is not limited to that first described by Kanner (1943), and the mushrooming of research into all aspects of the spectrum.

Memory research has grown in parallel with this general increase. One of us (JB) was heavily involved in the early phase of this growth, in particular developing the hypothesis that the patterning of memory functions, at least in lower-functioning individuals with ASD, had some parallels with that seen in the amnesic syndrome. This work continued into the 1980s but then diminished, partly because of the lack of a community of scholars interested in the topic, but also because memory was not seen as a particular problem in those high-functioning individuals who were becoming the main focus of research. These things changed, however, when in the late 1990s people such as Nancy Minshew and DB and his colleagues became interested in memory patterns in higher-functioning individuals including those with Asperger syndrome. At this time, modularist accounts of ASD were increasingly called into question, and researchers began to seek out other explanations for the patterning of autistic behaviour, this time in terms of more general psychological processes. It is this desire to understand ASD in terms of a developmentally unfolding patterning of general processes such as attention, learning and memory that has driven the approaches to research adopted by both of us. Our position contrasts with those who try to explain the surface patterning of behaviour by invoking damage to modular systems that were thought to drive such patterns in a highly specific way. From our different perspectives we both share the view that studying memory enables us to understand better the inner world of the person with ASD as well as to unpack the relation between language and cognition, especially in those whose language development is atypical. Increasing understanding in these areas will help to develop a clearer picture of underlying brain functioning in this population. Thus, for both of us, we do not see ASD as being 'due to a problem with memory'. Rather we see the unique patterning of memory functions in this population as providing a window into the causes of those behavioural characteristics that are defining features of conditions on the spectrum. For these reasons, we felt that it was time to bring together an up-to-date compendium of research on memory in ASD.

The organization of the book reflects different facets of current memory research in ASD. The Preface by Hobson and Hermelin sets the scene by reminding us of the importance of a consideration of memory to an understanding of ASD. It also serves as a link with the earlier work in the field. The introductory chapter by Gardiner outlines the important changes in how psychologists understand and conceptualize human memory and serves to up-date what for many of us is a relatively unreconstructed undergraduate knowledge of the topic. The later sections include chapters that cover neurobiological and psychological aspects of memory. These sections consist mostly of reports by scientists of their most recent work in specific areas and are designed to give readers a flavour of the latest findings and the development of ideas in the different fields. The final section broadens focus in three ways: by providing an applied perspective, by casting a critical eye and by attempting to identify recurrent and promising themes in the field.

As a compendium of approaches to different facets of the same underlying phenomenon, this is a book more to be dipped into than read from cover to cover. Acknowledging this aspect of the book has led to a number of editorial decisions on our part. For example, anyone reading the book right through will encounter quite a bit of repetition of material. As editors, we faced the choice of cutting much of this repetition by making heavy use of cross-referencing. However, we felt that this would be frustrating for people who wished to read only a subset of the contributions. We therefore decided to leave each author to provide what they thought was the best background against which to set their work. In this respect, we have limited our editorial interventions to ensuring that a reasonably consistent account of the earlier literature emerges across chapters.

We also had to make a number of decisions on how diagnosis, classi-fication and labelling should be reported. Terminology in the field of autism research has become a minefield. Forty years ago, research was limited to studies of 'autistic children' of the kind described by Kanner. Since then, the phenomenon of 'autism' (i.e. the symptomological cluster manifested by such children) has been extended to a spectrum of con-ditions that are now often referred to as 'autism spectrum disorders' or ASDs. In this book we have, as far as possible, allowed authors to use their preferred terminology, with the result that 'people with autism', 'people with ASD' or 'people with an ASD' are used interchangeably. We have also allowed interchangeable use of the terms 'autism' and 'ASD' to refer to the symptomological picture of these conditions. In all but one chapter, we have insisted that the formula 'people/children/adults/individuals with ...' be used. We have asked authors to avoid the use of 'patients' or 'suffering from'. The one exception to all this is in Chapter 17 by Mottron and colleagues who, for reasons that they explain, prefer the term 'autistics'.

Related to the question of how to describe autism in general terms is the issue of when and how to distinguish between high- and low-functioning autism (HFA and LFA) and, in the case of the former, how to treat the reporting of Asperger syndrome (AS). In general, HFA is used to refer to any individual with language and intellectual attainments currently within normal limits. In this respect, the term includes AS but is broader and less committed to the developmental history require-ments of current diagnostic systems. Where authors have chosen to use the term AS, we have tried to ensure that there is some clarification on whether this is on the basis of strict criteria including the requirements on language development or on looser criteria based solely on present-state evaluations. Terminological issues are not just limited to clinical groups. When reference is made to children, we have insisted on the use of 'typically developing' although we have allowed the use of 'normal adults'. We have also asked authors to use the term 'comparison' when referring to groups with whom the performance of an ASD group is compared. We prefer this term to the widely used 'control group/participants' because, technically, the investigator does not exercise any control as is the case when a control task is used (see Burack *et al.*, 2004 for further discussion).

We should both very much like to thank all the contributors to this volume, all of whom delivered their manuscripts and revisions in a timely fashion. During the preparation of the book, JB was supported by the Economic and Social Research Council and DB by the Wellcome Trust, the Medical Research Council and the Economic and Social

Research Council, as well as by the Psychology Department of City University, London.

Jill Boucher
City University, London

Dermot Bowler
City University, London

References

Burack, J. A., Iarocci, G., Flanagan, T. D. & Bowler, D. M. (2004). On Mosaics and melting pots: conceptual considerations of comparison and matching questions and strategies. *Journal of Autism and Developmental Disorders, 34,* 65–73.

Hermelin, B. & O'Connor, N. (1970). *Psychological experiments with autistic children.* Oxford: Pergamon Press.

Kanner, L. (1943). Autistic disturbances of affective contact. *Nervous Child, 2,* 217–250.

O'Connor, N. & Hermelin, B. (1978). *Seeing and hearing and space and time.* London: Academic Press.

Preface

Peter Hobson and Beate Hermelin

'It's a poor sort of memory that only works backwards', the Queen remarked.　　　　Lewis Carroll, *Through the Looking Glass* (1872), chapter 5

Memory is a funny thing. It is exercised in the present, but (we fondly suppose) it conjures up the past, or perhaps more accurately, what we register and recall from a time gone by. Sometimes it is only the effects of past experience that feature in memory – what we have come to know the world to be like, what we have learned words signify, what we feel we know is linked with what – and sometimes it seems more like revisiting what we experienced some while back (whether from a distant age, or from the moment just faded), how it was to be the person who we were then, seeing and feeling and thinking those things that we saw and felt and thought. Without memory of the world, or without memory of what we were when engaging with that world, we would become shadow-beings inhabiting a theatre of spectral forms.

As the Queen of *Through the Looking Glass* remarks, memory can't just be a matter of working backwards. Rather, it is the backward-seeming reach of personal experience that also exists in the present and the future, structured and understood by ways of knowing and communicating that are profoundly influenced by what we, the human community, share and judge alike. Memory shows us how we mentally reconstruct what has, and had, meaning.

But what has this rather abstract circumspection got to do with the experimental psychology of memory in individuals with autism? Rather a lot, we think. In order to explain why, perhaps we might begin by casting back . . .

Memoirs

Picture a time around fifty years ago, some twenty years or so after Kanner (1943) had described the syndrome of autism. By now the condition was widely acknowledged, but almost completely obscure. For some time, Neil O'Connor and Beate Hermelin had been working with severely learning-disabled children. In the course of this research, they came across some children who had the diagnosis of autism. When they explored the literature on autism, they found rich descriptions of the children's behaviour, but almost no experimental research. Just as dismaying, they were confronted with theoretical accounts that were mainly variations on the theme of autism as the outcome of aberrant parent–child relations. Quite simply, this did not square with what they encountered with the children and their parents. Indeed from what parents and teachers recounted, for example how their children looked at people's faces in the same way as they looked at the objects around them, it seemed that there was something fundamentally unusual in their perception of, as well as thinking about, the world.

So it was that Hermelin and O'Connor decided to explore in what respects these remarkable children differed from matched children without autism who were similar in chronological and mental age. They studied abnormalities that were not restricted to the domain of cognition, as narrowly conceived, but extended across a spectrum of abilities in perception, language, intellectual organization, and responsiveness to the animate (people) as well as inanimate world. Looking back, it is striking how others had not systematically investigated such psychological functions in and through children with autism – and rather brilliant that now, new vistas of uncharted territory could be mapped through the deployment of carefully controlled and specifically focused experiments. Here was a new way of looking at autism, and beyond this, through the application of the experimental method to an intriguing and perplexing condition, a new perspective on mental processes as such.

We shall not attempt to summarize findings from this work. By way of grounding the remainder of this preface, however, we shall quote the formulation that Hermelin and O'Connor offered at the conclusion of their book, *Psychological Experiments with Autistic Children* (1970): 'We regard the inability of autistic children to encode stimuli meaningfully as their basic cognitive deficit' (p. 129).

This formulation was both specific and prescient, yet it begged as many questions as it answered – as any self-respecting scientific advance needs to do. There is *something* about perceiving and organizing meaningful material that is essential to what makes autism 'autism'. With appropriate methodology, one can specify how the abnormality is manifest in a variety of settings. Moreover, this something is dissociable from other facets of intelligence that appear to be relatively unimpaired or, if impaired, less unusual in quality. But *the source* of the dysfunction remains an open question. In the ensuing years, Hermelin and O'Connor gave increasing prominence to the children's difficulties in perceiving and relating to people on the one hand (as in suggesting that autism is a logico-affective disorder), and to modular abilities that might be spared as well as impaired in autism, on the other.

To the present

The quest for understanding the psychology of autism continues to fire research enthusiasm and to inspire methodological ingenuity. After all, when we study memory we are discovering things about what is perceived; how what is perceived may be understood; how what is understood may be linked with other things that were registered previously, or at the time, or since; how what is retained is coloured by action and feeling and either integrated with or distanced from experiences of oneself and others; and, of course, how all this is reconstituted at a fresh time, often a fresh place, and even by a fresh (for instance, now more-grown-up) individual. By investigating low-functioning as well as high-functioning children, we may learn how intelligence may also bear upon the natural history of the disorder. By returning again and again to what we fail to encompass in our cherished theories, we might even be led to a radical rethink of the inter-relations among cognitive, conative and affective dimensions of human mental life.

Before coming to our own reflections on one future direction for research on memory in autism, it would be as well to identify some potential pitfalls that exist for ourselves and others who try to interpret whatever evidence is available. Firstly, there are the twin dangers of underplaying the neurological level of explanation of psychological dysfunction, or elbowing out psychology in favour of neurology. The organization of neural structures in the brain and psychological structures in the mind have complex interdependence in development. Experiences change brains, just as brains (and bodies) are needed for experiences. We should heed the cautionary messages contained in several chapters of this book (for example, those by Toichi, by Williams, Minshew & Goldstein, and by Webb) suggesting how memory impairments may be a downstream consequence of perceptual, information processing, executive functioning *or* social motivational deficits.

Secondly, we must try *not* to conclude that if a given strategy such as elaborative rehearsal (e.g. Smith & Gardiner, this volume) offsets certain memory deficits in autism, it follows that a relative absence of this strategy is the source of impaired memory. And even if it proves to be so, this does not preclude a quite different and additional account of how the strategy comes to be used, or not used, in the first place.

Thirdly, we need to respect the heterogeneity of autism, and reconcile this with findings of surprising homogeneity at certain levels of psychological functioning.

So if one is trying to account for such memory-related abnormalities as those in concept formation or retrieval, or in organizing information, or in drawing upon source memory, then one needs an account of typical development in relation to which one can identify derailments in developmental processes, whether in terms of neurology (e.g. frontal lobe functions), *or* those of cognitive development (e.g. central coherence), *or* those of social relatedness (e.g. intersubjectivity) – or in terms that may cross such domains, such as ... encoding stimuli meaningfully.

Thoughts for the future

What we would now like to offer is a kind of premonition for the future study of memory. This takes the form of a framework prefigured, but not yet fully explicated, in a number of the contributions to this book, perhaps most notably in the chapter by Lind and Bowler.

Consider the following excerpt from the writings of the most famous rememberer in literature:

Et tout d'un coup le souvenir m'est apparu. Ce goût c'était celui du petit morceau de madeleine que le dimanche matin à Combray ... ma tante Léonie m'offrait après l'avoir trempé dans son infusion de thé ou de tilleul.

And suddenly the memory revealed itself. The taste was that of the little piece of madeleine which on Sunday mornings at Combray ... my aunt Leonie used to give me, dipping it first in her own cup of tea or tisane. (Marcel Proust, *Du côte de chez Swann* (*Swann's Way*, 1913, 1, p. 99))

Why are we confident that Proust was not someone with autism? What this memory, and its remembering, makes manifest, is how human subjectivity is a web of relational experiences. Relations both to people and to things. Or more specifically, relations towards things as meaningfully connected with people (including oneself in the past, present and future), and people as meaningful in personal experience. And whatever it is that distinguishes this form of memory from memories typical of individuals with autism, it is difficult to see how it might be captured by accounts that focus upon theory of mind, or central coherence, or executive function, if these fail to encompass the subtle but powerful specialness of *personal* remembering so vividly conveyed by Proust.

Our suggestion for a theoretical framework is founded upon what has gone before: the ideas that there are certain modular processes that can develop and function relatively independently from much else in the brain/mind, but that beyond this, *interpersonal* processes profoundly influence what become intrapsychic processes (*à propos* of which, Neil O'Connor was always keen to stress the importance of what Pavlov called the 'second signalling system'). We have been struck by the relatively empty feel to the self-descriptions of children and adolescents with autism (Lee & Hobson, 1998), something that corresponds with what Bowler has studied in the form of a diminished involvement of a sense of self in their remembered experience. Or from a complementary perspective, is it not significant that those 'foolish wise ones' whose 'bright splinters of the mind' are sometimes dazzling, show so little interest in the artistic creations of others (Hermelin, 2002)? We are also impressed by the nature of what is, and what is not, achieved by way of 'encoding stimuli meaningfully' in the case of children with autism – and as an important corollary, how among children without autism, 'stimuli' may be conceptualized, grouped and regrouped, creatively and flexibly dealt with and thought about, embedded in but also disembedded from the settings in which they are experienced. What is it that usually supports memory in the minds of children who do not have autism, but which needs to be provided by *external* scaffolding in the case of children with autism? What is it that distinguishes 'concept identification', relatively intact among individuals with autism, from 'concept formation', the spontaneous organization of meaningful categories that can be reorganized and adjusted to context (Minshew, Meyer & Goldstein, 2002)?

Well, consider all those components of memory, such as registration, representation, and retrieval, as entailing positions or stances from which memories are entertained as memories. For example, episodic memory involves remembering according to self/other-anchored experience. We believe that a primary source of relating to one's own relations to the world is the interiorization of the many ways of relating to and identifying with *other people's* stances in relation to oneself and the world. At least to some degree, an individual arrives at the ability to move among and co-ordinate different perspectives on the world *and* him/her own self, including his or her own self as one who experiences and thinks, through adopting and assimilating other-centred attitudes.

So it is that Proust's memory entails him relating to himself as experiencing a set of events with feeling. In a sense, he *identifies with himself-as-represented* (and see how rich a concept of representation is involved here, so much more than a picture) – and lo! the feelings return in the modified form characteristic of identification. Then when he relates to his own relations with his aunt Leonie, she is experienced to have her own self-anchored orientation, as well as an orientation towards and significance for Proust himself. He identifies with her sufficiently to give her personal life, in his own mind. One can sense how the mental space needed to move from person to person, from stance to stance, from subjectivity to objectivity and back, is bound up with interpersonal linkage and differentiation. We suggest it is this interpersonal infrastructure to certain forms of memory that yields not only the phenomenology of what is recalled, but sometimes the fact that it is recalled at all.

Whether this framework will prove helpful, time will tell. Time, that is, filled with creative research and penetrating theoretical reflection – as represented in this book.

References

Hermelin, B. (2002). *Bright splinters of the mind*. London: Jessica Kingsley.

Hermelin, B. & O'Connor, N. (1970). *Psychological experiments with autistic children*. Oxford: Pergamon Press.

Kanner, L. (1943). Autistic disturbances of affective contact. *Nervous Child, 2,* 217–250.

Lee, A. & Hobson, R. P. (1998). On developing self-concepts: a controlled study of children and adolescents with autism. *Journal of Child Psychology and Psychiatry, 39,* 1131–1141.

Minshew, N. J., Meyer, J. A. & Goldstein, G. (2002). Abstract reasoning in autism: a dissociation between concept formation and concept identification. *Neuropsychology, 16,* 327–334.

Part I

Introduction

1   Concepts and theories of memory

John M. Gardiner

Concept. A thought, idea; disposition, frame of mind; imagination, fancy; .... an idea of a class of objects.

Theory. A scheme or system of ideas or statements held as an explanation or account of a group of facts or phenomena; a hypothesis that has been confirmed or established by observation or experiment, and is propounded or accepted as accounting for the known facts; a statement of what are known to be the general laws, principles, or causes of something known or observed.

From definitions given in the Oxford English Dictionary

The *Oxford Handbook of Memory*, edited by Endel Tulving and Fergus Craik, was published in the year 2000. It is the first such book to be devoted to the science of memory. It is perhaps the single most authoritative and exhaustive guide as to those concepts and theories of memory that are currently regarded as being most vital. It is instructive, with that in mind, to browse the exceptionally comprehensive subject index of this handbook for the most commonly used terms. Excluding those that name phenomena, patient groups, parts of the brain, or commonly used experimental procedures, by far the most commonly used terms are *encoding* and *retrieval processes*. Terms for different kinds of memory also feature prominently, as one would expect. Among the most frequently used are *short-term* and *long-term memory*; *explicit* and *implicit memory*; *working memory*; *episodic* and *semantic memory*; *verbal, visual* and *procedural memory*. All these terms may refer, among other things, to different memory systems and *memory systems theory* itself also has a lengthy entry in the index. Other commonly used terms are more disparate. They include such terms as *attention, consciousness, learning, forgetting, priming, recollection* and *remembering*.

It is important to distinguish between such terms and the concepts they may refer to, not least because any such term may be used in the literature to refer to several quite different concepts. One of the most notorious examples of such usage concerns explicit memory which, as Richardson-Klavehn and Bjork (1988) pointed out, has sometimes been used to refer to the conscious state of being aware of memory, sometimes to refer to an experimental procedure, or kind of test, and sometimes to refer to a kind of memory, or memory system. Similarly, the term episodic memory is often used to refer to a class of memory tasks (which was in fact its first usage historically) as well as to a mind/brain system. Even encoding, which might seem a more straightforward term, may refer to a memory task, or to an experimental manipulation, or to a class of hypothetical processes that are assumed to be involved in the performance of a task. This 'duality of patterning' in the usage of terminology has sometimes led to conceptual confusion. It is well to be alert to this potential problem and to be clear about which concepts terms refer to in any given context.

The concepts of encoding and retrieval processes, and memory systems, are the most fundamental hypothetical constructs in theory of memory. Brown and Craik (2000, p. 93) explained encoding and retrieval thus:

The terms *encoding* and *retrieval* have their origins in the information-processing framework of the 1960s, which characterized the human mind/brain as an information-processing device ... In this model, the mind – like the computer – receives informational input that it retains for a variable duration and subsequently outputs in some meaningful form. *Encoding*, therefore, refers to the process of acquiring information or placing it into memory, whereas *retrieval* refers to the process of recovering previously encoded information.

Though the distinction between encoding and retrieval seems relatively straightforward, it is less clearcut than it seems. Encoding entails retrieval. Retrieval entails encoding. The way new events are encoded is heavily dependent on previous experiences, the retrieval of which determines how the new events are perceived and interpreted. Subsequent retrieval of those events in itself creates new events and experiences, which are in turn encoded. Encoding and retrieval are continually interchangeable processes.

The definition of a memory system is more complex. Tulving (1985, pp. 386–387: see also Tulving, 2002) defined memory systems thus:

Memory systems are organized structures of more elementary operating components. An operating component of a system consists of a neural substrate and its behavioural or cognitive correlates. Some components are shared by all systems, others are shared by only some, and still others are unique to individual systems. Different learning and memory situations involve different concatenations of components from one or more systems ...

Memory systems tend to be defined by a set of criteria, such as differences in the kinds of information they process, in their rules of operation, some incompatibility in their evolved function, and in the conscious states they may give rise to (Sherry & Schacter, 1987). The biological concept of system offers a useful analogy. For example, organisms have digestive systems, cardiovascular systems, respiratory systems, excretory systems and reproductive systems, and these systems may have common properties and shared components, as well as unique properties and distinct components. And all these systems have certain specific functions, an evolutionary and developmental history, and, of course, physiological and anatomical substrates. Memory systems have much the same general characteristics.

For the last thirty years or so, theory of memory has been divided between theories based exclusively on the processing concepts of encoding and retrieval and theories based on the concept of memory systems. The contrast between these two approaches has generated a great deal of controversy over the years, but more recently there has been some rapprochement between them and an increasing recognition that the two approaches are complementary. Different memory systems all entail encoding and retrieval processes, some of which (or some components of which) they may have in common, some not.

The controversy between these two approaches followed the gradual abandonment of the belief that differences between short-term and long-term memory performance could be explained by a theoretical distinction between short-term and long-term memory stores (Atkinson & Shiffrin, 1968; Waugh & Norman, 1965), a theory that had been so generally accepted that it had become known as the *modal* model of memory. On the one hand, this theory was challenged by the levels-of-processing framework introduced by Craik and Lockhart (1972). On the other hand, this theory was challenged by a further fractionation of memory into additional short- and long-term memory systems, including the working memory model introduced by Baddeley and Hitch (1974) and the distinction between episodic and semantic memory systems introduced by Tulving (1983).

Process theorists have sometimes challenged the concept of memory systems on the grounds that there are no generally agreed 'rules' for proposing the existence of any new system, with the consequent danger of an undesirable proliferation of systems. Systems theorists have responded by suggesting that various criteria, taken together, might help reduce this risk. Process theorists might also be criticized on similar grounds, however, as there are also no generally agreed rules for proposing the existence of any new processes. It can equally well be argued that there has also been an undesirable proliferation of encoding and retrieval processes. But such is the rapid development of the field that no doubt many of the systems and processes that now seem central may soon be superseded by others, yet to be conceived.

Whatever their ultimate fate, however, current distinctions between different memory systems and memory processes most certainly have heuristic value in investigating memory in special populations such as that of individuals with ASD. These distinctions make the investigation of possible population differences in memory function more tractable. Instead of a global approach in which, perhaps, memory is conceived as a single, undifferentiated entity with memory performance determined largely by stronger or weaker 'trace strength', these distinctions encourage a finer-grained, qualitative approach. Hence, possible population differences in memory function may be found in some memory systems but not others, or in some memory processes but not others. And any differences in memory function that are found can be readily interpreted within an existing body of theoretical knowledge.

The remainder of this introductory chapter is intended to provide a guide to some of those memory systems and processes likely to be of the most immediate relevance to furthering our understanding of memory in ASD. It continues in the next section with a review of major memory systems. This is followed by a section that reviews several key process distinctions. In conclusion, some broader theoretical issues are discussed, including the importance of considering the nature of the memory tasks and of having convergent sources of evidence.

Memory systems

The five memory systems listed in Table 1.1 were identified as such by Schacter and Tulving (1994). Perceptual representation systems are those involved in the perception of objects and events and which represent their structure and form. They give rise to perceptual priming in tasks such as the perceptual identification of objects or of words. Procedural memory refers to those systems involved in skilled behaviour and action and it is usually acquired through extensive practice. Neither

Table 1.1. *Memory systems*

Perceptual representation
Procedural memory
Working memory
Semantic memory
Episodic memory

perceptual nor procedural systems are generally thought to be open to consciousness, in contrast with working memory, semantic memory and episodic memory, where consciousness has a crucial and (arguably) different role in each case. The distinction between these five systems embraces other similar distinctions that include the distinction between short-term and long-term memory (Atkinson & Shiffrin, 1968; Waugh & Norman, 1965) and the distinction between nondeclarative and declarative memory (Squire, 1987). Working memory refers to short-term memory whereas procedural, semantic and episodic memory systems all refer to long-term memory. Semantic and episodic memory systems both refer to declarative memory, whereas procedural and perceptual systems are nondeclarative.

The original working memory model was introduced by Baddeley and Hitch (1974) to replace the unitary view of short-term memory that had characterized the distinction between short-term and long-term memory stores (Atkinson & Shiffrin, 1968; Waugh & Norman, 1965). It has three components concerned with the temporary storage and manipulation of information, a central executive, a phonological loop and a visuo-spatial scratchpad. The central executive – the least well understood component of the model – is viewed as an attentional, supervisory system thought to co-ordinate the operation of the other two components. The phonological loop is involved with the maintenance of phonological information and is crucial for language learning. The visuo-spatial scratchpad is involved with the maintenance of visual and spatial information and is crucial for imagery. The major advantage of this model over the earlier unitary view of short-term memory is that it allows a finer-grained analysis of the functions of short-term memory, including the possibility of selective impairments among those component functions under different task conditions and in different populations.

Working memory depends on its interface with long-term memory systems, both in the retrieval of information from those systems and the encoding of information into them. Baddeley (2000, 2001) has recently introduced an additional component, the episodic buffer. This new subsystem provides temporary storage for the integration of information from other slave systems with information from long-term memory systems. The key point is that the combination of information from different sources itself requires some temporary holding mechanism to bind it together.

Semantic memory is the long-term memory system for general knowledge about the world. It includes information about language; about historical and geographical facts; about music, games, current affairs, and so on. It represents categorical knowledge about concepts. Semantic memory theories are concerned with how this categorical information is acquired, represented and retrieved. An early model of semantic memory assumed a network of nodes organized in a hierarchy, each node in which representing a discrete concept with links between nodes representing associations among them (Collins & Quillian, 1969). Encoding and retrieval in semantic memory were conceived in terms of spreading activation of nodes and of the connecting links. There are also feature comparison models in which the meaning of a concept is represented by semantic features that may be more or less defining of the concept (Rosch, 1975; Smith, Shoben & Rips, 1974). Later theories include connectionist, or neural network, models (McClelland & Rumelhart, 1985), one fundamental tenet of which is that representation is distributed across the network, in a pattern of activation, rather than being isolated in separate nodes.

Other key concepts in semantic memory are those of schema (Bartlett, 1932) and script (Schank & Abelson, 1977), both of which refer to sets of ideas relating to particular kinds of things such as what classical music sounds like compared with jazz and what clothes are worn in winter, or particular situations such as telling a story or going to the airport to catch a flight. Schemas and scripts represent generalized scenarios reflecting what has been learned about the way the world works and they contain much more information than any simple concept represented by a node in a semantic network. They have an important social role, both in the interpretation of events and in the planning and achievement of goals.

Episodic memory is the long-term memory system for personally experienced events, usually including information about where the events took place and when they occurred. Not all theorists have accepted the need to distinguish episodic from semantic systems, which are clearly closely related. Indeed, it is assumed that episodic memory is built on top of earlier systems, including semantic memory. The most critical feature that separates the two systems is the kind of consciousness experienced when retrieving information from either of them. Retrieval from semantic memory is accompanied by *noetic* awareness, which refers to a sense of knowing, whereas retrieval from episodic memory is accompanied by *autonoetic* awareness, which refers to recollective experiences that entail mentally reliving what was experienced at the time of the original event (Tulving, 1983; 1985). This sense of self in subjective time, or 'mental time travel' as it has been called, has become of increasing importance to the concept of episodic memory (Tulving, 2002) not merely in distinguishing it from semantic memory, but also with respect to its role in thinking about the future. Autonoetic awareness also enables one to project oneself into the future and it is crucial for the planning of, and for foreseeing the consequences of, personal decisions and actions.

It is important to appreciate that events are registered in semantic memory, as well as in episodic memory, and that according to Tulving's (1995) model of relations between these systems, encoding is serial, storage is parallel, and retrieval is independent. Thus, the occurrence of an event may be encoded in semantic memory without being encoded into episodic memory, but not vice versa. One can know that an event has occurred before without experiencing mental time travel with respect to its previous occurrence. One can know of many previous visits to Paris without re-experiencing anything that happened during any such visit. Semantic memory includes information about one's personal history that is known in a detached and factual way, without the experience of mental time travel. It is also assumed that episodic memory evolved more recently, and develops later in childhood, than semantic memory – perhaps at about the same time as theory of mind (Perner & Ruffman, 1995).

Encoding and retrieval processes

Six process distinctions are listed in Table 1.2. This selection of processes is inevitably more arbitrary than the selection of memory systems, but it does include some of those likely to be useful for investigating memory in ASD. All six distinctions are cast in the form of a dichotomy, though some of them have nonetheless been conceived more as a continuum of processing than as discontinuous categories. For process theorists who have often argued against a systems approach, memory is better approached as a unitary 'faculty' that can be explained in terms of a few broad descriptive and functional principles, such as these, rather than by partitioning it into separate memory systems.

Craik and Lockhart (1972) introduced the levels-of-processing approach as an alternative to theories that distinguished short-term from long-term memory stores (Atkinson & Shiffrin, 1968; Waugh & Norman, 1965). They proposed that memory is simply the by-product of

Table 1.2. *Encoding and retrieval processes*

Deep vs shallow level
Item-specific vs relational
Explicit vs implicit
Conceptual vs perceptual
Effortful vs automatic
Recollection vs familiarity

perception and that deeper levels of processing, in the sense of more meaningful semantic processing, makes for stronger, more durable memories than shallower, more superficial levels of processing. Information can also be maintained at any given level of processing, in short-term memory, but maintenance, *per se*, does not increase the durability of the memory trace. Only deeper, more meaningful processing can do this. This simple set of theoretical ideas has been hugely influential, despite some obvious limitations and shortcomings.

One limitation was that the approach was restricted to encoding. It did not include retrieval. Yet the effects of level of processing at encoding depend on retrieval conditions. Shallow levels of processing may give rise to superior memory performance if the overlap between retrieval and encoding conditions is greater for that level of processing than is the overlap for deeper levels of processing as, for example, when a test requires the retrieval of superficial stimulus features instead of semantic features (Morris, Bransford & Franks, 1977). Such evidence led to the formulation of another important principle, that of 'transfer appropriate processing'. According to this principle, memory performance depends on the extent to which the kind of processing engaged at encoding matches or overlaps with the kind of processing engaged at retrieval. The transfer appropriate processing principle is similar to the encoding specificity principle (Tulving & Thomson, 1973). Encoding specificity was formulated at the level of individual items. It states that no retrieval cue, however strongly related to its target in semantic memory, will aid episodic retrieval unless the information it provides was specifically encoded at the time of study. Transfer appropriate processing is encoding specificity writ large, at the level of the task as a whole, and of the kinds of processing induced by the task.

Levels of processing focuses on the encoding of specific items, and deeper levels of processing in the encoding of specific items makes those items more distinctive. The concept of distinctiveness is a relative concept, in the sense that distinctiveness depends on the context. What is distinctive in one context may not be distinctive in another context. Distinctiveness, like levels of processing, refers to item-specific encoding. It therefore ignores another important concept that had been the focus of much previous research, that of organization. Organization refers to groupings and relations among studied items, and the development of organization during study can greatly increase memory for those items (Bower, 1970; Mandler, 1967). The distinction between item-specific and relational processing usefully embraces both the item-centred focus of levels of processing and the relational focus of organization. In practice, there is often a trade-off between the two. Experimental conditions, or individual biases, may foster greater relational encoding at the cost of reduced item-specific encoding, or greater item-specific encoding at the cost of reduced relational encoding (Hunt & McDaniel, 1993; Hunt & Seta, 1984).

The use of the terms explicit and implicit memory to refer to different memory systems has now been largely discredited, partly because of the conceptual confusion these terms engendered and partly because of more recent theoretical developments, such as the distinction between semantic and episodic systems, both of which are explicit in the sense that they are both open to consciousness. In contrast with explicit processes, implicit processes are not open to consciousness. Thus, implicit processes refer to the nonconscious forms of memory that are assumed to be reflected in implicit memory tests. But people may often be well aware that they are retrieving studied items in implicit tests, even if they did not intend to retrieve studied items. In view of this, it has been suggested that it is retrieval intention that is critical to comparisons between explicit and implicit tests, rather than awareness that retrieved items were encountered earlier (Richardson-Klavehn et al., 1994; Schacter, Bowers & Booker, 1989).

Perceptual fluency is one implicit process that has been of some theoretical importance in shaping attributional views of memory (Jacoby, 1988; Jacoby, Kelley & Dywan, 1989). Perceptual fluency refers to the perceptual facilitation – some item is perceived more quickly, or more readily if in a degraded form – following a prior act of perception. It has been argued that perceptual fluency gives rise to priming effects in tasks like perceptual identification. Moreover, in recognition memory, the effects of perceptual fluency may be attributed to having encountered the test item in a previously studied list, in the absence of any awareness of the actual occurrence of the item there. Thus, memory is inferred from some other experience. In other circumstances, implicit processes may drive the perception of the stimulus. Thus, a word heard recently may sound louder next time than one not heard recently, or the previously studied name of a nonfamous person may seem famous, when making fame judgements about those names in the context of names of other moderately famous people. An attributional view of memory is concerned with how memory may be inferred from other kinds of experiences and with how memory may influence other kinds of experiences (Jacoby, 1988; Jacoby, Kelley & Dywan, 1989).

The distinction between conceptual and perceptual processes was largely developed in order to provide an alternative account of dissociations between memory performance in explicit and implicit tests to the account provided by the theory that the two kinds of tests involve different memory systems (Jacoby, 1983; Roediger, Weldon & Challis, 1989). In this alternative account it is assumed that task conditions, both at encoding and at retrieval, may bias processing towards being more conceptual, or more perceptual in nature. Many explicit tests, such as free recall or recognition, depend largely on conceptual processing, whereas many implicit tests, such as perceptual identification or word-stem completion, depend largely on perceptual processing. Given those assumptions, coupled with the transfer-appropriate processing principle, then much of the evidence can be explained. Encoding tasks that rely on greater perceptual analyses may promote more effective performance in tests that also rely more on perceptual processing. Conversely, encoding tasks that rely on greater conceptual analyses may promote more effective performance in tests that also rely more on conceptual processing. As with the original levels-of-processing distinction, a continuum between perceptual and conceptual processing is envisaged rather than a more discrete contrast, since most tasks necessarily involve both kinds of pro-cesses to varying extents. The emphasis on the relation between encoding and retrieval processes is one great advantage of this approach. Another is its ability to provide a framework for understanding dissociations between performance *within* different explicit or different implicit mem-ory tests which are sometimes observed when comparing perceptual with conceptual explicit tests, or when comparing perceptual with conceptual implicit tests (Blaxton, 1989).

The distinction between effortful and automatic processing refers nei-ther to the qualitative nature of encoding and retrieval processes nor to the relation between them, but rather to the extent to which those processes seem to demand attention and conscious resources (Hasher & Zacks, 1979). This distinction therefore cuts across some of the other process distinctions, although it is related to them. Shallow levels of processing, for example, may normally be more automatic than deeper levels of processing, but this is not always so. Some superficial encoding tasks can be quite difficult and time-consuming. Implicit processing may normally be more automatic than explicit processing, but again this is not always so. Some implicit tasks, particularly some conceptual implicit tasks such as general knowledge tests, can also be quite difficult and time-consuming. Indeed, there has been some controversy about which tasks may or may not entail relatively automatic processing, and the effects of normal ageing have been used as a kind of litmus test for this, on the grounds that automatic processes will be spared the effects of normal ageing whereas attention-demanding effortful processing will not. Another litmus test for this distinction is the extent to which the performance of a task can be improved with practice. The assumption is that more attention-demanding effortful processing will improve with practice whereas automatic processing, by definition, will not. Regardless of some evidential problems that have arisen from attempts to classify tasks (or kinds of information within tasks) with respect to this process distinction, encoding and retrieval processes do vary considerably in the extent to which they seem to demand consciously controlled and limited attentional resources.

The final process distinction listed in Table 1.2 originated largely in the context of recognition memory tests and it relates to dual-process theories of recognition memory (Jacoby, 1991; Mandler, 1980) that assume recognition may be accomplished on the basis of two independent processes, recollection and familiarity. These processes are assumed to give rise to the corresponding states of awareness. There is an obvious parallel between these assumptions and those made in distinguishing episodic from semantic memory systems. Recollection, as a state of awareness, corresponds to autonoetic awareness. Familiarity, as a state of awareness, corresponds to noetic awareness. Dual-process theories also generally assume that the processes of recollection and familiarity correspond closely with the distinction between effortful and automatic processes. Recollection is effortful and consciously controlled, whereas familiarity is automatic and not open to conscious control. These assumptions, though, have not gone unchallenged and, despite a great deal of evidence in support of these dual-process theories, unidimensional models of various kinds, including signal detection models and global memory models (Gillund & Shiffrin, 1984; Hintzman, 1986) have also proved quite successful in accounting for recognition performance.

Memory systems and components of processing

The systems approach to memory theory and the process approach have frequently been viewed as alternative ways of conceptualizing memory. Much research has been generated within one or other of these two approaches, internally, as it were, rather than in an attempt to directly contrast them empirically (though see Blaxton, 1989). But though each of the two approaches stands alone as a way of thinking about memory, and of hypothesizing about memory function, they can also be regarded as being complementary. Memory systems necessarily entail memory processes. Some theoretical rapprochement along these lines has been proposed by Roediger, Buckner and McDermott (1999), amongst others. Roediger *et al.* (1999) argued that neither systems nor processing theories have fared all that well, considered alone, and argued instead for a components-of-processing approach based largely on ideas developed by Moscovitch (1994). This approach is concerned with how different information-processing systems and modules interact and give rise to different memory traces that include not only the features of the event, but also those elements that enable one to become conscious of that event.

Theories depend more directly on evidence than do concepts, which may both transcend and survive their instantiation in any particular theory. And evidence depends upon tasks. One virtue of the components-of-processing idea is that it focuses on the characteristics of memory tasks and it assumes that task performance typically involves a number of different processing components, both at a cognitive and at neuro-anatomical levels. Performance in any two different tasks may involve some shared components and some components that are not shared. Associations between performances in the two tasks implicate shared components; dissociations between performances in the two tasks implicate distinct components. Tasks are rarely, if ever, 'process-pure' in the sense that they involve only one process, or only one system.

A focus on memory tasks also suggests a more 'functional' approach to memory theory in which consideration of the nature of the task, and of task demands, is at least as important as any other theoretical consideration. The environment has to be taken into account, as well as the organism. Craik (1986), for example, argued that whether or not memory performance declines with normal ageing will depend on task demands, and that such age-related effects will be more likely when task demands are high, and less likely when the tasks provide a more supportive environment. The important factor here is the extent to which the task requires encoding and retrieval processes that are largely self-initiated, or encoding and retrieval processes that are strongly constrained and determined by the nature of the task. If the former, age-related effects are more likely; if the latter, age-related effects are less likely. This approach cuts across interpretations of age-related effects such as that provided by the distinction between episodic and semantic systems, according to which episodic memory is particularly vulnerable to such effects, because the degree of environmental support provided can vary considerably within either episodic or semantic memory tasks.

Converging sources of evidence

Two other, recent developments in research on memory are of great theoretical importance. Both of these developments result from the availability of new sources of evidence. The first new source of evidence comes from recently developed techniques for scanning brain activity. The concepts and theories reviewed in this chapter have largely arisen in the context of cognitive information-processing ideas, rather than in the context of ideas about brain function. But there are of course many other theories that have arisen largely in the context of ideas about brain function. These have included the idea of a hierarchical organization of cognitive memory, particularly in relation to the medial temporal lobe and the hippocampus (Mishkin *et al.*, 1997), with the hippocampus being most crucial for episodic memory. They have also included the idea that there is an encoding/retrieval asymmetry in the frontal cortex, reflecting evidence that episodic encoding produced greater activation in the left hemisphere than in the right, whereas episodic retrieval produced greater activation in the right hemisphere than in the left (Tulving *et al.*, 1994; see too Buckner, 1996). If nothing else, evidence of this kind places an important constraint on cognitive information-processing theories, which is that no cognitive information-processing theory should entail any proposals or assumptions that are *inconsistent* with what is known about neuroanatomical function. And in the longer run, cognitive information-processing theories that do not additionally address neuroanatomical function will increasingly seem incomplete.

The second new source of evidence is phenomenological, and for that reason its use is more controversial. But there has been an increasing willingness amongst memory theorists to take on board mental life as experienced, and reported verbally, by participants in memory research. In the laboratory, this development includes, amongst much else, the widespread use of reports of remembering and of knowing to measure, respectively, experiences of autonoetic and noetic consciousness, in systems theory, or of recollection and familiarity in dual-process theories of recognition. It also includes the source-monitoring framework (Johnson, Hashtroudi & Lindsay, 1993), which focuses in a much more detailed way on the qualitative features of experiences of memory and the uses to which they are put. In this framework, attributional judgements are made about the origin of various mental experiences – whether, for example, those experiences reflect reality or only previously imagined experiences. Experiences that entail a great deal of perceptual detail are more likely to be attributed to the real world than those that do not. The amount and qualitative nature of the information experienced mentally is diagnostic of its origin, and serves as a basis for decision and action. Metamemory, too, which refers to the self-monitoring and strategic control of memory performance, is essentially concerned with what people are aware of during memory tasks (Nelson & Narens, 1990).

Experiences of memory are also central to the study of autobiographical memories, which may be both episodic, when accompanied by autonoetic awareness, or semantic, when accompanied by noetic awareness. Theories of autobiographical memory typically involve assumptions about several levels of representation which may range from highly detailed episodic memories to more general memories covering much longer time periods (such as life as a student). They also include more generic kinds of memories (such as early childhood holidays at the seaside) that seem to reflect the merging of many similar experiences into a few more generally representative experiences. In Conway's model of autobiographical memory (Conway, 2001; Conway & Pleydell-Pearce, 2000), there is a structurally organized autobiographical memory knowledge base, extending over different time periods, which is identified with the concept of self. This autobiographical knowledge base is crucial for the planning and attainment of personal and social goals. And, in a significant revision of Tulving's (1983) concept of episodic memory, episodic memories are conceived to be largely sensory and perceptual in nature and to last for a comparatively short time period (a matter of hours) unless linked to more permanent autobiographical memory structures. Importantly, these theoretical ideas about episodic and autobiographical memories and about the concept of self are supported by all three kinds of converging evidence illustrated by Figure 1.1, not least by phenomenology.

Other major theories, also, including the distinction between episodic and semantic memory, and at least some of the process distinctions listed in Table 1.2, are concerned with phenomenological evidence as well as with other sources of evidence. In the longer run, cognitive information processing theories that do not additionally take on board phenomenological evidence will also increasingly seem incomplete.

BEHAVIOUR		MIND
Memory performance	←	Conscious experience
Overt responses	→	Verbal reports
↖		↗
↘	BRAIN	↙
	Neuronal activation	
	Physiological indices	

Note. The figure (from Gardiner, 2001, with permission) shows three different sources of evidence. Arrows may be loosely interpreted as 'influence'.

Figure 1.1 Three kinds of converging evidence

Conclusion

This chapter has attempted to provide an introductory review of those concepts and theories of memory that might be helpful in furthering our understanding of memory in ASD. Two major theoretical approaches have been contrasted, one based on the concept of memory systems, the other based on the concepts of encoding and retrieval processes. Neither of these approaches is complete in and of itself, though each may nonetheless be of heuristic value, and there has recently been some rapprochement between them. Environmental considerations must also be taken into account, particularly the degree of environmental support provided by memory tasks. Theoretical advances will increasingly depend on converging sources of evidence, not on cognitive information-processing ideas based solely on traditional measures of memory.

The most important adaptive functions of memory, both as it has evolved, and for any one individual, have not to do with memory, *per se*, in the sense of simply being able to know or remember things about the past. They have to do with the decisions and actions that are taken on the basis of memory, most especially on the basis of conscious experiences of memory, and with the personal and social uses to which memory is put. Therein lies the importance of memory to understanding ASD.

References

Atkinson, R. C. & Shiffrin, R. M. (1968). Human memory: a proposed system and its control processes. In K. W. Spence (ed.), *The psychology of learning and motivation: advances in research and theory*, vol. 2, pp. 89–195. New York: Academic Press.

Baddeley, A. D. (2000). The episodic buffer: a new component of working memory? *Trends in Cognitive Sciences*, 4, 417–423.

(2001). Levels of working memory. In M. Naveh-Benjamin, M. Moscovitch & H. L. Roediger (eds.), *Perspectives on human memory and cognitive ageing: essays in honour of Fergus Craik*, pp. 111–123. New York: Psychology Press.

Baddeley, A. D. & Hitch, G. (1974). Working memory. In G. A. Bower (ed.), *Recent advances in learning and motivation*, vol. 8, pp. 47–89. New York: Academic Press.

Bartlett, F. C. (1932). *Remembering*. Cambridge: Cambridge University Press.

Blaxton, T. A. (1989). Investigating dissociations among memory measures: support for a transfer-appropriate processing framework. *Journal of Experimental Psychology: Learning, Memory, and Cognition*, 10, 3–9.

Bower, G. H. (1970). Imagery as a relational organizer in associational learning. *Journal of Verbal Learning and Verbal Behavior*, 9, 529–533.

Brown, S. C. & Craik, F. I. M. (2000). Encoding and retrieval of information. In E. Tulving and F. I. M. Craik (eds.), *The Oxford handbook of memory*, pp. 93–107. New York: Oxford University Press.

Buckner, R. L. (1996). Beyond HERA: contributions of specific prefrontal brain areas to long-term memory retrieval. *Psychonomic Bulletin & Review, 3*, 149–158.

Collins, A. M. & Quillian, A. R. (1969). Retrieval time from semantic memory. *Journal of Verbal Learning and Verbal Behavior, 8*, 240–247.

Conway, M. A. (2001). Sensory-perceptual memory and its context: autobiographical memory. *Philosophical Transactions of the Royal Society London B, 356*, 1375–1384.

Conway, M. A. & Pleydell-Pearce, C. W. (2000). The construction of autobiographical memories in the self-memory system. *Psychological Review, 107*, 261–288.

Craik, F. I. M. (1986). A functional account of age differences in memory. In F. Klix & H. Hagendorf (eds.), *Human memory and cognitive capabilities, mechanisms, and performances*, pp. 409–422. Amsterdam: Elsevier/North Holland.

Craik, F. I. M. & Lockhart, R. S. (1972). Levels of processing: a framework for memory research. *Journal of Verbal Learning and Verbal Behavior, 11*, 671–684.

Gardiner, J. M. (2001). On the objectivity of subjective experiences of autonoetic and noetic consciousness. In E. Tulving (ed.), *Memory, consciousness, and the brain: the Tallinn conference*, pp. 159–172. Philadelphia, PA: Psychology Press.

Gillund, G. & Shiffrin, R. M. (1984). A retrieval model for both recognition and recall. *Psychological Review, 91*, 1–67.

Hasher, L. & Zacks, R. T. (1979). Automatic and effortful processes in memory. *Journal of Experimental Psychology: General, 108*, 356–388.

Hintzman, D. (1986). 'Schema abstraction' in a multiple-trace memory model. *Psychological Review, 93*, 411–428.

Hunt, R. R. & McDaniel, M. A. (1993). The enigma of organization and distinctiveness. *Journal of Memory and Language, 32*, 421–445.

Hunt, R. R. & Seta, C. E. (1984). Category size effects in recall: the roles of relational and individual item information. *Journal of Experimental Psychology: Learning, Memory and Cognition, 10*, 454–464.

Jacoby, L. L. (1983). Remembering the data: analyzing interactive processes in reading. *Journal of Verbal Learning and Verbal Behavior, 22*, 485–508.

(1988). Memory observed and memory unobserved. In U. Neisser & E. Winograd (eds.), *Remembering reconsidered: ecological and traditional approaches to the study of memory*, pp. 145–177. New York: Cambridge University Press.

(1991). A process dissociation framework: separating automatic from intentional uses of memory. *Journal of Memory and Language, 30*, 513–541.

Jacoby, L. L., Kelley, C. M. & Dywan, J. (1989). Memory attributions. In H. L. Roediger & F. I. M. Craik (eds.), *Varieties of memory and consciousness: Essays in honour of Endel Tulving*, pp. 391–422. Hillsdale, NJ: Erlbaum.

Johnson, M. C., Hashtroudi, S. & Lindsay, D. S. (1993). Source monitoring. *Psychological Bulletin, 114*, 3–28.

Mandler, G. A. (1967). Organization in memory. In K. W. Spence & J. T. Spence (eds.), *The psychology of learning and motivation*, vol. 1, pp. 327–372. New York: Academic Press.

(1980). Recognizing: the judgment of previous occurrence. *Psychological Review, 87*, 252–271.

McClelland, J. L. & Rumelhart, D. E. (1985). Distributed memory and the representation of general and specific information. *Journal of Experimental Psychology: General, 114*, 159–188.

Mishkin, M., Suzuki, W., Gadian, D. G. & Vargha-Khadem, F. (1997). Hierarchical organization of cognitive memory. *Philosophical Transactions of the Royal Society London B, 352*, 1461–1467.

Morris, C. D., Bransford, J. D. & Franks, J. J. (1977). Levels of processing versus transfer appropriate processing. *Journal of Verbal Learning and Verbal Behavior, 16*, 519–533.

Moscovitch, M. (1994). Memory and working with memory: evaluation of a component process model and comparison with other models. In D. L. Schacter & E. Tulving (eds.), *Memory systems 1994*, pp. 369–394. Cambridge, MA: MIT Press.

Nelson, T. O. & Narens, L. (1990). Metamemory: a theoretical framework and some new findings. In G. H. Bower (ed.), *The psychology of learning and motivation*, vol. 26, pp. 125–173. New York: Academic Press.

Perner, J. & Ruffman, T. (1995). Episodic memory and autonoetic consciousness: developmental evidence and a theory of childhood amnesia. *Journal of Experimental Child Psychology, 59*, 516–548.

Richardson-Klavehn, A. & Bjork, R. A. (1988). Measures of memory. *Annual Review of Psychology, 39*, 475–543.

Richardson-Klavehn, A., Lee, M. G., Joubran, R. & Bjork, R. A. (1994). Intention and awareness in perceptual identification priming. *Memory & Cognition, 22*, 293–312.

Roediger, H. L., Weldon, M. S. & Challis, B. H. (1989). Explaining dissociations between implicit and explicit measures of retention: a processing account. In H. L. Roediger & F. I. M. Craik (eds.), *Varieties of memory and consciousness: essays in honour of Endel Tulving*, pp. 391–422. Hillsdale, NJ: Erlbaum.

Roediger, H. L., Buckner, R. & McDermott, K. B. (1999). Components of processing. In J. K. Foster & M. Jelicic (eds.), *Memory: systems, process, or function?*, pp. 31–65. Oxford: Oxford University Press.

Rosch, E. H. (1975). Cognitive representations of semantic categories. *Journal of Experimental Psychology, 104*, 192–233.

Schacter, D. L., Bowers, J. & Booker, J. (1989). Intention, awareness, and implicit memory: the retrieval intentionality criterion. In S. Lewandowsky, J. C. Dunn & K. Kirsner (eds.), *Implicit memory: theoretical issues*, pp. 47–65. Hillsdale, NJ: Erlbaum.

Schacter, D. L. & Tulving, E. (1994). What are the memory systems of 1994? In D. L. Schacter & E. Tulving (eds.), *Memory systems 1994*, pp. 1–38. Cambridge, MA: MIT Press.

Schank, R. C. & Abelson, R. (1977). *Scripts, plans, goals, and understanding.* Hillsdale, NJ: Erlbaum.

Sherry, D. F. & Schacter, D. L. (1987). The evolution of multiple memory systems. *Psychological Review, 94,* 439–454.

Smith, E. E., Shoben, E. J. & Rips, L. J. (1974). Structure and process in semantic memory: a featural model for semantic decisions. *Psychological Review, 81,* 214–241.

Squire, L. R. (1987). *Memory and brain.* New York: Oxford University Press.

Tulving, E. (1983). *Elements of episodic memory.* New York: Oxford University Press.

(1985). How many memory systems are there? *American Psychologist, 40,* 385–398.

(1995). Organization of memory: quo vadis? In M. S. Gazzaniga (ed.), *The cognitive neurosciences,* pp. 839–847. Cambridge, MA: MIT Press.

(2002). Episodic memory: from mind to brain. *Annual Review of Psychology, 53,* 1–25.

Tulving, E. & Craik, F. I. M. (eds.) (2000). *The Oxford handbook of memory.* New York: Oxford University Press.

Tulving, E., Kapur, S., Craik, F. I. M., Moscovitch, M. & Houle, S. (1994). Hemispheric encoding/retrieval asymmetry in episodic memory: positron emission tomography findings. *Proceedings of the National Academy of Sciences, USA, 91,* 2016–2020.

Tulving, E. & Thomson, D. M. (1973). Encoding specificity and retrieval processes in episodic memory. *Psychological Review, 80,* 352–373.

Waugh, N. C. & Norman, D. A. (1965). Primary memory. *Psychological Review, 72,* 89–104.

Part II

The neurobiology of memory in autism

2 Temporal lobe structures and memory in nonhuman primates: implications for autism

Jocelyne Bachevalier

Introduction

The medial temporal lobe (MTL), which includes the amygdala, hippo-campal formation (dentate gyrus, CA fields and subicular complex) and a set of cortical areas (i.e. entorhinal, perirhinal and parahippocampal areas TH and TF) on the parahippocampal gyrus, has long been known to be implicated in memory processes and regulation of emotional behaviours. In experimental work with animals, the development of new surgical tools that have allowed more selective lesions of the amygdala and hippocampus (e.g. sparing adjacent temporal cortical areas), together with neuropsychological studies of the functions of the various medial temporal cortical areas have helped to clarify the contributions of each of these medial temporal lobe components to cognitive functions (Baxter & Murray, 2000; Brown & Aggleton, 2001; Eichenbaum, 2001; Lavenex & Amaral, 2000; Mishkin *et al.*, 1997; Murray & Bussey, 1999; O'Reilly & Rudy, 2001; Yonelinas, 2002). Although controversies still exist in the field, the general picture that emerges can be summarized as follows. The perirhinal cortex, which receives perceptual information about objects, mediates item-specific memory, as well as learning of stimulus–stimulus, cross-modal and stimulus–reward associations. In turn, areas TH and TF, which receive more extensive spatial information about objects, are involved in spatial memory. Thus, these temporal cortical areas are involved in the storage and retrieval of stimulus representations, and are viewed as storing information or knowledge independently of the context in which they are learned (fact or semantic memory). By comparison, the hippocampal formation is needed to acquire, store and recollect inter-item relations and their context and supports recollection of specific events (relational, configural and/or episodic memory). Finally, although the amygdala is not involved in stimulus memory and in learning stimulus–stimulus, cross-modal and stimulus–reward associations *per se*, it plays a critical role in a specific class of stimulus–reward associations, namely the associations of a stimulus with the specific or current value of a reinforcer. In addition, the amygdala acts as an interface between stimulus, both animate and inanimate, and emotional responses. Thus, selective amygdala lesions result in emotional changes (e.g. reduced fear and aggressiveness, increased submission, and excessive manual and oral exploration), whilst sparing behavioural and physiological components of anxious temperament (Kalin *et al.*, 2001, 2004; Meunier *et al.*, 1999). Further, the magnitude of these emotional changes is generally greater in monkeys with aspiration lesions of the amygdala that include portions of the medial temporal cortex in addition to the amygdala, suggesting a role for these cortical areas in emotional behaviour as well. This is supported by recent findings in monkeys showing that selective damage to the ento- and perirhinal cortex is accompanied by emotional changes that are in fact the opposite of those found after neurotoxic lesions of the amygdala, namely enhanced fearful reactions (Meunier & Bachevalier, 2002; Meunier, Cirilli & Bachevalier, 2006).

Much less emphasis has been placed, however, on the development of cognitive functions mediated by the medial temporal structures in primates. This chapter will begin with a brief review of the maturation of MTL structures in primates. Current knowledge on the functional development of MTL structures will then be summarized, relying mostly on developmental neuropsychological studies in nonhuman primates as well as in humans when applicable. The possible relevance of these experimental findings for autism will be discussed in a final section.

Maturation of medial temporal lobe structures in primates

As reviewed recently (Alvarado & Bachevalier, 2000; Bachevalier & Vargha-Khadem, 2005; Machado & Bachevalier, 2003a), most of the neurogenesis within the hippocampus occurs before birth in primates. Nevertheless, neurogenesis in the dentate gyrus continues throughout gestation, and even postnatally until the fourth and sixth postnatal months. Yet, despite this early neurogenesis, hippocampal neurons undergo significant postnatal changes, suggesting prolonged morphological maturation during the first postnatal year in monkeys and up to 5–6 years of age in humans. This postnatal development of the hippocampus has also been shown by an increase in hippocampal volume as well as changes in the ratio of grey to white matter in neuroimaging studies in infant monkeys and humans. Conversely, morphological maturation of the allocortical areas, such as entorhinal and perirhinal cortex, precedes that of the hippocampus, and at birth these cortical areas can be clearly identified cytoarchitectonically and display adult-like chemoanatomical characteristics. Thus, these cortical areas may be available to support some memory processes (e.g. fact or semantic memory) early in life, whereas memory processes mediated by the hippocampus (relational or episodic memory) may mature progressively over a longer period of time. Finally, neurogenesis in the amygdala occurs early in gestation and proceeds in a smooth dorsal-to-ventral wave in both nonhuman primates and humans. Also, most afferent and efferent connections of amygdala neurons are already established by the time of birth, and by the second postnatal week in primates, amygdala efferent connections largely resemble those seen in adult monkeys. However, there is still some immaturity in the pattern of afferent cortical projections in the first few postnatal months, suggesting that refinement of cortico-amygdalar projections provides infant monkeys with increasingly detailed information about complex socioemotional stimuli as they mature. This protracted refinement in the sensory inputs to the amygdala is accompanied by progressive myelination of the amygdala until the fourth postnatal week, indicating that the influence of the amygdala on other neural systems increases slowly in infancy.

These data suggest that the medial temporal cortical areas and the structural elements and synaptic connections within the hippocampus necessary for memory formation are present in newborn primates, although the modifications of hippocampal circuits from birth to adulthood provide a basis for memory processes to continue to mature during development. Similarly, although structural elements within the amygdala necessary for regulation of emotions are present at birth, postnatal changes in its connectivity with other neural systems could support further maturation of a modulatory role of the amygdala in emotional responses to environmental stimuli.

Given the early development of MTL structures, it could be argued that any insult to this neural system in the perinatal period may result in profound deficits in memory processes and emotional responses. Conversely, given the significant sparing of functions known to occur after early brain damage, it is possible that any early insult to this neural system may result in significant functional compensation. The data reviewed below tend to support the former, rather than the latter, proposal.

Neonatal damage to the medial temporal lobe

My colleagues and I began our exploration of the long-term behavioural and cognitive consequences of neonatal MTL damage by characterizing the memory impairment and socioemotional changes of newborn monkeys that had received extensive MTL lesions (amygdala, hippo-campal formation and adjacent cortical areas) in the first weeks of life. In these early studies (see review Bachevalier & Málková, 2000), we found that neonatal MTL damage resulted in a profound anterograde amnesia, closely resembling the anterograde amnesia that follows similar MTL damage in adult monkeys and humans (Mishkin *et al.*, 1982; Zola-Morgan & Squire, 1985). Thus, unlike age-matched controls, the oper-ated infant monkeys showed impaired performance on item-specific recognition tasks (visual paired comparison and delayed nonmatching-to-sample), as well as in tasks measuring tactual and spatial location recognition. By contrast, they displayed normal immediate memory abil-ities as well as normal performance on tasks of procedural learning, such as concurrent discrimination learning tasks.

Altogether these earlier findings indicated that MTL structures are required for some types of learning and memory processes (fact and episodic memory) but not others (short-term memory, procedural mem-ory or skill learning). This early MTL damage was also accompanied by profound changes in emotionality and social interactions that were greater in magnitude than those found after MTL lesions incurred in adulthood. They were also accompanied by the presence of stereotyped behaviours (Bachevalier, Málková & Mishkin, 2001; Málková *et al.*, 1997).

These behavioural changes led us to suggest that any neural reorgan-ization that occurs after early damage to the MTL structures may be more harmful than beneficial, perhaps because it disrupts the functioning of late-maturing neural systems. This view is now supported by recent data on the same neonatally MTL-operated monkeys and their age-matched controls demonstrating that this early damage interferes with the func-tions of neural systems remote from the site of injury, namely the dorso-lateral prefrontal cortex (Bertolino *et al.*, 1997; Chlan-Fourney *et al.*, 2000, 2003) and the anatomically related portion of the neostriatum (Heinz *et al.*, 2000; Saunders *et al.*, 1998). In addition, the neonatally operated monkeys displayed a dysregulation of prefrontal–striatal dopa-mine transmission that could provide an explanation for the presence of ritualistic and stereotyped behaviours in these animals. Thus, the lack of functional inputs from MTL structures could prevent the prefrontal cortex from undergoing proper neuronal development. However, it is not known at the present time whether these early MTL lesions affect other neural systems; nor is it known which MTL structures are respon-sible for such a prefrontal immaturity.

To learn more about the underlying neural substrate of the behavioural disorders resulting from the early MTL damage, we investigated whether or not the complex behavioural syndrome described above might be fractionated by damaging specific MTL components. We began this set of studies by producing infant monkeys with damage to the amygdala and hippocampal formation, which were behaviourally tested until adulthood using the same procedures as those used in the previous studies. However, it is important to note that, since the neonatal lesions were produced by aspiration procedures, amygdala damage also included damage to the ento- and perirhinal cortex, and hippocampal damage also included areas TH and TF (for further information on the extent of these neonatal lesions see Bachevalier, Beauregard & Alvarado, 1999). In a preliminary report (Bachevalier, 1994), it was concluded that neonatal amygdala damage yielded mild deficits in memory function and a pattern of socioemotional deficits almost identical to that found after complete MTL lesions, although the magnitude of the deficits was less. By contrast, early hippocampal damage largely spared memory and resulted in reduced social interactions and locomotor stereotypies only when the monkeys reached adulthood (Beauregard, Málková & Bachevalier, 1995).

Further investigations of these operated animals and their unoperated controls as well as more recent developmental studies of either selective neurotoxic damage to the amygdala and hippocampal formation avoiding the adjacent cortices, or direct damage to the entorhinal and perirhinal cortex avoiding the two subcortical structures, allow more specific characterization of the memory and behavioural deficits that follow neonatal damage to different MTL structures. Findings from these recent studies are presented next, subdivided into findings relating first to the amygdala, then to the hippocampal formation, and finally to the temporal cortical areas.

Neonatal damage to the amygdala

Effects on memory

Monkeys with neonatal aspiration lesions of the amygdala (Bachevalier, Beauregard & Alvarado, 1999) showed a mild and transient deficit in procedural learning that was in fact similar to that found earlier in monkeys with neonatal MTL damage. In addition, this early damage yielded significant recognition memory impairment (as assessed using delayed nonmatching-to-sample – DNMS) that persisted when the neonatally operated animals were re-tested on the same recognition task upon reaching adulthood. As reviewed above, the role of the amygdala in learning stimulus–reward associations such as concurrent discriminations, as well as in recognition memory as measured by the DNMS, has been recently called into question by findings in adult monkeys indicating that most of the memory impairment resulting from an aspiration lesion of the amygdala appears to be due instead to direct or indirect damage to the ento- and perirhinal cortices (Baxter & Murray, 2000). Thus, the mild and transient impairment in concurrent discrimination learning, and the moderate and long-lasting impairment in the DNMS seen after neonatal amygdaloid lesions and reported by Bachevalier and colleagues (1999), could have resulted from additional damage to cortical areas surrounding the amygdala. This suggestion is supported by recent evidence showing severe recognition memory impairment following direct damage to the ento- and perirhinal cortex in infant monkeys (Málková *et al.*, 1998).

Recent findings on the same neonatally amygdalectomized animals (Alvarado, Wright & Bachevalier, 2002) demonstrated normal abilities on tasks sensitive to selective neurotoxic hippocampal lesions, such as a transverse patterning task (measuring the ability to learn the relationship between three different objects) and a spatial locations recognition task. In addition, our current investigations of the effects of neonatal neurotoxic lesions of the amygdala, which spare the adjacent cortical areas, demonstrate that these early lesions affect neither the learning of stimulus–reward associations, as measured by an object discrimination reversal task, nor the ability to recognize objects over extended delays, as measured by visual paired comparison (VPC). Thus, altogether the data suggest that damage to the amygdala in early infancy, like the same damage in adulthood, does not affect stimulus memory and stimulus–reward associations. However, given that in adult monkeys the amygdala plays a critical role in a particular class of stimulus–reward associations, namely the association of a stimulus with its intrinsic reward value (whether it is pleasant or not), it will be of particular interest to investigate whether the same deficit will be evident in the animals with selective neonatal amygdala damage.

Effects on socioemotional behaviour

Given that the primate amygdala develops early in infancy and plays a critical role in the regulation of emotional responses and social cognition (see for review Adolphs 2001; Bachevalier & Meunier, 2005), it is not surprising to observe that neonatal amygdala lesions also alter emotional responses and social behaviour. Earlier studies (Thompson, Schwartzbaum & Harlow, 1969; Thompson, 1981) have shown that infant monkeys with aspiration amygdala lesions displayed more fear responses during social encounters than did control monkeys with whom they were paired, and these fear responses became more profound whenever control animals became more active. By contrast, responses to novel objects in the absence of other monkeys revealed an opposite pattern of results, with operated monkeys displaying fewer fear responses than controls. These results suggest that the neonatally operated animals have difficulty in evaluating potentially threatening social situations, although they seem uninhibited when confronted with novel objects. When observed in dyadic social interactions as they reached adulthood, monkeys with neonatal aspiration lesions of the amygdala, like those with similar lesions in adulthood, showed transient hyperactivity and were subordinate to control animals during social interactions, suggesting that the amygdala lesions may have affected the normal development of aggressive responses (Bachevalier, 1994; Thompson, 1981; Thompson, Bergland & Towfighi, 1977).

Interestingly, recent investigations of social interactions in monkeys with neonatal neurotoxic amygdala lesions and age-matched controls (Bauman et al., 2004; Prather et al., 2001) have demonstrated that the neonatally operated monkeys retained their ability to produce all affiliative and social gestures, although they expressed more fear, reduced amount of physical contacts with partners and more submissive responses at both 6 and 9 months. Thus, although the social changes following selective neonatal amygdala lesions were much less severe in magnitude than those found when the amygdala damage was associated with cortical damage (as in the case of aspiration lesions), it still remains to be seen whether greater emotional and social changes will emerge as the operated animals from these more recent reports reach maturity.

Summary

Neonatal damage to the amygdala does not alter object recognition memory or stimulus–reward associations, but severely impairs the regulation of emotional responses to animate and inanimate stimuli. In addition, although neonatal aspiration lesions of the amygdala that included portions of the medial temporal cortical areas resulted in enhanced social fear and alteration in social interactions that became more severe as the animals reached adulthood, amygdala lesions that spared the cortical areas yielded similar enhanced social fear but milder changes in social interactions. Thus, the data suggest that the behavioural changes seen after neonatal amygdala lesions are exacerbated by additional damage to the adjacent cortical areas. However, future investigations are required to directly assess whether the different behavioural outcomes between these developmental studies reflect variations in lesion extent, rearing conditions, timing of social testing, or a combination of these factors.

Neonatal damage to the hippocampal formation

Effects on memory

Monkeys with neonatal aspiration lesions of the hippocampal formation showed no deficits in procedural learning or item-specific recognition memory (Bachevalier, Beauregard & Alvarado, 1999). This lack of memory impairment, however, does not imply that neonatal hippocampal damage spares all memory processes. Indeed, these same neonatally operated animals showed severe impairments on three memory tasks that have been shown to be sensitive to neurotoxic hippocampal lesions in adult monkeys (Alvarado & Bachevalier, 2005; Nemanic, Alvarado & Bachevalier, 2004): recognition memory (VPC task) when long delays are used (Pascalis & Bachevalier, 1999), transverse patterning problems, and recognition of the locations of rewards on a testing board (Alvarado, Wright & Bachevalier, 2002). Because these memory tasks tax recognition-based incidental memory (VPC) and relational memory based on conjunctive representations linking an item with other items (transverse patterning) or with spatial information (spatial DNMS), they have also been thought to measure a precursor form of episodic memory processes in animals (Eichenbaum, 2001). Thus, monkeys with neonatal hippocampal lesions demonstrated a specific loss in relational (or episodic) memory processes, sparing familiarity-based object recognition as measured by object DNMS (see Nemanic, Alvarado & Bachevalier, 2004 for a discussion of the different declarative memory processes taxed by the VPC and DNMS).

These data on monkeys with neonatal hippocampal lesions parallel those found in children with developmental amnesia who suffer from pathology of the hippocampal formation associated with severe impairment in declarative memory processes (see for review Bachevalier & Vargha-Khadem 2005; see also Salmond *et al.*, this volume, Chapter 4). Thus, after early hippocampal pathology, both children and monkeys show a pronounced impairment in context-rich memory processes, including memory for unique events. In individuals with developmental amnesia this impairment in the recall of events and episodes prevails despite the relative preservation of semantic memory and recognition memory (Vargha-Khadem *et al.*, 1997). Furthermore, in at least one individual, neonatal hippocampal pathology appears to selectively impair recollection-based as compared with familiarity-based recognition abilities. Whether the deficit in monkeys with neonatal hippocampal lesions in incidental item recognition (VPC), particularly at long delays, is due to the same distinction between familiarity-based and recollection-based recognition remains to be determined. In the same way, it has yet to be demonstrated whether individuals with developmental amnesia will be impaired in recognition of incidental unique items, especially at long delays, although this is true for adults with acquired damage to the hippocampus (Pascalis *et al.*, 2004).

Effects on socioemotional behaviours

While there is little evidence of behavioural changes following hippo-campal lesions in adult monkeys, a decreased fear towards a human observer has previously been reported (Butter, Mishkin & Mirsky, 1968). Recent studies from our laboratory have shown that selective neurotoxic hippocampal lesions in the adult monkeys result in increased production of tense or anxious signals and activity (hyperlocomotion), as well as reduced affiliative signals with familiar and unfamiliar peers. By contrast, neither behavioural and physiological emotional reactivity to aversive stimuli nor the learning of association between a stimulus and its current reward value were affected (Machado & Bachevalier, 2002, 2003b, 2006). Thus, it is possible that an inability to accurately represent, retain and recollect stimuli, especially complex social stimuli, in their proper contextual environment after hippocampal lesions (see above) might result in inappropriate responses to social signals and altered social relationships. Similarly, a protracted emergence of behavioural abnor-malities following early nonselective hippocampal damage was observed in our developmental studies in monkeys (Beauregard, Málková & Bachevalier, 1995). Thus, although monkeys with neonatal hippocampal damage presented few changes in emotional and social behaviour when they were evaluated in infancy (at 2 months and 6 months), in adulthood they displayed less social contact with their normal peers and exhibited more motor stereotypies than normal controls.

In a more recent study investigating the effects of more selective neo-natal hippocampal damage in social interactions in monkeys, Bauman and colleagues (2004) reported no changes in emotional and social behaviours but greater activity levels when the animals were tested in infancy (at 3, 6 and 9 months), although further investigations of these operated animals when they reached adolescence (i.e. 18 months of age) indicated the presence of stereotypic behaviours (Babineau *et al.*, 2005). It is not yet known whether the animals with these more selective hippo-campal lesions, like those with aspiration hippocampal lesions described above, will show more changes in social behaviours as they mature. Likewise, although children with neonatal hippocampal pathology do not show changes in behaviours other than memory, it remains to be seen whether some of these individuals will demonstrate other behavioural changes as they reach adulthood. It is clear, however, that these children with profound memory impairment do not suffer from autism (see Salmond *et al.*, this volume, Chapter 4).

Summary

Neonatal damage to the hippocampal formation in monkeys does not affect item-specific recognition, but severely impairs recognition of incidental unique items at long delays as well as object and spatial relational memory. In addition, neonatal hippocampal lesions seem to produce anxious behaviours and enhanced locomotion that could in turn alter normal social interactions.

Neonatal damage to the temporal cortical areas

The only primate study that has begun to investigate the effects of neonatal damage to the ento- and perirhinal cortex on cognitive functions has indicated that, unlike neonatal damage to the amygdala and hippocampal formation, these early cortical lesions profoundly altered item-specific recognition memory (Málková *et al.*, 1998). In addition, recent reports suggest that these medial temporal cortical areas may also contribute to the regulation of emotional responses and motivational states in both monkeys and humans (Liu & Richmond, 2000; Liu, Murray & Richmond, 2000; Meunier & Bachevalier, 2002; Meunier, Cirilli & Bachevalier, 2006). For example, as discussed in our recent report (Meunier, Cirilli & Bachevalier, 2006), aside from its important role in perceptual and mnemonic functions, and congruent with its dual position as the first multimodal station of the ventral visual ('what') pathway, and gateway to the hippocampus, the perirhinal cortex also possesses intimate connections with both the amygdala and orbital frontal cortex (Suzuki, 1996). It is thus critically placed to integrate emotional and perceptual-mnemonic processes, perhaps by storing the emotional significance of prior experience. Thus, it will not be surprising to find significant changes in emotional reactions and social interactions after early damage to this medial temporal cortical area, although this remains to be tested.

Implications for autism

The developmental studies reviewed here have provided several important results with implications for autism. The first of these results concerns the effects of neonatal as compared with later lesions. None of the neonatal lesions resulted in significant sparing of functions even when the damage occurred in the first two postnatal weeks, suggesting that these structures operate in early infancy to support cognitive processes. Thus, despite the greater plasticity of the brain in early infancy, no other neural regions can assume these functions even when the damage occurs neonatally. Moreover, in the case of behavioural and emotional responses, the neonatal lesions yielded changes that were either not present, or less severe, in animals with the same lesions acquired in adulthood, presumably because brain reorganization that follows these early lesions alters the maturation of developing neural systems remote from the lesion site, as was demonstrated for the prefrontal–striatal system in the case of extensive neonatal MTL damage. Evidence concerning the severity of the effects of neonatal lesions as compared with later lesions confirms the validity of inferring implications for autism from the work on primates, as was done in an earlier report (Bachevalier, 1994).

In this earlier report it was concluded that extensive neonatal damage to the medial temporal lobe region might be related to the critical determinants of autistic behaviour. Based on the experimental evidence at that time, it was also postulated that the amygdala was likely to be involved in the social dysfunction of all cases of autism, but that the hippocampus may only be involved in people with autism who demonstrate additional impairments in language acquisition and overall cognitive abilities. Given the more recent experimental data reported above, this view can be updated and revised in three ways relating to (1) the effects of neonatal damage to specific structures; (2) the effects of more extensive MTL neonatal lesions; and (3) the effects of more extensive lesions on other neural systems.

The effects of neonatal damage to specific structures

Neonatal damage to any one specific MTL structure does not yield a behavioural profile fully resembling autism. However, damage to each structure individually can be associated with several specific symptoms observed in autism, as outlined below.

Selective neonatal amygdala lesions spared both memory processes and the production of social signals and behaviours. However, this early insult did result in heightened fear of social stimuli and submissive gestures, greater tendency to flee others and reduced social contacts (Bachevalier, 1994; Bauman et al., 2004), although it did not yield complete social withdrawal or lack of social interest. This pattern of behavioural changes is reminiscent not only of the high degree of anxiety observed in people with autism (Amaral 2002; Bradley et al., 2004; Kim et al., 2000) but also of the social perception deficits that have been observed. Thus, compared with persons without autism of similar verbal level, persons with autism are poorer at recognizing emotional expressions and gestures; reasoning about what others think, know or believe; and making social attributions and judgements. In addition, even when they are aware of the mental states of others, they do not modify their behaviour according to the perceived emotional states of others (see for review Loveland 2001, 2005). Thus, an early amygdala dysfunction could be associated with some of the social deficits found in autistic individuals.

This view is supported by recent evidence suggesting morphological and functional changes in the amygdalae of persons with autism. Postmortem investigations of the brain of people with autism indicate neuropathological changes in the amygdala (Bauman & Kemper, 2004) and abnormal amygdala volume has now been demonstrated in several studies (see for review Bachevalier & Loveland 2006; Cody, Pelphrey & Piven, 2002). Furthermore, recent functional neuroimaging studies demonstrate weak or absent amygdala activation in individuals with autism compared to matched controls during tasks involving face perception or the implicit processing of facial expressions (Critchley *et al.*, 2000; Pierce *et al.*, 2004). Similarly, increased amygdala activation has been shown to occur when healthy participants are asked to make judgements about a person's mental state based on eye expression, but this increased activation does not occur in individuals with autism (Baron-Cohen *et al.*, 1999).

Nevertheless, the social impairment in autism is greater than the social impairment that follows selective neonatal amygdala lesions. Thus, it is likely that additional neuropathology to adjacent medial temporal cortical areas could exacerbate the social deficit. In addition, other neural systems, which are known to participate in the regulation of social cognition (i.e. orbital frontal, cingulate and parietal cortex), may also be affected in people with autism. This latter view is supported by the findings that individuals with autism are not only impaired in recognizing other people's emotions and reactions in social situations, lack insight into the mental life of other people, and do not appreciate others' points of view (functions that could be supported by the amygdala, Adolphs, 2001), but they are also less able to use information about others to guide their own behaviour (Loveland, 2001, 2005). This difficulty in self-regulation of socioemotional behaviour in autism has recently been linked to a malfunction of the orbital frontal cortex that is known to regulate decision-making behaviours (Bachevalier & Loveland, 2006).

Selective neonatal hippocampal damage causes profound impairment in relational and declarative memory processes, sparing immediate memory and item-specific recognition memory. However, selective neonatal hippocampal damages causes little or no impairment in social interactions, at least in early development. A number of reports have now indicated that individuals with autism show normal or near normal performance in recognition and free-recall tasks (Bennetto, Pennington & Rogers, 1996; Minshew & Goldstein 1993; Renner, Klinger & Klinger, 2000), but impaired performance on tasks measuring episodic memory (Boucher, 1981; Boucher & Lewis, 1989; Bowler, Gardiner & Grice, 2000; Klein, Chan & Loftus, 1999; Millward *et al.*, 2000; Toichi & Kamio, 2003).

These findings are confirmed and extended in a recent study (Loveland *et al.*, 2008). In this study we compared the performance of individuals with low-functioning autism (LFA), high-functioning autism (HFA), or no autism (NA) in an object memory span task measuring item-specific recognition memory, and a spatial memory span task measuring spatial relational memory. Both the LFA and the HFA groups obtained a memory span similar to that of the NA group in the object condition, whereas both groups obtained a span less than that of the NA group in the spatial condition. The normal span obtained by all participants with autism in the object version of the task indicates that item-specific memory is not substantially affected in autism. By contrast, relational memory processes as measured by the spatial memory span appear to be affected in the low-functioning group and in the high-functioning group. These findings parallel those of a recent study (Minshew & Goldstein, 2001) reporting poorer performance of individuals with autism as compared to controls on maze learning tasks and on spatial span tasks (see Williams, Minshew & Goldstein, this volume, Chapter 7). Further, in a recent review of memory functions in autism, Ben Shalom (2003) concluded that, for memory tasks that do not depend on episodic (relational) memory but on perceptual representation system or semantic memory, individuals with autism show intact performance. Given the critical role of the hippocampus in relational memory tasks, but a less critical role in item-specific memory tasks (Alvarado & Bachevalier, 2005; Mishkin *et al.*, 1997; Nemanic, Alvarado & Bachevalier, 2004), these data imply a dysfunction of a system involving the hippocampus in persons with autism (see also DeLong, this volume, Chapter 6). This conclusion is supported by volumetric (Aylward *et al.*, 1999; Schumann *et al.*, 2004; Sparks *et al.*, 2002) and neuropathological (Saitoh, Karns & Courchesne, 2001; Bauman & Kemper, 2004) changes in the hippocampus in individuals with autism.

The effects of more extensive MTL neonatal lesions

The developmental data from nonhuman primates (Bachevalier, 1994) indicate that more profound behavioural and cognitive changes occur when neonatal damage to the medial temporal cortical areas and/or the hippocampus is associated with damage to the amygdala. In the case of the extensive neonatal MTL lesions, the insult resulted in severe memory loss, involving both relational and item-specific memory processes, though preserving procedural learning. The memory deficit was associated with profound changes in socioemotional behaviour as well as motor stereotypies.

Increased magnitude of the behavioural changes following more extensive MTL lesions has also been demonstrated in the case of emotional responses to animate and inanimate stimuli in adult monkeys (Meunier *et al.*, 1999). In this study, we showed that monkeys with aspiration lesions of the amygdala that included the ento- and perirhinal cortex yielded behavioural changes that were greater in magnitude than those found after neurotoxic amygdala lesions which spared these cortical areas.

Thus, damage to the cortical areas on the parahippocampal gyrus and to the hippocampal formation appears to exacerbate the behavioural changes seen after damage to the amygdala. This pattern of results suggests that the extent of damage to the amygdala, hippocampus and adjacent cortical areas might critically correlate with the severity of the social and behavioural symptoms as well as with the extent of learning disabilities and language impairment seen in people with autism. This interpretation has recently been espoused by Boucher and colleagues (2005).

The effects of more extensive lesions on other neural systems

The nonhuman primate findings show that extensive neonatal damage to the medial temporal region alters the maturation and proper functioning of at least one neural system remote from the site of the lesion, namely the prefrontal–striatal dopamine system. Such dysregulation of prefrontal–striatal dopamine transmission could have an interesting relationship with the ritualistic and stereotyped behaviours (Bachevalier, Málková & Mishkin, 2001) as well as the impaired working memory ability (J. Bachevalier, unpublished data) found in these same operated animals. Although it remains to be determined whether the prefrontal–striatal dysregulation results from combined damage to all structures or rather from damage to specific structures within the MTL region, these experimental data suggest that the impairment in certain executive functions mediated by the prefrontal cortex, as well as the structural and functional abnormalities in the prefrontal cortex found in individuals with autism (see for review Bachevalier & Loveland, 2006), could likewise be related to abnormalities in the medial temporal inputs to the prefrontal cortex in early infancy. These dysfunctional temporal–prefrontal connections may result in maldevelopment of the prefrontal cortex, a cortical area known for its protracted maturation well into adolescence.

Summary

The experimental findings lead to several hypotheses concerning potential configurations of underlying brain dysfunction that may be related to differing outcomes in autism. They have the potential to illuminate some of the most persistent issues in the field of autism research. Among these are the origins of the developmental differences observed in persons with autism with and without mental retardation, those who do or do not exhibit early regression, and those with differing severity of autism.

Acknowledgements

The work reviewed here is supported in part by grants MH58846 (NIMH), HD35471 (NICHD), Yerkes Base Grant 00165 (NIH), and the Center for Behavioural Neuroscience IBN9876754 (NSF).

References

Adolphs, R. (2001). The neurobiology of social cognition. *Current Opinion in Neurobiology*, *11*, 231–239.

Alvarado, M. C. & Bachevalier, J. (2000). Revisiting the maturation of medial temporal lobe memory functions in primates. *Learning & Memory*, *7*, 244–256.

Alvarado, M. & Bachevalier, J. (2005). Selective neurotoxic damage to the hippocampal formation impairs acquisition and performance of the transverse patterning task and location memory in rhesus macaques. *Hippocampus*, *15*, 118–131.

Alvarado, M. C., Wright, A. A. & Bachevalier, J. (2002). Object and spatial relational memory in adult rhesus monkeys is impaired by neonatal lesions of the hippocampal formation but not the amygdaloid complex. *Hippocampus*, *12*, 421–433.

Amaral, D. G. (2002). The primate amygdala and the neurobiology of social behaviour: implications for understanding social anxiety. *Biological Psychiatry*, *51*, 11–17.

Aylward, E. H., Minshew, N. J., Goldstein, G., Honeycutt, N. A., Augustine, A. M., Yates, K. O. *et al.* (1999). MRI volumes of amygdala and hippocampus in non-mentally retarded autistic adolescents and adults. *Neurology*, *53*, 2145–2150.

Babineau, B. A., Bauman, M. D., Toscana, J. E. *et al.* (2005). Juvenile macaque monkeys with neonatal lesions of the amygdala and hippocampus display higher frequencies of stereotypies than control subjects. *Society for Neuroscience Abstracts*, *31*. Retrieved from http://sfn.scholarone.com.

Bachevalier, J. (1994). Medial temporal lobe structures and autism: a review of clinical and experimental findings. *Neuropsychologia 32*, 627–648.

Bachevalier, J., Beauregard, M. & Alvarado, M. (1999). Long-term effect of neonatal damage to the hippocampal formation and amygdaloid cortex on object discrimination learning and object recognition memory in monkeys. *Behavioural Neuroscience*, *113*, 1127–1151.

Bachevalier, J. & Loveland, K. (2006). The orbitofrontal-amygdala circuit and self-regulation of social-emotional behaviour in autism. *Neuroscience and Biobehavioural Reviews*, *30*, 97–117.

Bachevalier, J. & Málková, M. (2000). Behavioural indices of early medial temporal lobe dysfunction in nonhuman primates. In H. S. Levin & J. Grafman (eds.), *Neuroplasticity and reorganization of function after brain injury*. pp. 27–48. Oxford: Oxford University Press.

Bachevalier, J., Málková, M. & Mishkin, M. (2001). Effects of selective neonatal temporal lobe lesions on socioemotional behaviour in infant rhesus monkeys (Macaca mulatta). *Behavioural Neuroscience*, *115*, 545–559.

Bachevalier, J. & Meunier, M. (2005). Neurobiology of socio-emotional cognition in primates. In A. Eaton & N. Emery (eds.), *Cognitive neuroscience of social behaviour*, pp. 19–58. Hove: Psychology Press.

Bachevalier, J. & Vargha-Khadem, F. (2005). The primate hippocampus: ontogeny, early insult and memory. *Current Opinion in Neurobiology*, *15*, 168–174.

Baron-Cohen, S., Ring, H. A., Wheelwright, S., Bullmore, E. T., Brammer, M. J., Simmons, A. & Williams, S. C. R. (1999). Social intelligence in the normal and autistic brain: an fMRI study. *European Journal of Neuroscience*, *11*, 1891–1898.

Bauman, M. L. & Kemper, T. L. (2004). Structural brain anatomy in autism: What is the evidence? In M. L. Bauman & T. L. Kemper (eds.), *The neurobiology of autism* pp. 119–145. Baltimore: Johns Hopkins Press.

Bauman, M. D., Lavenex, P., Mason, W. A., Capitanio, J. P. & Amaral, D. G. (2004). The development of social behaviour following neonatal amygdala lesions in rhesus monkeys. *Journal of Cognitive Neuroscience*, *16*, 1388–1411.

Baxter, M. G. & Murray, E. A. (2000). Reinterpreting the behavioural effects of amygdala lesions in nonhuman primates. In J. P. Aggleton (ed.), *The amygdala: A functional analysis*, pp. 545–568. Oxford: Oxford University Press.

Beauregard, M., Málková, L. & Bachevalier, J. (1995). Stereotypies and loss of social affiliation after early hippocampectomy in monkeys. *NeuroReport*, *6*, 2521–2526.

Bennetto, L., Pennington, B. F. & Rogers, S. J. (1996). Intact and impaired memory functions in autism. *Child Development*, *67*, 1816–1835.

Ben Shalom, D. (2003). Memory in autism: review and synthesis. *Cortex*, *39*, 1129–1138.

Bertolino, A., Saunders, R. C., Mattay, V. S., Bachevalier, J., Frank, J. A. & Weinberger, D. R. (1997). Altered development of prefrontal neurons in rhesus monkeys with neonatal mesial temporo-limbic lesions: a proton magnetic resonance spectroscopic imaging study. *Cerebral Cortex*, *7*, 740–748.

Boucher, J. (1981). Memory for recent events in autistic children. *Journal of Autism and Developmental Disorders*, *11*, 293–301.

Boucher, J., Cowell, P., Howard, M., Broks, P., Farrant, A., Roberts, N. & Mayes, A. (2005). A combined clinical neuropsychological and neuroanatomical study of adults with high-functioning autism. *Cognitive Neuropsychiatry*, *10*, 165–214.

Boucher, J. & Lewis, V. (1989). Memory impairments and communication in relatively able autistic children. *Journal of Child Psychology and Psychiatry*, *30*, 99–122.

Bowler, D. M., Gardiner, J. M. & Grice, S. J. (2000). Episodic memory and remembering in adults with Asperger syndrome. *Journal of Autism and Developmental Disorders*, *30*, 295–304.

Bradley, E., Summers, J., Wood, H. & Bryson, S. (2004). Comparing rates of psychiatric and behaviour disorders in adolescents and young adults with severe intellectual disability with and without autism. *Journal of Autism and Developmental Disorders*, *34*, 151–161.

Brown, M. W. & Aggleton, J. P. (2001). Recognition memory: what are the roles of the perirhinal cortex and hippocampus? *Nature Review Neuroscience*, *2*, 51–61.

Butter, C. M., Mishkin, M. & Mirsky, A. F. (1968). Emotional responses toward humans in monkeys with selective frontal lesions. *Physiology & Behaviour*, *3*, 213–215.

Chlan-Fourney, J., Webster, M. J., Felleman, D. J. & Bachevalier, J. (2000). Neonatal medial temporal lobe lesions alter the distribution of tyrosine hydroxylase immunoreactive varicosities in the macaque prefrontal cortex. *Society for Neuroscience Abstracts*, *26*, 609.

Chlan-Fourney, J., Webster, M. J., Jung, J. & Bachevalier, J. (2003) Neonatal medial temporal lobe lesions decrease GABAergic interneuron densities in macaque prefrontal cortex: implications for schizophrenia and autism. *Society for Neuroscience Abstracts*, *29*. Retrieved from http://sfn.scholarone.com

Cody, H., Pelphrey, K. & Piven, J. (2002). Structural and functional magnetic resonance imaging of autism. *International Journal of Developmental Neuroscience*, *766*, 1–18.

Critchley, H. D., Daly, E. M., Bullmore, E. T., Williams, S. C., Van Amelsvoort, T., Robertson, D. M., Rowe, A., Phillips, M., McAlonan, G., Howlin, P. & Murphy, D. G. (2000). The functional neuroanatomy of social behaviour: Changes in cerebral blood flow when people with autistic disorder process facial expressions. *Brain*, *123*, 2203–2212.

Eichenbaum, H. (2001). The hippocampus and declarative memory: cognitive mechanisms and neural codes. *Behavioural Brain Research*, *127*, 199–207.

Heinz, A., Saunders, R. C., Kolachana, B. S., Jones, D. W., Gorey, J. G., Bachevalier, J. & Weinberger, D. R. (2000). Striatal dopamine receptors and transporters in monkeys with neonatal temporal limbic damage. *Synapse*, *32*, 71–79.

Kalin, N. H., Shelton, S. E. & Davidson, R. J. (2004). The role of the central nucleus of the amygdala in mediating fear and anxiety in the primate. *Journal of Neuroscience*, *24*, 5506–5515.

Kalin, N. H., Shelton, S. E., Davidson, R. J. & Kelly, A. E. (2001). The primate amygdala mediates acute fear but not the behavioural and physiological components of anxious temperament. *Journal of Neuroscience*, *21*, 2067–2074.

Kim, J., Szatmari, P., Bryson, S., Streiner, D. & Wilson, F. (2000). The prevalence of anxiety and mood problems among children with autism and Asperger syndrome. *Autism*, *4*, 117–126.

Klein, B., Chan, R. & Loftus, J. (1999). Independence of episodic and semantic knowledge: The case from autism. *Social Cognition*, *17*, 413–436.

Lavenex, P. & Amaral, D. G. (2000). Hippocampal-neocortical interaction: a hierarchy of associativity. *Hippocampus*, *10*, 420–30.

Liu, Z. & Richmond, B. J. (2000). Response differences in monkey TE and perirhinal cortex: stimulus association related to reward schedules. *Journal of Neurophysiology*, *83*, 1677–1692.

Liu, Z., Murray, E. A. & Richmond, B. J. (2000). Learning motivational significance of visual cues for reward schedules requires rhinal cortex. *Nature Neuroscience*, *3*, 1307–1315.

Loveland, K. (2001). Toward an ecological theory of autism. In J. A. Burack, T. Charman, N. Yirmiya & P. R. Zelazo (eds.), *The development of autism: perspectives from theory and research*, pp. 17–37. Mahwah, NJ: Erlbaum.

(2005). Social-emotional impairment and self-regulation in autism spectrum disorders. In J. Nadel & D. Muir (eds.), *Typical and impaired emotional development*, pp. 365–382. Oxford: Oxford University Press.

Loveland, K. A., Bachevalier, J., Pearson, D. A. & Lane, D. M. (2008). Fronto-limbic functioning in children and adolescents with and without autism. *Neuropsychologia*, *46*, 49–62.

Machado, C. J. & Bachevalier, J. (2002). Selective lesions to the amygdala, hippocampus or orbital frontal cortex alter reactivity to a human intruder in monkeys. *Society for Neuroscience Abstracts*, *26*. Retrieved from http://sfn.scholarone.com.

(2003a). Nonhuman primate models of childhood psychopathology: the promise and the limitations. *Journal of Child Psychology and Psychiatry: Annual Research Review*, *44*, 1–24.

(2003b). Impact of amygdaloid, hippocampal and orbital frontal cortex lesions on approach/avoidance responses in monkeys. *Society for Neuroscience Abstracts*, *29*. Retrieved from http://sfn.scholarone.com.

(2006). The impact of selective amygdala, orbital frontal or hippocampal formation lesions on established social relationship in monkeys. *Behavioral Neuroscience*, *120*, 761–786.

Málková, L., Mishkin, M., Suomi, S. J. & Bachevalier, J. (1997). Socioemotional behaviour in adult rhesus monkeys after early versus late lesions of the medial temporal lobe. *Annals of the New York Academy of Science 807*, 538–540.

Málková, L., Pixley, G. I., Webster, M. J., Mishkin, M. & Bachevalier, J. (1998). The effects of early rhinal lesions on visual recognition memory in rhesus monkeys. *Society for Neuroscience Abstracts*, *24*, 1906.

Meunier, M. & Bachevalier, J. (2002). Comparison of emotional responses in monkeys with rhinal cortex and amygdala lesions. *Emotion*, *2*, 147–161.

Meunier, M., Cirilli, L. & Bachevalier, J. (2006). Responses to affective stimuli with entorhinal or perirhinal cortex lesions. *The Journal of Neuroscience*, *26*, 7718–7722.

Meunier, M., Bachevalier, J., Murray E. A., Málková, L. & Mishkin, M. (1999). Effects of aspiration vs neurotoxic lesions of the amygdala on emotional responses in monkeys. *European Journal of Neuroscience*, *11*, 4403–4418.

Millward, C., Powell, S., Messer, D. & Jordan, R. (2000). Recall for self and other in autism: children's memory for events experienced by themselves and their peers. *Journal of Autism and Developmental Disorders*, *30*, 15–28.

Minshew, N. J. & Goldstein, G. (1993). Is autism an amnesic disorder? Evidence from the California Verbal Learning Test. *Neuropsychologia*, *7*, 209–216.

(2001). The pattern of intact and impaired memory functions in autism. *Journal of Child Psychology & Psychiatry*, *42*, 1095–1101.

Mishkin, M., Spiegler, B. J., Saunders, R. C. & Malamut, B. L. (1982). An animal model of global amnesia. In S. Corkin, K. L. Davis, J. H. Growdon, E. Usdin & R. J. Wurtman (eds.), *Alzheimer's disease: a report of progress*, pp. 235–247. New York: Raven Press.

Mishkin, M., Suzuki, W. A., Gadian, D. G. & Vargha-Khadem, F. (1997). Hierarchical organization of cognitive memory. *Philosophy Transactions of the Royal Society of London B: Biological Sciences*, *352*, 1461–1467.

Murray, E. A. & Bussey, T. J. (1999). Perceptual-mnemonic functions of the perirhinal cortex. *Trends in Cognitive Sciences*, *3*, 142–151.

Nemanic, S., Alvarado, M. & Bachevalier, J. (2004). The hippocampal/ parahippocampal regions and recognition memory: insights from visual paired-comparison versus object delayed nonmatching in monkeys. *Journal of Neuroscience*, *24*, 2013–2026.

O'Reilly, R. C. & Rudy, J. W. (2001). Conjunctive representations in learning and memory: principles of cortical and hippocampal function. *Psychological Review*, *108*, 311–345.

Pascalis, O. & Bachevalier, J. (1999). Neonatal aspiration lesions of the hippocampal formation impair visual recognition memory when assessed by paired-comparison task but not by delayed nonmatching-to-sample task. *Hippocampus*, *9*, 609–616.

Pascalis, O., Hunkin, N. M., Holdstock, J. S., Isaac, C. L. & Mayes, A. R. (2004). Visual paired comparison performance is impaired in a patient with selective hippocampal lesions and relatively intact item recognition. *Neuropsychologia*, *42*, 1293–1300.

Pierce, K., Haist, F., Sedaghat, F. & Courchesne, E. (2004). The brain response to personally familiar faces in autism: findings of fusiform activity and beyond. *Brain*, *127*, 2703–2716.

Prather, M. D., Lavenex, P., Mauldin-Jourdain, M. L., Mason, W. A., Capitanio, J. P., Mendoza, S. P. & Amaral, D. G. (2001). Increased social fear and decreased fear of objects in monkeys with neonatal amygdala lesions. *Neuroscience*, *106*, 653–658.

Renner, P., Klinger, L. G. & Klinger, M. R. (2000). Implicit and explicit memory in autism: is autism an amnesic disorder? *Journal of Autism and Developmental Disorders*, *30*, 3–14.

Saitoh, O., Karns, C. & Courchesne, E. (2001). Development of the hippocampal formation from 2 to 42 years: MRI evidence of smaller area. *Brain, 124,* 1317–1324.

Saunders, R. C., Kolachana, B. S., Bachevalier, J. & Weinberger, D. R. (1998). Neonatal lesions of the medial temporal lobe disrupt prefrontal cortical regulation of striatal dopamine. *Nature, 393,* 169–171.

Schumann, C. M., Hamstra, J., Goodlin-Jones, B. L., Lotspeich, L. J., Kwon, H., Buonocore, M. H. *et al.* (2004). The amygdala is enlarged in children but not adolescents with autism; the hippocampus is enlarged at all ages. *Journal of Neuroscience, 24,* 6392–6401.

Sparks, B. F., Friedman, S. D., Shaw, D. W., Aylward, E. H., Echelard, D., Artru, A. A. *et al.* (2002). Brain structural abnormalities in young children with autism spectrum disorder. *Neurology, 59,* 184–192.

Suzuki, W. A. (1996). Neuroanatomy of the monkey entorhinal, perirhinal and parahippocampal cortices: organization of cortical inputs and interconnections with amygdala and striatum. *Seminars in the Neurosciences, 8,* 3–12.

Thompson, C. I. (1981). Long-term behavioural development of rhesus monkeys after amygdalectomy in infancy. In Y. Ben-Ari (ed.), *The amygdaloid complex,* pp. 259–270. Amsterdam: Elsevier.

Thompson, C. I., Bergland, R. M. & Towfighi, J. T. (1977). Social and nonsocial behaviours of adult rhesus monkeys after amygdalectomy in infancy or adulthood. *Journal of Comparative and Physiological Psychology, 91,* 533–548.

Thompson, C. I., Schwartzbaum, J. S. & Harlow, H. F. (1969). Development of social fear after amygdalectomy in infant rhesus monkeys. *Physiology and Behaviour, 4,* 249–254.

Toichi, M. & Kamio, Y. (2003). Long-term memory in high-functioning autism: Controversy on episodic memory in autism reconsidered. *Journal of Autism and Developmental Disorders, 33,* 151–161.

Vargha-Khadem, F., Gadian, D. G., Watkins, K. E., Connelly, A., Van Paesschen, W. & Mishkin, M. (1997). Differential effects of early hippocampal pathology on episodic and semantic memory. *Science, 277,* 376–380.

Yonelinas, A. P. (2002). The nature of recollection and familiarity: a review of 30 years of research. *Journal of Memory and Language, 46,* 441–517.

Zola-Morgan, S. & Squire, L. R. (1985). Complementary approaches to the study of memory: human amnesia and animal models. In N. W. Weinberger, J. L. McGaugh and G. Lynch (eds.), *Memory systems of the brain: animal and human cognitive processes,* pp. 463–477. New York: Guilford.

3 Acquired memory disorders in adults: implications for autism

Andrew Mayes and Jill Boucher

Introduction

Memory can be impaired by brain damage at any age. Developmental memory disorders can result from genetic factors or genetic/environmental interactions which prevent the brain from developing normally; or from early-acquired brain lesions. Developmental memory problems are likely to resemble adult memory problems with respect to specific deficits in information processing that depend on dedicated brain structures where there is little scope for transfer of function, as may be true of the medial temporal lobes (MTL) (Bachevalier, this volume, Chapter 2).

The effects of developmental memory problems are, however, likely to differ from the effects of adult-acquired memory problems in several ways. On the one hand, they may have a cumulative effect in so far as they slow or prevent the acquisition of knowledge critical for the development of social skills, language and crystallized intelligence. As a result, developmental memory problems may produce much more severe social, linguistic and cognitive disruption than adult memory problems, as appears to be the case in infant-lesioned as opposed to adult-lesioned primates (Bachevalier, this volume, Chapter 2). Conversely, early-acquired disorders could allow the acquisition of better compensatory strategies and coping skills than occurs in adult-acquired disorders. Also, if a structure has never been functional or even present, other brain structures will not have to adapt to working with it and then without it, so that their functioning may be more optimal.

Despite the differences between the effects of early-acquired as opposed to late-acquired memory deficits, the likely similarities of the actual deficits themselves and their brain bases suggest that the rich set of findings and theories relating to adult-acquired memory disorders can be profitably used as a heuristic to guide research into developmental memory impairments and anomalies. This argument applies to any neuro-developmental disorders in which atypical memory function occurs. However, it particularly applies to autistic spectrum disorders (ASDs) for two reasons.

43

First: despite the fact that high-functioning individuals have normal or superior intelligence overall, they nevertheless have certain subtle memory impairments, as documented in several chapters of the present book. Second: from the 1970s to the present day there have been persistent suggestions concerning possible parallels between the profile of memory strengths and weaknesses in autism and the memory profile associated with the adult-acquired amnesic syndrome. Early versions of this hypothesis (e.g. Boucher & Warrington, 1976; DeLong, 1978) were proposed at a time when autism was defined partly in terms of learning and language difficulties, such as might result from severe memory deficits. Moreover, it was widely argued at that time that the social impairments in autism might be secondary to severely delayed language, or to cognitive processes underlying the acquisition of language (e.g. Rutter, 1968; Churchill, 1972; Ricks & Wing, 1976). Severe memory deficits could therefore be seen as a possible cause of the social, as well as the intellectual and linguistic impairments of autism as then defined.

Changes in the definition of autism in the 1980s to exclude learning and language difficulties as core impairments, and abandonment of the suggestion that social impairments might result from language-related deficits, made the hypothesis that autism constitutes a developmental form of the amnesic syndrome untenable. This conclusion was reinforced by empirical studies of memory in individuals with high-functioning autism (HFA, used here to include Asperger syndrome) showing that memory is predominantly, though not wholly, intact (see Williams, Minshew & Goldstein, this volume, Chapter 7). Moreover, Vargha-Khadem *et al.*'s (1997) case studies of developmental amnesia showed that bilateral hippocampal lesions of early origin cause severe episodic memory impairments *not* accompanied by autism (see Salmond *et al.*, this volume, Chapter 4). Finally, many studies have demonstrated structural and functional abnormalities of the amygdala and associated prefrontal structures in people with autism, sufficient to explain the core social impairments (see e.g. Baron-Cohen *et al.*, 1999; Howard *et al.*, 2000). None of these developments, however, rules out the possibility that a developmental condition analogous to the adult-acquired global amnesic syndrome (associated with impaired semantic as well as episodic memory) causes the learning and language difficulties associated with low-functioning autism (LFA), as suggested within the original hypothesis, and as currently proposed by various authors (Bauman & Kemper, 2004; Boucher *et al.* 2005; Bachevalier, 1994; also Bachevalier, this volume, Chapter 2 and DeLong, this volume, Chapter 6).

The purpose of this chapter is, therefore, to present a summary of empirical findings and theories from the literature on adult-acquired organic memory impairments, particularly focusing on those aspects of memory that may have most relevance to autism, including an extended section on the amnesic syndrome. Following this summary, we suggest ways in which insights from the literature reviewed may illuminate autism itself, as manifested across the whole spectrum, including individuals with HFA; and also how this literature might be fruitful in guiding research into the causes of learning and language impairments in LFA.

Adult-acquired organic memory disorders

The idea that there are different kinds of memory, each supported by different sets of brain structures, is mainly based on evidence that non-overlapping brain lesions in human adults cause different memory disorders. The initial distinction is between forms of memory that only last for a few seconds (short-term or working memory) and longer-lasting forms of memory (long-term memory). Working memory involves several distinct slave systems that briefly hold very specific kinds of information, such as phonological or visuospatial information (perhaps by continued activity of the representing neurons), and a central executive that processes what is held in the slave systems and so enables complex thinking to occur (Baddeley, 1992). Working memory is disrupted by lesions of particular parts of the neocortex, prominently including the parietal cortex and probably the frontal cortex. When a specific slave system is disrupted by a lesion, long-term memory is not pervasively disrupted, but long-term memory for the kind of information held in the slave system is devastated (see Mayes, 2000).

Within long-term memory, the major distinction is between declarative and procedural memory (see Gardiner, this volume, Chapter 1). Declarative memory includes episodic memory, which is memory for personally experienced episodes; and semantic memory, which is memory for the kind of factual information available in dictionaries or encyclopedias. A defining feature of declarative memory is that those remembering know that they are remembering, i.e. recall or recognition is accompanied by a *feeling of memory*. Procedural memories are not accompanied by such a feeling and include memory for motor, perceptual and cognitive skills, various kinds of conditioning, and priming. Procedural memories are, therefore, heterogeneous and only share the feature of not being accompanied by a feeling of memory.

Lesions of the basal ganglia and cerebellum disrupt certain types of procedural memory. In particular, memory for certain kinds of skill is disrupted by basal ganglia and, more controversially, by cerebellar lesions (Mayes, 2000). Cerebellar lesions also disrupt motoric classical conditioning (Daum & Schugens, 1995; Mayes, 2000). Emotion conditioning is disrupted by amygdala lesions (for example, Bechara *et al.*, 1995). Although individuals with lesions of the amygdala can explicitly remember pairings of previously neutral events with aversive stimuli, they do not show learned development of autonomic responses (such as a change in skin conductance). In other words, they do not learn to associate automatic emotional responses with the neutral event. Although basal ganglia, cerebellar and amygdala lesions disrupt different kinds of skill and conditioning, they do not disrupt priming, some forms of which seem to be disrupted by lesions to those sensory neocortex regions which underlie representation of the primed information (e.g. Keane *et al.*, 1995). Nor is there convincing evidence that any of the above lesions disrupt declarative memory. The one partial exception may be amygdala lesions, which abolish the usual memory advantage shown for emotional over neutral stimuli, because such lesions reduce emotional arousal and hence the boost to the consolidation of declarative memory that emotion-related stimuli produce in typical individuals (Adolphs *et al.*, 1997).

In contrast, declarative memory is disrupted in a small number of memory disorders involving loss of memory for specific kinds of information – the agnosias, including prosopagnosia, or loss of memory for faces (Benson, Segara & Albert, 1974); also, and most notably, in a condition called the amnesic syndrome. The agnosias are associated with lesions of neocortex specific to the kind of information being processed. For example, prosopagnosia is often associated with lesions of the fusiform face area (Barton *et al.*, 2002). The amnesic syndrome, on the other hand, is associated with damage to any of a number of strongly interconnected brain regions, which include the structures of the MTL, the midline diencephalon and the basal forebrain. There is also evidence that damage to fibre tracts that connect these regions, such as the fornix, which interconnects parts of the MTL with parts of the midline diencephalon (for example, McMackin *et al.*, 1995), causes amnesia. This suggests that normal declarative memory depends on a system of connected structures working together in a highly organized way (Tranel & Damasio, 2002).

Evidence and theories relating to the adult-acquired amnesic syndrome are considered in more detail below.

The amnesic syndrome: empirical findings

The amnesic syndrome is sometimes confusingly referred to as 'organic amnesia'. To ensure clarity, 'organic amnesia' is used here to include any kind of memory disorder that is caused by brain damage or dysfunction, whereas 'amnesic syndrome' is used as the name of a specific kind of disorder of declarative memory as outlined above. It is called a syndrome because it comprises a collection of memory disorders that are in principle dissociable, and because it has many clinical causes including stroke, viral or bacterial brain diseases, alcoholism, various causes of hypoxia (e.g. cardiac arrest) and several others.

Anterograde and retrograde amnesia

The amnesic syndrome is thought to affect, either mainly or solely, declarative memory. The syndrome has two main features. First, affected individuals are very impaired at recalling and recognizing personal episodes or facts that they encountered often only seconds previously prior to being distracted. This symptom is known as anterograde amnesia and life, for people with anterograde amnesia, feels as if they are continually waking from a dream the contents of which fade from view almost as soon as they are grasped. Although people with amnesia are very poor at learning new facts or remembering what they have just experienced, many of them can hold information in immediate or working memory quite normally. For example, their digit spans are often normal. They can also show normal intelligence and, consistent with this, they seem to represent and manipulate incoming information fairly normally.

Second, individuals with the amnesic syndrome have impaired recall and recognition for facts and personal episodes that were encountered prior to their brain damage and were learned normally when they were encountered – retrograde amnesia. It is unclear to what extent anterograde and retrograde amnesia co-occur and how strongly they are correlated with each other. Although it is accepted that anterograde amnesia can sometimes occur in relative isolation, reports of focal retrograde amnesia have been more contentious (Kopelman, 1991, 2002).

Dissociation from procedural memory impairments

Amnesic individuals can show normal procedural memory, whether this is simple motoric classical conditioning or skill learning. However, they are often unable to recall the learning experience and so deny that they will be able to show conditioning or skill memory (Weiskrantz & Warrington, 1979). There is also evidence that amnesic individuals are unimpaired at some kinds of priming, although it is unresolved whether they show impairments with priming for novel information (Gooding, Mayes & van Eijk, 2000).

Possible subtypes based on processes

It has proved difficult to establish whether or not the amnesic syndrome comprises distinct subtypes, each caused by specific kinds of brain damage. If the syndrome does subdivide into several disorders, the division could relate to the different kinds of processes that are disrupted, the different kinds of information for which long-term memory is disrupted, or both. Possible subtypes based on processes are considered first.

Evidence related to process dissociations within the amnesic syndrome is currently inconclusive. As indicated above, there is some evidence that retrograde and anterograde amnesia may dissociate from each other in some individuals, although evidence for selective retrograde amnesia, in particular, is difficult to assess (Kapur, 2000; Kopelman, 2000). Furthermore, even if genuine double dissociations between anterograde and retrograde amnesia exist, little is known about their neuroanatomical bases. Also, most cases of the amnesic syndrome show both anterograde and retrograde amnesia even where damage seems relatively focal, so a single processing deficit may often underlie both post- and premorbid memory problems.

In recent years, most attention has been given to the possibility that recollection and familiarity memory can be separately disrupted by different brain lesions. Familiarity is a feeling that a target stimulus has been encountered before – a feeling that is not accompanied by recall of associated information. Recollection, on the other hand, involves recall of a target stimulus plus recall of associated information, and a feeling of memory for both the target stimulus and the associated information. Recognition depends on both recollection and familiarity, although the relative contribution of recollection and familiarity varies greatly for different recognition tests.

There is currently controversy about whether lesions of the hippocampus disrupt recollection but not familiarity and, relatedly, disrupt recall test performance, but have little effect on recognition except where it depends mainly on recollection. Some people with relatively selective hippocampal damage have shown good recognition and impaired recall, and tests suggest that familiarity has been preserved in the face of very impaired recollection (for example, Mayes *et al.*, 2002; Aggleton *et al.*, 2005). Others with relatively selective hippocampal damage have shown more or less equally impaired recollection and familiarity (Manns *et al.*, 2003). At present, there is no accepted explanation of why these different memory impairments are found in individuals with apparently similar lesions. However, one closely adjacent MTL structure that may be affected in cases such as those described by Manns *et al.* is the perirhinal cortex. Large lesions that include this structure disrupt familiarity, and its activity changes when human and monkey subjects show familiarity (Brown & Xiang, 1998). The fact that lesions of the perirhinal cortex often also disrupt recollection does not prove that this region mediates recollection. This is because it projects to the hippocampus, so perirhinal cortex damage partially disconnects the hippocampus.

Finally, whilst bearing the above problem in mind, it is important to realize that, although selective disorders of recollection and recall, caused by hippocampal lesions, may occur, there is not yet evidence that recollection can be impaired without familiarity also being disrupted.

Possible subtypes based on material specificity

As indicated above, research has also examined whether the amnesic syndrome can be divided up according to the kind of information memory for which is disrupted. Related to the controversy discussed above, involving the functional roles of certain MTL structures, some researchers believe that either episodic or semantic memory may be selectively disrupted in different subtypes of the amnesic syndrome. Large lesions that include the perirhinal cortex and other parts of the anterior MTLs severely disrupt acquisition of new semantic as well as episodic memories. However, Vargha-Khadem et al. (1997) found that three young people, who had suffered very early hypoxic damage to the hippocampus, not only showed good recognition and clearly impaired recall and recollection, but had also been able to acquire normal or relatively normal levels of semantic knowledge during the years in school. This suggested that hippocampal damage may impair the ability to put new episodic experiences into memory, but leave the ability to acquire new factual memories intact.

Subsequent work, however (for example, Holdstock et al., 2002), found that the ability to acquire new semantic memories is not completely preserved after selective hippocampal damage in adults. Nevertheless, there may be some protection for memories that can be acquired slowly across long periods of time and multiple exposures. Such slow acquisition of factual memories may depend less on the hippocampus, which is critical for rapid learning, than on neocortical structures that acquire memories slowly over widely spaced, multiple exposures. People who have relatively selective hippocampal damage should be very impaired at acquiring episodic memories, which typically depend on a single exposure, but will be less impaired at acquiring those semantic memories which can be acquired slowly. They will not show completely typical semantic memories, however, because the rapid learning abilities of the hippocampus also contribute to building these memories.

It should also be pointed out that there is no strong evidence that individuals who have a subset of the lesions that cause the amnesic syndrome ever show a selective deficit in the ability to *acquire* new semantic memories. Some researchers have argued, however, that semantic dementia (a condition caused by progressive atrophy of the anterior temporal lobes, involving a gradually worsening impairment of memory for previously well-established semantic information (Snowden, Goulding & Neary, 1989)) can be associated with relatively greater *loss* of semantic as compared to episodic memories.

The strongest evidence for subtypes based on material specificity is that which supports the view that amnesia is material-specific in a way that depends mainly on the laterality of lesion location. Thus, it is generally accepted that damage to memory structures in the left hemisphere particularly disrupts verbal memory, whereas right-sided damage particularly disrupts nonverbal kinds of memory (e.g. Milner, 1971). It is plausible to argue that small lesions to the association neocortex may disconnect part of these information representation and processing regions from the MTL-midline diencephalon-basal forebrain complex, which is prevented from performing its vital memory operations on very specific kinds of information. Ross (1982) reported several cases of this kind.

Other, more controversial, claims of subtypes of the amnesic syndrome relating to material specificity concern whether individuals with MTL damage have completely typical encoding abilities (which is a processing issue). Although most individuals seem to be able to encode (process and represent information at input) normally, it has recently been argued that specific MTL lesions cause subtle high-level visual processing impairments for specific kinds of information. Thus, some believe that perirhinal lesions not only disrupt the ability to remember recently encountered facts and experiences, but also subtly disrupt the ability to process feature conjunctions or make high-level viewer-independent visual representations of objects or faces at input; and that hippocampal lesions not only cause memory disruption, but also subtly disturb the ability to make viewer-independent scene, but not object and face, representations (Lee *et al.*, 2005a, b).

The amnesic syndrome: explanatory theories

Any theory of the amnesic syndrome needs to link specific lesions to a functional deficit that leads to *some or all* of the symptoms of amnesia. Such a theory would have implications both for how the human brain normally mediates episodic and semantic memory, and for how and why these kinds of memory may not function properly in developmental disorders such as autism. The global form of the amnesic syndrome, in which both episodic and semantic memory are affected, could relate to disorders of encoding, consolidation and storage, and/or retrieval of some or all components of semantic and/or episodic information. Over the past thirty years, theories of all of these kinds have been proposed. These will be considered in turn, below.

Theories implicating impaired encoding

Encoding views have had something of a resurgence, with recent claims that MTL structures may be critical for representing high-level kinds of perceptual information (Lee *et al.*, 2005a, b). However, even if these claims are correct, it seems unlikely – and remains to be shown – that these specific encoding deficits underlie the nonperceptual as well as the perceptual memory deficits of amnesic individuals. As most researchers believe that the sites where information is represented and stored in the brain are identical, it would also be the case that an encoding deficit for specific information would be expected to be accompanied by a comparable storage deficit (Gaffan & Hornak, 1997).

Theories implicating impaired storage

Any claim that amnesia is caused by a *selective* deficit in storing certain kinds of information seems to contradict the above assumption. The contradiction is avoided if it is proposed that an individual's lesion disrupts a structure that modulates consolidation into long-term memory of information represented and stored in another, but connected, brain region. This has been proposed for amygdala lesions, which are postulated to disrupt the modulation of consolidation in the hippocampus (and other structures) that the amygdala normally facilitates in response to emotional stimuli. Without this support, memory for emotional, but not neutral stimuli, declines abnormally fast (Phelps *et al.*, 1998). The deficit is mild, specific and not the same as amnesia, which is not caused by amygdala lesions. Only Gaffan, Parker and Easton (2001) have suggested that amnesia itself may be caused by disruption of the facilitation of consolidation in the MTL and temporal neocortex when brain damage disconnects them from the basal forebrain and midbrain. The disconnected structures are hypothesized to work suboptimally so that they represent information normally, but fail to consolidate it into long-term memory.

However, the two main selective storage theories of the amnesic syndrome are in tension with the assumption that representation and storage occur in identical sites. The first theory proposes that key aspects of factual and episodic information are consolidated and stored within the MTL, but that, through rehearsal and repetition, the information is slowly consolidated and stored within the neocortex where it is always represented. Once this transfer has occurred, the MTLs are no longer needed for retrieval (Squire & Alvarez, 1995). The second theory proposes that, although semantic memories transfer entirely in this way to the neocortex, components of episodic memories remain stored in the MTLs for as long as the memories last. Repetition and rehearsal lead to these components being more redundantly stored, but still in the MTLs (Nadel & Moscovitch, 1997). Both kinds of theory are compatible with the idea that information rapidly stored in the MTLs initially links together information that is represented in the neocortex, and that, over time, all of the links (first theory) or only some of them (second theory) are slowly stored in the neocortical representing sites.

Theories implicating impaired retrieval

In recent years, retrieval deficit views of amnesia have not been argued for except by Gray and McNaughton (2000), who suggest that people with amnesia are unable to inhibit competition that operates at retrieval. This deficit should have effects in competitive situations even when memory is minimally involved. These authors, like others, emphasize the role of the hippocampus and related structures as a comparator with a role in producing an arousal response to novelty, which is likely to have at least some effect on memory.

Conclusion

At present, none of the above theories concerning the functional deficits that underlie amnesia can be eliminated with confidence, although probably more than one functional deficit contributes to the syndrome. For example, as indicated above, it is likely that hippocampal encoding/storage/retrieval deficits primarily cause recollection/recall impairments whereas perirhinal cortex and other lesions primarily cause familiarity impairments.

Implications for autism: introduction

This part of the chapter will comprise two main sections: one on ways in which the literature on adult-acquired memory disorders may or may not relate to and illuminate what is already known about the patterns of memory found in autism; and one on ways in which this literature may be a useful source of hypotheses concerning other possible anomalies of memory function in autism which have not to date been directly investigated.

Adult-acquired memory disorders and known anomalies of memory in autism

Studies of individuals with HFA demonstrate that memory is largely unimpaired, with the exception of three areas of material-specific declarative memory impairment. These are impairments of: (a) face recognition (see Webb, this volume, Chapter 10); (b) recall of the kinds of episode-specific contextual information associated with the process of recollection (Lind & Bowler, this volume, Chapter 9); (c) memory for complex information of the kind that would normally be memorized utilizing organizational strategies, and especially strategies involving semantic organization (Williams, Minshew & Goldstein, this volume, Chapter 7 and Toichi, this volume, Chapter 8). It can be assumed that individuals with LFA have *at least* these same memory impairments. How the adult-acquired memory disorders literature may or may not relate to each of these impairments is considered next.

Face recognition impairment

An analogy with adult-acquired disorders suggests that this might be associated with fusiform gyrus lesions, and this is supported in as far as numerous studies have shown that the fusiform area does not show normal activity during face processing by people with autism (Schultz *et al.*, 2000; Pierce *et al.*, 2005). It is uncertain, however, that impaired face recognition in people with autism results from a primary lesion of the fusiform area (for discussion, see Webb, this volume, Chapter 10). The causes of adult-acquired prosopagnosia and the face recognition impairment in autism may, therefore, be unrelated, with the adult condition having little to offer to an understanding of the descriptively similar impairment in autism.[1]

---

[1] Occasional cases of developmental (as opposed to adult-acquired) prosopagnosia have been reported. Some but not all of these cases occur in individuals who have social impairments resembling those seen in people with Asperger syndrome, but without the additional behavioural impairments diagnostic of autism (Kracke, 1994; Barton *et al.*, 2004). These cases probably have more potential than cases of adult-acquired prosopagnosia to shed light on the origins of the face recognition impairment in autism.

Selectively impaired recall of episodic information

This impairment is inferred from reports of impaired performance on sensitive tests of recall (the 'remember' component of the 'remember-know' task; Bowler, Gardiner & Grice, 2000) and on uncued source memory tasks (Bowler, Gardiner & Bertholier, 2004). It is unclear whether impaired recollection in HFA has the same cause as the partial amnesic syndrome associated with selective hippocampal lesions.[2] The similarities could be superficial, resulting from quite different sets of psychological and neurobiological deficits (Renner, Klinger & Klinger, 2000; see also Lind & Bowler, this volume, Chapter 9). Moreover, the recollection impairment in people with HFA is mild compared to that which occurs in adult-acquired amnesia or developmental amnesia (Vargha-Khadem *et al.*, 1997; see also Salmond *et al.*, this volume, Chapter 4). This suggests that any hippocampal damage or dysfunction in people with HFA is more circumscribed, or different in kind, compared to that associated with the adult and developmental forms of the amnesic syndrome. Nevertheless, given that hippocampal abnormalities have been reported in people with HFA (e.g. Boucher *et al.*, 2005) as well as in less selective groups of individuals with ASDs (e.g. Bauman & Kemper, 2004), it remains possible that impaired recollection in autism is associated with selective hippocampal lesions.

If this proved to be the case, it would be more fruitful to describe the memory impairment in the terms used here, rather than in terms of a selective impairment of episodic memory. This is because studies of the adult-acquired amnesic syndrome suggest that equations between recollection and a putative episodic memory system are inexact. To recapitulate: the hippocampus not only mediates the ability to recall and recollect personally experienced episodes, but probably also contributes to the rapid acquisition of semantic information (although the gradual acquisition of facts via repetition is mediated by neocortical structures that probably include the perirhinal cortex). If declarative memory deficits in HFA do resemble those caused by hippocampal damage in adulthood, then HFA may be associated with a deficit in the rapid learning mechanism so that semantic memories are not learned at a normal rate. The slow learning mechanism will function normally, so that with time and practice, semantic memories may become strong and effectively normal. Subtle deficits should, however, be apparent in HFA with

---

[2] Relatively normal performance on standard recall tasks might argue against this. However, when recall (or recollection) is only mildly impaired, recall of unrelated items might be achieved by a strategy of randomly generating candidate targets, and using preserved familiarity to identify targets.

memory for less practised facts. This is a novel hypothesis which could shed light on some of the anomalies of both language and semantic knowledge which occur even in people with HFA, and which suggests that semantic memory in HFA may differ in certain ways from semantic memory in typically developing individuals.

Impaired memory for complex or semantically rich material

Evidence about this type of memory impairment is presented in the chapters by Williams, Minshew and Goldstein, and by Toichi, later in this book. Williams and her colleagues argue that impaired memory for complex material is just one manifestation of a more general impairment in the ability to process complex information: in other words, this aspect of anomalous memory function in people with autism is not seen as originating in a mnestic deficit of the kinds discussed in the section on adult-acquired memory disorders. Instead, Williams *et al.* propose an explanation in terms of defective binding.

Problems of neural binding and connectivity are increasingly proposed as fundamental to autism (Brock *et al.*, 2002; Dawson *et al.*, 2002; Just *et al.*, 2004). Without wishing to make a strong case for the connection, we note that the hippocampus, which shows tissue anomalies in cases of autism (e.g. Sparks *et al.*, 2002; Bauman & Kemper, 2004) plays a critical role in binding together multiple components of complex experience into memory (cf. DeLong, this volume, Chapter 6). It was also suggested above that impaired episodic memory would have subtle effects on the acquisition of semantic knowledge because of an absence of the ability to acquire factual information from a single episodic experience. Factual, or semantic, information derived from episodic memory will be multimodal and contextually rich, whereas factual or semantic information derived exclusively from repetition and familiarity will lack such associative richness. There is a possibility, therefore, that the well-documented problems people with autism have in utilizing rich semantic networks derive from limitations in the memory systems that can be used to acquire semantic information. This in turn may derive from a problem of neural binding, as suggested (but without reference to memory systems) by Williams, Minshew and Goldstein in Chapter 7.

Adult-acquired memory disorders as a source of hypotheses concerning other possible memory impairments in autism

In this section, some novel hypotheses derived from the literature on adult-acquired memory disorders will be proposed. One of these has already been introduced, and will not be discussed further: namely that impaired recollection associated with selective hippocampal damage will disrupt the rapid acquisition of factual information in all individuals with autism, including those with HFA. Three further hypotheses are introduced below.

Impaired emotion conditioning across the spectrum

At the outset of the section on adult-acquired memory disorders, four distinct types of procedural memory and related brain systems were identified:

(a) priming, associated with the sensory neocortex regions which underlie representation of the primed information;
(b) motoric classical conditioning, dependent on the cerebellum;
(c) skill learning dependent on basal ganglia and possibly cerebellar structures;
(d) emotion conditioning associated with amygdala function.

It is often stated that procedural memory is unimpaired in autism. This is almost certainly true for priming (Renner, Klinger & Klinger, 2000; see also Toichi, this volume, Chapter 8), and probably true for most forms of conditioning. It may be true for the acquisition of skills, although this is more difficult to determine because of the common occurrence of motor impairments in association with autism (Ghaziuddin & Butler, 1998). It is much less certainly true for emotion conditioning, given that both structural and functional abnormalities of the amygdala have been found in numerous studies involving individuals with HFA as well as LFA (see e.g. Baron-Cohen *et al.*, 1999; Howard *et al.*, 2000). The possibility that the particular form of conditioning which involves associating emotional significance with an experience is impaired is of particular interest because several authors have recently suggested that a lack of salience, or reward value, of social stimuli underlies the indifference of infants with autism to social stimuli, with cascading effects on social interaction and social learning (Dawson *et al.*, 2002; Loveland, 2001; Mundy, 2005). Moreover, if, as argued in the literature on adult-acquired disorders, the consolidation of memories involving emotional stimuli is facilitated by input from the amygdala to the hippocampus, it could be the case that experiences which carry emotional valency are inefficiently stored in memory by people with autism, including those with HFA (see Gaigg & Bowler, 2007, for some evidence supporting this speculation).

Specific visual encoding impairments

The literature on adult-acquired memory disorders suggests that hippocampal lesions may impair the ability to form viewer-independent visual representations of scenes, whereas perirhinal lesions may impair the ability to form viewer-independent visual representations of objects or faces (Lee *et al.*, 2005a, b). If our hypothesis that all individuals with autism have at least some degree of hippocampal dysfunction, and that individuals with LFA have additional perirhinal and other MTL damage is correct, then all individuals with autism may have impaired ability to encode scenes; and individuals with LFA (but not those with HFA) will have additional problems in encoding viewer-independent representations of objects and faces. There is some support for the first part of this hypothesis (Williams, Goldstein & Minshew, 2005).

As pointed out in the section on explanatory theories of the amnesic syndrome, Lee's work also has implications for the controversy concerning the roles of encoding, storage, and retrieval deficits in declarative memory impairments. There has been no systematic attempt to discriminate between encoding, storage, or retrieval deficits as possible causes of impaired memory in autism, as demonstrated in studies of HFA. Such attempts would, of course, only be relevant if the memory impairments in HFA were reliably shown to be mnestic in origin, and of kinds that are analogous to adult-acquired declarative memory impairments. We have argued that both impaired recollection of episodic information and impaired memory for complex information in HFA could derive from fundamental memory deficits analogous to those known to occur in adults. We have also hypothesized that a developmental form of global amnesia may occur in LFA. If we are correct about any of this, then the literature on theories of the amnesic syndrome will have significance for autism.

Combined impairments of recollection and familiarity as a cause of learning and language impairment in low-functioning autism

The hypothesis proposed here is that individuals with LFA have a dual impairment of recollection associated with hippocampal dysfunction (and secondary involvement of prefrontal systems), plus impaired familiarity associated with additional perirhinal and possible other MTL lesions/dysfunction, and that this dual impairment causes or contributes to the learning and language impairments in LFA. A dual impairment of recollection and familiarity would cause an acquisition deficit for both episodic and factual information, analogous to that which occurs in the global form of the adult-acquired amnesic syndrome. It is hard to see how a developmental form of the global amnesic syndrome could fail to result in learning impairments if, as argued in the introduction to this chapter, developmental memory problems have cumulative effects on knowledge acquisition and crystallized intelligence – effects which are more severe than the effects of memory loss in adults.

However, the precise mechanisms underlying impaired language acquisition, in particular, would have to be established. Moreover, the hypothesis does not rule out the possible contribution of other fundamental deficits which might also contribute to the language and learning impairments. It is also likely that combined deficits of recollection and familiarity are implicated in other intellectual disability syndromes. Fragile-X syndrome, for example, is characterized by marked impairments of declarative memory in association with brain tissue abnormalities affecting hippocampal regions and extending into the parahippocampal gyrus (Shapiro *et al.*, 1995; Jäkälä *et al.*, 1997). Hippocampal malfunction is also central to Turner's syndrome (Murphy *et al.*, 1993), one form of which can co-occur with autism (as does Fragile-X in a small proportion of cases).

The hypothesis that combined impairments of recollection and familiarity are a critical cause of the language impairment and intellectual disability in low-functioning autism is presented and discussed more fully later by Boucher, Mayes and Bigham in Chapter 14.

Summary

Developmental memory disorders may resemble adult-acquired memory disorders with respect to specific deficits in information processing where these arise from lesions of dedicated MTL brain structures with little scope for transfer of function. Developmental disorders will, however, have more serious consequences than adult disorders, affecting new learning of many kinds. Individuals with autism have selective memory impairments. They also have MTL abnormalities, notably of the amygdala (implicated in the core social impairments), but also in the hippocampal and perirhinal regions subserving memory. The aim of this chapter was, therefore, to consider ways in which the literature on adult-acquired organic memory disorders may illuminate problems of memory and learning in autism.

Several types of adult-acquired organic memory disorders were described in brief, followed by a more extensive summary of current knowledge and theories relating to the amnesic syndrome, a disorder of memory for episodes and facts caused by MTL and other lesions. Possible implications for autism were then discussed. These include the resemblance of features of HFA to those produced by hippocampal lesions in adults, with especial reference to recollection problems; possible emotional conditioning problems in ASDs that may be linked to amygdala dysfunction; the possible role of more extensive MTL dysfunction and wider ranging, more severe memory deficits in the language and learning impairments in LFA; and the possibility that more extensive MTL dysfunction could underlie visual encoding impairments especially in LFA.

References

Adolphs, R., Cahill, L., Schul, R. & Babinsky, R. (1997). Impaired declarative memory for emotional material following bilateral amygdala damage in humans. *Learning & Memory, 4,* 291–300.

Aggleton, J. P., Vann, S. D., Denby, C., Dix, S., Mayes, A. R., Roberts, N. & Yonelinas, A. P. (2005). Sparing of the familiarity component of recognition memory in a patient with hippocampal pathology. *Neuropsychologia, 43,* 1810–1823.

Bachevalier, J. (1994). Medial temporal lobe structures and autism: A review of clinical and experimental findings. *Neuropsychologia, 32,* 627–648.

Baddeley, A. D. (1992). Working memory. *Science, 255,* 556–559.

Baron-Cohen, S., Ring, H. A., Wheelwright, S., Bullmore, E. T., Brammer, M. J., Simmons, A. & Williams, S. (1999). Social intelligence in the normal and autistic brain: An fMRI study. *European Journal of Neuroscience, 11,* 1891.

Barton, J. J., Press, D. Z., Keenan, J. P. & O'Connor, M. (2002). Lesions of the fusiform face area impair perception of face configuration in prosopagnosia. *Neurology, 58,* 71–78.

Barton, J. J., Cherkasova, M., Hefter, R., Cox, T., O'Connor, M. & Manoach, D. S. (2004). *Brain, 127,* 1706–1716.

Bauman, M. L. & Kemper, T. L. (2004). Structural brain anatomy in autism: what is the evidence? In M. L. Bauman & T. L. Kemper (eds.), *The neurobiology of autism,* pp. 119–145. Baltimore: Johns Hopkins University Press.

Bechara, A., Tranel, D., Damasio, H., Adolphs, R., Rockland, C. & Damasio, R. A. R. (1995). Double dissociation of conditioning and declarative knowledge relative to the amygdala and hippocampus in humans. *Science, 269,* 1115–1118.

Benson, D. F., Segara, J. & Albert, M. L. (1974). Visual-agnosia-prosopagnosia, a clinicopathological correlation. *Archives of Neurology, 30,* 307–310.

Boucher J. & Warrington, E. K. (1976). Memory deficits in early infantile autism: Some similarities to the amnesic syndrome. *British Journal of Psychology, 67,* 73–87.

Boucher, J., Cowell, P., Howard, M., Broks, P., Farrant, A., Roberts, N. & Mayes, A. (2005). A combined clinical neuropsychological and neuroanatomical study of adults with high-functioning autism. *Cognitive Neuropsychiatry, 10,* 165–214.

Bowler, D. M., Gardiner, J. M. & Berthollier, N. (2004). Source memory in adolescents and adults with Asperger's syndrome. *Journal of Autism and Developmental Disorders, 34,* 533–542.

Bowler, D. M., Gardiner, J. M. & Grice, S. (2000). Episodic memory and remembering in adults with Asperger's syndrome. *Journal of Autism and Developmental Disorders, 30,* 305–316.

Brock, J., Brown, C. C., Boucher, J. & Rippon, G. (2002). The temporal binding deficit hypothesis of autism. *Development and Psychopathology, 14*, 209–224.

Brown, M. W. & Xiang, J. Z. (1998). Recognition memory: neuronal substrates of the judgement of prior occurrence. *Progress in Neurobiology, 55*, 149–189.

Churchill, D. W. (1972). The relation of infantile autism and early childhood schizophrenia to developmental language disorders of childhood. *Journal of Autism and Childhood Schizophrenia, 2*, 182–197.

Daum, I. & Schugens, M. M. (1995). Classical conditioning after brain lesions in humans: the contribution of neuropsychology. *Journal of Psychophysiology, 9*, 109–118.

Dawson, G., Webb, S., Schellenberg, G. D., Dager, S., Friedman, S., Aylward, E. & Richards, T. (2002). Defining the broader phenotype of autism: genetic, brain, and behavioural perspectives. *Development and Psychopathology, 14*, 581–611.

DeLong, G. R. (1978). A neuropsychological interpretation of infantile autism. In M. Rutter and E. Schopler (eds.), *Autism*, pp. 207–218. New York: Plenum Press.

Gaffan, D. & Hornak, J. (1997). Amnesia and neglect: beyond the Delay-Brion system and the Hebb synapse. *Philosophical Transactions of the Royal Society, London B, 352*, 1481–1488.

Gaffan, D., Parker, A. & Easton, A. (2001). Dense amnesia in the monkey after transection of fornix, amygdala and anterior temporal stem. *Neuropsychologia, 39*, 51–70.

Gaigg, S. & Bowler, D. (2007). Differential fear-conditioning in Asperger syndrome: implications for an amygdala theory of autism. *Neuropsychologia, 45*, 2125–2134.

Ghaziuddin, M. & Butler, E. (1998). Clumsiness in autism and Asperger syndrome: a further report. *Journal of Intellectual Disability Research, 42*, 1365–2788.

Gooding, P. A., Mayes, A. R. & van Eijk, R. (2000). A meta-analysis of indirect memory tests for novel material in organic amnesics. *Neuropsychologia, 38*, 666–676.

Gray, J. A. & McNaughton, N. (2000). *The neuropsychology of anxiety*, 2nd edition. Oxford: Oxford University Press.

Holdstock, J. S., Mayes, A. R., Isaac, C. L. & Roberts, J. N. (2002). Differential involvement of the hippocampus and temporal cortices in rapid and slow learning of new semantic information. *Neuropsychologia, 40*, 748–768.

Howard, M., Cowell, P., Boucher, J., Broks, P., Mayes, A., Farrant, A. & Roberts, N. (2000). Convergent neuroanatomical and behavioural evidence of an amygdala hypothesis of autism. *NeuroReport, 11*, 2931–2935.

Jäkälä, P., Hänninen, T., Ryynänen, M., Laakso, M., Partanen, K., Mannermaa, A. & Soininen, H. (1997). Fragile-X: neuropsychological test performance, CGG triplet repeat lengths, and hippocampal volumes. *Journal of Clinical Investigations, 100*, 331–338.

Just, M. A., Cherkassky, V. L., Keller, T. A. & Minshew, N. J. (2004). Cortical activation and synchronization during sentence comprehension in high-functioning autism: evidence of underconnectivity. *Brain, 127*, 1811–1821.

Kapur, N. (2000). Focal retrograde amnesia and the attribution of causality: an exceptionally benign commentary. *Cognitive Neuropsychology*, *17*, 623–637.

Keane, M. M., Gabrieli, J. D. E., Mapstone, H. C., Johnston, K. A. & Corkin, S. (1995). Double dissociation of memory capacities after bilateral occipital-lobe or medial temporal-lobe lesions. *Brain*, *118*, 1129–1148.

Kopelman, M. D. (1991). Frontal lobe dysfunction and memory deficits in the alcoholic Korsakoff syndrome and Alzheimer-type dementia. *Brain*, *114*, 117–137.

(2000). Focal retrograde amnesia and the attribution of causality: an exceptionally critical review. *Cognitive Neuropsychology*, *17*, 585–621.

(2002). Retrograde amnesia. In A. D. Baddeley, M. D. Kopelman & B. A. Wilson (eds.), *The handbook of memory disorders*, 2nd edn, pp. 189–207. Chichester: Wiley.

Kracke, I. (1994). Developmental prosopagnosia in Asperger syndrome: presentation and discussion of an individual case. *Developmental Medicine and Child Neurology*, *36*, 873–886.

Lee, A. C. H., Buckley, M. J., Pegman, S. J., Spiers, H., Scahill, V. L., Gaffan, D., Bussey, T. J., Davies, R. R., Kapur, N., Hodges, J. R. & Graham, K. S. (2005a). Specialization in the medial temporal lobe for processing of objects and scenes. *Hippocampus*, *15*, 782–797.

Lee, A. C. H., Bussey, T. J., Murray, E. A., Saksida, L. M., Epstein, R. A., Kapur, N., Hodges, J. R. & Graham, K. S. (2005b). Perceptual deficits in amnesia: challenging the medial temporal 'mnemonic' view. *Neuropsychologia*, *43*, 1–11.

Loveland, K. A. (2001). Toward an ecological theory of autism. In J. Burack, T. Charman, N. Yirmiya & P. R. Zelazo (eds.), *The development of autism: perspectives from theory and research*, pp. 17–38. Mahwah, NJ: Erlbaum.

Manns, J. R., Hopkins, R. O., Reed, J. M., Kitchener, E. G. & Squire, L. R. (2003). Recognition memory and the human hippocampus. *Neuron*, *37*, 171–180.

Mayes, A. R. (2000). Selective memory disorders. In E. Tulving & F. I. M. Craik (eds.), *The Oxford handbook of memory*, pp. 427–440. Oxford: Oxford University Press.

Mayes, A. R., Holdstock, J. S., Isaac, C. L., Hunkin, N. M. & Roberts, N. (2002). Relative sparing of item recognition memory in a patient with adult-onset damage limited to the hippocampus. *Hippocampus*, *12*, 325–340.

McMackin, D., Cockburn, J., Anslow, P. & Gaffan, D. (1995). Correlation of fornix damage with memory impairments of six cases of colloid cyst removal. *Acta Neurochirurgie* (Vienna), *135*, 12–18.

Milner, B. (1971). Interhemispheric differences in the localisation of psychological processes in man. *British Medical Bulletin*, *27*, 272–277.

Mundy, P. (2005). The neural basis of social impairments in autism: the role of the dorsal medial-frontal cortex and anterior cingulate system. *Journal of Child Psychology and Psychiatry*, *44*, 793–809.

Murphy, D. G., DeCarli, C., Daly, E., Haxby, J. V., Allen, G., White, B. J., McIntosh, A. R., Powell, C. M., Horwitz, B., Rapoport, S. I. *et al.* (1993).

X-chromosome effects on female brain: a magnetic resonance imaging study of Turner's syndrome. *Lancet, 342,* 1188–1189.

Nadel, L. & Moscovitch, M. (1997). Memory consolidation, retrograde amnesia and the hippocampal complex. *Current Opinion in Neurobiology, 7,* 217 227.

Phelps, E. A., LaBar, K. S., Anderson, A. K. *et al.* (1998). Specifying the contributions of the human amygdala to emotional memory: a case study. *Neurocase, 4,* 527–540.

Pierce, K., Muller, R. A., Ambrose, J., Allen, G. & Courchesne, E. (2005). Face processing occurs outside the fusiform 'face area' in autism: evidence from functional MRI. *Brain, 124,* 2059–2073.

Renner, P., Klinger, L. G. & Klinger, M. (2000). Implicit and explicit memory in autism: is autism an amnesic disorder? *Journal of Autism and Developmental disorders, 30,* 3–14.

Ricks, D. M. & Wing, L. (1976). Language, communication, and the use of symbols. In L.Wing (ed.), *Early childhood autism,* pp. 93–134. Oxford: Pergamon Press.

Ross, E. D. (1982). Disorders of recent memory in humans. *Trends in Neurosciences, 5,* 170–172.

Rutter, M. (1968). Concepts of autism: a review of research. *Journal of Child Psychology and Psychiatry, 9,* 1–25.

Schultz, R. T., Gauthier, I., Klin, A., Fulbright, R., Anderson, A., Volkmar, F., Skudlarski, P., Lacadie, C., Cohen, D. & Gore, J. (2000). Abnormal ventral temporal cortical activity during face discrimination among individuals with autism and Asperger syndrome. *Archives of General Psychiatry, 57,* 331–340.

Shapiro, M. B., Murphy, D. G., Hagerman, R. J., Azari, N. P., Alexander, G. E., Miezejeski, C. M., Hinton, V. J., Horwitz, B., Haxby, J. V. & Kumar, A. (1995). Adult fragile X syndrome: neuropsychology, brain anatomy, and metabolism. *American Journal of Medical Genetics, 60,* 480–493.

Snowden, J. S., Goulding, H. L. & Neary, D. (1989). Semantic dementia: a form of circumscribed cerebral atrophy. *Behavioural Neurology, 2,* 167–182.

Sparks, B. F., Friedman, S. D., Shaw, D. W., Aylward, E. H., Echelard, D., Artru, A. A. *et al.,* (2002). Brain structural abnormalities in young children with autism spectrum disorder. *Neurology, 59,* 184–192.

Squire, L. R. & Alvarez, P. (1995). Retrograde amnesia and memory consolidation: a neurobiological perspective. *Current Opinion in Neurobiology, 5,* 169–177.

Tranel, D. & Damasio, A. R. (2002). Neurobiological foundations of human memory. In A. D. Baddeley, M. D. Kopelman & B. A. Wilson (eds.), *The handbook of memory disorders,* 2nd edn, pp. 17–56. Chichester: Wiley.

Vargha-Khadem, F., Gadian, D. G., Watkins, K. E., Connelly, A., Van Paesschen, W. & Mishkin, M. (1997). Differential effects of early hippocampal pathology on episodic and semantic memory. *Science, 277,* 376–380.

Weiskrantz, L. & Warrington, E. K. (1979). Conditioning in amnesic patients. *Neuropsychologia, 17,* 187–194.

Williams, D., Goldstein, G. & Minshew, N. J. (2005). Impaired memory for faces and social scenes in autism: clinical implications of memory dysfunction. *Archives of Clinical Neuropsychology, 20,* 1–15.

4 A comparison of memory profiles in relation to neuropathology in autism, developmental amnesia and children born prematurely

Claire H. Salmond, Anna-Lynne R. Adlam,
David G. Gadian and Faraneh Vargha-Khadem

Introduction

Autistic spectrum disorders (ASDs) are characterized by impairments in social interaction and communication, and by restricted or repetitive behaviours and interests. The degree of impairment varies enormously. For example, individuals with low-functioning autism (LFA) may be mute or have atypical language, whilst individuals with high-functioning autism (HFA – used here to include individuals with Asperger syndrome) may have good language but nevertheless suffer from communication problems including impaired nonverbal communication. The underlying neural abnormalities associated with autism-related disorders are not well understood.

In addition to investigations of the defining behavioural impairments, as listed above, a number of studies have examined memory functions in people with ASDs. These have revealed an impairment in episodic memory (i.e. memory for events and episodes; Russell 1996; Bowler, Gardiner & Grice, 2000; Millward *et al.*, 2000; Gardiner, Bowler & Grice, 2003), but not semantic memory (i.e. memory for facts or world knowledge – Tulving, 1972), at least in higher-functioning individuals (e.g. Ameli *et al.*, 1988; Minshew *et al.*, 1992; Bennetto, Pennington & Rogers, 1996; Siegel, Minshew & Goldstein, 1996; Farrant, Blades & Boucher, 1998).

Previous reports of individuals with developmental amnesia (DA) and a group of children born preterm (PT) have revealed a similar dissociation between episodic memory, which is selectively impaired, and factual memory, which is relatively preserved (e.g. Vargha-Khadem *et al.*, 1997, 2003; Gadian *et al.*, 2000; Isaacs *et al.*, 2000, 2003). The neuropathology underlying the dissociation in mnemonic ability in developmental amnesia has been well documented (i.e. severe bilateral hippocampal atrophy in the presence of relatively preserved parahippocampal cortices; Mishkin *et al.*, 1997; Vargha-Khadem *et al.*, 1997; Schoppik *et al.*, 2001; Isaacs *et al.*, 2003).

This chapter reviews the data on memory impairments in individuals with autism-related disorders, and compares the cognitive and neural abnormalities to those in children with DA and children born prematurely.

The anatomy of declarative memory

Memory is not the function of a unitary system but of many systems that vary in the type of information they store and the length of time they store it. The present chapter will be restricted to a discussion of long-term declarative memory: primarily episodic memory (e.g. remembering climbing the Eiffel tower last spring) and semantic memory (e.g. knowing that Paris is the capital of France) (see Gardiner, this volume, Chapter 1, for definitions and discussion of these concepts).

Long-term declarative memory is dependent on the medial temporal–diencephalic circuit (Aggleton & Brown, 1999). In particular, the medial temporal lobe is essential for declarative memory (e.g. Scoville & Milner, 1957). One model of medial temporal lobe function suggests a hierarchical organization: perceptual information from the different sensory modalities cascades into the perirhinal and parahippocampal cortices, which reciprocally connect with the entorhinal cortex, which in turn reciprocally connects with the hippocampus (Mishkin *et al.*, 1997, 1998; Aggleton & Brown, 1999; Brown & Aggleton, 2001). According to this model, the hippocampus is necessary for episodic memory and therefore recollection, whereas the parahippocampal cortices can support semantic memory and therefore familiarity-based recognition (for a more detailed discussion see Mishkin *et al.*, 1997, 1998). This model predicts dissociations in declarative memory following selective hippocampal damage. For an alternative view see Squire (1987, 1992, 1994), Squire and Knowlton (1995), Squire and Zola-Morgan (1991, 1996, 1998), and Manns and Squire (2002).

The following sections describe previous research findings on declarative memory in individuals with autism, those with DA, and children born preterm (PT). Declarative memory in each of these three groups is considered separately, with subsections ordered in such a way that there is a decreasing reliance on familiarity-based recognition of factual, or context-free information (not mediated by the hippocampal formation) and correspondingly increasing dependence on the recollection of personally experienced, episodic information, mediated by the hippocampal formation.

Memory in individuals with autism

Although there have been a large number of studies investigating declarative memory skills in people with ASDs, few have assessed memory for personally experienced episodes and memory for facts within the same sample. This, combined with the wide variety of ability levels in people with autism, makes it difficult to establish the characteristic declarative memory profile of such individuals. However, the evidence summarized below is consistent with a selective impairment in episodic memory. In view of the importance of the functioning levels of the study participants, wherever possible details of the intellectual abilities of the participants of the studies reviewed are included in brackets. Where available, chronological age (CA), verbal IQ (VIQ) and nonverbal IQ (NVIQ) (or performance IQ (PIQ)) are quoted. Some studies do not provide IQ details, and so verbal mental age (VMA) and nonverbal mental age (NVMA) are quoted instead.

Recognition

Individuals with high-functioning autism have been shown to have good recognition skills for a variety of different types of stimuli. Recognition isheavily dependent on familiarity, and is thus less dependent on the hippocampus than some other modes of recall (see Mayes and Boucher, this volume, Chapter 3). For example, Farrant, Blades and Boucher (1998) showed that children with autism (CA 12;7, VMA 7;8) were able to correctly recognize words that were previously presented to them. Similarly, Bennetto, Pennington and Rogers (1996) found that children with autism (CA 16;0, VIQ 82) were able to recognize previously presented pictures and words, even though they were unable to temporally order them. Good picture recognition has also been reported by Ameli et al. (1988) (CA 22;7, PIQ 91) and Brian and Bryson (1996) (CA 19;5, Raven's Percentile Score 33.9).

However, comparisons between recognition of objects with and without agency (defined as objects capable of self-propelled motion, both animate and inanimate) have led to suggestions that individuals with autism have a recognition deficit for objects with agency. For example studies by Boucher and Lewis (1992) and Blair et al. (2002) reported deficits in recognition of stimuli with agency (such as faces) but intact recognition for objects without agency (such as leaves and buildings) in individuals with ASDs (CA 13;6, VMA 6/7 years in the former study; CA 30;0, VIQ 88, PIQ 95 in the latter study). Ellis et al. (1994) showed typical word recognition but impaired face recognition in a group of individuals with HFA (CA 15;6, VIQ 96, NVIQ 86) (see also Boucher *et al.*, 2005). Although recognition of faces in general shows a less consistent pattern (e.g. Boucher, Lewis & Collis, 1998; Langdell, 1978), it should be noted that it is likely that impaired encoding of faces influences recognition.

The recognition impairment in individuals with low-functioning autism (LFA) has been found to extend to nonagency objects. For example, Boucher and Warrington (1976) found evidence of impairment in a group of children with LFA (CA 13;0, VMA 5;0, NVMA 9;0) for recognition of pictures of common objects. Similarly, Barth, Fein and Waterhouse (1995) found impaired performance on a delayed match-to-sample task with brightly coloured shape stimuli, in an LFA group (CA 5;0, VIQ 66, NVIQ 64) but not in an HFA group (CA 5;0, VIQ 82, NVIQ 101).

Semantic memory

Semantic memory has not been explicitly investigated in individuals with ASDs. However, most verbal intelligence scales include subtests of semantic memory (such as general knowledge or vocabulary) and therefore many studies contain information regarding semantic memory in children with ASDs. It should be highlighted that scores on such subtests are influenced not only by semantic memory, but also by educational experience and language ability. Nevertheless, scores within the average (or above) range infer that semantic memory is intact. There are many reports of individuals with ASDs and typical (or even superior) intelligence (e.g. Minshew *et al.*, 1992). Thus, at least some individuals with ASDs can be expected to have typical semantic memory. Further, studies providing subtest scores on the intelligence scale have found that scores on semantic memory subtests are on average higher than other subtests contributing to the verbal IQ score, at least in high-functioning individuals (e.g. Siegel, Minshew & Goldstein, 1996).

Cued recall

Individuals with ASDs have been shown to have good cued recall. For example, in a study by Bowler, Matthews and Gardiner (1997) individuals with ASDs (CA 33;0, VIQ 99) performed similarly to a comparison group on explicit word-stem recall tasks. Boucher and Warrington (1976) demonstrated that individuals with ASDs (CA 9;11, VMA 5;5, NVMA 9;0) are able to recall pictures they have seen if they are given either a semantic cue (e.g. 'something you sit on') or a phonetic cue (e.g. 'st-' – both cues referring to 'stool'). Boucher and Lewis (1989) demonstrated that children with ASDs (CA 13;1, VMA 7;4, NVMA 11;3) are able to recall recent events if they are cued with contextual questions.

Delayed free recall of stimuli following repeated presentation

Similarly, paradigms that use repeated presentation of stimuli have generally found no gross impairment in the free recall ability of individuals with ASDs. For example, Boucher and Warrington (1976) found no impairment in paired associate word learning, using a repeated presentation paradigm (CA 9;11, VMA 5;5, NVMA 9;0). This finding was replicated by Minshew et al. (1993) (CA 20;2, VIQ 101, PIQ 94). Studies investigating word-list recall after repeated presentation have also found no impairment (Minshew et al., 1992; Minshew & Goldstein, 1993; Bennetto, Pennington & Rogers, 1996; Buitelaar et al., 1999).

Delayed free recall of stimuli following single presentation

Studies using single presentation paradigms (with their increased dependence on episodic memory) have found deficits in individuals with ASDs. Bowler, Matthews and Gardiner (1997) (CA 33;0, VIQ 99) and Boucher (1978) (CA 14;2, VMA 5;9) demonstrated that both adults and children with ASDs were impaired at recalling a list of words after a single presentation. Boucher and Lewis (1989) showed that low-functioning children with autism (CA 13;1, VMA 7;4, NVMA 11;3) were impaired at following instructions presented once, but not when given instructions without a memory load. Deficits in repeating novel actions were also noted by DeMeyer et al. (1972) in children with LFA (CA < 7;0, IQ ~ 50).

Studies of recall of once-presented pictures have produced inconsistent results. For example, Boucher and Warrington (1976) found that lower-functioning children with autism (CA 9;1, VMA 5;5, NVMA 9;0) were impaired at free recall of pictures presented once. Using a similar paradigm, Renner and colleagues (2000) found that higher-functioning children (CA 10;2, VIQ 101, NVIQ 97) were able to recall pictures presented once as well as children in a comparison group. Factors that may contribute to these mixed findings include differing intellectual ability, varied proportions of agent and nonagent stimuli (see the section on recognition, above), and differing degrees of relatedness of the pictures. This latter possibility is raised by the finding that children with ASDs benefit less than other children from the stimuli being semantically related (see Williams, Minshew & Goldstein, this volume, Chapter 7, and Toichi, this volume, Chapter 8).

Related to this, a number of studies have shown that individuals with ASDs have difficulty with contextual memory. Boucher and colleagues showed that children with LFA (CA 13;2, VMA 7;2, NVMA 10;6) were significantly less able than children in a comparison group to recall the context and order of recent activities in which they had participated. The same children, however, performed at levels similar to the participants without autism when asked questions about the events of the testing, which included contextual cues (Boucher, 1981; Boucher & Lewis, 1989). In the more extensive of these two studies, children participated in four experiments over a period of six to twelve months. At least one month after completing the last experiment, the child was then asked to recall the activities previously completed with the experimenter (Boucher & Lewis, 1989).

Other studies have shown impaired event memory in individuals with ASDs. Russell (1996) asked children how they knew what was in a box (were they told or did they see) and who had placed a card into a grid (either the child, the experimenter or a doll manipulated by the experimenter or child). The children with ASDs were severely impaired on this task in contrast to the comparison group. Millward *et al.* (2000) further showed that children with ASDs (CA 13;1, VMA 6;3) had more difficulties recalling events that they had personally experienced than events that they saw another child experience. This last finding may be argued to be more a reflection of a lack of insight into self, rather than a memory deficit *per se*. However, the study has an important confound. Children's memories for events are enhanced by narration (Tessler & Nelson, 1994), and it might be expected that comparison children are more likely than children with ASDs to provide a spontaneous narration of the events happening to them. Thus the children with ASDs might have recalled events occurring to other children better due to the benefits of narration.

Further, Bowler, Gardiner and Grice (2000) have reported deficits in high-functioning adults with ASDs in recollection-based recognition (associated with episodic memory) but not familiarity-based recognition.

Summary of behavioural findings

This literature review suggests that the memory profile of children with ASDs in the absence of marked intellectual disability is consistent with a relatively selective episodic memory deficit and comparative preservation of semantic memory (see also Bowler & Gaigg, this volume, Chapter 17). This memory profile was recently confirmed by a study of both episodic and semantic memory in children with ASDs (Salmond *et al.*, 2005). In this study a cohort of high-functioning individuals with autism

(VIQ = 102) and matched comparison participants completed a comprehensive neuropsychological memory battery. A selective deficit in episodic memory with relative preservation of semantic memory was found.

Neuropathology relating to memory in autism

Given the memory profile of individuals with ASDs as summarized above, abnormality in the hippocampal formation might be suspected (see above; also Bachevalier, this volume, Chapter 2; Mayes & Boucher, this volume, Chapter 3). A number of studies have investigated the integrity of the hippocampal formation in ASDs, with mixed results. Some structural imaging studies have reported decreased hippocampal volumes (Aylward et al., 1999; Saitoh, Karns & Courchesne, 2001; Boucher et al., 2005) whilst others have found no detectable change (e.g. Piven et al., 1998; Haznedar et al., 2000; Sparks et al., 2002). Post-mortem studies have revealed increased cell density and decreased cell size in the hippocampal formation (Raymond, Bauman & Kemper, 1996).

We recently reported bilateral abnormality in the hippocampal formation in high-functioning children with ASDs (Salmond et al., 2005). In this study, the children with autism and matched comparison participants underwent magnetic resonance imaging for the purpose of voxel-based morphometric analyses. Our analysis searched explicitly for bilateral abnormalities using a conjunction analysis (see Salmond et al., 2000a). This method was chosen because bilateral abnormality is consistent with the nature of autism, a neurodevelopmental disorder with a strong genetic component (Shallice, 1988; McCarthy & Warrington, 1990; Vargha-Khadem et al., 1994). Bilateral abnormalities were detected in grey matter in several areas including the hippocampal formation.

It is important to acknowledge that many studies have highlighted abnormality in other neural regions, including the cerebellum, the amygdala, the frontal cortex and fusiform gyrus (Courchesne et al., 1988; Minshew et al., 1993; Pierce et al., 2001; Howard et al., 2000; Sparks et al., 2002; Aylward et al., 1999; Salmond et al., 2005). Considerable variation in findings highlights the heterogeneity of the autistic population and the need for large samples (Brambilla et al., 2003). However, these findings do not detract from the possibility that hippocampal formation abnormalities may be related to the memory profile described above. The abnormalities outside the hippocampal formation may be associated with other behavioural aspects of autism (such as the amygdala and frontal cortex abnormalities being associated with social difficulties).

The finding of a relatively selective episodic memory impairment in higher-functioning individuals with autism raises the question of how this deficit might be related to the diagnostic symptoms. One possibility is that the social impairments diagnostic of autism lead to the memory problems (Salmond *et al.*, 2005). For example, episodic memory may have a greater dependency on attending to inherently social aspects of the world than does semantic memory. Indirect evidence supporting this possibility comes from reports of superior abilities for the recall of spatial arrangements in the environment (Caron *et al.*, 2004), a task typically thought to depend on episodic memory.

From an anatomical perspective, this memory profile would be consistent with autism being attributable to a neural abnormality elsewhere in the brain, presumably connected to the hippocampal formation (perhaps the amygdala, or potentially multiple areas). The aberrant connections to the hippocampal formation would then potentially lead to the abnormalities in the hippocampal formation itself. Such 'knock-on' effects occurring in areas connected to atypical areas have been noted in animal studies (Hanlon & Sutherland, 2000).

Developmental amnesia

There have been relatively few reported cases of amnesia originating in childhood (for a review see Temple, 2002). However, of the few studies reported, the main focus of the literature has been on investigating the presence or absence of dissociations in memory (e.g. Ostergaard, 1987; Wood, Brown & Felton, 1989; De Renzi & Lucchelli, 1990; Broman *et al.*, 1997; Temple, 1997; Vargha-Khadem *et al.*, 1997; Benedict *et al.*, 1998; Casalini *et al.*, 1999; Meguro *et al.*, 1999; Gadian *et al.*, 2000; Hughes *et al.*, 2002). For the purpose of this chapter, and in order to compare the memory profile associated with DA to that associated with autism, the following section is divided according to the same subheadings as used above.

Recognition

Children with developmental amnesia have been reported to have preserved single item (words, nonwords, unknown faces, famous faces) and intra-modal (same item pairs) associative recognition (Vargha-Khadem *et al.*, 1997). The recall and recognition performance of one young man, Jon, was also assessed using the Doors and People test (Baddeley, Vargha-Khadem & Mishkin, 2001). Jon's performance was compared to that of two age-, sex- and IQ-matched typically developing adolescents. For visual and verbal recall, Jon scored between the 1st and 5th percentile, indicating severe impairments, while he scored between the

50th and 75th percentile, i.e. within the typical range, on the verbal and visual recognition subtests. More complex recognition tasks (such as cross-modal recognition), however, have been reported to be impaired in children with DA (Vargha-Khadem *et al.*, 1997).

Semantic memory

As in the high-functioning children with ASDs, semantic memory in children with DA (as reflected by intellectual abilities) has been reported to be within the average range (e.g. Wood, Brown & Felton, 1989; Broman *et al.*, 1997; Vargha-Khadem *et al.*, 1997; and Gadian *et al.*, 2000). For example, individuals with DA (e.g. Vargha-Khadem *et al.*, 1997; Gadian *et al.*, 2000), have shown preserved performance on tests of semantic memory including the comprehension and vocabulary subtests of verbal IQ, and academic attainments (but see Broman *et al.*, 1997).

Cued recall and recall of stimuli following repeated presentation

Both cued recall and recall of stimuli following repeated presentation rely less on episodic or contextual memory than recall of stimuli presented only once (see above). Again, given the rarity of the condition, very few studies have reported cued recall performance in individuals with DA. However, in contrast to individuals with autism, it seems that individuals with DA are impaired at cued recall of words (i.e. when required to recall the target word when presented with the first item of a word pair, Vargha-Khadem *et al.*, 2003).

A small number of studies have investigated learning of new information with repeated exposure in individuals with DA (e.g. Benedict *et al.*, 1998; Baddeley, Vargha-Khadem & Mishkin, 2001) For example, Baddeley and colleagues attempted to assess the ability of Jon, the young man mentioned above, to learn novel information from a video with repeated exposure over distributed study sessions. Jon was presented with two videos based on newsreels of events from the years 1937 and 1957. Both of these videos contained information that depicted events that occurred before Jon was born (1977), and therefore information that was likely to be not well known to him. Briefly, one of these videos (1937) was presented four times distributed over a two-day period, whilst the other (1957) was presented only once. Both recall and recognition were tested immediately after the final presentation of each video and were retested the following morning after a delay of ~18 hours. After one presentation, Jon's immediate recall score was much lower than that of his matched comparison group. However, after four presentations, Jon's immediate recall score rose considerably, to a level similar to that of his comparison group. Jon's delayed (overnight) recall after four presentations, although slightly lower than comparison group, was better than delayed recall after one presentation. His immediate and delayed recognition after one and four presentations was at a similar level to that of the comparison participants, with only delayed recognition after one presentation being slightly below theirs. The recognition performance of Jon and the comparison group improved slightly with repetition. Jon's performance indicates that his immediate and delayed recall and recognition benefited from repeated exposure. This is reminiscent of the pattern seen in the autism groups. Furthermore, these findings show that Jon is able to retain the information he has acquired across an overnight delay of 18 hours, whether tested by recall or recognition. An increase in knowledge with repetition, and the retention of newly acquired knowledge, are both necessary features for the incrementation of semantic memory.

Recall of stimuli following single presentation

Individuals with DA show impairments on episodic memory measures, such as tests of everyday memory and delayed verbal and visual recall (Vargha-Khadem et al., 1997; Gadian et al., 2000). Moreover, individuals with DA show a deficit in recall both after an imposed delay and immediately after presentation if the stimuli exceed short-term memory capacity (e.g. story recall). This is consistent with the findings of poor verbal and visual immediate and delayed recall but preserved short-term memory span, in case MS (Broman et al., 1997). Event memory has also been reported to be impaired in the DA group (Vargha-Khadem et al., 1997; Gadian et al., 2000; Isaacs et al., 2003). More recently we have shown that these impairments extend to measures of nonverbal recall, such as remembering an action sequence (Adlam et al., 2005).

Summary of behavioural findings

Overall the memory profile of individuals with DA is one of relative preservation of semantic memory and substantial impairment in episodic memory.

Neuropathology associated with developmental amnesia

Structural MRI studies of DA have identified severe bilateral hippocampal atrophy in all cases, using volumetric region of interest analyses (Vargha-Khadem et al., 1997; Gadian et al., 2000). Voxel-based morphometry studies have confirmed this with findings of bilateral reductions in grey matter in the hippocampal formation. It should be emphasized that the nature of these abnormalities were decreases in the proportional amount of grey matter, in contrast to the finding of increases in grey matter in the HFA group, as reported above (see Salmond *et al.* 2005). Additional abnormalities have also been identified in other aspects of the medial temporal lobe–cortical circuit including the putamen and the ventral part of the thalamus (Vargha-Khadem *et al.*, 1997; Gadian *et al.*, 2000; Salmond *et al.*, 2000a, 2000b). These structural abnormalities are consistent with the known pathology associated with hypoxic-ischaemic episodes (e.g. Volpe, 2001; Singhal, Topcuoglu & Koroshetz, 2002), the common aetiology of the previously reported DA cases, and were found to be independent of age at injury (Salmond *et al.*, 2000b). Behavioural correlates of these additional brain abnormalities have yet to be identified.

Memory in children born prematurely

The importance of the hippocampal formation in episodic memory is further highlighted by studies of a group of children who were born prematurely (Isaacs *et al.*, 2000, 2003). These preterm (PT) children show a similar type of cognitive profile to the developmental amnesic group, with impaired episodic memory and preservation of semantic memory. However, the episodic memory impairment is very much milder than that seen in the DA group. This is consistent with the disparity in hippocampal volume reduction in the DA group (~40% reduction bilaterally) and the PT group (~8% reduction). Presumably, the greater preservation of the hippocampal volume supports the preterm children's superior episodic memory function.

A direct comparison of the episodic memory impairment in autism, developmental amnesia and in children born preterm

In order to directly compare the episodic memory deficits in children with ASDs with children with DA and children born prematurely, the Rivermead Behavioural Memory Test (RBMT) was administered to children from all three groups and to two comparison groups. Participant details are shown in Table 4.1, and the RBMT is described in Box 1. Scores for the three groups for each of the eleven subtests are shown in Table 4.2 and the composite prospective memory score is plotted in Figure 4.1. Whilst the severity of the impairment in episodic memory

Table 4.1. *Participants' details (from Isaacs* et al., *2003; Salmond* et al., *2005)*

Group	Sex	Verbal IQ WISC-III (Bracken, 1992)	Age (years; months)
ASD	13 male, 1 female	102	12;11
TD (ASD comparison group)	6 male, 12 female	104	12;7
DA	6 male, 4 female	92	14;1
PT	8 male, 3 female	92	13;6
TD (DA/PT comparison group)	3 male, 5 female	110	13;8

Box 1: Rivermead Behavioural Memory Test

The Rivermead Behavioural Memory Test (Wilson, Cockburn & Baddeley, 1991), designed to measure recognition and recall of events closer to real-life situations, was used to quantify everyday memory. A Standardized Profile Score was obtained by assigning a score of 0, 1, or 2 to each of eleven subtests: immediate and delayed memory for a name, face, picture, story and route, and measures of prospective memory (appointment, message and a personal belonging), plus orientation to time and place. A twelfth subtest, knowledge of the date, was not given to some of the younger children and was therefore omitted from the analysis, reducing the maximum Standardized Profile Score from 24 to 22. A composite score was created by summing the scores for prospective memory (appointment, message and belonging), and these are displayed in Figure 4.1. Prospective memory is considered to rely heavily on episodic memory (Isaacs *et al.*, 2003).

---

was markedly less than that in the DA group, the memory profile of the children with ASDs nevertheless shows similarities with those of the DA and PT groups, particularly in relation to the prospective memory composite.

Cognitive differences between individuals with autism, those with developmental amnesia and children born preterm

As a contrast to the above similarities it is interesting to note that differences in the cognitive profile between the children with ASDs and the children with DA are evident in other cognitive domains. For example,

Table 4.2. *RBMT subtest scores for the three participant groups and the two comparison groups (from Isaacs et al., 2003; Salmond, 2001)*

Subtest	DA Mean (sd)	PT Mean (sd)	TD (DA/PT) mean (sd)	ASD mean (sd)	TD (ASD) mean (sd)
Standardized profile	8.6	17.7	21.4	16.8	20.9
Score (max = 22)	(3.4)	(2.4)	(1.2)	(3.1)	(1.1)
Name recall	0.2	1.8	2.0	0.9	1.8
(max = 2)	(0.63)	(0.6)	(0.0)	(1.0)	(0.6)
Belonging	0.5	1.9	2.0	1.3	2.0
(max = 2)	(0.7)	(0.3)	(0.0)	(0.8)	(0.0)
Appointment	0.6	1.6	2.0	1.4	1.9
(max = 2)	(0.7)	(0.5)	(0.0)	(0.7)	(0.3)
Picture recognition	0.8	1.9	1.9	1.7	1.9
(max = 2)	(0.9)	(0.3)	(0.4)	(0.5)	(0.3)
Immediate story recall	1.0	1.8	2.0	1.4	1.9
(max = 2)	(0.8)	(0.4)	(0.0)	(0.8)	(0.4)
Delayed story recall	0.3	2.0	2.0	1.5	1.9
(max = 2)	(0.7)	(0.0)	(0.0)	(0.7)	(0.5)
Face recognition	1.6	1.8	1.9	1.9	1.9
(max = 2)	(0.7)	(0.6)	(0.4)	(0.3)	(0.4)
Immediate route recall	0.9	1.2	1.9	1.8	1.9
(max = 2)	(0.9)	(0.9)	(0.4)	(0.4)	(0.4)
Delayed route recall	0.4	1.2	1.9	1.8	2.0
(max = 2)	(0.7)	(0.8)	(0.4)	(0.6)	(0.0)
Message	0.8	1.2	2.0	1.9	2.0
(max = 2)	(0.9)	(0.9)	(0.0)	(0.4)	(0.0)
Orientation	1.5	1.2	1.9	1.4	1.9
(max = 2)	(0.5)	(0.9)	(0.4)	(0.7)	(0.5)
Prospective composite	1.9	4.7	6.0	4.5	5.9
(max = 6)	(1.5)	(1.3)	(0.0)	(1.6)	(0.3)

DA = developmental amnesia group; PT = preterm group; TD (DA/PT) = typically developing comparison participants for DA and PT groups; ASD = ASDs group; TD (ASD) = typically developing comparison participants for ASD group. Prospective memory composite = sum of appointment, message and belonging.
© National Academy of Sciences, USA, 2003

children with DA do not show symptoms of 'executive dysfunction', although formal test results have not yet been reported (Adlam *et al.*, unpublished data). This is consistent with findings in adult amnesic individuals with MTL damage who generally do not demonstrate deficits on putative measures of prefrontal function (e.g. Wisconsin Card Sorting Test – Milner, Corkin & Teuber, 1968; Tulving, Hayman & Macdonald, 1991; Rempel-Clower *et al.*, 1996; Kitchener, Hodges & McCarthy, 1998; Henke *et al.*, 1999; Verfaellie, Koseff & Alexander, 2000; Van der Linden *et al.*, 2001).

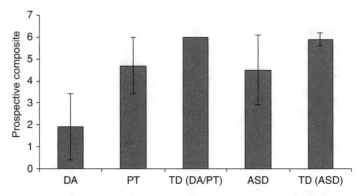

Figure 4.1 Prospective memory composite score from the RBMT in the DA, PT and ASD groups. Error bars represent Standard Deviation. (Data from Isaacs *et al.*, 2003, Salmond *et al.*, 2005) © National Academy of Sciences, USA, 2003

By contrast, children with ASDs have been reported to have difficulty with executive functions, as measured on a number of tests, including the Wisconsin Card Sorting Test (Rumsey & Hamburger, 1990; Ozonoff, Pennington & Rogers, 1991), maze learning (Prior & Hoffmann, 1990) and Tower of London (Hughes, Russell & Robbins, 1994). These differences in the cognitive profile are likely to reflect the different patterns of neural abnormality in the two groups (see above).

Discussion

Neuropathology

It has been shown that high-functioning individuals with autism have impaired episodic memory with relative preservation of semantic memory. Comparison with the DA and PT children, using similar measures, suggests that the hippocampal formation may be involved in this memory profile. However, the literature to date suggests that the nature of any hippocampal abnormality in autism contrasts with findings in the DA and preterm children. Whilst the latter two groups have been found to have decreased hippocampal volumes, findings in the autistic population are less consistent, possibly reflecting the heterogeneity of the population or the subtle nature of hippocampal abnormalities associated with autism. Moreover, there are additional differences in the pattern of neural abnormality in the two groups. For example, individuals with developmental amnesia have been reported to have bilateral abnormalities in the thalamus, putamen and hippocampal formation (Gadian *et al.*,

2000; Vargha-Khadem *et al.*, 2003), whilst abnormalities in the autistic population are more diverse including regions such as the amygdala, the cerebellum and the frontal lobes (see above). In addition, whilst the hippocampal abnormality in the DA children is visible on radiological examination, the abnormalities evident in individuals with ASDs are only evident using quantitative techniques (such as voxel-based morphometry).

Cognitive profiles: memory

The memory profile of children with ASDs (at least high-functioning individuals) appears to be similar to, but less severe than, that of the DA group. Further it is particularly similar to that of the preterm children (i.e. no evidence of recognition impairment and a mild, but significant, impairment on the Rivermead Test). However, although the mean score of the preterm group on the Rivermead Test is similar to that of the ASDs group, the individual subtests the ASDs group found difficult are not the same as those the preterm children are impaired on (as shown in Table 4.2, Isaacs *et al.*, 2000, 2003; Salmond *et al.*, 2005)

These differences might be a reflection of the social deficits associated with the syndrome of ASDs. Indeed the episodic memory impairment was particularly pronounced for prospective memory items pertaining to the 'self'. For example, aspects of episodic memory may have a greater dependency on attending to inherently social aspects of the world than semantic memory. This proposal is supported by inspection of the ASDs children's performance on individual subtests of the Rivermead Behavioural Memory Test, where particular difficulty is shown with those subtests that have a heavy social demand (e.g. memorizing someone's name, remembering to ask for a belonging, remembering an appointment and orientation to time and place). This is in contrast to performance on other subtests, even those thought to depend heavily on episodic memory (e.g. memorizing a route).

Cognitive profiles: social skills

Deficits in social skills, communication and interaction are hallmark features of ASDs. However, no such difficulties have been noted in children with developmental amnesia (Vargha-Khadem *et al.*, 1997). To date, there has been no formal assessment of skills such as theory of mind in the developmental amnesic population, making direct comparison between the two groups once again difficult. However, there have been no parental reports of difficulties with social situations, pretend play, maintaining friendships, etc. in the developmental amnesia group. Moreover, individuals with DA are often reported by parents and teachers to be sociable and confident, experiencing no difficulty in relating to others, and often spontaneously using their social skills to compensate for their profound memory difficulties (see Gadian *et al.*, 2000 for an anecdotal report).

This important contrast between the two groups suggests that hippocampal abnormality alone is not sufficient to induce social deficits. Indeed it appears that it is combined abnormality in multiple neural areas that produces the symptoms of ASDs.

Summary

Recent evidence has suggested that high-functioning individuals with autistic spectrum disorders (ASDs) show impaired episodic memory and relatively preserved semantic memory (Bowler, Gardiner & Grice, 2000; Salmond *et al.*, 2005). This pattern is reminiscent of the profile associated with developmental amnesia (Vargha-Khadem *et al.*, 1997) and also with children born preterm (Isaacs *et al.*, 2000). Individuals with developmental amnesia show marked reduction in hippocampal formation volumes attributable to a hypoxic-ischaemic episode (Gadian *et al.*, 2000). Children born preterm also have reduced hippocampal volume, although the reduction is considerably less than in developmental amnesia.

This chapter first reviewed the data on memory impairments and on neuropathology in individuals with ASDs and compared the cognitive and neural abnormalities to those in children with DA and children born prematurely. Whilst the behavioural findings suggest similarities between the three groups, all of whom have selective episodic memory impairments, the evidence for comparable neural substrates to the memory impairments is less compelling. Specifically, whilst there is some evidence of hippocampal abnormality in ASDs, findings have yet to be consistently replicated.

A direct comparison of episodic and semantic memory in the three groups using the Rivermead Behavioural Memory Test (Wilson, Cockburn & Baddeley, 1991) was then reported. The results suggest that the broad pattern of episodic memory impairment and intact semantic memory is consistent between the three groups. However, the individuals with ASDs show a much less severe deficit in episodic memory than that seen in individuals with developmental amnesia, and more comparable to that which occurs in children born preterm. In addition, there are differences of detail between the memory profiles of the children with ASDs and those born preterm. Finally, some other cognitive differences between individuals with autism, those with developmental amnesia, and those born preterm were noted, in particular in the areas of social interaction and executive function. The possible significance of these differences for understanding memory impairments in autism was discussed.

Acknowledgements

ARA and CHS contributed equally to this chapter. This work was funded by the Wellcome Trust and the Medical Research Council. Research at the Institute of Child Health and Great Ormond Street Hospital for Children NHS Trust benefits from Research and Development Funding from the NHS Executive. Thanks to Jane Ho and Lindy McWhirter for performing the MRI scans, to the National Autistic Society for help with recruitment and to the children and families who participated.

References

Adlam, A. L., Vargha-Khadem, F., Mishkin, M. & de Haan, M. (2005). Deferred imitation of action sequences in developmental amnesia. *Journal of Cognitive Neuroscience*, *17*, 240–248.

Aggleton, J. P. & Brown, M. W. (1999). Episodic memory, amnesia, and the hippocampal–anterior thalamic axis. *Behavioral Brain Sciences*, *22*, 425–444.

Ameli, R., Courchesne, E., Lincoln, A., Kaufman, A. S. & Grillon, C. (1988). Visual memory processes in high-functioning individuals with autism. *Journal of Autism and Developmental Disorders*, *18*, 601–615.

Aylward, E. H., Minshew, N. J., Goldstein, G., Honeycutt, N. A., Augustine, A. M., Yates, K. O., Barta, P. E. & Pearlson, G. D. (1999). MRI volumes of amygdala and hippocampus in non-mentally retarded autistic adolescents and adults. *Neurology*, *52*, 2145–2150.

Baddeley, A., Vargha-Khadem, F. & Mishkin, M. (2001). Preserved recognition in a case of developmental amnesia: implications for the acquisition of semantic memory? *Journal of Cognitive Neuroscience*, *13*, 357–369.

Barth, C., Fein, D. & Waterhouse, L. (1995). Delayed match-to-sample performance in autistic children. *Developmental Neuropsychology*, *11*, 53–69.

Benedict, R. H. B., Shapiro, A., Duffner, P. & Jaeger, J. J. (1998). Acquired oral reading vocabulary following the onset of amnesia in childhood. *Journal of the International Neuropsychological Society*, *4*, 179–189.

Bennetto, L., Pennington, B. F. & Rogers, S. J. (1996). Intact and impaired memory functions in autism. *Child Development*, *67*, 1816–1835.

Blair, R. J. R., Frith, U., Smith, N., Abell, F. & Cipolotti, L. (2002). Fractionation of visual memory: agency detection and its impairment in Autism. *Neuropsychologia*, *40*, 108–18.

Boucher, J. (1978). Echoic memory capacity in autistic children. *Journal of Child Psychology and Psychiatry*, 19, 161–166.

(1981). Memory for recent events in autistic children. *Journal of Autism and Developmental Disorders*, 11, 293–301.

Boucher, J., Cowell, P., Howard, M., Broks, P., Farrant, A., Roberts, N. & Mayes, A. (2005). A combined clinical, neuropsychological and neuroanatomical study of adults with high functioning autism. *Cognitive Neuropsychiatry*, 10, 165–213.

Boucher, J., Lewis, V. & Collis, G. (1998). Familiar face and voice matching and recognition in children with autism. *Journal of Child Psychology and Psychiatry*, 39, 171–181.

Boucher, J. & Lewis, V. (1989). Memory impairments and communication in relatively able autistic children. *Journal of Child Psychology and Psychiatry*, 30, 99–122.

(1992). Unfamiliar face recognition in relatively able autistic children. *Journal of Child Psychology and Psychiatry*, 33, 843–859.

Boucher, J. & Warrington, E. K. (1976). Memory deficits in early infantile autism: some similarities to the amnesic syndrome. *British Journal of Psychology*, 67, 73–87.

Bowler, D. M., Gardiner, J. M. & Grice, S. J. (2000). Episodic memory and remembering in adults with Asperger syndrome. *Journal of Autism and Developmental Disorders*, 30, 295–304.

Bowler, D. M., Matthews, N. J. & Gardiner, J. M. (1997). Asperger's syndrome and memory: similarity to autism but not amnesia. *Neuropsychologia*, 35, 65–70.

Bracken, B. A. (ed.) (1992). *Wechsler Intelligence Scale for Children*, 3rd UK edn. Sidcup: Psychological Corporation.

Brambilla, P., Hardan, A., di Nemi, S. U., Perez, J., Soares, J. C. & Barale, F. (2003). Brain anatomy and development in autism: review of structural MRI studies. *Brain Research Bulletin*, 61, 557–69.

Brian, J. A. & Bryson, S. E. (1996). Disembedding performance and recognition memory in autism/PDD. *Journal of Child Psychology and Psychiatry*, 37, 865–872.

Broman, M., Rose, A. L., Hotson, G. & Casey, C. M. (1997). Severe anterograde amnesia with onset in childhood as a result of anoxic encephalopathy. *Brain*, 120, 417–433.

Brown, M. W. & Aggleton, J. P. (2001). Recognition memory: what are the roles of the perirhinal cortex and hippocampus? *Nature Reviews Neuroscience*, 2, 51–61.

Buitelaar, J. K., van der Wees, M., Swaab, B. H. & van der Gaag, R. J. (1999). Verbal memory and Performance IQ predict theory of mind and emotion recognition ability in children with autistic spectrum disorders and in psychiatric control children. *Journal of Child Psychology and Psychiatry*, 40, 869–881.

Caron, M. J., Mottron, L., Rainville, C. & Chouinard, S. (2004). Do high functioning persons with autism present superior spatial abilities? *Neuropsychologia*, 42, 467–481.

Casalini, C., Brizzolara, D., Cavallaro, M. C. & Cipriani, P. (1999). 'Developmental dysmnesia': a case report. *Cortex*, 35, 713–727.

Courchesne, E., Yeung-Courchesne, R., Press, G. A., Hesselink, J. R. & Jernigan, T. L. (1988). Hypoplasia of cerebellar vermal lobules VI and VII in autism. *New England Journal of Medicine, 318,* 1349–1354.

De Renzi, E. & Lucchelli, F. (1990). Developmental dysmnesia in a poor reader. *Brain, 113,* 1337–1345.

DeMeyer, M. K., Alpern, G. D., Barton, S., DeMyer, W. E., Churchill, D. W., Hingtgen, J. N., Bryson, C. Q., Pontius, W. & Kimberlin, C. (1972). Imitation in autistic, early schizophrenic, and non-psychotic subnormal children. *Journal of Autism and Childhood Schizophrenia, 2,* 264–287.

Ellis, H. D., Ellis, D. M., Fraser, W. & Deb, S. (1994). A preliminary study of right hemisphere cognitive deficits and impaired social judgements among young people with Asperger syndrome. *European Child and Adolescent Psychiatry, 3,* 255–266.

Farrant, A., Blades, M. & Boucher, J. (1998). Source monitoring by children with autism. *Journal of Autism and Developmental Disorders, 28,* 43–50.

Gadian, D. G., Aicardi, J., Watkins, K. E., Porter, D. A., Mishkin, M. & Vargha-Khadem, F. (2000). Developmental amnesia associated with early hypoxic-ischaemic injury. *Brain, 123,* 499–507.

Gardiner, J. M., Bowler, D. M. & Grice, S. J. (2003). Further evidence of preserved priming and impaired recall in adults with Asperger's syndrome. *Journal of Autism and Developmental Disorders, 33,* 259–269.

Hanlon, F. M. & Sutherland, R. J. (2000). Changes in adult brain and behaviour caused by neonatal limbic damage: implications for the etiology of schizophrenia. *Behavioral Brain Research, 107,* 71–83.

Haznedar, M. M., Buchsbaum, M. S., Wei, T. C., Hof, P. R., Cartwright, C., Bienstock, C. A. & Hollander, E. (2000). Limbic circuitry in patients with autism spectrum disorders studied with positron emission tomography and magnetic resonance imaging. *American Journal of Psychiatry, 157,* 1994–2001.

Henke, K., Kroll, N. E., Behniea, H., Amaral, D. G., Miller, M. B., Rafal, R. *et al.* (1999). Memory lost and regained following bilateral hippocampal damage. *Journal of Cognitive Neuroscience, 11,* 682–697.

Howard, M. A., Cowell, P. E., Boucher, J., Broks, P., Mayes, A., Farrant, A. & Roberts, N. (2000). Convergent neuroanatomical and behavioural evidence of an amygdala hypothesis of autism. *Neuroreport, 11,* 2931–2935.

Hughes, C., Russell, J. & Robbins, T. W. (1994). Evidence for executive dysfunction in autism. *Neuropsychologia, 32,* 477–492.

Hughes, S. K., Nilsson, D. E., Boyer, R. S., Bolte, R. G., Hoffman, R. O., Lewine, J. D. *et al.* (2002). Neurodevelopmental outcome for extended cold water drowning: a longitudinal case study. *Journal of the International Neuropsychological Society, 8,* 588–595.

Isaacs, E. B., Lucas, A., Chong, W. C., Wood, S. J., Johnson, C. L., Marshall, C., Vargha-Khadem, F. & Gadian, D. G. (2000). Hippocampal volume and everyday memory in children of very low birth weight. *Pediatric Research, 47,* 713–720.

Isaacs, E. B., Vargha-Khadem, F., Watkins, K. E., Lucas, A., Mishkin, M. & Gadian, D. G. (2003). Developmental amnesia and its relationship to degree of hippocampal atrophy. *Proceedings of the National Academy of Science USA*, *100*, 13060–13063.

Kitchener, E. G., Hodges, J. R. & McCarthy, R. (1998). Acquisition of post-morbid vocabulary and semantic facts in the absence of episodic memory. *Brain*, *121*, 1313–1327.

Langdell, T. (1978). Recognition of faces: an approach to the study of autism. *Journal of Child Psychology and Psychiatry*, *19*, 255–268.

Manns, J. R. & Squire, L. R. (2002). The medial temporal lobe and memory for facts and events. In A. Baddeley, M. D. Kopelman & B. A. Wilson (eds.), *The handbook of memory disorders*, 2nd edn, pp. 81–99. Chichester: Wiley.

McCarthy, R. A. & Warrington, E. K. (1990). *Cognitive neuropsychology: a clinical introduction*. San Diego: Academic Press.

Meguro, Y., Suzuki, K., Tsukiura, T., Fujii, T., Yamadori, A. & Kudoh, M. (1999). Episodic and semantic memory after traumatic brain injury in a child [in Japanese]. *No To Shinkei*, *51*, 985–990.

Millward, C., Powell, S., Messer, D. & Jordan, R. (2000). Recall for self and other in autism: children's memory for events experienced by themselves and their peers. *Journal of Autism and Developmental Disorders*, *30*, 15–28.

Milner, B., Corkin, S. & Teuber, H. L. (1968). Further analysis of the hippocampal amnesic syndrome: 14-year follow-up study of H.M. *Neuropsychologia*, *6*, 215–234.

Minshew, N. J., Goldstein, G., Dombrowski, S. M., Panchalingam, K. & Pettegrew, J. W. (1993). A preliminary (31)P MRS study of autism: evidence for undersynthesis and increased degradation of brain membranes. *Biological Psychiatry*, *33*, 762–773.

Minshew, N. J., Goldstein, G., Muenz, L. R. & Payton, J. B. (1992). Neuropsychological functioning in nonmentally retarded autistic individuals. *Journal of Clinical and Experimental Neuropsychology*, *14*, 749–761.

Minshew, N. J. & Goldstein, G. (1993). Is autism an amnesic disorder? Evidence from the California Verbal Learning Test. *Neuropsychology*, *7*, 209–216.

Mishkin, M., Vargha-Khadem, F. & Gadian, D. G. (1998). Amnesia and the organization of the hippocampal system. *Hippocampus*, *8*, 212–216.

Mishkin, M., Suzuki, W. A., Gadian, D. G. & Vargha-Khadem, F. (1997). Hierarchical organization of cognitive memory. *Philosophical Transactions of the Royal Society London, Biological Sciences*, *352*, 1461–1467.

Ostergaard, A. L. (1987). Episodic, semantic and procedural memory in a case of amnesia at an early age. *Neuropsychologia*, *25*, 341–357.

Ozonoff, S., Pennington, B. F. & Rogers, S. J. (1991). Executive function deficits in high-functioning autistic children: relationship to theory of mind. *Journal of Child Psychology and Psychiatry*, *32*, 1081–1105.

Pierce, K., Muller, R. A., Ambrose, J., Allen, G. & Courchesne, E. (2001). Face processing occurs outside the fusiform 'face area' in autism: evidence from functional MRI. *Brain*, *124*, 2059–2073.

Piven, J., Bailey, J., Ranson, B. J. & Arndt, S. (1998). No difference in hippocampus volume detected on magnetic resonance imaging in autistic individuals. *Journal of Autism and Developmental Disorders*, *28*, 105–110.

Prior, M. & Hoffmann, W. (1990). Brief report: neuropsychological testing of autistic children through an exploration of frontal lobe tests. *Journal of Autism and Developmental Disorders*, 20, 581–590.

Raymond, G. V., Bauman, M. L. & Kemper, T. L. (1996). Hippocampus in autism: a Golgi analysis. *Acta Neuropathologica Berlina*, 91, 117–119.

Reed, L. J., Marsden, P., Lasserson, D., Sheldon, N., Lewis, P., Stanhope, N. et al. (1999). FDG-PET analysis and findings in amnesia resulting from hypoxia. *Memory*, 7, 599–612.

Rempel-Clower, N. L., Zola, S. M., Squire, L. R. & Amaral, D. G. (1996). Three cases of enduring memory impairment after bilateral damage limited to the hippocampal formation. *Journal of Neuroscience*, 16, 5233–5255.

Renner, P., Klinger, L. G. & Klinger, M. R. (2000). Implicit and explicit memory in autism: is autism an amnesic disorder? *Journal of Autism and Developmental Disorders*, 30, 3–14.

Rumsey, J. M. & Hamburger, S. D. (1990). Neuropsychological divergence of high-level autism and severe dyslexia. *Journal of Autism and Developmental Disorders*, 20, 155–168.

Russell, J. (ed.) (1996). *Agency: its role in mental development*. Hove: Erlbaum.

Saitoh, O., Karns, C. M. & Courchesne, E. (2001). Development of the hippocampal formation from 2 to 42 years: MRI evidence of smaller area dentata in autism. *Brain*, 124, 1317–1324.

Salmond, C. H. (2001). The role of the medial temporal lobes in high functioning autism. PhD thesis, University of London.

Salmond, C., Ashburner, J., Vargha-Khadem, F., Gadian, D. G. & Friston, K. (2000a). Detecting bilateral abnormalities with voxel-based morphometry. *Human Brain Mapping*, 11(3), 223–232.

Salmond, C. H., Vargha-Khadem, F., Friston, K., Mishkin, M. & Gadian, D. G. (2000b). Age at hypoxia and neuropathology in children with developmental amnesia. *Society for Neuroscience Abstracts*, 26, 1242.

Salmond, C. H., Ashburner, A., Connelly, A., Friston, K. J., Gadian, D. G. & Vargha-Khadem, F. (2005). The role of the medial temporal lobes in autistic spectrum disorders. *European Journal of Neuroscience*, 22, 764–772.

Schoppik, D., Gadian, D. G., Connelly, A., Mishkin, M., Vargha-Khadem, F. & Saunders, R. C. (2001). Volumetric measurement of the subhippocampal cortices in patients with developmental amnesia. *Society for Neuroscience Abstracts*, 27, 1400.

Scoville, W. B. & Milner, B. (1957). Loss of recent memory after bilateral hippocampal lesions. *Journal of Neuropsychiatry and Clinical Neuroscience*, 12, 103–113.

Shallice, T. (1988). *From neuropsychology to mental structure*. Cambridge: Cambridge University Press.

Siegel, D. J., Minshew, N. J. & Goldstein, G. (1996). Wechsler IQ profiles in diagnosis of high-functioning autism. *Journal of Autism and Developmental Disorders*, 26, 389–406.

Singhal, A. B., Topcuoglu, M. A. & Koroshetz, W. J. (2002). Diffusion MRI in three types of anoxic encephalopathy. *Journal of Neurological Science*, 196, 37–40.

Sparks, B. F., Friedman, S. D., Shaw, D. W. W., Aylward, E. H., Echelard, D., Artru, A. A., Maravilla, K. R., Giedd, J. N., Munson, J., Dawson, G. & Dager, S. R. (2002). Brain structural abnormalities to young children with autism spectrum disorder. *Neurology*, *59*, 184–192.

Squire, L. R. & Knowlton, B. J. (1995). Memory, hippocampus, and brain systems. In M. S. Gazzaniga (ed.), *The cognitive neurosciences*, pp. 825–837. Cambridge, MA: MIT Press.

Squire, L. R. & Zola-Morgan, S. (1991). The medial temporal lobe memory system. *Science*, *253*(5026), 1380–1386.

Squire, L. R. & Zola, S. M. (1996). Structure and function of declarative and nondeclarative memory systems. *Proceedings of the National Academy of Science of the USA*, *93*, 13515–13522.

(1998). Episodic memory, semantic memory, and amnesia. *Hippocampus*, *8*, 205–211.

Squire, L. R. (1987). *Memory and the brain*. New York: Oxford University Press.

(1992). Declarative and nondeclarative memory: multiple brain systems supporting learning and memory. *Journal of Cognitive Neuroscience*, 232–243.

(1994). Memory and forgetting: long-term and gradual changes in memory storage. *International Review of Neurobiology*, *37*, 243–269.

Temple, C. M. (1997). Memory disorders. In *Developmental cognitive neuropsychology*, pp. 83–110. Hove: Psychology Press.

(2002). Developmental amnesias and acquired amnesias of childhood. In A. Baddeley, M. D. Kopelman & B. A. Wilson (eds.), *The handbook of memory disorders*, 2nd edn, pp. 521–542. Chichester: Wiley.

Tessler, M. & Nelson, K. (1994). Making memories: the influence of joint encoding on later recall by young children. *Consciousness and Cognition*, *3*, 307–326.

Tulving, E. (1972). Episodic and semantic memory. In E. Tulving & W. Donaldson (eds.), *Organization of memory*, pp. 161–163. New York: Academic Press.

Tulving, E., Hayman, C. A. & Macdonald, C. A. (1991). Long-lasting perceptual priming and semantic learning in amnesia: a case experiment. *Journal of Experimental Psychology Learning, Memory and Cognition*, *17*, 595–617.

Van der Linden, M., Cornil, V., Meulemans, T., Ivanoiu, A., Salmon, E. & Coyette, F. (2001). Acquisition of a novel vocabulary in an amnesic patient. *Neurocase*, *7*, 283–293.

Vargha-Khadem, F., Gadian, D. G., Watkins, K. E., Connelly, A., Van Paesschen, W. & Mishkin, M. (1997). Differential effects of early hippocampal pathology on episodic and semantic memory. *Science*, *277*, 376–380.

Vargha-Khadem, F., Isaacs, E. & Muter, V. (1994). A review of cognitive outcome after unilateral lesions sustained during childhood. *Journal of Child Neurology*, *9*, 67–73.

Vargha-Khadem, F., Salmond, C. H., Watkins, K. E., Friston, K. J., Gadian, D. G. & Mishkin, M. (2003). Developmental amnesia: effect of age at injury. *Proceedings of the National Academy of Science USA*, *100*, 10055–10060.

Verfaellie, M., Koseff, P. & Alexander, M. P. (2000). Acquisition of novel semantic information in amnesia: effects of lesion location. *Neuropsychologia*, *38*, 484–492.

Volpe, J. J. (2001). Perinatal brain injury: from pathogenesis to neuroprotection. *Mental Retardation and Developmental Disabilities Research Review*, *7*, 56–64.

Wilson, B., Cockburn, J. & Baddeley, A. D. (1991). *The Rivermead behavioural memory test*. Bury St Edmonds: Thames Valley Test Company.

Wood, F. B., Brown, I. S. & Felton, R. H. (1989). Long-term follow-up of a childhood amnesic syndrome. *Brain and Cognition*, *10*, 76–86.

5 Possible parallels between memory and emotion processing in autism: a neuropsychological perspective

Yifat Faran and Dorit Ben Shalom

Introduction

In this chapter it is argued that the socioemotional and memory profiles in autism may be consistent with an abnormality in two systems both of which involve an interaction between the limbic system and the medial prefrontal cortex. The first system, which is probably critical for a diagnosis of autism, includes the pathway from the amygdala to the medial prefrontal cortex. This system is involved in the generation of basic and complex feelings, and in the successful performance of theory of mind tasks. The other system is the one including the pathway from the hippocampus to the medial prefrontal cortex (including the medial orbital prefrontal cortex). This system is arguably necessary for episodic memory. It is also perhaps involved in some of the 'coherence' impaired in 'weak coherence'. In the case of both of these systems, it is suggested that autism involves an impairment in the interaction between the limbic system and the medial prefrontal cortex.

The chapter is organized as follows. First there is a brief review of findings on memory in autism, using Tulving's (1995) analysis of different memory systems as a framework (for a fuller review, see Ben Shalom, 2003). This brief review focuses in particular on the episodic memory impairment in autism, and its likely brain bases. There follows a detailed account of what is known about emotion processing in autism, and the likely brain bases of the processing of emotions and feelings. The chapter closes with a brief discussion of the possible parallel between memory impairment and emotion-processing impairments in autism.

Intact and impaired memory systems in autism

Behavioural findings

In his 1995 review, Tulving distinguishes five types of memory systems: the procedural memory system, working memory, the perceptual representation system, semantic memory and episodic memory (see Gardiner, this volume, Chapter 1). Procedural memory includes non-declarative motor and cognitive skills, as well as simple conditioning. This type of memory will not be dealt with in this chapter. Likewise, the chapter does not deal with working memory, whose subsystems hold 'on-line' information during the execution of cognitive tasks (see Poirier & Martin, this volume, Chapter 12). The chapter focuses on the last three memory systems on Tulving's list: the perceptual representation system, semantic memory and episodic memory. Of these three memory systems, the perceptual representation system is clearly the most basic – a limbic (probably rhinal cortex) representation of 'raw', nondeclarative, perceptual and cognitive information. Declarative information is derived from the perceptual representation system through at least two different pathways (Tulving & Markowitsch, 1998; Aggleton & Brown, 1999). One, from the rhinal cortex to the inferior frontal gyrus derives fact information (semantic memory); the other, from the rhinal cortex to the hippocampus and then the medial prefrontal cortex (including the medial orbital pre-frontal cortex), derives event information (episodic memory).

The perceptual representation system is probably unimodal, and is sensitive to transformations that semantic and episodic memory are not sensitive to (such as the orientation of three-dimensional objects). Items in the perceptual representation system are rich in context, as are items in episodic memory. The within-item context in the perceptual representation system is, however, unimodal, as are the core items themselves. In addition, whereas context and item are bound together in the perceptual memory system, contextual information is factored out of individual items in episodic memory and can be used to create organization between different items. Items in semantic memory are, by contrast, relatively context free. Semantic and episodic memory differ in that episodic memory has to do with conscious recollection of previous experiences of events, whereas semantic memory is concerned with the acquisition and use of the knowledge of what is, or could be, in the world (Tulving & Markowitsch, 1998).

It has been argued in an earlier paper (Ben Shalom, 2003) that the perceptual representation system and the semantic memory system are relatively intact in people with high-functioning autism (HFA – used here to include people with a diagnosis of Asperger syndrome), whereas the episodic memory system is selectively impaired. This hypothesis, which would probably be accepted by most of the authors contributing to the present volume, gives rise to the following three predictions (Ben Shalom, 2003):

1. Memory tasks that do not depend on episodic memory but on the perceptual representation system or semantic memory, such as

rote memory and memory for facts, will show intact performance in autism.

2. Memory tasks that depend on episodic memory, and that cannot be compensated for using compensatory strategies involving either the perceptual representation system or semantic memory, will show impaired performance in autism. Such tasks would include tests of source memory, temporal order memory and memory for personally experienced events.

3. Memory tasks that depend partly or wholly on episodic memory but which can be compensated for by the perceptual representation system or semantic memory, such as free recall and recognition, will show a mixed performance in participants with autism. The level of performance may depend on many factors, including the test methods used and the cognitive level of the participants tested. Qualitatively, there should be signs of the use of atypical strategies.

The successful use of compensatory strategies, at least by more able individuals with autism, may derive from the fact that autism is a developmental disorder. These types of compensations may be harder to acquire when a memory disorder is acquired in adulthood.

The evidence reviewed in Ben Shalom (2003) and reported in other chapters in the present volume seems largely compatible with these predictions, as summarized below:

1. Performance on memory tasks that do not depend on episodic memory but on the perceptual representation system or semantic memory, such as rote memory and memory for facts, is intact in people with HFA. People with low-functioning autism (LFA) rely less on semantic memory and more on the perceptual memory system. Memory in people with LFA is famously rote, restricted and inflexible (e.g. O'Connor & Hermelin, 1988), all hallmarks of the perceptual representation system (Tulving & Schacter, 1990). In fact, both Toichi and Kamio (2002) and Mottron, Morasse and Belleville (2001) have reported that despite comparable levels of performance, individuals with high-functioning autism or Asperger syndrome show an equal memory gain from semantic as compared to perceptual or phonological processing. Mottron and Burack (2001) interpret these findings in terms of an enhancement of low-level perceptual processing in autism.

2. Memory tasks that are episodic in nature, and which cannot be compensated for using strategies involving semantic memory or the perceptual representation system, are universally impaired in participants with autism. In particular, source memory and temporal order memory have been shown to be impaired even in high-functioning

individuals (Bennetto, Pennington & Rogers, 1996). Deficits in the organization of information in memory, arguably related to episodic learning, are also consistently found in individuals with HFA (Minshew & Goldstein, 1993; Bennetto, Pennington & Rogers, 1996; Renner, Klinger & Klinger, 2000). Memory for personally experienced events has been shown to be impaired in people with LFA (Boucher, 1981a; Boucher & Lewis, 1989) as well as those with HFA (Klein, Chan & Loftus, 1999; Millward et al., 2000).

3. Memory tasks that depend partly or wholly on episodic memory, but for which it is possible to compensate using the perceptual representation system or semantic memory, show a mixed pattern of performance in participants with autism. The level of performance may depend on the cognitive level of the participants tested. Thus, in low-functioning children with autism, Boucher and Warrington (1976) found delayed free recall to be impaired relative to both normal and ability-matched comparison groups. Recognition, often argued to be less dependent on episodic memory than is free recall, was also impaired, but to a lesser degree. By contrast, Boucher (1981b) found immediate free recall to be intact in low-functioning children. In higher-functioning individuals, delayed free recall and recognition are unimpaired or close to unimpaired relative to ability-matched controls (Ameli et al., 1988; Minshew & Goldstein, 1993; Bennetto, Pennington & Rogers, 1996; Renner, Klinger & Klinger, 2000).

The difference between immediate and delayed free recall in low-functioning autism can be explained if the perceptual representation system can be used in immediate but not delayed recall. The difference between delayed recall in LFA as compared to that in HFA might be explained if a higher IQ facilitates the existence and efficacy of semantic compensatory strategies (perhaps similar to the effects of cognitive ability on the ability to perform tasks that require empathy in participants with autism, Yirmiya et al., 1992).

It was also predicted that there should be qualitative signs of the use of atypical strategies. Reduced or absent primacy effects in the face of intact recency effects have been reported in both high-functioning (Renner, Klinger & Klinger, 2000) and low-functioning autism (Boucher, 1981b). Performance in high-functioning autism is reduced on the late but not the early trials of the California Verbal Learning Test (Minshew & Goldstein, 1993; Bennetto, Pennington & Rogers, 1996). Finally, despite similar levels of performance, participants with HFA (as used here to include Asperger syndrome) show more 'know' responses and fewer 'remember' responses in recognition compared to a comparison group (Bowler, Gardiner & Grice, 2000).

A neuropsychological perspective

A general role for the hippocampus and prefrontal cortex in episodic memory is well established (e.g. Tulving & Markowitsch, 1998; Aggleton & Brown, 1999). Whilst the above memory profile in autism is largely consistent with a selective deficit in episodic memory, it does not allow localization of the anatomical abnormality to either the hippocampus or the prefrontal cortex. All three predictions are consistent with abnormalities in either of these locations, while specific comparisons with other clinical groups sometimes point to the one and sometimes to the other.

One possible cause of this ambiguity is a variation in the location of the abnormality among individuals with autism (perhaps contributing to some of the variation between the autopsy findings reported by Kemper and Bauman (1993), who found abnormalities in the hippocampal region in a postmortem study in people with autism, and by Bailey *et al.*, 1998, who did not find such abnormalities in the majority of their cases).

Intact and impaired emotion-processing systems in autism

Terminology

Turning to affective processing in autism, two different distinctions about affective processing have been developed within different areas of psychology. One, arising within neuropsychology (e.g. LeDoux, 1996), distinguishes between physiological emotions such as being in the physiological state of fear: for example, the way our body responds when we see a snake (fast heart beats, cold sweat, etc.); and cognitive feelings such as feeling afraid: for example, explaining to ourselves and to others that we felt afraid because we saw a snake.

Another distinction, arising within social psychology, distinguishes between basic emotions (feeling afraid, angry, happy, sad or disgusted; in our example feeling afraid of the snake) and more complex mental states, including the more properly 'social' emotions (e.g. feeling embarrassed, guilty, proud or ashamed; for example, being embarrassed that you were afraid of such a small snake).

The fact that there are two theories that have different terminologies makes it hard to formulate hypotheses and test their predictions. To preserve both distinctions the following terminology will be adopted in the present chapter. Physiological *emotions* will denote only the physiological signs of emotions (i.e. heart pounding, cold sweat, etc.). *Basic feelings* will refer to the cognitive counterparts of these physiological emotions (i.e. feeling afraid, angry, happy, sad or disgusted). More complex, 'social' feeling will be called *complex feelings* (e.g. feeling guilty, embarrassed, proud or ashamed). Going back to the example given above, when we see the snake and our heart beats faster and we are covered with cold sweat this is a physiological emotion; when we are conscious of these body reactions as feeling afraid this is a basic feeling; after a while when we get embarrassed that we reacted in panic to such a small snake this is a complex feeling. That is, complex feelings must include the understanding of other people's reaction to our feelings. Thus, the result is a three-way distinction within affective processing (physiological emotions vs basic feelings vs complex feelings), instead of a pair of two-way distinctions. Armed with this less ambiguous terminology, we can describe two major hypotheses concerning affective processing in autism. These are presented next, followed by a review of the relevant current evidence and finally a neuropsychological perspective on the findings.

Hypotheses

Whilst many different hypotheses about affective processing in autism are in principle possible, it seems current debate centres around the following two hypotheses. One approach, revolving around the work of Baron-Cohen and his colleagues, makes the following three predictions concerning the three-way distinction outlined above: physiological emotions should be intact in autism; basic feelings should be intact, at least in high-functioning autism; complex feelings, on the other hand, should be impaired even in high-functioning autism. This latter prediction stems from the assumption that people with autism cannot appreciate another person's point of view. Going back to our example, people with autism will have all the physical signs of fear when they see a snake and they will also feel afraid; however, they are not able to be embarrassed about feeling afraid, because they cannot appreciate how they may appear to another person.

A different approach, expressed in Ben Shalom (2000) and, perhaps, in Grossman *et al.* (2000), makes the following three predictions: physiological emotions should be intact in autism; all feelings, including basic and complex alike, should be atypical even in high-functioning autism (but not necessarily in PDD-NOS (pervasive developmental disorder – not otherwise specified)). Instances of intact performance by high-functioning individuals on tests of basic feelings should be achieved by using atypical compensation strategies, rather than by using hard-wired brain mechanisms. Thus, for our example, people with autism will experience the normal physiological signs of fear when they see the snake; but if they say to themselves or to someone else that they are afraid, this reflects a compensation they have acquired either for themselves, or through instruction: the feeling (as opposed to the raw emotion) of fear is not something a person with autism will automatically experience. The difference between these two different approaches stems from differences in the assumptions they make about the locus of impairment in autism. While the first approach traces the disorder to an impaired processing of complex mental states, the second hypothesis claims that all feelings (as opposed to emotions) are processed atypically by people with autism. Thus, while both approaches would agree that both social and affective processing may be atypical in autism, they differ with respect to whether the primary impairment is social or rather cognitive-affective.

Current evidence relating to the two hypotheses

Physiological emotions

Not much is known about physiological emotions in autism. Three recent studies are all suggestive, but none of them are completely convincing.

Willemsen-Swinkels *et al.* (2000) compared heart rate changes in children with autism spectrum disorders and typically developing children during separation and reunion with a parent. Children with autism spectrum disorders and disorganized attachment showed an increase in heart rate during separation, and a decrease during reunion, a pattern familiar from younger typically developing infants (e.g. Spangler & Grossman, 1993). The number of children in this part of the study was however very small. Blair (1999) showed pictures of distress, threatening pictures and neutral pictures to children with LFA, children with mental retardation without autism and typically developing children, matched on verbal mental age. He measured electrodermal responses following presentation of the pictures. Like the children with mental retardation and the normally developing children, the children with autism showed larger electrodermal responses to the pictures depicting distress than to the neutral pictures. Unlike the children with mental retardation and the typically developing children, the children with autism did not show larger electrodermal responses to the threatening pictures than to the pictures with neutral affective content. It is not entirely clear why this is the case. Ben Shalom *et al.* (2006) showed pleasant, unpleasant and neutral pictures to children with HFA and a typically developing comparison group. They measured electrodermal responses following presentation of the pictures.

All children showed larger electrodermal responses to the unpleasant pictures than to the pleasant ones. The main effect of picture type, however, was only marginally significant.

Complex feelings

In contrast, a lot is known about complex feelings in autism, which have been extensively studied by Baron-Cohen and his colleagues, in particular. For example, Baron-Cohen, Spitz and Cross (1993) matched children with autism, children with mental retardation and typically developing children on verbal mental age. They tested the ability to recognize the feelings of people from faces. The children with autism were impaired relative to both comparison groups in recognizing the complex feeling of surprise. Baron-Cohen, Wheelwright and Jolliffe (1997) compared adults with high-functioning autism and an IQ-matched normal comparison group on the ability to recognize complex feelings from photographs of faces. The participants with autism were impaired relative to the comparison group, and this impairment was even more pronounced in a condition in which the stimuli included the eye region alone. This finding may suggest that when participants with autism did manage to perform the task with the faces, they were using a strategy different from that of participants in the comparison group. Baron-Cohen *et al.* (1999) compared adults with HFA with typical adults on their ability to recognize complex feeling from the same type of stimuli of the eye region as the ones in Baron-Cohen, Wheelwright and Jolliffe (1997). The participants with autism performed less well than the normal adults. They also showed less activation of the amygdala during the task, as measured by functional magnetic resonance imaging. Concerning individual complex feelings, Capps, Yirmiya and Sigman (1992) compared children with high-functioning autism and verbal and nonverbal ability-matched typically developing children on the ability to talk about complex feelings of pride and embarrassment. The children with autism had more difficulty than children in the comparison groups in talking about these complex emotions. Similarly, Hillier and Allinson (2002) compared children with LFA to children with mental retardation and typically developing children, matched for verbal and mental age. They tested the ability to understand scenarios describing embarrassing situations. The children with autism were impaired relative to the typically developing children on scenarios describing empathic embarrassment.

These kinds of results were given a comprehensive theoretical treatment in the theory of mind hypothesis of autism (Baron-Cohen, 1995). According to this hypothesis, people with autism have difficulty in ascribing mental states to themselves and to others.

Basic feelings

The third, and perhaps most important line of evidence in deciding between the two hypotheses outlined above concerns basic feelings in autism. In contrast to physiological emotions, a large number of studies have been conducted about basic feelings in autism. Their results are for the most part, however, still subject to conflicting interpretations.

Earlier studies seem to suggest an impairment in the processing of basic feelings in autism. Hobson (1986) compared groups of mental-age-matched children with autism, mental retardation and normal children on the ability to choose drawn and photographed facial expressions of basic feelings that matched the gestures and vocalizations of video-taped persons in terms of four basic feelings (happy, sad, angry and afraid). The children with autism were markedly impaired in selecting the appropriate faces for the videotaped gestures and vocalizations. Similarly, Bormann-Kischkel, Vilsmeier and Baude (1995) compared individuals with autism between the ages of 7;0 and 36;0 and an age- and intelligence-matched comparison group on the ability to recognize basic feelings in photographs of faces. The autism group was significantly impaired, relative to the comparison group.

Later studies have argued, however, that the impairment disappears once participants with autism and participants without autism are matched on verbal as opposed to nonverbal mental age. So, for example, Ozonoff, Pennington and Rogers (1990) compared young children with autism with a comparison group matched on verbal mental age, and a comparison group matched on nonverbal mental age on the ability to perceive different basic feelings. The children with autism showed deficits in the perception of basic feelings only when compared to the group matched on nonverbal mental age. Compared to the group matched on verbal ability the children with autism did not show an impairment. Similarly, Prior, Dahlstrom and Squires (1990) compared children with autism with children matched pairwise on chronological age and verbal mental age, on recognition of basic feelings using the same task as Hobson (1986). No differences were found between the two groups. In the Baron-Cohen, Spitz and Cross (1993) study described above, which compared verbal mental-age-matched children with autism, children with mental retardation and typically developing children on the ability to recognize the feelings of others from faces, no differences were found between groups on recognition of the basic feelings of happiness and sadness. Similarly, in the Capps, Yirmiya and Sigman (1992) study described above, which compared high-functioning children with autism and verbal-ability-matched typically developing children on the ability to understand basic and complex feelings, no differences were found between the two groups on the understanding of the basic feelings of sadness and happiness.

One important study on basic feelings in autism is that of Grossman *et al.* (2000). Starting at least as early as Hermelin and O'Connor (1985), it has been conjectured that people with autism learn ways to recognize and express feelings that 'come naturally' to people without autism. No direct evidence of such compensation had, however, been available. Grossman *et al.* compared children with HFA and typically developing children matched for verbal intelligence on the ability to recognize basic feelings in faces alone and, in another condition, in faces paired with matching, mismatching or irrelevant words. They showed that while children with autism performed as well as the comparison group on the pictures of faces without words, they were significantly impaired relative to controls when the faces were matched with mismatching words. One possibility raised by Grossman *et al.* is that this finding suggests that the children with HFA used compensatory strategies (probably involving some kind of verbal mediation) to carry out recognition of facial expressions of basic feelings, in contrast to the typical, hard-wired, nonverbal mechanisms of the typically developing children.

Another important study in this context is that of Hill, Berthoz and Frith (2004). These authors studied difficulties in the cognitive processing of emotions in adults with high-functioning autism and normal adults using a self-report scale. The scale included items that clearly target basic feelings, such as 'When I am upset, I don't know if I am sad, frightened or angry.' The individuals with autism were significantly more impaired in their emotion processing compared with the normal adults.

In sum, while more work is clearly needed, it seems physiological emotions are relatively intact in autism, while basic and complex feelings are either atypical or impaired.

A neuropsychological perspective

The amygdala is a small subcortical structure, located in the temporal lobe. It is comprised of thirteen nuclei, traditionally classified into deep, superficial and other nuclei. It receives a great deal of sensory input from somatosensory, visual, auditory and all types of visceral input. The amygdala has extensive connections with the hypothalamus, affecting drive-directed behavior (sexual, feeding, cardio-vascular and respiratory changes). When an animal's amygdala is electrically stimulated, the animal typically stops what it is doing and becomes attentive. This may be followed by defensiveness, fight or flight. Conversely, bilateral destruction of the amygdala causes decrease in aggression, resulting in animals that are described as tame and placid. The amygdala plays a major role in affiliative behaviours in primates, via grooming (Kling & Brothers, 1992), and lesions of the amygdala impair these kinds of social behaviours (see Bachevalier, this volume, Chapter 2). The prefrontal cortex is the most anterior part of the frontal lobe, and the medial prefrontal cortex is one of its three major subdivisions (the medial, orbitofrontal and dorsolateral prefrontal cortex). Broadly speaking, the medial prefrontal cortex (including the medial orbital prefrontal cortex) is thought to be implicated in social, affective and memory processing; the lateral orbitofrontal in inhibition of impulses; and the dorsolateral prefrontal cortex in classical working memory. Ghashghaei and Barbas (2002) investigated the neural pathways between the amygdala and the medial prefrontal cortex in rhesus monkeys. They found that connections of the amygdala with the medial prefrontal areas were robust and bidirectional. Moreover, medial prefrontal axonal terminations in the amygdala were expansive, spreading into the parvicellular basolateral nucleus, which is robustly connected with hypothalamic autonomic structures, suggesting that they may influence the expressive emotional system of the amygdala.

There is considerable evidence that the amygdala is crucial for physiological emotions. For example, Kubota *et al.* (2000) showed negative and neutral affective pictures to participants with unilateral lobectomy of the temporal lobe. They measured electrodermal responses, a measure of physiological emotion. To reduce conscious feelings, presentation was subliminal. In other words, the pictures were masked and presented using brief exposure times, so that participants could not report the content of the presented pictures. Kubota *et al.* found the typical pattern of larger electrodermal responses to the negative compared to the neutral pictures, but only when pictures were presented to the hemisphere with the intact temporal lobe and hence the intact amygdala. In contrast, there is considerable evidence that the medial prefrontal cortex is involved in basic feelings. Phan *et al.* (2002) reviewed fifty-five PET and fMRI studies of basic feelings (feelings of happiness, fear, anger, sadness and disgust). They concluded that beyond specific areas involved in the processing of individual basic feelings, the one brain area with a general role in the processing of basic feelings was the medial prefrontal cortex.

There is also considerable evidence that the medial prefrontal cortex is involved in complex feelings. For example, Berthoz *et al.* (2002) explored the neural basis of the complex feeling of embarrassment. They presented stories describing neutral and embarrassing situations to twelve normal volunteers. The medial prefrontal cortex showed increased activation during the processing of stories involving embarrassing situations, when compared to those with neutral content.

There is some evidence for abnormality of the medial prefrontal cortex in autism. For example, Ohnishi *et al.* (2000) compared blood flow at rest in children with LFA and children with mental retardation, and discovered a reduction in blood flow in the medial prefrontal cortex in the children with LFA. Happé *et al.* (1996) found that adults with HFA activated a different subarea of the medial prefrontal cortex to that activated in normal adults during a theory of mind task.

In a postmortem study, Bauman and Kemper (1985) found increased cell packing in the medial temporal lobe in low-functioning individuals with autism. Some structural imaging studies have found increases or decreases of the size of the amygdala in autism spectrum disorders relative to comparison groups (e.g. Howard *et al.*, 2000). Baron-Cohen *et al.* (1999) compared adults with high-functioning autism to normal adults and found no activation of the amygdala in the HFA adults during a task of recognition of complex feelings.

Based on this type of evidence, Baron-Cohen *et al.* (2000) proposed the amygdala theory of autism, according to which the amygdala is a brain area necessarily abnormal in autism.

Note, however, that both the hypotheses concerning emotion processing in autism described above predict that physiological emotions are intact in autism. If this is true, there is an apparent contradiction. On the one hand there is evidence of abnormalities of the amygdala in autism spectrum disorders. On the other hand, the amygdala has to be intact enough to produce physiological emotions in autism. One way to resolve this contradiction is to use LeDoux's (1996) distinction between physiological emotions and feelings, according to which physiological emotions can be generated by the amygdala without input from the medial prefrontal cortex, while both basic and complex feelings depend on both the amygdala and the medial prefrontal cortex (or perhaps other higher-order cortical structures – see Critchley *et al.*, 2000). Utilizing this distinction it can be hypothesized that activity that can be carried out by the amygdala itself without involvement of the medial prefrontal cortex is relatively intact in autism, while performance on tasks that crucially depend on an interaction between the amygdala and the medial prefrontal cortex is atypical in autism spectrum disorders.[1]

Thus, if basic feelings are atypical in autism, there is a simple characterization of intact and atypical affective processing in autism. If basic

---

[1] Notwithstanding, it could still be the case that developmental impairments of the amygdala affect the development of the medial prefrontal cortex – cf. Fine, Lumsden and Blair, 2001.

feelings are typical, no such simple neuropsychological characterization is available at the present time.

Summary

Two hypotheses about affective functioning in autism have been outlined in this section. One predicts that of the three affective processing categories – physiological emotions, basic feelings and complex feeling, physiological emotions and basic feelings are intact in autism, but complex feelings are impaired. The other hypothesis predicts that whilst physiological emotions are intact, both basic and complex feelings are atypical in autism. It was argued that current evidence provides more support for the second hypothesis, and that this hypothesis is consistent with an abnormality of the interaction between the amygdala and the medial prefrontal cortex in autism.

Conclusion

This chapter argues that there are some parallels between memory processing and emotion processing in autism. In both cases a 'raw' representation (single-item perceptual and conceptual information in the case of memory, physiological emotions in the case of emotion) is converted in normally developing people into 'mental states' (memory episodes in the case of memory and basic feelings in the case of emotions). In both cases it seems that these 'mental states' are impaired in autism (universally in the case of emotion, to a variable degree in the case of memory), and in both cases it is argued that people with low-functioning autism rely more on the raw representations themselves, whereas people with high-functioning autism add to these raw representations a general-purpose reasoning mechanism that relies on *facts* (semantic or fact-based memory in the case of memory; fact-based reasoning about emotions in the case of emotion). Finally, it is argued that in both cases, there are some parallels in the neural substrates of these deficits – namely an impaired conversion of limbic system representations (hippocampal and amygdaloid, respectively), into medial prefrontal representations.

References

Aggleton, J. P. & Brown, M. W. (1999). Episodic memory, amnesia, and the hippocampal-anterior thalamic axis. *Behavioral and Brain Sciences, 22,* 425–444.

Ameli, R., Courchesne, E., Lincoln, A., Kaufman, A. S. & Grillon, C. (1988). Visual memory processes in high functioning individuals with autism. *Journal of Autism and Developmental Disorders, 18,* 601–615.

Bailey, A., Luthert, P., Dean, A., Harding, B., Janota, I., Montgomery, M., Rutter, M. & Lantos, P. (1998). A clinicopathological study of autism. *Brain 121,* 889–905.

Baron-Cohen, S. (1995). *Mindblindness: an essay on autism and theory of mind.* Cambridge, MA: MIT Press.

Baron-Cohen, S., Ring, H. A., Bullmore, E. T., Wheelwright, S., Ashwin, C. & Williams, S. C. (2000). The amygdala theory of autism. *Neuroscience and Biobehavioral Reviews, 24,* 355–364.

Baron-Cohen, S., Ring, H. A., Wheelwright, S., Bullmore, E. T., Brammer, M. J., Simmons, A. & Williams, S. C. (1999). Social intelligence in the normal and autistic brain: an fMRI study. *European Journal of Neuroscience, 11,* 1891–1898.

Baron-Cohen, S., Spitz, A. & Cross, P. (1993). Do children with autism recognize surprise? A research note. *Cognition and Emotion, 7,* 507–516.

Baron-Cohen, S., Wheelwright, S. & Jolliffe, T. (1997). Is there a 'language of the eyes'? Evidence from normal adults, and adults with autism or Asperger syndrome. *Visual Cognition, 4,* 311–331.

Bauman, M. & Kemper, T. L. (1985). Histoanatomic observations of the brain in early infantile autism. *Neurology, 35,* 866–874.

Bennetto, L., Pennington, B. F. & Rogers, S. J. (1996). Intact and impaired memory functions in autism. *Child Development, 67,* 1816–1835.

Ben Shalom, D. (2000). Autism: emotions without feelings. *Autism, 4,* 205–206.

(2003). Memory in autism: review and synthesis. *Cortex, 39,* 1129–1138.

Ben Shalom, D., Mostofsky, S. H., Hazlett, R. L., Goldberg, M. C., Landa, R. J., Faran, Y., McLeod, D. R. & Hoehn-Saric, R. (2006). Normal physiological emotions but differences in expression of conscious feelings in children with high functioning autism. *Journal of Autism and Developmental Disorders, 36,* 395–400.

Berthoz, S., Armony, J. L., Blair, R. J. & Dolan, R. J. (2002). An fMRI study of intentional and unintentional (embarrassing) violations of social norms. *Brain, 125,* 1696–1708.

Blair, R. J. R. (1999). Psychophysiological responsiveness to the distress of others in children with autism. *Personality and Individual Differences, 26,* 477–485.

Bormann-Kischkel, C., Vilsmeier, M. & Baude, B. (1995). The development of emotional concepts in autism. *Journal of Child Psychology and Psychiatry, 36,* 1243–1259.

Boucher J. (1981a), Memory for recent events in autistic children. *Journal of Autism and Developmental Disorders, 11,* 293–301.

(1981b). Immediate free recall in early childhood autism: another point of behavioural similarity with the amnesic syndrome. *British Journal of Psychology, 72,* 211–215.

Boucher J. & Lewis V. (1989). Memory impairments and communication in relatively able autistic children. *Journal of Child Psychology and Psychiatry, 30,* 99–122.

Boucher J. & Warrington, E. K. (1976). Memory deficits in early infantile autism: some similarities to the amnesic syndrome. *British Journal of Psychology*, 67, 73–87.

Bowler, D. M., Gardiner, J. M. & Grice, S. J. (2000). Episodic memory and remembering in adults with Asperger syndrome. *Journal of Autism and Develomental Disorders*, 30, 295–304.

Capps, L., Yirmiya, N. & Sigman, M. (1992). Understanding of simple and complex emotions in non-retarded children with autism. *Journal of Child Psychology and Psychiatry*, 33, 1169–1182.

Critchley, H. D., Daly, E. M., Bullmore, E. T., Williams, S. C., van Amelsvoort, T., Robertson, D. M., Rowe, A., Phillips, M., McAlonan, G., Howlin, P. & Murphy, D. G. (2000). The functional neuroanatomy of social behaviour: changes in cerebral blood flow when people with autistic disorder process facial expressions. *Brain*, 123, 2203–2212.

Fine, C., Lumsden, J. & Blair, R. J. (2001). Dissociation between 'theory of mind' and executive functions in a patient with early left amygdala damage. *Brain*, 124, 287–298.

Ghashghaei, H. T. & Barbas, H. (2002). Pathways for emotion: interactions of prefrontal and anterior temporal pathways in the amygdala of the rhesus monkey. *Neuroscience*, 115, 1261–1279.

Grossman, J. B., Klin, A., Carter, A. S. & Volkmar, F. R. (2000). Verbal bias in recognition of facial emotions in children with Asperger syndrome. *Journal of Child Psychology and Psychiatry*, 41, 369–379.

Happé, F., Ehlers, S., Fletcher, P., Frith, U., Johansson, M., Gillberg, C., Dolan, R., Frackowiak, R. & Frith, C. (1996). 'Theory of mind' in the brain: evidence from a PET scan study of Asperger syndrome. *Neuroreport*, 8, 197–201.

Hermelin, B. & O'Connor, N. (1985). The logico-affective disorder in autism. In E. Schopler & G. B. Mesibov (eds.), *Communication problems in autism*, pp. 283–310. New York: Plenum Press.

Hill, E., Berthoz, S. & Frith, U. (2004). Brief report: cognitive processing of own emotions in individuals with autistic spectrum disorder and in their relatives. *Journal of Autism and Developmental Disorders*, 34, 229–235.

Hillier, A. & Allinson L. (2002). Understanding embarrassment among those with autism: breaking down the complex emotion of embarrassment among those with autism. *Journal of Autism and Developmental Disorders*, 32, 583–592.

Hobson, R. P. (1986). The autistic child's appraisal of expressions of emotion. *Journal of Child Psychology and Psychiatry*, 27, 321–342.

Howard, M. A., Cowell, P. E., Boucher, J., Broks, P., Mayes, A., Farrant, A. & Roberts, N. (2000). Convergent neuroanatomical and behavioural evidence of an amygdala hypothesis of autism. *Neuroreport*, 11, 2931–2935.

Kemper, T. L. & Bauman, M. L. (1993). The contribution of neuropathologic studies to the understanding of autism. *Neurologic Clinics*, 11, 175–187.

Klein, B., Chan, R. & Loftus, J. (1999). Independence of episodic and semantic self-knowledge: the case from autism. *Social Cognition*, 17, 413–436.

Kling, A. & Brothers, L. (1992). The amygdala in social behavior. In J. P. Aggleton (ed.), *Neurobiological aspects of emotion, memory, and mental dysfunction*, pp. 353–377. New York: Wiley.

Kubota, Y., Sato, W., Murai, T., Toichi, M., Ikeda, A. & Sengoku, A. (2000). Emotional cognition without awareness after unilateral temporal lobectomy in humans. *Journal of Neuroscience*, *20*, RC97.

LeDoux, J. (1996). *The emotional brain*. New York: Simon & Schuster.

Millward, C., Powell, S., Messer, D. & Jordan, R. (2000). Recall for self and other in autism: children's memory for events experienced by themselves and their peers. *Journal of Autism and Developmental Disorders*, *30*, 15–28.

Minshew, N. J. & Goldstein, G. (1993). Is autism an amnesic disorder? Evidence from the California Verbal Learning Test. *Neuropsychology*, *7*, 209–216.

Mottron, L. & Burack, J. A. (2001). Enhanced perceptual functioning in the development of autism. In J. A. Burack, T. Charman, N. Yirmiya & P. Zelazo (eds.), *The development of autism: perspectives from theory and research*, pp. 131–148. Mahwah, NJ: Erlbaum.

Mottron, L., Morasse, K. & Belleville, S. (2001). A study of memory functioning in individuals with autism. *Journal of Child Psychology and Psychiatry*, *42*, 253–260.

O'Connor, N. & Hermelin, B. (1988). Low intelligence and special abilities. *Journal of Child Psychology and Psychiatry*, *29*, 391–396.

Ohnishi, T., Matsuda, H., Hashimoto, T., Kunihiro, T., Nishikawa, M., Uema, T. & Sasaki, M. (2000). Abnormal regional cerebral blood flow in childhood autism. *Brain*, *123*, 1838–1844.

Ozonoff, S., Pennington, B. F. & Rogers, S. J. (1990). Are there emotion perception deficits in young autistic children? *Journal of Child Psychology and Psychiatry*, *31*, 343–361.

Phan, K. L., Wager, T., Taylor, S. F. & Liberzon, I. (2002). Functional neuroanatomy of emotion: a meta-analysis of emotion activation studies in PET and fMRI. *Neuroimage*, *16*, 331–348.

Prior, M., Dahlstrom, B. & Squires T. L. (1990). Autistic children's knowledge of thinking and feeling states in other people. *Journal of Child Psychology and Psychiatry*, *31*, 587–601.

Renner, P., Klinger, L. G. & Klinger, M. R. (2000). Implicit and explicit memory in autism: is autism an amnesic disorder? *Journal of Autism and Developmental Disorders*, *30*, 3–14.

Spangler, G. & Grossmann, K. E. (1993). Biobehavioral organization in securely and insecurely attached infants. *Child Development*, *64*, 1439–1450.

Tager-Flusberg, H. (1986). The semantic deficit hypothesis of autistic children's language. *Australian Journal of Human Communication Disorders*, *14*, 51–58.

Toichi, M. & Kamio, Y. (2002). Long-term memory and levels-of-processing in autism. *Neuropsychologia*, *40*, 964–969.

Tulving, E. (1995). Organization of memory: quo vadis? In S. Gazzaniga (ed.), *The cognitive neurosciences*, pp. 839–847. Cambridge, MA: MIT Press.

Tulving, E. & Markowitsch, H. J. (1998). Episodic and declarative memory: role of the hippocampus. *Hippocampus*, *8*, 198–204.

Tulving, E. & Schacter, D. L. (1990). Priming and human memory systems. *Science*, *247*, 301–306.

Willemsen-Swinkels, S. H., Bakermans-Kranenburg, M. J., Buitelaar, J. K., van IJzendoorn, M. H. & van Engeland, H. (2000). Insecure and disorganised attachment in children with a pervasive developmental disorder: relationship with social interaction and heart rate. *Journal of Child Psychology and Psychiatry*, *41*, 759–767.

Yirmiya, N., Sigman, M. D., Kasari, C. & Mundy, P. (1992). Empathy and cognition in high functioning children with autism. *Child Development*, *63*, 150–160.

6   Dysfunction and hyperfunction of the hippocampus in autism?

G. Robert DeLong

Introduction

Autism encompasses wide disparities of memory and learning: at one extreme, some children with autism learn virtually no language and very little about the world around them; at the opposite extreme, other children with autism may show prodigious memorization and savant abilities. In family members of individuals with autism, unusual intellectual abilities are over-represented (DeLong, Ritch & Burch, 2002; Dor-Shav & Horowitz, 1984). Memory ability – but not cognitive profiles of visualization and reasoning – has been found to differentiate high- and low-functioning individuals with autism (Russo *et al.*, 2005). This suggests that the most disabling cognitive aspects of low-functioning autism may be due to memory disability (and raises the question whether the common research focus on high-functioning autism may tend to obscure the role of memory in the cognitive deficits of autism).

The hippocampus has a unique role in memory and cognition – a role that is still being clarified, and is directly pertinent to autism. In this chapter a genetic hypothesis will be presented, focused on hippocampal function and bringing together many seemingly unrelated aspects of autism. The hypothesis relates to the role of the GABA(A) receptor subunit gene GABRA5. This gene, located in chromosome 15q11–13, has been closely associated with autism in genetic linkage studies (McCauley *et al.*, 2004; Shao *et al.*, 2003). The same gene has been associated independently with bipolar disorder, a fact that is relevant to the hypothesis to be proposed (Otani *et al.*, 2005; Papadimitriou *et al.*, 2001). GABRA5 is expressed almost exclusively in the hippocampus (Sur *et al.*, 1999; Wisden *et al.*, 1992), where it controls an extra-synaptic tonic inhibitory chloride current into hippocampal pyramidal neurons in fields CA1 and CA3 (Caraiscos *et al.*, 2004). Deletion or mutation of this gene in mice *enhances* hippocampal-dependent learning and memory (Collinson *et al.*, 2002; Crestani *et al.*, 2002). Such gain-of-function of learning and memory is of potential interest with regard to autism, inasmuch as any complete theory of autism must take into account increased memory and learning ability to explain savant characteristics, and also the notable intellectual abilities found in family members (especially fathers) of individuals with autism (Dor-Shav & Horowitz, 1984). It is argued below that a different expression of this gene could produce an excessive or distorted gain-of-function resulting in dysfunction resembling autism.

The evidence relating to the genetic hypothesis to be proposed is complex, and includes analysis of the specific characteristics of the memory impairments and also the language impairments associated with autism; an account of specific abnormalities of brain lateralization and brain chemistry in autism, including evidence of similarities between neurochemical abnormalities in autism and those associated with certain psychiatric disorders; and finally consideration of the possible genetic origins of the neurochemical and ultimately the cognitive abnormalities earlier described. At the outset, however, it is necessary to review emerging concepts of hippocampal function, as a basis for understanding the memory and language impairments associated with autism. This review is undertaken next.

The hippocampus and memory

The organization of information in memory

There is general agreement that the hippocampus and related brain areas mediate declarative memory in humans. However, only now are neurophysiologists clarifying the neural network underlying the fundamental cognitive mechanisms supported by the hippocampus. Learning experiments in humans show that the hippocampal formation is important for establishing associations between components of episodes in memory (Henke et al., 1999). Henke et al. argue that the experience of an episode may involve the simultaneous processing of diverse sensory inputs, bodily sensations, thoughts and emotions in distributed cortical regions. These diverse activations must be brought together as a coherent event and stored in memory for the later recovery of some or all aspects of that episode. PET scans reveal that the hippocampal formation is activated by learning tasks that induce the deep encoding of single words, and more so by the creation and storage of semantic associations between two semantically unrelated nouns (Henke et al., 1999). This and other results demonstrate that the process of semantically associating items activates the hippocampal formation, that associating originally unrelated items challenges the hippocampal formation more than deep single-item encoding and novelty detection, and that this effect is independent of the kind of stimulus material used: similar results have been found with visual and olfactory material as well as verbal (Eichenbaum, 2004). These results substantiate the hypothesized role of the hippocampus as essential for semantic association of items in memory, and correspond to neuropsychological findings that patients with hippocampal damage are most impaired in complex associative learning (spatial and nonspatial). Thus, the function of the hippocampus is progressively revealed as a fundamental central cognitive processor that permits flexible multidimensional association of perceptual stimuli, stored information and motivational states (DeLong, 1992; Eichenbaum, 2004).

It is recognized however that individuals suffering from the amnesic syndrome (see Mayes & Boucher, this volume, Chapter 2) are capable of some limited kinds of new learning; it is also possible to demonstrate retrieval of stored material by means of cueing. Nevertheless, when learning can be demonstrated in amnesic humans it tends to be rigid, hyperspecific, pairwise and rote. Thus, Schacter (1985, p. 373) states that amnesic patients 'may be limited to the acquisition of rigid pair-wise associations that represent linkages between pre-existing unitised structures, and *they may be unable to acquire flexible new configurations in which multiple relations are formed among constituent units*' (emphasis added). Failure of this process results in rigid, invariant and rote behaviour, thought and language – at least as far as new information is concerned. The parallel with autism is obvious.

Eichenbaum's model of hippocampal function

Eichenbaum (2004) has developed a model, supported by elegant physiological evidence, which may elucidate the cognitive function of the hippocampus. According to Eichenbaum's model, the principal neurons of each subdivision of the hippocampus receive convergent inputs from virtually all cortical association areas; these afferents contain highly preprocessed information from the final stages of all the hierarchical streams of sensory, motor, emotional and cognitive processing; and these inputs are widely distributed on the various subfields of the hippocampus. Some describe these fields as being 'equipotential fields' on which all the inputs can work together to form 'conjunctive representations' of an episode of experience (Hampson, Simeral & Deadwyler, 1999). Thus the hippocampal field can encode highly complex combinations of the stimuli, behavioural actions and spatial cues that constitute an event and the place where it occurs. (I think of it simplistically as a jig or stage where the elements of a job are temporarily juxtaposed.) This is the highest level of synthesis of elements of an 'episode' of experience. The elements of this configured 'episode' are conveyed back to neocortex where they are stored, though with the hippocampus retaining the address for future reference. In fact, it takes several weeks before the cortical representation becomes independent of the hippocampus, as demonstrated by the phenomenon of permanent retrograde amnesia after head injury.

Another key part of Eichenbaum's concept of hippocampal function is a mechanism to support memory for the flow of events in experience: when elements of one episodic representation are activated, elements of other linked representations may also become activated. This organization of linked memory representations is called a 'relational memory network'. Relational networks can encode and retrieve the flow of events in episodic memories, and can encode and retrieve information that is common across experiences – information that constitutes semantic memory. Eichenbaum (2004) notes that this framework is consistent with the common view that episodic memory is the 'gateway' through which we initially encode everyday events, and that semantic memories are composed of a synthesis of episodic memories. This perspective is consistent with findings indicating that the hippocampus plays a role in the networking of semantic information (Bayley & Squire, 2002).

In support of this model, Eichenbaum has conducted a series of experiments to demonstrate the behavioural and cognitive deficits of hippocampectomized rats. Some of these studies examined whether the hippocampus is critical for remembering the flow of events in unique experiences and for the organization and flexible expression of related memories. Animals with hippocampal lesions were able to learn associations involving odour stimuli but were unable to learn the order of appearance of odour stimuli. From this and similar experiments, it was clear that some form of stimulus–stimulus representations can be acquired independent of the hippocampus. However, these representations are 'hyperspecific'. Only a hippocampally mediated representation can support the linkage and flexible expression of memories within a relational organization.

Evidence indicates that hippocampal neurons respond to a large range of feature conjunctions, such as those defining spatial locations, stimulus configurations and task-relevant behaviours. This suggests that the hippocampus represents experiences as a series of encodings of sequential events and the places where they occur.

Memory and language deficits in autism

The memory deficit

Hermelin and O'Connor (1970, p. 140) gave a classic description of the cognitive failure in children with low-functioning autism, recognizing the autistic child's 'generally very restricted and repetitive behaviour repertoire' and limited ability to process verbal sequences. They found that children with autism 'had immediate auditory rote memories as good as or better than those of typically developing children of similar mental age. However, the recall capacity of the control group improved significantly more when syntactical and meaningfully related material was presented than did that of the autistic children.' They concluded that children with autism hold information in a relatively 'raw' or unprocessed form due to a central deficiency in the processing of information, and 'are deficient in the capacity to appreciate order or pattern where this involves extracting the structure from sequences of stimuli'. (Note the similarity to the finding of Eichenbaum that hippocampectomized rats were unable to learn the order of appearance of stimuli.) The problem posed by Hermelin and O'Connor: *What is the cause of the limited ability of children with autism to process verbal sequences, and to recall meaningfully related material?* remains a central problem concerning autism and cognition, as Hobson and Hermelin point out in the Preface to the current volume.

Even in high-functioning individuals with autism, memory testing consistently shows increased difficulty with (1) increased complexity of material, (2) depth of semantic processing, (3) tasks requiring organization of information in memory, (4) verbal material, and (5) encoding information about themselves (personal episodic memory) (Millward *et al.*, 2000; Minshew & Goldstein, 2001; Toichi & Kamio, 2002; see also this volume, Chapters 5, 6 and 7). Toichi and Kamio (2002) found that people with autism do not perform better when verbal materials to be remembered are semantically related, and semantic processing of verbal materials did not facilitate memory in individuals with autism as it did in ability-matched comparison groups. At the same time, rote memory was superior in the individuals with autism. The contrast between impaired semantic processing of verbal information and superior rote memory is vital to understanding the cognitive memory deficit in autism and, as noted by Toichi and Kamio, may be unique to autism. It presumably involves a 'loss of central (cognitive) coherence' (Miyashita, 2004).

Language limitations

Limitations of language learning in low-functioning autism vividly demonstrate the characteristic deficits of autistic cognition. Two older descriptions classically summarize autistic language limitations. Prior (1979, p. 368) states that 'some autistic children can learn to speak via operant procedures ... However, problems of creativity, spontaneity, and generalization are rarely overcome even with carefully planned additional training extending into all facets of the child's life ... Speech may be relatively competent but language and communication of any but the most concrete type continue to be limited.' In autism, as shown by children who have partially acquired language, the simplest tasks – requiring the least relational processing – may be accomplished satisfactorily; more complex demands of language, however, produce only failure. Churchill (1978) has given an elegant analysis of the language processing incapacities of children with autism that remains pertinent today.

Relations between memory and language

Studies of memory and language have traditionally been rather separate. However, that is changing, with some authors beginning to argue that there is no dividing line between language and memory for verbal materials (see, for example, MacKay, Stewart & Burke, 1998). These authors suggest that the hippocampus is responsible for 'binding': that is, new experiences are comprehended by binding with old data, to form new memories. MacKay *et al.* (1998) have shown that binding is impaired in the language of adult patients with bilateral hippocampal lesions, as evidenced by impairments of comprehension and of semantic-level language production. According to this conception, every new sentence of language that an individual generates, and every new sentence understood, involves the semantic memory system and requires hippocampal system function. This idea about hippocampal activation in language is reminiscent of the finding of hippocampal activation in sensorimotor integration (Tesche & Karhu, 1999); that is, it begins to describe a finer grain of hippocampal activity than previously known.

In sum: the core cognitive defect in autism appears to involve a deficit in the same semantic function of the hippocampus elucidated by Henke, Eichenbaum and others (see above). The memory of individuals is defective or limited in capacity for multidimensional associations, constituting meaning or understanding of complex material, including verbal material. By contrast, rote memory and the processing of nonmeaningful or visual–spatial material may be supernormal in some high-functioning individuals with autism.

Neurochemical abnormalities in autism: similarities to schizophrenia and bipolar mood disorder

Abnormal lateralization of cognitive functions and of serotonin synthesis in autism

An important aspect of autism is the disparity between left- and right-hemisphere cognitive function: defective language function, poor

abstraction and generalization, and poor sequential function are suggestive of left hemisphere deficits; conversely, normal visual–spatial skills,
ability to solve visual puzzles, excellent topographic ability, musical sense
and certain other abilities are suggestive of intact right-hemisphere function (Dawson, 1983). (Low-functioning autism may well involve bilateral
deficits.)

Several studies have produced evidence of abnormal lateralization of
serotonin synthesis in autism. Chugani *et al.* (1997) and Chugani (2004)
found interhemispheric differences in putative serotonin synthesis in PET
scans using a serotonin precursor (alpha(C-11) methyl-L-tryptophan)
(AMT). Castelloe and Dawson (1993) found very low levels of serotonin
synthesis in the left cerebral hemisphere (except for the occipital lobes),
particularly in the subgroup of children with autism characterized as
'passive'. Finally, in a study of seven boys with autism between 5 and
7 years of age, Chugani *et al.* (1997) found that five of the boys had
markedly decreased serotonin synthesis in the left-hemisphere cortex
(most marked in frontal cortex, but also decreased in temporal and parietal cortex), along with increased serotonin synthesis in the right (con-
tralateral) cerebellum. In the remaining two children, whose clinical
picture did not differ from that of the other five, the asymmetry was
reversed. In further studies that included girls, a delay in the development
of serotonin synthesis in frontal cortex was found, compared to typical
children. This was often bilateral, especially in the girls studied (Chugani
et al., 1999). Autism is less common in girls than in boys, but girls tend to
be more severely affected.

These studies raise two important points: (1) The role of serotonin in
autism. (2) The lateralization of serotonin synthesis in autism, which
appears to parallel the abnormal lateralization of function. The origin of
lateralized deficits in autism is unexplained. However, it may relate to
psychiatric disorder, particularly bipolar disorder, which is prominent in
families of people with autism and associated with aberrant cerebral
functional lateralization (DeLong, 2004). Evidence in support of this
suggestion is reviewed next.

Responsivity to SSRIs in children with autism

There is increasing recognition that childhood autism can be favourably
modified by psychotropic medications used for mood disorder in the
nonautistic population. Such medications are SSRIs (specific serotonin
reuptake inhibitors, potentiating serotonin at serotonergic synapses)
(DeLong, Teague & McSwain Kamran, 1998); also atypical antipsy-
chotic medications combining dopaminergic antagonism and 5HT1 A

receptor activation (McDougle *et al.*, 2005). This observation suggests that the neurotransmitter and receptor characteristics of autism and mood disorder may be similar.

The alpha-methyltryptophan (AMT) PET data of the Chuganis (see above) provide a rationale for treating children with autism using SSRI medications, which increase serotonin at serotonergic synaptic receptors. Serotonin has many effects in the developing nervous system, acting as a neurotrophic agent as well as a neurotransmitter (Chandana *et al.*, 2005). In addition, serotonergic neurons have intimate interactions with other transmitter systems, especially GABergic interneurons. The use of SSRIs in autism therefore has an underlying rationale based on known neuro-biology. There is an additional rationale in the parallelism of autism with familial affective disorders, seen in symptoms associated with autism and in family histories of children with autism. So, for example, a recent epidemiological study of antecedents of autism found familial psychiatric disorders (affective and psychotic) to be the strongest epidemiologic factors associated with autism (Larsson *et al.*, 2005). (For a fuller account of the argument for an association between autism and familial affective disorders see DeLong, 2004).

In my clinic we have extensive experience of treating young idiopathic children with autism with fluoxetine, a prototypical SSRI, over ten years (DeLong, Ritch & Burch, 2002). From a research point of view, this work has the limitations of all open trials, and the data reported below must be viewed cautiously. However, our trials have been continued for long durations, controlled by intermittent drug holidays, and compared to trials of other interventions in the same children. Data from these trials are summarized below.

Outcomes for the whole group of children treated
Of 129 children in whom treatment could be evaluated, global clinical outcome measures indicated 22 (17%) had an excellent response; 67 (52%) had a good response; 10 (8%) had a fair response; and 30 (23%) had a poor response. The mean age of starting treatment was 54 months (4 years 6 months). The mean length of treatment to date is 36.6 months (range 13 to 76 months) for excellent responders, and 32.3 months (range 5 to 76 months) for good responders.

Outcomes for the subgroup of children treated for at least 36 months
Thirty children were maintained on fluoxetine for 36 months or more (range 36 to 76 months). Twenty were good and 10 were excellent responders. Twenty-five of the original group of 30 children were continuing treatment when last encountered.

Effects of discontinuation trials

Twenty of the 30 children treated for at least 36 months had trial(s) of discontinuing treatment. Of these, 18 resumed treatment after clinical regression; one had no regression; one was lost to follow-up. Six parents refused discontinuation trials, and data regarding discontinuation are not available for the remaining 4 children.

Follow-up of the 30 children

With regard to educational placement, 14 were in regular classes (some with an aide), 5 in classes for children with autism, 3 in other special classes. There was no information for the remaining 8 children. Five boys were later diagnosed independently with bipolar disorder; 4 of these were no longer considered autistic – 3 were in regular classes and one was in a learning disability class; one was still clearly autistic and in a class for children with autism. Four of the 5 boys with bipolar disorder were treated with lithium, one with valproate.

Correlations within the proband group and between probands and other family members

Response to fluoxetine correlated with the occurrence of major mood disorder in the proband's family: of probands with a positive family history, 67 of 86 had a good/excellent response (78%), while of those with a negative family history, 12 of 31 (39%) had a good/excellent response ($X^2 = 17.2$, df = 1, p < .001). Fluoxetine response likewise correlated with special intellectual abilities in the autistic proband's family: 52 of 68 probands (76%) with a positive family history of special abilities had good/excellent fluoxetine response, while 32 of 53 with no family history of special abilities (60%) had a good/excellent response ($X^2 = 3.8$, df = 1, p = .05). However, selecting only those with excellent responses, 21 of 22 had family history of special ability.

A strong correlation was found between major mood disorder and unusual intellectual ability in families ($X^2 = 20.8$, df = 1, p < .0001). If only bipolar disorder in the families is considered, the correlation with unusual intellectual ability is even stronger ($X^2 = 38$, df = 1, p < .00001). In addition, hyperlexia in the probands (defined as precocious interest in letters and numbers) correlated robustly with treatment response. Of children with autistic spectrum disorder and hyperlexia, 24 of 25 showed an excellent (10) or good (14) response.

It is commonly stated that neuropharmacologic agents do not ameliorate the core symptoms of autism, but only modify comorbid or incidental features. Our clinical experience suggests otherwise: improvement in socialization, language, adaptive skills, praxis, attention and mood indicate that in many cases medication does modify, though not cure, some of the core symptoms of autism, as well as some incidental features. Most notably, SSRIs given to young children with autism have produced an important, though incomplete, improvement in the quality, spontaneity and communicativeness of some children's language, as formally assessed. Anecdotally, some parents also noted 'normalization' of memory with treatment: the obsessive, rote features faded as memory became more 'normal'. These findings have not, however, been adequately systematized and must therefore be considered encouraging but not proven.

Abnormalities of glutamate and reelin in schizophrenia, bipolar disorder and autism

An emerging understanding of the neuropathology of psychotic disorders, focusing on synapses and synaptic plasticity, is revealing a convergence of findings in schizophrenia, bipolar disorder and autism. Abnormal markers in prefrontal cortical areas in postmortem specimens from patients with bipolar disorder or schizophrenia have been summarized by Knable *et al.* (2002). The markers identified pertain to a variety of neural systems and processes including neuronal plasticity, neurotransmission, signal transduction, inhibitory interneuron function and glial cells. However, the most salient markers pertain to aspects of glutamatergic, GABAergic and dopaminergic neurotransmission. In particular, the neuropathology of schizophrenia includes decreased reelin and glutamic acid decarboxylase (GAD67) expression, increased neuronal packing density and decreased neuropil and dendritic spine number (Costa *et al.*, 2002).

Decreased dendritic spine counts in frontal cortex of individuals with schizophrenia or bipolar disorder have also been reported by Rodriguez *et al.* (2000), and (most relevant to the current argument) individuals with autism (Costa *et al.*, 2001). Decreased BDNF (brain-derived neurotrophic factor) and decreased reelin (both involved in synaptic and dendritic spine plasticity) have also been described in prefrontal cortex of all three groups (Fatemi, 2001).

Abnormalities of GABA in autism, bipolar disorder and schizophrenia

GABA receptors are decreased in the hippocampus in autism (Blatt *et al.*, 2001). GABA receptor abnormalities may determine mood disorders (see below). The GABergic and serotonergic systems have extensive and complex interactions, which may be important both in autism and in bipolar disorder. Serotonergic neurons extensively modulate GABA action in prefrontal and hippocampal cortex. This interaction is mediated by 5HT1, 5HT2 and 5HT3 receptors on GABA interneuron cell bodies; by 5HT1, 5HT2 and 5HT4 receptors on pyramidal cell bodies; by 5HT2 and 5HT4 synapses near GABA-receptive dendritic spines; and by 5HT1 A receptors on proximal pyramidal cell axons, adjacent to GABA inhibitory synapses (Cai et al., 2002; Feng et al., 2001). Mice lacking 5HT1 A receptors (5HT1 A knockout mice) show impaired hippocampal-dependent learning (Sarnyai et al., 2000); and a deficiency of 5HT1 A receptors has been reproducibly found in the limbic system of people with mood disorders (Drevets et al., 2000). Stimulation of 5HT1 A receptors by serotonin (5HT) results in hyperpolarization and inhibition of neuronal activity in the hippocampus (Schmitz et al., 1998). These interactions may mediate the efficacy of fluoxetine and related SSRIs in treatment of autism (see above). Finally, GABAergic receptors have a special role in establishing the computational architecture of cortical columns (Ferster, 2004; Hensch & Stryker, 2004). Abnormalities in the organization of cortical minicolumns have been demonstrated in autism (Acosta & Pearl, 2003).

Reelin and GAD67 are co-localized in GABergic interneurons. Reelin is found at GABergic synapses, co-localized with clusters of alpha3integrin molecules in postsynaptic densities located on apical dendritic spines. Reelin and integrin activate a cascade that modulates cytoskeletal elements thought to mediate synaptic and spine plasticity (Costa et al., 2002). These interactions are presumably important in SSRI-responsive autism as well as in depression. Mutations of X-linked genes encoding neuroligands NLGN3 and NLGN4 have been associated with autism; these mutations affect cell-adhesion molecules localized at synapses, and suggest that various defects of synaptogenesis may predispose to autism (Jamain et al., 2003).

The foregoing account of chemical and synaptic abnormalities in autism offers only a sketchy look at this rapidly advancing field. However, it suggests a congruence of findings in schizophrenia, bipolar disorder and autism. This congruence may be explicable in terms of shared genetic factors, as outlined next.

Genetics, hippocampus, memory and autism

Genomic linkage studies support a linkage of one subgroup of people with autism to chromosome 15q11–13, the region associated with Prader-Willi and Angelman's syndromes and subject to imprinting (parent-specific methylation of genes inhibiting gene expression (Cassidy, Dykens & Williams, 2000)). Existing genetic data for autism in this region converge on a cluster of three GABA(A) receptor subunit genes

(GABRB3, GABRA5 and GABRG3), most specifically with a marker in the GABRB3 gene but including GABRA5 (McCauley et al., 2004). Linkage data selecting for a specific phenotypic trait ('insistence on sameness') to enhance homogeneity showed increased linkage evidence for the 15q11–13 region at the GABRB3 locus (Shao et al., 2003). These authors suggest that 'insistence on sameness' is a trait related to obsessive–compulsive disorder (OCD), and thus to mood disorder (OCD has a large comorbidity with bipolar disorder (Angst et al., 2005)). A similar strategy based on savant skills in families of children with autism likewise improved evidence of genetic linkage to 15q11–13 (Nurmi et al., 2003). These data are consistent with a genetic contribution of a 15q11–13 locus to autism susceptibility in a subset of affected individuals exhibiting savant skills. Similar special visuospatial skills (recognized as proficiency at jigsaw puzzles) have been noted in individuals with Prader-Willi syndrome resulting from deletions of this chromosomal region (Dykens, 2002; Whittington et al., 2004).

In Prader-Willi syndrome a parent-of-origin effect has been described ('grandmatrilineal inheritance' (Ming et al., 2000)), in which a small deletion in 15q11–13 was not expressed when transmitted from grandmother to her two sons (because of maternal imprinting, blocking gene expression), but when transmitted by those two sons resulted in Prader-Willi syndrome in their offspring. We have observed a similar pattern of inheritance in certain families of children with autism. In one such family the grandmother was an artist and had depression; her two sons showed special nonverbal abilities (one an artist with photographic memory, one with remarkable mathematical ability) and affective disorders (one had bipolar disorder and one depression). Each brother has a son with classical autism and severe affective disorder. One father–son dyad has oculocutaneous albinism, consistent with a chromosome 15q abnormality (Manga et al., 2001). Karyotypes were normal and comparative genomic hybridization revealed no abnormality.

The foregoing observations take on special significance in light of the recent demonstration that knockout mice lacking the alpha5 subunit of the GABA(A) receptor (GABRA5) show enhanced learning and memory, specifically in the water maze model of spatial learning, a hippocampus-dependent learning task (Collinson et al., 2002). Expression of GABRA5 is virtually restricted to the hippocampus (Sur, 1999; Wisden, 1992). Moreover, mice carrying a point mutation at position 105 of the alpha5 subunit (H105R) have a selective reduction of GABRA5-containing receptors in hippocampal pyramidal neurons and demonstrate facilitation of a particular form of associative learning, trace fear conditioning (Crestani et al., 2002). GABRA5 subunit-containing receptors mediate tonic inhibition in mouse hippocampal CA1 and CA3 pyramidal neurons, which play a key role in hippocampal cognitive processes (Caraiscos *et al.*, 2004). It is noteworthy that in GABRA5-knockout mice, gamma frequency oscillations in the electroencephalogram, evoked by increased network drive, are significantly greater than in normals (Towers *et al.*, 2004). Similar increased gamma activity is found in individuals with autism identifying the presence or absence of an illusory Kanizsa shape (Brown *et al.*, 2005). Abnormal gamma activity has been hypothesized to underlie certain cognitive deficits in autism (Bayly, 2005; Brock *et al.*, 2002).

Consistent with the hypothesis advanced here, there is evidence using a microcell-mediated chromosome transfer technique that human GABA(A) receptor subunit genes on chromosome 15q11–13 (GABRB3, GABRA5, and GABRG3) are expressed exclusively from the paternal allele (Meguro *et al.*, 1997). Papadimitriou *et al.* (2001) found an association between the GABRA5 gene locus and bipolar affective disorder, a finding recently confirmed independently by Otani *et al.* (2005). In clinical studies of 151 families of children with autism, we found a strong correlation among fluoxetine response in autistic probands, special intellectual ability in family members, and major affective disorders (especially bipolar disorder and related comorbidities) in family members (DeLong *et al.*, 2002; see above). The hypothesis of grandmatrilineal inheritance (specifically of a paternal parent-of-origin effect affecting expression of the GABRA5 gene) may inter-relate autism, mood disorder, and special intellectual abilities to a specific genetic locus or region. It suggests that these different manifestations may depend on differences in GABRA5 gene expression. There is evidence that GABRA5 may be expressed only on the paternal allele; that its mutation or deletion produces a gain of spatial memory and learning function; that it has independently been associated with bipolar affective disorder; and most importantly that it has been associated with autism in genetic linkage studies. While additional colouration of the autistic picture associated with 15q11–13 may come from effects of adjacent genes, especially GABRB3, the GABRA5 hypothesis is compelling in light of these recent findings.

The precise forms of behavioural disturbance that might result from altered expression of GABRA5 can only be guessed at this point, but they would likely include disturbances of memory (particularly enhanced or distorted memory function) and elements of heightened anxiety and/or other disturbances of mood, all of which are salient features of classical autism. These possibilities will be worked out by careful correlation of clinical observations with genetic data. Also, it must be remembered that this or any specific genetic hypothesis, if shown to be valid, would likely only pertain to one subtype of autism.

Summary

Autism may be the developmental syndrome of the hippocampus, at least as regards cognition. Memory ability is claimed to be a critical factor differentiating high- and low-functioning individuals with autism. The hippocampus appears to be essential for multidimensional combinatorial processes essential for semantic learning. The most distinctive function of the hippocampus is as a central cognitive processor: the hippocampus creates and stores deep and extensive semantic associations among diverse inputs. Flexible and generative language likewise appears to be dependent on these hippocampal processes. These processes are curtailed in autism, and this failure may be unique to autism.

A second concept central to autism is the role of serotonin, because of the dramatic lateralized abnormality of its synthesis in the brains of children with autism; its role in brain development (controlling growth of corticopetal axons, cortical columns and synapse formation); and because specific serotonin reuptake inhibitors (SSRIs) markedly benefit some children with autism. Serotonin is implicated in major affective disorders as well as autism, and familial affective disorder is a major risk factor for autism. The lateralized abnormalities in autism may relate to the same (unknown) factors causing lateralized abnormalities in major affective disorders.

The serotonin story converges with the hippocampus story: mice lacking 5HT1 A receptors show impaired hippocampal-dependent learning; and a deficiency of 5HT1 A receptors has been reproducibly found in the limbic system of people with mood disorders. Closely related is the new neuropathology, finding abnormalities of synapse formation and plasticity involving serotonin, GABA, reelin and others; and showing a convergence of pathologic findings in autism and psychiatric disorders (bipolar disorder and schizophrenia).

Lastly, we put forward a genetic hypothesis potentially linking the major themes listed above: the GABA receptor subunit gene GABRA5 (in chromosome 15q11–13 and expressed virtually exclusively in the hippocampus) when deleted or mutated in experimental animals produces a gain in learning and memory function. This is particularly compelling as it pertains to one of the most remarkable features of autism: the areas of enhanced memory and ability (such as savant characteristics and supernormal visual–spatial abilities of some individuals with autism), and the unusual intellectual abilities commonly found in the families – particularly the fathers – of children with autism. Independently, in humans the GABRA5 gene has been linked with bipolar disorder. Certain families of children with autism reveal a conjunction of bipolar disorder and unusual intellectual abilities (memory, visual–spatial or mathematical) in fathers of children with autism; linkage to chromosome 15q11–13; and evidence of a parent-of-origin effect by which autism is expressed when genetic transmission occurs through the father. These features suggest the hypothesis that a defect in GABRA5 expression induced by genetic mutation and/or imprinting could cause a gain in memory and learning ability and/or bipolar disorder in the fathers; while altered expression of the same gene by paternal imprinting could produce autism in their children. Whether right or not, the hypothesis emphasizes that familial affective psychopathology, and unusual memory and intellectual abilities, must be taken into account in any comprehensive hypothesis of autism. However, it must be remembered that this or any specific genetic hypothesis, if shown to be valid, would likely only pertain to one subtype of autism.

References

Acosta, M. T. & Pearl, P. L. (2003). The neurobiology of autism: new pieces of the puzzle. *Current Neurology & Neuroscience Reports*, *3*(2), 149–156.

Aman, M. G., Arnold, M. D. L., McDougle, C. J., Vitiello, B., Scahill, L., Davies, M. *et al.* (2005). Acute and long-term safety and tolerability of risperidone in children with autism. *Journal of Child and Adolescent Psychopharmacology*, *15*(6), 869–884.

Angst, J., Gamma, A., Endrass, J., Hantouche, E., Goodwin, R., Ajdacic, V. *et al.* (2005). Obsessive–compulsive syndromes and disorders: significance of comorbidity with bipolar and anxiety syndromes. *European Archives of Psychiatry and Clinical Neuroscience*, *255*(1), 65–71.

Bayley, P. J. & Squire, L. R. (2002). Medial temporal lobe amnesia: gradual acquisition of factual information by nondeclarative memory. *Journal of Neuroscience*, *22*(13), 5741–5748.

Bayly, M. B. (2005). Concept-matching in the brain depends on serotonin and gamma-frequency shifts. *Medical Hypotheses*, *65*(1), 149–151.

Blatt, G. J., Fitzgerald, C. M., Guptill, J. T., Booker, A. B., Kemper, T. L. & Bauman, M. L. (2001). Density and distribution of hippocampal neurotransmitter receptors in autism: an autoradiographic study. *Journal of Autism & Developmental Disorders*, *31*(6), 537–543.

Brock, J., Brown, C. C., Boucher, J. & Rippon, G. (2002). The temporal binding deficit hypothesis of autism. *Developmental Psychopathology*, *14*(2), 209–224.

Brown, C., Gruber, T., Boucher, J., Rippon, G. & Brock, J. (2005). Gamma abnormalities during perception of illusory figures in autism. *Cortex*, *41*(3), 364–376.

Cai, X., Flores-Hernandez, J., Feng, J. & Yan, Z. (2002). Activity-dependent bidirectional regulation of GABA(A) receptor channels by the 5-HT(4) receptor-mediated signalling in rat prefrontal cortical pyramidal neurons. *Journal of Physiology*, *540*(3), 743–759.

Caraiscos, V. B., Elliott, E. M., You-Ten, K. E., Cheng, V. Y., Belelli, D., Newell, J. G. *et al.* (2004). Tonic inhibition in mouse hippocampal CA1 pyramidal neurons is mediated by alpha5 subunit-containing gamma-aminobutyric acid type A receptors. *Proceedings of the National Academy of Sciences,* *101*(10), 3662–3667.

Cassidy, S. B., Dykens, E. & Williams, C. A. (2000). Prader-Willi and Angelman syndromes: sister imprinted disorders. *American Journal of Medical Genetics,* *97*(2), 136–146.

Castelloe, P. & Dawson, G. (1993). Subclassification of children with autism and pervasive developmental disorder: a questionnaire based on Wing's sub-grouping scheme. *Journal of Autism & Developmental Disorders,* *23*(2), 229–241.

Chandana, S. R., Behen, M. E., Juhasz, C., Muzik, O., Rothermel, R. D., Mangner, T. J. *et al.* (2005). Significance of abnormalities in developmental trajectory and asymmetry of cortical serotonin synthesis in autism. *International Journal of Developmental Neuroscience,* *23*(2–3), 171–182.

Chugani, D. C. (2004). Serotonin in autism and pediatric epilepsies. *Mental Retardation & Developmental Disabilities Research,* *10*(2), 112–116.

Chugani, D. C., Muzik, O., Behen, M., Rothermel, R., Janisse, J. J., Lee, J. *et al.* (1999). Developmental changes in brain serotonin synthesis capacity in autistic and nonautistic children. *Annals of Neurology,* *45*(3), 287–295.

Chugani, D. C., Muzik, O., Rothermel, R., Behen, M., Chakraborty, P., Mangner, T. *et al.* (1997). Altered serotonin synthesis in the dentatothala-mocortical pathway in autistic boys. *Annals of Neurology,* *42*(4), 666–669.

Churchill, D. W. (1978). Language: the problem beyond conditioning. In M. Rutter & E. Schopler (eds.), *Autism, a reappraisal of concepts and treatment,* pp. 73–84. New York: Plenum Press.

Collinson, N., Kuenzi, F. M., Jarolimek, W., Maubach, K. A., Cothliff, R., Sur, C. *et al.* (2002). Enhanced learning and memory and altered GABAergic synaptic transmission in mice lacking the alpha 5 subunit of the GABAA receptor. *Journal of Neuroscience 22,* 5572–5580.

Costa, E., Davis, J., Grayson, D. R., Guidotti, A., Pappas, G. D. & Pesold, C. (2001). Dendritic spine hypoplasticity and downregulation of reelin and GABAergic tone in schizophrenia vulnerability. *Neurobiology of Disease,* *8*(5), 723–742.

Costa, E., Davis, J., Pesold, C., Tueting, P. & Guidotti, A. (2002). The hetero-zygote reeler mouse as a model for the development of a new generation of antipsychotics. *Current Opinions in Pharmacology,* *2*(1), 56–62.

Crestani, F., Keist, R., Fritschy, J. M., Benke, D., Vogt, K., Prut, L. *et al.* (2002). Trace fear conditioning involves hippocampal alpha5 GABA(A) receptors. *Proceedings of the National Academy of Sciences,* *99*(13), 8980–8985.

Dawson, G. (1983). Lateralized brain dysfunction in autism: evidence from the Halstead–Reitan neuropsychological battery. *Journal of Autism & Developmental Disorders,* *13*(3), 269–286.

DeLong, G. R. (1992). Autism, amnesia, hippocampus, and learning. *Neuroscience & Biobehavioural Reviews,* *16*(1), 63–70.

DeLong, G. R., Teague, L. A. & McSwain Kamran, M. (1998). Effects of fluoxetine treatment in young children with idiopathic autism. *Developmental Medicine & Child Neurology*, 40(8), 551–562.

DeLong, G. R., Ritch, C. R. & Burch, S. (2002). Fluoxetine response in children with autistic spectrum disorders: correlation with familial major affective disorder and intellectual achievement. *Developmental Medicine & Child Neurology*, 44(10), 652–659.

DeLong, R. (2004). Autism and familial major mood disorder: are they related? *Journal of Neuropsychiatry & Clinical Neurosciences*, 16(2), 199–213.

Dor-Shav, N. K. & Horowitz, Z. (1984). Intelligence and personality variables of parents of autistic children. *Journal of Genetic Psychology*, 144(1), 39–50.

Drevets, W. C., Frank, E., Price, J. C., Kupfer, D. J., Greer, P. J. & Mathis, C. (2000). Serotonin type-1 A receptor imaging in depression. *Nuclear Medicine & Biology*, 27(5), 499–507.

Dykens, E. M. (2002). Are jigsaw puzzle skills 'spared' in persons with Prader-Willi syndrome? *Journal of Child Psychology & Psychiatry*, 43(3), 343–352.

Eichenbaum, H. (2004). An information processing framework for memory representation by the hippocampus. In M. S. Gazzaniga (ed.), *The cognitive neurosciences*, 3rd edn, pp. 679–690. Cambridge, MA: MIT Press.

Fatemi, S. H. (2001). Reelin mutations in mouse and man: from reeler mouse to schizophrenia, mood disorders, autism and lissencephaly. *Molecular Psychiatry*, 6(2), 129–133.

Feng, J., Cai, X., Zhao, J. & Yan, Z. (2001). Serotonin receptors modulate GABA(A) receptor channels through activation of anchored protein kinase C in prefrontal cortical neurons. *Journal of Neuroscience*, 21(17), 6502–6511.

Ferster, D. (2004). Neuroscience. Blocking plasticity in the visual cortex. *Science*, 303(5664), 1619–1621.

Hampson, R. E., Simeral, J. D. & Deadwyler, S. A. (1999). Distribution of spatial and nonspatial information in dorsal hippocampus. *Nature*, 402(6762), 610–614.

Henke, K., Weber, B., Kneifel, S., Wieser, H. G. & Buck, A. (1999). Human hippocampus associates information in memory. *Proceedings of the National Academy of Sciences*, 96(10), 5884–5889.

Hensch, T. K. & Stryker, M. P. (2004). Columnar architecture sculpted by GABA circuits in developing cat visual cortex. *Science*, 303(5664), 1678–1681.

Hermelin, B. & O'Connor, N. (1970). *Psychological experiments with autistic children*. Oxford and New York: Pergamon Press.

Jamain, S., Quach, H., Betancur, C., Rastam, M., Colineaux, C., Gillberg, I. C. *et al.* (2003). Mutations of the X-linked genes encoding neuroligins NLGN3 and NLGN4 are associated with autism. *Nature Genetics*, 34(1), 27–29.

Knable, M. B., Barci, B. M., Bartko, J. J., Webster, M. J. & Torrey, E. F. (2002). Molecular abnormalities in the major psychiatric illnesses: Classification and Regression Tree (CRT) analysis of post-mortem prefrontal markers. *Molecular Psychiatry*, 7(4), 392–404.

Larsson, H. J., Eaton, W. W., Madsen, K. M., Vestergaard, M., Olesen, A. V., Agerbo, E. *et al.* (2005). Risk factors for autism: perinatal factors, parental psychiatric history, and socioeconomic status. *American Journal of Epidemiology, 161*(10), 916–925; discussion 918–926.

MacKay, D. G., Stewart, R. & Burke, D. M. (1998). H.M. revisited: relations between language comprehension, memory, and the hippocampal system. *Journal of Cognitive Neuroscience, 10*(3), 377–394.

Manga, P., Kromberg, J., Turner, A., Jenkins, T. & Ramsay, M. (2001). In Southern Africa, brown oculocutaneous albinism (BOCA) maps to the OCA2 locus on chromosome 15q: P-gene mutations identified. *American Journal of Human Genetics, 68*(3), 782–787.

McCauley, J. L., Olson, L. M., Delahanty, R., Amin, T., Nurmi, E. L., Organ, E. L. *et al.* (2004). A linkage disequilibrium map of the 1-Mb 15q12 GABA(A) receptor subunit cluster and association to autism. *American Journal of Medical Genetics B Neuropsychiatric Genetics, 131*(1), 51–59.

McDougle, C. J., Scahill, L., Aman, M. G., McCracken, J. T., Tierney, E., Davies, M. *et al.* (2005). Risperidone for the core symptom domains of autism: results from the study by the autism network of the research units on pediatric psychopharmacology. *American Journal of Psychiatry, 162*(6), 1142–1148.

Meguro, M., Mitsuya, K., Sui, H., Shigenami, K., Kugoh, H., Nakao, M. *et al.* (1997). Evidence for uniparental, paternal expression of the human GABAA receptor subunit genes, using microcell-mediated chromosome transfer. *Human Molecular Genetics, 6*(12), 2127–2133.

Millward, C., Powell, S., Messer, D. & Jordan, R. (2000). Recall for self and other in autism: children's memory for events experienced by themselves and their peers. *Journal of Autism & Developmental Disorders, 30*(1), 15–28.

Ming, J. E., Blagowidow, N., Knoll, J. H., Rollings, L., Fortina, P., McDonald-McGinn, D. M. *et al.* (2000). Submicroscopic deletion in cousins with Prader-Willi syndrome causes a grandmatrilineal inheritance pattern: effects of imprinting. *American Journal of Medical Genetics, 92*(1), 19–24.

Minshew, N. J. & Goldstein, G. (2001). The pattern of intact and impaired memory functions in autism. *Journal of Child Psychology & Psychiatry, 42*(8), 1095–1101.

Miyashita, Y. (2004). Cognitive memory: cellular and network machineries and their top-down control. *Science, 306*(5695), 435–440.

Nurmi, E. L., Dowd, M., Tadevosyan-Leyfer, O., Haines, J. L., Folstein, S. E. & Sutcliffe, J. S. (2003). Exploratory subsetting of autism families based on savant skills improves evidence of genetic linkage to 15q11-q13. *Journal of the American Academy of Child & Adolescent Psychiatry, 42*(7), 856–863.

Otani, K., Ujike, H., Tanaka, Y., Morita, Y., Katsu, T., Nomura, A. *et al.* (2005). The GABA type A receptor alpha5 subunit gene is associated with bipolar I disorder. *Neuroscience Letters, 381*(1–2), 108–113.

Papadimitriou, G. N., Dikeos, D. G., Karadima, G., Avramopoulos, D., Daskalopoulou, E. G. & Stefanis, C. N. (2001). GABA-A receptor beta3 and alpha5 subunit gene cluster on chromosome 15q11-q13 and bipolar disorder: a genetic association study. *American Journal of Medical Genetics, 105*(4), 317–320.

Prior M. R. (1979). Cognitive abilities and disabilities in infantile autism: a review. *Journal of Abnormal Child Psychology*, 7(4), 357–380.

Rodriguez, M. A., Pesold, C., Liu, W. S., Kriho, V., Guidotti, A., Pappas, G. D. *et al.* (2000). Colocalization of integrin receptors and reelin in dendritic spine postsynaptic densities of adult nonhuman primate cortex. *Proceedings of the National Academy of Sciences*, 97(7), 3550–3555.

Russo, N., Flanagan, T., Blidner, I., Berringer, D. & Burack, J. (2005). Nonverbal cognitive and memory profiles of high and low functioning children with autism. Paper presented at the International Meeting for Autism Research Boston, MA.

Sarnyai, Z., Sibille, E. L., Pavlides, C., Fenster, R. J., McEwen, B. S. & Toth, M. (2000). Impaired hippocampal-dependent learning and functional abnormalities in the hippocampus in mice lacking serotonin(1A) receptors. *Proceedings of the National Academy of Sciences*, 97(26), 14731–14736.

Schacter, D. L. (1985). Multiple forms of memory in humans and animals. In N. M. Weinberger, J. L. McGaugh & G. Lynch (eds.), *Memory systems of the brain*, pp. 351–379. New York: Guilford Press.

Schmitz, D., Gloveli, T., Empson, R. M. & Heinemann, U. (1998). Comparison of the effects of serotonin in the hippocampus and the entorhinal cortex. *Molecular Neurobiology*, 17(1–3), 59–72.

Shao, Y., Cuccaro, M. L., Hauser, E. R., Raiford, K. L., Menold, M. M., Wolpert, C. M. *et al.* (2003). Fine mapping of autistic disorder to chromosome 15q11-q13 by use of phenotypic subtypes. *American Journal of Human Genetics*, 72(3), 539–548.

Sur, C., Fresu, L., Howell, O., McKernan, R. M. & Atack, J. R. (1999). Autoradiographic localization of alpha5 subunit-containing GABAA receptors in rat brain. *Brain Research*, 822(1–2), 265–270.

Tesche, C. D. & Karhu, J. (1999). Interactive processing of sensory input and motor output in the human hippocampus. *Journal of Cognitive Neuroscience*, 11(4), 424–436.

Toichi, M. & Kamio, Y. (2002). Long-term memory and levels-of-processing in autism. *Neuropsychologia*, 40(7), 964–969.

Towers, S. K., Gloveli, T., Traub, R. D., Driver, J. E., Engel, D., Fradley, R. *et al.* (2004). Alpha 5 subunit-containing GABAA receptors affect the dynamic range of mouse hippocampal kainate-induced gamma frequency oscillations in vitro. *Journal of Physiology*, 559(3), 721–728.

Whittington, J., Holland, A., Webb, T., Butler, J., Clarke, D. & Boer, H. (2004). Cognitive abilities and genotype in a population-based sample of people with Prader-Willi syndrome. *Journal of Intellectual Disability Research*, 48(2), 172–187.

Wisden, W., Laurie, D. J., Monyer, H. & Seeburg, P. H. (1992). The distribution of 13 GABAA receptor subunit mRNAs in the rat brain. I. Telencephalon, diencephalon, mesencephalon. *Journal of Neuroscience*, 12(3), 1040–1062.

Part III

The psychology of memory in autism

7 Memory within a complex information processing model of autism

*Diane L. Williams, Nancy J. Minshew
and Gerald Goldstein*

Introduction

Clinical neuropsychologists have often commented that sometimes a memory problem is not a problem with memory. The implication of this remark is that what appears to be a difficulty with remembering is actually the result of a deficit in some other domain of cognitive functioning, influencing memory only indirectly. Our studies of the profile of neuropsychological functioning in autism have provided evidence of multiple primary coexisting deficits with one of the affected cognitive processes being memory (Minshew, Goldstein & Siegel, 1997; Williams, Goldstein & Minshew, 2006a). Over the past fifteen years, we have performed comprehensive studies of memory functioning in over 100 children, adolescents and adults, all of whom met Autism Diagnostic Interview (ADI & ADI-Revised, Le Couteur *et al.*, 1989; Lord, Rutter & Le Couteur, 1994), Autism Diagnostic Observation Schedule (ADOS; Lord *et al.*, 1989, 1999), and expert opinion criteria for autistic disorder (AD), including onset prior to age 3 years. The lower limit of Full-Scale and Verbal IQ scores varied between 70 and 80 depending on the study. The results of this research have led us to conclude that the memory impairment is universal across participants with high-functioning autism (HFA), but is selective in that it does not involve all aspects of memory functioning. The memory processes in HFA are differentially affected by domain, demands of the memory task, and the cognitive abilities of the individual. However, individuals with HFA demonstrate consistent patterns with respect to the nature of their memory difficulties so that a pattern of intact and impaired memory processes in HFA can be described. Furthermore, the memory problems in HFA are but one manifestation of a broader underlying problem with the processing of complex information that appears to characterize this disorder.

125

Autism as an amnesic disorder

An early proposed theory of the memory deficit in autism was that it was an amnesic disorder similar to that seen in adults with lesions of the limbic lobe, which result in a global deficit in long-term memory with relative sparing of other cognitive abilities (Boucher & Warrington, 1976). To address the hypothesis that autism was an amnesic disorder, we compared a group of adolescents and adults with HFA to a matched comparison[1] group using the California Verbal Learning Test (CVLT; Delis *et al.*, 1987) (Minshew & Goldstein, 1993). The CVLT is a standardized word list learning measure that is designed to provide a process analysis of memory and to assess strategies and error types to characterize the individual's way of remembering new material. The autism group consisted of 21 males between the ages of 12 and 40 years who had Full-Scale and Verbal IQ scores higher than 72 and who met the Diagnostic and Statistical Manual of Mental Disorders (DSM) criteria for autistic disorder (American Psychiatric Association, 1987). The comparison group consisted of 21 participants matched on age, Full-Scale IQ, gender and race. The scores obtained on 33 variables of the CVLT were compared between the two groups. The results of paired-comparison t-tests showed uncorrected statistically significant differences between the autism and comparison groups on six of the variables: (1) Trial 5 free recall of List A; (2) total intrusions on List A; (3) free recall of List B; (4) the semantic-cluster ratio for List B; (5) the global-cluster ratio for List B; and (6) total intrusions after a short delay. However, after Bonferroni correction, the comparisons did not retain significance. When the relative group performance on the 33 scores was evaluated, there were only 3 scores on which the autism group did better than or tied with the comparison group, with 30 scores on which the autism group did worse. Thus, while the study failed to reveal evidence of an amnesic disorder or of a subgroup of individuals with autism who had poor memories, the variables for which there were initially statistically significant differences between the autism and comparison groups and the fact that the autism group consistently did less well than the comparison group led to the

---

[1] The comparison participants for our studies are typically developing (TD) children and normal adolescents and adults recruited in response to advertisements placed in communities of the same socioeconomic level as the families of origin of the individuals with autism. They were screened to exclude personal and family history of learning and language disability, autistic spectrum disorders (ASDs), depression, anxiety disorder, obsessive–compulsive disorder, attention deficit disorder or other heritable psychiatric and neurologic disorders of relevance to the study.

suggestion that the autism participants had less efficient mechanisms for organizing information.

Renner, Klinger and Klinger (2000) also examined whether autism was an amnesic disorder and obtained the same answer as our earlier study. They argued that in medial temporal lobe amnesic disorders there is impaired explicit memory with intact implicit or procedural memory. Tests of both forms of memory were administered to autism and comparison groups. Significant differences between groups were not found, but the autism group did show a recency effect with better recall at the end than at the beginning of the lists of materials presented. They attributed this finding to differences in organizational strategies. Bennetto, Pennington and Rogers (1996) and Rumsey and Hamburger (1988) have reported intact recall and recognition memory in autism. Notably, the findings of Bennetto and colleagues for children with HFA using the CVLT produced nearly identical results to those we obtained for our sample of adolescents and adults with HFA.

It appears that on standard procedures assessing serial and paired-associate learning, individuals with HFA demonstrate functioning that is not statistically reliably different from typically developing (TD) children. However, in evaluating these results, we have stated that, while they rule out the characterization of autism as an amnesic disorder, it cannot be concluded that memory is intact in autism. Differences in the way in which individuals with HFA memorize the material were evident, leading us to further exploration of the memory skills in this population.

Pattern of intact and impaired memory skills in autism

In subsequent research, the conceptual framework we used was based upon the consideration that, although many memory abilities are intact, there were others that were not, and that a pattern of intact and impaired memory abilities specific to autism, and therefore present in high-functioning as well as low-functioning individuals, could be discerned. We attempted to demonstrate the presence of this pattern, hypothesizing that if procedures assessing a number of kinds of memory were used, individuals with autism would not perform normally on all of these procedures but would generate a profile showing widely varying levels of performance among the tests. To test such a hypothesis, we needed not only to consider basic scores from serial learning and associative memory tasks, but also to examine other characteristics of performance on such tasks, particularly those involving acquisition schemas and learning patterns. Furthermore, more elaborate forms of memory, such as recall of extended text or complex visual material, needed to be assessed.

Storage processes as measured by retention of information following extended delays and the effects of interference on memory formation were also of interest. Another issue to be considered was modality specificity. Memory for verbal and memory for visual, pictorial material might be mediated by different systems. The reported integrity of visuospatial abilities in autism in contrast to limited language development suggested that visual memory might be more intact than verbal memory.

Using a battery of tests that yielded 18 separate measures of memory function in a sample of individuals with autism and a comparison group matched on age and cognitive level, we explored the pattern of memory skills in HFA (Minshew & Goldstein, 2001). We proposed the general hypothesis that memory dysfunction is present in autism but is not modality specific and is produced by poor utilization of organizing strategies. More specifically, we hypothesized that:

(1) Inefficiency in recall would be manifested in incremental learning across trials in individuals with autism compared to a group of matched controls.

(2) Memory performance of individuals with autism would become increasingly impaired as the complexity of task material increased. Such complexity could be produced by (a) increasing the number of elements in a single type of task or (b) increasing the inherent semantic or visual complexity of the content material.

(3) There would be a greater reduction in recall by the autism group than in the comparison group under delayed recall conditions relative to immediate recall.

These hypotheses were tested by comparing a group of 52 individuals with HFA between the ages of 12 and 40 with a normal comparison group of 40 individuals all of whom had Verbal and Full-Scale Wechsler IQ scores above 80. The groups did not differ significantly in age, Verbal Quotient, Performance Quotient, or Full-Scale IQ scores, gender distribution, race, or socioeconomic (SES) evaluations.

The experiment conducted to test the first hypothesis utilized three-word short-term memory and paired-associate learning tasks described in Ryan *et al.* (1980), which consisted of single, unrelated words, and the five learning trials from the adult CVLT (the children's version was not available at that time), which consisted of semantically related words. Part (a) of the second hypothesis was tested using a visual memory procedure consisting of three stylus mazes of increasing size with more choice point elements in each maze. Part (b) was tested using the Detroit Test of Learning Aptitude – Revised letter sequences, word sequences and oral directions subtests (DTLA-2; Hammill, 1985). Hypothesis 3 was tested using immediate and delayed recall of the paired-associate learning task, the 5th A List trial, short delayed recall and uncued long delayed recall scores from the CVLT, the immediate and delayed recall of one of the stories from the logical memory subtest of the Wechsler Memory Scale – Revised (WMS-R; Wechsler, 1987), and the immediate and delayed recall conditions of the Rey–Osterrieth Complex Figure (Osterrieth, 1944).

Tests of the first hypothesis showed that the autism group did worse than the comparison group on most of the CVLT trials. However, the difference did not increase or decrease in magnitude across trials, so there were no trials by group interaction. The remaining two learning tasks placed little (paired-associate learning) or no (three-word short-term memory) demand on organizational strategies, and no differences were demonstrated between the autism and comparison groups. The first hypothesis was therefore supported. Basic associative memory abilities were demonstrated to be intact, and the group with HFA apparently encoded words semantically rather than phonemically. However, they used semantic meaning less efficiently, resulting in a general inefficiency of learning of semantically related words. This lack of efficiency was demonstrated by the autism group consistently recalling fewer words than the comparison group on the learning trials of the CVLT. The important role of semantic complexity was also demonstrated by the finding that, while the autism group did not differ from the comparison group on recall of sequences of letters, they did less well than the comparison group on recall of words and much less well on grammatically complex sentences.

Tests of the second hypothesis showed that the autism group did increasingly poorly on maze learning as the task became more complex. This finding provides strong support for the hypothesis that the memory performance of individuals with autism becomes increasingly impaired as the complexity of the material increases. Because this task involved three tests of the same type but of increasing difficulty, it was possible to demonstrate the direct relationship between increasingly impaired memory performance and increasing complexity or difficulty of the material to be remembered. Combining the results for recalling verbal sequences (letters, words, sentences of increasing grammatical complexity) and maze learning, memory appeared to deteriorate consistently as complexity increased regardless of whether the stimuli were auditory and linguistic or visual and spatial. Hypotheses 2a and 2b were therefore supported.

The findings from tests of the third hypothesis were more complex. The autism group only differed from the comparison group on story recall from the WMS-R. Apparently delayed recall itself is not impaired, and information may be retained over a lengthy period of time during which other activities take place. Impairment in delayed recall relative to the participants in the comparison group was only noted when the delay was combined with a complex linguistic task placing demands on encoding strategies. It is of note, though, that these stories were quite simple and short, especially given the IQ level of these participants. The extent to which they challenged the need to extract themes to reduce processing load as opposed to recalling all of the details was very minimal for individuals of this ability level.

In sum, this study demonstrated that there is a pattern of uneven memory function in HFA consisting of normal performance in some areas with other areas in which individuals with HFA do less well than demographically matched, normal individuals. Basic encoding, storage and retrieval abilities are intact, but there is a problem that exists at the encoding level, or possibly at the level of retrieval, or both. This difficulty appears to be one of applying acquisition schemas that support learning and memory, particularly memory of complex material. These schemas are not as important for remembering single elements in a series, but recall of complex linguistic or spatial material is greatly benefited by use of organizing strategies. These strategies are apparently not available to, or utilized by, individuals with HFA. The question may be raised as to whether the failure is in the application of the strategy at the time of learning or encoding, or in memory search during retrieval. Recent research has demonstrated that retrieval failures can be produced by poor initial learning, particularly involving depth of encoding (DeLuca & Chiaravalloti, 2004); therefore, establishing an experimental distinction between encoding/storage and retrieval is problematic. Evidence in the autism literature documenting failure to spontaneously organize incoming information even for tasks that do not involve memory suggests the likelihood that organizational and planning strategies are not effectively applied at time of encoding (e.g. Smith & Bryson, 1994; see also Smith & Gardiner, this volume, Chapter 13). Studies demonstrating a recency effect in recall in autism also support reduced encoding because stronger encoding is reflected in a primacy effect.

Clinical memory batteries

Adults

In a follow-up study, an effort was made to provide an elaboration of these results (Williams, Goldstein & Minshew, 2005). We used the Wechsler Memory Scale III (WMS-III; Wechsler, 1997), a clinical memory test battery assessing auditory and visual memory in adults. The WMS-III consists of tests of associative learning, story recall, memory span and visual memory. The span tests are constructed to allow for the evaluation of working memory, an ability involving brief retention of verbal or spatial material while performing a task (Baddeley, 1998). The visual memory tests include recall of faces, recall of common family scenes, and a spatial span task. Delayed recall is assessed for several of the tests with a time interval of approximately 30 minutes after the original subtest is given.

The sample consisted of 29 adults (26 males and 3 females) with HFA and 34 matched normal adults (30 males and 4 females). Participants did not differ significantly in age (all were between the ages of 16 and 53 years) and Verbal or Full-Scale IQ (all had Verbal and Full-Scale Wechsler IQ scores above 80), gender, race or socioeconomic status. The results again reflected a pattern of intact and impaired abilities. The autism and comparison groups did not differ on immediate or delayed recall of word-paired associates, nor, unlike previous results, did they differ on immediate or delayed recall of stories. Letter–number sequences, a measure of verbal working memory, also did not produce a significant difference. The autism group did less well than the comparison group on immediate and delayed recall of faces and family scenes, but there was no worsening under the delayed condition. The family scenes subtest involves faces but also recall of activities of the people in the pictures; the identity of the people can be determined from clothing and hair cues and is not dependent on faces. Spatial memory, assessed with a spatial span test, was also performed significantly less well by the autism than by the comparison group. A statistically significant difference on the visual memory tests was obtained even when the analyses were repeated using Performance IQ as a covariate. Thus, none of the verbal memory tests produced significant differences between the groups, but all of the visual memory tests generated significant differences.

The presence or absence of impairment on story recall has varied across studies within our research and that of others. This variability may reflect the differences in the IQ scores and ability level of the autism groups. Thus, ability to recall text (relatively simple stories) may not be impaired in individuals with autism and high intellectual levels. The WMS-III stories were apparently not sufficiently challenging to produce significant differences in the HFA participants involved in this study, in which the mean Verbal IQs were 109 for the autism group and 108 for the comparison group. The difficulty in recalling faces documented in the above study is consistent with an extensive literature on impaired memory for faces in autism, an impairment that is independent of IQ score. Difficulty with face recognition is also consistent with the findings of abnormal functional magnetic resonance imaging (fMRI) activity of the fusiform gyrus, the brain area thought to be responsible for face recognition (Schultz *et al.*, 2000). Face recognition appears to be a separate neuro-psychological module based on the evidence that brain lesions may produce the syndrome of prosopagnosia, or the specific loss of the ability to recognize faces. However, the impaired recognition of family scenes is not fully explicable on the basis of difficulties with facial recognition, since location and activities must be recognized and the individuals could be recognized by hair cues and clothing. Some time ago Boucher (1981) found that children with autism recalled less about recently experienced events than did typically developing children. The suggestion from these two findings is that there may be some impairment of encoding of complex environmental activity. The impaired performance on the social scenes task may reflect the failure of individuals with autism to automatically organize and categorize the scenes, people and activities thematically (but see Chapter 2, this volume, for an alternative, neurologically based interpretation of this finding). Importantly, the deficits in memory for faces and common social scenes, and of complex visual/spatial stimuli, demonstrate the contribution of memory dysfunction in autism to deficits in real-life function.

Children

In a companion study, we examined the memory pattern in children with autism (Williams, Goldstein & Minshew, 2006b). Since autism is a developmental disorder existing from early life, it was possible that the pattern of memory functioning observed in adolescents and adults had been altered by life experiences, and that the pattern in children would appear considerably different. This hypothesis was therefore tested in a study of children's memory abilities. A review of the children's memory literature in autism identified numerous studies in which impairment of organizational strategies and the detrimental influence of increasing complexity had been noted. The tests used in our previous studies with adolescents and adults were not appropriate for children. Therefore, we used the Wide Range Assessment of Memory and Learning (WRAML; Sheslow & Adams, 1990), a standardized memory test battery specifically designed for children, but which assesses many of the areas of memory evaluated in our adult studies. The WRAML is normed for children aged 5 to 17 and contains 9 subtests that evaluate auditory and visual tests of associative learning, serial learning, story memory and memory for complex visual material.

This instrument was administered to 38 children with HFA and 38 individually matched TD children, 8 to 16 years of age, with Wechsler

Full-Scale and Verbal IQ scores above 80. Measures used were the scaled scores from the 9 individual subtests plus delayed-recall subtest scores, and the story memory recognition score. T-tests showed significant results for the sentence memory, story memory, finger windows, design memory and picture memory subtests, with the autism group performing relatively worse than the comparison group. Significant group differences were not found for the number/letter, verbal learning, sound symbol and visual learning subtests. Hence, the autism group performed less well than the comparison group on measures of visual memory, verbal memory involving syntactic and discourse elements, and spatial working memory. The groups did not differ on measures of associative memory and immediate memory span.

Kappa analysis showed that the WRAML profile as a whole produced a statistically significant but not a highly accurate classification of autism and comparison participants. However, there were numerous significant group differences for the individual subtests. The most powerful discriminator was finger windows, a test that assesses spatial working memory. A Principal Components analysis showed that the comparison group subtests loaded on three factors which, while somewhat different from the factor solution obtained by the WRAML normative sample, can reasonably be interpreted as Visual, Verbal and Learning factors. The autism group subtests only loaded on two factors showing no resemblance to the Visual, Verbal and Learning structure. The first factor contained high loadings from seven of the nine subtests, while the second factor only received high loadings from picture memory and story memory. The factor structure can probably be best described as representing a distinction between thematic social and nonsocial components of memory. The HFA group showed a difference in delayed recall for complex thematic verbal material and did not show a specific problem with retrieval of information.

The results indicate differing profiles of memory abilities between the HFA and TD groups. The memory profile of the autism group was characterized by relatively poorer memory for both complex visual and complex verbal stimuli, with relatively intact associative learning ability, verbal working memory and recognition memory. Spatial working memory of the children with HFA was also poorer than that of the TD group; however, spatial memory as defined as memory for location was not. The factor analytic results also indicated that the organization of memory in autism was not consistent with relationships between skills found in individuals who are not autistic. The implications of this distinction for understanding the possibility of differing encoding, storage and retrieval processing in autism is clear, but has yet to be studied in detail. Delayed recall of the children with HFA was not generally different from that of the matched TD children, with the exception of thematic verbal material as assessed by recall of stories. Thus, the memory profile for the children with HFA as measured by the WRAML was similar but not identical to that previously obtained for our group of adults with HFA.

Conclusions based on memory profile studies

In the research reviewed thus far, we have demonstrated that, contrary to early views, autism is not an amnesic disorder characterized by severely impaired declarative memory. However, the memory of individuals with HFA does not function like that of TD children. A memory pattern is consistently present in both children and adults with HFA. The pattern is characterized by intact associative processes with relative impairment of more complex memory that involves high-level information processing. This information-processing component is involved in spontaneous formation of acquisition schemas and organizational strategies that may be applied at encoding to support learning, and perhaps at retrieval while searching for stored material. Neurobiologically, this form of memory disorder would not appear to involve a localized hippocampal or subcortical locus but would be more consistent with a widespread neocortical memory system difference.

Working memory

A finding of particular interest from both the adult and the child memory battery studies was the dissociation between intact verbal working memory and impaired spatial working memory. The literature contains reports proposing that working memory may be an important consideration in explaining impairments in cognition in autism, although findings regarding the status of verbal working memory have been inconsistent.

We studied verbal and spatial working memory in samples of children, adolescents, and adults with HFA compared to individuals without autism matched in all cases for age, Verbal and Performance IQ, and Full-Scale IQ (Williams et al., 2005). Participants were divided into two groups based on age: an adult group consisting of 31 individuals with autism (29 males and 2 females) and 25 normal controls (21 males and 4 females) between the ages of 17 and 48 years; and a child and adolescent group composed of 24 children with autism (22 males and 2 females) and 44 TD children (33 males and 11 females) from 8 to 16 years of age. All participants had Verbal and Full-Scale Wechsler IQ scores above 72 and at least second-grade reading skills. Three verbal working memory tasks were administered. In the N-back letter task, letter stimuli were presented in three conditions, baseline, 1-back and 2-back. In each condition, letters appeared on a screen one at a time. In the baseline condition, participants responded by pressing a button when they saw the letter X on the screen. For the 1-back condition, the participants responded when the current letter matched the letter immediately preceding it. For the 2-back condition, the participants responded when the current letter matched the letter that was viewed two letters back. In addition, the WMS-III letter–number sequencing subtest was used for adults, and the WRAML number/letter sequencing was used for adolescents and children. The spatial working memory tasks consisted of the WMS-III spatial span subtest (adults) and the WRAML finger windows subtest (children).

For the N-back letter task, neither of the autism age groups performed significantly differently from the matched participants in any of the three conditions. For the WMS-III, taken by the adults, a statistically significant difference between the HFA and comparison groups was not found for letter/number sequencing but was found for spatial span, with the HFA group performing relatively worse. In the WRAML subtests, taken by adolescents and children, the number/letter task did not discriminate significantly between the HFA and comparison groups. However, there was a statistically reliable difference for finger windows, again, with relatively poorer performance by the HFA group.

In summary, significant differences between the HFA and comparison groups in both age ranges were not obtained for the verbal working memory tests but were found for the spatial working memory tests. Correlations with IQ indicated the same level of association between the verbal and spatial tasks, indicating that the groups with autism did less well than controls on the spatial working memory tasks for reasons other than differing levels of task difficulty. Overall, the findings demonstrate a dissociation between verbal and spatial working memory in the same individuals with HFA.

The discrepancy between verbal and spatial working memory in individuals with HFA may have several explanations. At the most basic level, the computational demands of the spatial task used in our comparisons may be greater than that of the verbal task. The distinction would then become an artifact of task difficulty. However, eye movement studies employing a task that measures the ability of the eyes to look at the location of a target that is no longer present (oculomotor delayed response task) have also documented an impairment in spatial working memory in HFA using a neurophysiologic method that does not have the multiple contributing cognitive components typical of neuropsychologic tasks. The results indicate that individuals with autism move their eyes close to the target location but do not get to the precise location (Minshew, Luna & Sweeney, 1999). The documentation of a spatial working memory deficit using this classical, elegant but simple neurophysiological task would suggest that the deficit in spatial working memory reflects underlying dysfunction of dorsolateral prefrontal cortex (DLPFC).

The question then becomes why is there no impairment present with a letter working memory task that supposedly also relies on DLPFC function. There are several possible explanations. The first is that verbal working memory allows compensatory strategies by virtue of the presence of visual cues or letters. These letters could provide a scaffolding or support structure to facilitate memory. They are highly familiar, over practised, stored scripts. There is no analogue to letters in the spatial working memory tasks. The brain must move to the location with no cues or previously stored strategy. Therefore, the brain may have to utilize a higher degree of computation to achieve the same degree of task accuracy for spatial working memory. The specific brain process that accomplishes this task has been called corollary motor discharge, and has been shown in animal models to involve complex pathways between the visual areas of the brain and the frontal lobes (Teuber, 1964). Alternatively, the dissociation between verbal working memory and spatial working memory could represent some other factor. These issues led us to the further examination of working memory in autism using fMRI methodology.

An fMRI study involving an N-back letter verbal working memory task showed that, even though their behavioural performance did not differ from that of matched normal adults, different regions of the brain were used by adults with HFA to perform this task (Koshino et al., 2005). Specifically, the group with autism had an activation pattern that suggested they were performing the task using more right-lateralized prefrontal and parietal regions and more posterior visual spatial regions bilaterally rather than relying on the expected left DLPFC and language areas. If the adult with HFA had to rely on prefrontal regions for this task, as in the spatial working memory oculomotor task, they may have also exhibited impaired verbal working memory performance. Therefore, unimpaired performance on the verbal working memory task should not be interpreted to mean that left DLPFC is intact in autism. The dissociation between the status of verbal and spatial working memory in autism appears to reflect the capacity of the brain in individuals with autism to use visual areas to perform the verbal working memory task rather than the usual left prefrontal areas, which have proven dysfunctional with all imaging and neurophysiologic measures employed thus far. The findings of this study are supported by another fMRI study of spatial working memory in autism, which demonstrated functional disconnectivity of the neural circuitry underlying spatial working memory (Luna *et al.*, 2002).

Relation of pattern of impaired and intact memory to other cognitive domains

This series of studies of memory in HFA appears to have left us with some definitive findings and a remaining puzzle. The definitive findings are that autism is not an amnesic disorder and many areas of memory in HFA are intact. The areas of intactness are among those that would be significantly impaired in individuals with frank amnesia. Second, the absence of amnesia does not mean that memory is normal in HFA: groups of individuals with HFA do significantly worse than normal controls on many tests of memory. In particular, they often have poor recall of extended text, sequences of words, sentences and stories. They also have relatively poor performance on numerous tests of spatial working memory and poor recall of spatial patterns when these patterns are complex. Nor do our findings rule out the possibility that memory in low-functioning autism (LFA) may be more impaired than in HFA, as suggested in Chapter 14, this volume.

With the possible exception of spatial working memory tasks, there is a consistent pattern indicating that memory deficit is seen largely on complex tasks that benefit from organizing material through the spontaneous application of some scheme or strategy. Perhaps the most well-known example of such a process is encoding verbal material semantically rather than phonetically. It is much easier to recall a list of words when they are organized categorically than when they are recalled verbatim as presented. Our findings suggest that the failures of memory that occur in HFA are to a great extent based on a failure to spontaneously develop organizing strategies.

In work done in cognitive domains other than memory, we have also found that there is difficulty in strategy formation. This is most apparent in the domain of conceptual reasoning. In a study of that area, we utilized a distinction between concept identification and concept formation (Minshew, Meyer & Goldstein, 2002). In concept identification, the correct solution is inherent in the task and the problem solver has to identify it based on experience with exemplars. Thus, in some tests of conceptual reasoning, such as the Halstead Category Test (Reitan & Wolfson, 1993), the correct answer is pre-established and the test-taker must discover what it is through a trial-and-error procedure. In concept formation there is no inherent correct solution and the problem solver has to spontaneously generate hypotheses. Free object sorting tests have this characteristic, since there is no correct answer and the test taker has to generate and test hypotheses on a spontaneous basis. As predicted, our group with HFA did relatively well on the Halstead Category Test and poorly on concept formation abstraction tasks such as the Goldstein–Scheerer Object Sorting Test (Goldstein & Scheerer, 1941) and the verbal absurdities and picture absurdities subtests from the Stanford–Binet Scales (Thorndike, Hagen & Sattler, 1986). We concluded that the abstraction deficit in individuals with HFA is characterized by a dissociation between concept formation and concept identification. The deficit in concept formation results in cognitive inflexibility (incomplete apprehension of the concept and thus inability to apply it flexibly) and in the inability to spontaneously form schemata or paradigms that solve problems.

We are suggesting that the same function of spontaneously generating organizational structures underlies both conceptual reasoning and memory when the memory task involves more than basic associative processes. In Baddeley's (1998) theory of working memory, the central executive has a role that is not restricted to regulation of behavior involving the brief storage and retrieval of information while engaged in an activity. The central executive is also involved in numerous tasks in which there are conflicting schemas, the need for planning and scheduling, or performing concurrent tasks. The complexity of the information that needs to be encoded, stored and retrieved to complete the tasks may be the crucial consideration. Basic memory processes may fail to function when the complexity or amount of information to be processed becomes too great. This may occur in HFA because of the lack of regulatory processes to manage and reduce the amount of information through cognitive processes such as recoding, concept formation and schemas that reduce the memory load. Baddeley's model of the central executive is consistent with our view that the memory deficits in HFA are clearly relevant to understanding the cognitive deficits that characterize this population.

Summary

These studies have led us to a number of conclusions regarding the memory of individuals with HFA. While associative memory abilities are intact in individuals with HFA, memory dysfunction appears universal. Demonstration of memory failure does not always occur for the same test or type of task, since increasing general level of ability, as occurs in a group of individuals with HFA, requires increasingly challenging tasks to demonstrate the deficit. This memory impairment in HFA is not modality specific: qualitatively similar impairments are seen in both auditory and visual modalities. Delayed recall is not impaired, but delayed recall is adversely impacted when the level of semantic complexity is sufficiently challenged and demands are placed on depth of encoding and, in turn, on organizing strategy. Verbal working memory appears intact; however, the underlying neurofunctional basis of verbal working memory appears to be different from that of neurotypical controls and may involve reliance on visual cortex rather than prefrontal cortex. Individuals with HFA have difficulty with spatial working memory reflecting dysfunction of prefrontal cortex.

We argue that the memory impairments in HFA are related to the failure of the automatic use of organizing strategies or meaning to support memory; therefore, the memory performance of individuals with HFA becomes increasingly impaired as the complexity of the material increases. This impairment in the memory domain is but one of many in a consistent pattern we have observed across domains in HFA suggesting a fundamental neurobiological disturbance in how the brain processes more complex information, either large amounts or inherently complex, regardless of domain. Hence, we have found impairments in higher cortical sensory, skilled motor, memory for complex material, complex language (interpretive aspects), and concept formation but not elementary sensory, elementary motor, associative memory, formal language (spelling, fluency, grammar, decoding) or rule learning. The primary characteristic of this pattern is that information processing is constrained across domains and the constraint begins with the highest demands within each domain, with the most symptoms in those domains with the highest information-processing demands, e.g. the social, communication and reasoning domains. Nonetheless, there are less prominent symptoms in other domains such as the sensory, motor and memory domains that also place substantial demands on integration of information.

If individuals with HFA have difficulty with processing complex information, this difficulty must result from a neurobiologic difference. The search at the brain level is for differences in the organization of neural networks that support this type of processing. In the first of many studies, Just and colleagues (2004; see also Brock *et al.*, 2002) have proposed that there is a fundamental problem with functional underconnectivity of the neural systems of the brain in HFA. The reduction in connectivity or synchrony among the cortical regions involved in a function results in reduced integration of information at the neural and cognitive level. Clearly, whatever is going on with cognition and the brain in autism extends considerably outside the social, language and range of activities domains constituting the DSM diagnostic triad of autism. Further imaging and cognitive studies of the memory impairments in autism are likely to provide important insights into the neurobiology of autism.

Acknowledgements

This research was supported by National Institute of Child Health and Human Development (NICHD) Grant HD35469, National Institute of Neurological Disorders and Stroke (NINDS) Grant NS33355, National Institute of Deafness and Other Communication Disorders (NIDCD) Grant K23DC006691, and by an NICHD Collaborative Program of Excellence in Autism (CPEA). We also acknowledge the Medical Research Service, Department of Veterans Affairs, for support of this research. We thank the participants and their families who gave generously of their time and the research staff who diligently collected the data. We also thank Kelsey Woods for her assistance with preparation of this chapter.

References

American Psychiatric Association (1987). *Diagnostic and statistical manual of mental disorders*, 3rd edn (DSM-III-R). Washington, DC: American Psychiatric Association.

(1994). *Diagnostic and statistical manual of mental disorders*, 4th edn (DSM-IV). Washington, DC: American Psychiatric Association.

(2000). *Diagnostic and statistical manual of mental disorders*, 4th edn, revised (DSM-IV-TR). Washington, DC: American Psychiatric Association.

Baddeley, A. (1998). *Human memory: theory and practice*, rev. edn. Boston: Allyn and Bacon.

Bennetto, L., Pennington, B. F. & Rogers, S. J. (1996). Intact and impaired memory function in autism. *Child Development*, 67, 1816–1835.

Boucher, J. (1981). Memory for recent events in autistic children. *Journal of Autism and Developmental Disorders*, 11, 293–302.

Boucher, J. & Warrington, E. K. (1976). Memory deficits in early infantile autism: some similarities to the amnesic syndrome. *British Journal of Psychology*, 67, 73–87.

Brock, J., Brown, C. C., Boucher, J. & Rippon, G. (2002). The temporal binding deficit hypothesis of autism. *Development and Psychopathology*, 14, 209–224.

Delis, D. C., Kramer, J. H., Kaplan, E. & Ober, B. A. (1987). *California Verbal Learning Test: adult version*. San Antonio, TX: Psychological Corporation.

DeLuca, J. & Chiaravalloti, N. D. (2004). Memory and learning in adults. In G. Goldstein & S. R. Beers (eds.), *Comprehensive handbook of psychological assessment, vol. 1: Intellectual and neuropsychological assessment*, pp. 217–236. Hoboken, NJ: Wiley.

Goldstein, K. & Scheerer, M. (1941). Abstract and concrete behavior: an experimental study with special tests. *Psychological Monographs*, 53 (2, whole no. 239).

Hammill, D. D. (1985). *DTLA-2: Detroit Tests of Learning Aptitude*. Austin, TX: Pro-Ed.

Just, M. A., Cherkassky, V. L., Keller, T. A. & Minshew, N. J. (2004). Cortical activation and synchronization during sentence comprehension in high-functioning autism: evidence of underconnectivity. *Brain, 127*, 1811–1821.

Koshino, H., Carpenter, P. A., Minshew, N. J., Cherkassky, V. L., Keller, T. A. & Just, M. A. (2005). Functional connectivity in an fMRI working memory task in high-functioning autism. *NeuroImage, 24*, 810–821.

Le Couteur, A., Rutter, M., Lord, C., Rios, P., Robertson, S., Holdgrafer, M. & McLennan, J. (1989). Autism Diagnostic Interview: a standardized investigator-based instrument. *Journal of Autism and Developmental Disorders, 19*, 363–387.

Lord, C., Rutter, M., Goode, S., Heemsbergen, J., Jordan, H., Mawhood, L. & Schopler, E. (1989). Autism Diagnostic Observation Schedule: a standardized observation of communicative and social behavior. *Journal of Autism and Developmental Disorders, 19*, 185–212.

Lord, C., Rutter, M. & Le Couteur, A. (1994). Autism Diagnostic Interview–Revised: a revised version of a diagnostic interview for caregivers of individuals with possible pervasive developmental disorders. *Journal of Autism and Developmental Disorders, 24*, 659–685.

Lord, C., Rutter, M., DiLavore, P. C. & Risi, S. (1999). *Autism diagnostic observation schedule (ADOS).* Los Angeles: Western Psychological Services.

Luna, B., Minshew, N. J., Garver, K. E., Lazar, N. A., Thulborn, K. R., Eddy, W. F. & Sweeney, J. A. (2002). Neocortical system abnormalities in autism: an fMRI study of spatial working memory. *Neurology, 59*, 834–840.

Minshew, N. J. & Goldstein, G. (1993). Is autism an amnesic disorder? Evidence from the California Verbal Learning Test. *Neuropsychology, 7*, 209–216.

(2001). The pattern of intact and impaired memory functions in autism. *The Journal of Child Psychology and Psychiatry and Allied Disciplines, 42*, 1095–1101.

Minshew, N. J., Goldstein, G. & Siegel, D. J. (1997). Neuropsychologic functioning in autism: profile of a complex information processing disorder. *Journal of the International Neuropsychological Society, 3*, 303–316.

Minshew, N. J., Meyer, J. & Goldstein, G. (2002). Abstract reasoning in autism: a dissociation between concept formation and concept identification. *Neuropsychology, 16*, 327–334.

Minshew, N. J., Luna, B. & Sweeney, J. A. (1999). Oculomotor evidence for neocortical systems but not cerebellar dysfunction in autism. *Neurology, 52*, 917–922.

Osterrieth, P. A. (1944). Le test de copie d'une figure complexe [The Complex Figure Copy Test]. *Archives de Psychologie, 30*, 206–356.

Reitan, R. M. & Wolfson, D. (1993). *The Halstead–Reitan Neuropsychological Test Battery: theory and clinical interpretation*, 2nd edn. Tucson, AZ: Neuropsychology Press.

Renner, P., Klinger. L. G. & Klinger, M. R. (2000). Implicit and explicit memory in autism: Is autism an amnesic disorder? *Journal of Autism and Developmental Disorders, 30*, 3–14.

Rumsey, J. M. & Hamburger, S. D. (1988). Neuropsychological findings in high-functioning men with infantile autism, residual state. *Journal of Clinical and Experimental Neuropsychology, 10*, 201–221.

Ryan, C., Butters, N., Montgomery, K., Adinolfi, A. & Didario, B. (1980). Memory deficits in chronic alcoholics: continuities between the 'intact' alcoholic and the alcoholic Korsakoff patient. In H. Begleiter (ed.), *Biological effects of alcohol*, pp. 701–718. New York: Plenum Press.

Schultz, R. T., Gauthier, I., Klin, A., Fulbright, R. K., Anderson, A. W., Volkmar, F., Skudlarski, P., Lacadie, C., Cohen, D. J. & Gore, J. C. (2000). Abnormal ventral temporal cortical activity during face discrimination among individuals with autism and Asperger syndrome. *Archives of General Psychiatry*, 57, 344–346.

Sheslow, D. & Adams, W. (1990). *WRAML: Wide Range Assessment of Memory and Learning*. Wilmington, DE: Jastak Assessment Systems.

Smith, I. M. & Bryson, S. E. (1994). Imitation and action in autism: a critical review. *Psychological Bulletin*, 116, 259–273.

Teuber, H. L. (1964). The riddle of frontal lobe function in man. In J. M. Warren & K. Akert (eds.), *The frontal granular cortex and behavior*, pp. 410–444. New York: McGraw-Hill.

Thorndike, R. L., Hagen, E. P. & Sattler, J. M. (1986). *The Stanford–Binet Intelligence Scale*, 4th edn. Chicago: Riverside Publishing.

Wechsler, D. (1987). *Wechsler Memory Scale – Revised*. San Antonio, TX: Psychological Corporation.

(1997). *Wechsler Memory Scale*, 3rd edn. San Antonio, TX: Psychological Corporation.

Williams, D. L., Goldstein, G. & Minshew, N. J. (2006a). Neuropsychologic functioning in children with autism: further evidence for disordered complex information-processing. *Child Neuropsychology*, 12, 279–298.

(2006b). The profile of memory function in children with autism. *Neuropsychology*, 20, 21–29.

(2005). Impaired memory for faces and social scenes in autism: clinical implications of the memory disorder. *Archives of Clinical Neuropsychology*, 20, 1–15.

Williams, D. L., Goldstein, G., Carpenter, P. A. & Minshew, N. J. (2005). Verbal and spatial working memory in autism [Electronic version]. *Journal of Autism and Developmental Disorders*, 35, 747–756.

8 Episodic memory, semantic memory and self-awareness in high-functioning autism

Motomi Toichi

Introduction

The superior memory of people with autism has been commented on for over thirty years. Kanner, in his first report on autism, mentioned the 'excellent rote memory' of autism children (Kanner, 1943). Clinicians who are familiar with these conditions never fail to come across examples of outstanding memory for particular subjects (such as birthdays, the academic names of fish, and so on). However, early studies that used conventional neuropsychological tests reported impairments on various measures of memory in children with autism. So, for example, Boucher and Warrington (1976; see also Boucher 1978, 1981a) found that performance in memory tasks by participants with autism was similar to that of adults with the acquired amnesic syndrome, showing impaired recall from long-term memory (LTM), combined with relatively intact cued recall from LTM as well as intact short-term memory (STM). Thus, there is a discrepancy between the clinical observations and experimental findings.

One possible explanation for this discrepancy is differences between the individuals observed or tested. The participants with autism in early psychological studies were primarily children with varying degrees of intellectual disability (low-functioning autism, or LFA). More recent studies that examined individuals without intellectual disability (high-functioning autism, or HFA) have reported basically unimpaired performance on tasks thought to measure episodic memory (Bennetto, Pennington & Rogers, 1996; Minshew *et al.*, 1992; Minshew & Goldstein, 1993; Renner, Klinger & Klinger, 2000; Summers & Craik, 1994) (but see Bowler, Gardiner & Grice, 2000). This suggests that autism and intellectual disability may have a negative interactive influence on the development of episodic memory. Age may also affect episodic memory since performance tends to be less impaired as age advances in people with HFA (e.g. Fein *et al.*, 1996; Beversdorf *et al.*, 1998). Therefore, in addressing the issue of the core specificity of memory in autism, it seems important to examine adults with HFA.

The nature of memory tasks used in psychological studies appears to be another factor in accounting for the above discrepancy. For example, performance impairment tends to be striking when verbal materials to be remembered have rich semantic cues (Toichi & Kamio, 2003), and when they are semantically or contextually related (O'Connor & Hermelin, 1967; Ramondo & Milech, 1984; Tager-Flusberg, 1991; Wolff & Barlow, 1979), even when participants are those with HFA (Fein *et al.*, 1996; Minshew & Goldstein, 1993) or Asperger syndrome (Bowler, Matthews & Gardiner, 1997). This suggests that individuals with autism may have problems using conceptual relationships in memory. On the other hand, the author's previous study (Toichi & Kamio, 2002) found that memory performance on tasks not reliant on semantic information was unimpaired or even better than that of age- and ability-matched controls. This leads to the hypothesis that people with autism may be good at remembering stimuli based on sensory information, such as phonological traits or visual characteristics. It follows that in memory tasks it is important to control the type of processing used in encoding to-be-remembered materials.

Also relevant is the role of 'autonoetic consciousness', which, according to Tulving, is necessary for episodic memory (Tulving, 1985; see also Chapter 9, this volume). It has been consistently reported that individuals with autism perform worse than ability-matched comparison participants in remembering what they themselves have done (Boucher, 1981b; Boucher & Lewis, 1989; Millward, Powell & Messer, 2000). A study that directly addressed this issue also reported evidence of reduced autonoetic consciousness in individuals with Asperger syndrome (Bowler, Gardiner & Grice, 2000). These findings suggest that inconsistent results in previous studies may be partly attributed to the degree to which autonoetic consciouness was involved in the tasks.

The aim of the studies reported here was to examine different aspects of memory in autism taking all of the above points into account. Thus, the participants were adults with HFA; Study 1 re-examined free recall using a conventional memory task; Study 2 examined conceptual relationships in semantic knowledge, using a verbal association task; Study 3 employed a levels-of-processing task to examine the influence of semantic processing on episodic memory, as compared to nonsemantic processing; and Study 4 examined the influence of self-related processing on episodic memory. Studies 1 to 4 employed the same autism and comparison participants to exclude confounding factors related to individual differences.

Study 1

In this study, immediate free recall of supraspan unrelated word lists was tested. It is well known that, in this paradigm, typical individuals show superior recall for the first and last few items of a word list, relative to items presented in the middle of the list, phenomena known as the 'primacy effect' and 'recency effect', respectively. Performance in the primacy and middle regions of the serial position reflects long-term memory (LTM), and performance in the recency region contains both short-term memory (STM) and LTM components (e.g. Craik, 1971). It has also been demonstrated that STM is mediated mainly through auditory or phonological components, and LTM primarily through semantic components (for a review see e.g. Baddeley, 1999). Memory performance was analysed for the three regions (primacy, middle and recency) of word lists.

Methods

Participants

The participants were 18 individuals with high-functioning autism (16 men, 2 women) and 18 comparison participants (15 men, 3 women). The autism and comparison groups were matched for age (mean + SD; 23.0 + 5.2 and 24.5 + 7.9, respectively), and for verbal IQ (M = 95.3 + 17.9 and 97.2 + 19.5) and performance IQ (M = 92.1 + 14.8 and 91.2 + 19.0) on the Wechsler Adult Intelligence Scale – Revised (Shinagawa et al., 1990). The diagnosis of 'autism disorder' was made according to *Diagnostic and Statistical Manual of Mental Disorders*, 4th edition (DSM-IV; American Psychiatric Association, 1994) criteria by a child psychiatrist, and the experimental participants' scores on the Childhood Autism Rating Scale (Schopler, Reichler & Renner, 1986) (modified for adult use) ranged between 31 and 46.5 (M = 37.4), as assessed by the parents or professional psychologists. None of the participants had neurological problems or were taking medication, as confirmed by physical examination and interviews. All participants gave written informed consent prior to participation.

Materials

Two types of word lists (Type A and Type B) were used. Type A lists consisted of abstract nouns such as 'convenience' and 'satisfaction', and Type B lists consisted of concrete nouns such as 'orange' and 'blackboard' (see Table 1 of Toichi & Kamio, 2003). Two lists were prepared for each list type, producing four different lists (A-1, A-2, B-1, B-2), and each list contained fifteen words of three or four syllables (mean 3.47 syllables for

Type A, 3.6 for Type B). List items were selected to avoid a phonological or semantic relationship between any two items in the same list. The average word frequency (the occurrence in ninety magazines) was higher for the abstract lists (82.7 and 63.2 for A-1 and A-2, respectively) than for the concrete lists (18.9 and 22.7 for B-1 and B-2, respectively), with no significant differences between lists of the same type. The average 'meaningfulness' (the number of associated words within ten seconds to a stimulus word) was 3.22 and 2.17 per word for the concrete and abstract word lists respectively, with the difference being significant ($t = 8.2$, $p < 0.0001$). All the items in these lists were common words among Japanese adolescents and adults.

Procedure

Participants were tested individually. Words were spoken by an experimenter at the rate of one per two seconds, and the participant was instructed to write down all the items recalled within two minutes immediately following the learning phase. Two free-recall trials were conducted successively with a one-minute inter-trial interval. Half the participants in each group were tested using lists A-1 and B-1, and half using lists A-2 and B-2. The order of presentation of list-type was counterbalanced. The word order of the list was chosen from three randomizations, counterbalanced across participants.

Analysis

The primacy and recency regions were defined as the first three and the last six items (e.g. Craik, 1971 for review) in the serial positions, respectively. The area between the two regions, which included six items, was called the middle region. The mean probability of correct recall was calculated for each region in each participant. Statistical analyses were conducted using a Group (autism, comparison) × Type (concrete, abstract) × Position (primacy, middle, recency) analysis of variance (ANOVA).

Results

Figure 8.1 shows correct performance in the two groups in the three regions of interest. The number of recall errors (including intrusions) was small in both groups. The mean (SD) number of errors (per list) was 0.33 (0.59) and 0.22 (0.48) in the autism and comparison groups, respectively, with no significant difference between groups ($t < 1$, $df = 34$). Concerning correct recall, ANOVA revealed a significant main effect of Group ($F = 4.2$, $df = 1$, 204, $p < 0.05$), Position ($F = 46.6$, $df = 2$, 204, $p < 0.0001$) and Type ($F = 4.1$, $df = 1$, 204, $p = < 0.05$). There was a significant Group × Type interaction ($F = 4.2$, $df = 1$, 204, $p = 0.04$),

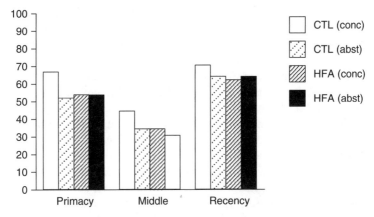

Figure 8.1 Correct recall (%) in the three regions. CTL: comparison participants; HFA: participants with high-functioning autism; conc, abst: concrete and abstract word lists, respectively

with no other significant interactions or double interactions. Post hoc comparisons (Fisher's PLSD) showed that the recall performances of the primacy region and recency region were better than that of the middle region (p < 0.0001), with better recognition in the recency than primacy region (p = 0.005). This indicates that the two groups showed similar serial position effects (i.e. primacy and recency effects) across list types.

The Group × Type interaction was attributable to a difference between the two groups in the superiority of recall of concrete as compared to abstract nouns. Post hoc comparisons (Fisher's PLSD) revealed that concrete noun recall in the comparison group was significantly better than abstract noun recall in the same group (p < 0.02), and concrete and abstract noun recall in the autism group (p = 0.02 and p = 0.02, respectively). On the other hand, there was no significant difference between abstract noun recall in the comparison group and either type of noun recall in the autism group, or between recall of the two word types in the autism group. This indicates that the significant main effect of Type was attributable primarily to the superior recall of concrete over abstract nouns in the comparison group. In summary, performance was better for concrete than abstract nouns in the comparison group, but the two types in the autism group were comparable, and similar to abstract nouns in the comparison group.

Discussion

The main findings of Study 1 replicated those of the author's previous study (Toichi & Kamio, 2003) which examined individuals with autism with a lower IQ than the participants in this study. In the present study, the main effect of Type and that of Group, as well as the Group × Type interaction, reached significance. For concrete nouns, the experimental group performed worse than the comparison group in all three serial positions (primacy, middle and recency). Considering that the primacy and middle regions exclusively reflect LTM, with the recency region including STM plus LTM components, the result suggests an impaired LTM for concrete nouns in the autism group. Abstract noun recall in both groups, however, was comparable, suggesting unimpaired memory for abstract nouns in the autism group. It is of interest that abstract noun recall in the two groups was similar to concrete noun recall in the autism group. As explained in the introduction, the nouns in the concrete word lists had higher 'meaningfulness' (i.e. they elicited more semantic associations) than those in the abstract word lists. Furthermore, in our previous study (Toichi & Kamio, 2003), the meaningfulness of words was found to correlate with the LTM performance of words in comparison participants but not in those with autism. Considering these findings, along with the semantic nature of LTM described in the introduction, a lack of superiority in the recall of concrete over abstract nouns in the autism group appears to suggest a problem using semantic knowledge at encoding. The next study examined the basic structure of semantic memory knowledge in autism.

Study 2

This study investigated semantic knowledge with a focus on semantic relationships between common words, using an indirect priming technique. Semantic priming refers to a phenomenon in which a preceding stimulus (prime) facilitates the processing of a subsequent target stimulus when the prime and target are semantically related (such as 'robin' and 'swallow'). It is believed that this phenomenon is mediated through the associative processing of concepts in semantic memory (Collins & Loftus, 1975). Two components of associative processing have been identified: fast automatic (unconscious) association, which occurs within a few hundred milliseconds, and slow voluntary (conscious) association (Neeley, 1977; Posner & Snyder, 1975). Of the two components of association, this study examined the slow component, using a semantic priming task with a word completion paradigm requiring participants to generate words to fit the word fragments. In the paradigm, targets were word fragments that were difficult to complete without semantic cues. If the semantic relationships between concepts were underdeveloped, the effect of semantic cues to facilitate correct responses (i.e. semantic priming effect) should be small.

The advantage of using a priming task is that it requires little explicit memory ability. Thus it is possible to examine semantic abilities independent of explicit memory function.

Methods

Materials

Single words and word fragments (36 points in size) were presented on a computer display approximately 70 cm from the participant. Letters appeared in black in the centre of the display against a white background. The prime and target words were written in Katakana, which is a set of phonograms used in written Japanese. Each 'character' in this syllabary conveys one syllable corresponding to one vowel or a consonant–vowel pair in English. The priming words were nouns and verbs, consisting of three to five letters. The target words were nouns and adjectives, consisting of three to five letters with the first letter always presented, and each missing letter replaced by a circle. Two letters were missing from four-letter words, and two or three from five-letter words, with two successive letters never presented. Only one word could be made from each target. Therefore errors, if present, would be due to producing nonwords or incorrect words that did not match the word fragments. College students found it difficult to complete the word fragments without semantic cues. Thirty pairs of primes + targets were used for the test trial. Twenty pairs were semantically related (e.g. 'bus'–'train', 'war'–'army', 'ice'–'cold' and 'tear'–'sad'); and ten pairs were semantically unrelated (e.g. 'television'–'necktie'). A preparatory study confirmed that the correct response for related and unrelated target words without primes and that for unrelated target words with primes did not differ significantly. Priming effects were therefore evaluated in terms of the ability of related primes, as compared with unrelated primes, to facilitate correct word completion.

Procedure

Participants were tested individually. Prior to test trials, three practice pairs which did not appear in the test trials were presented so that the participants could understand the test procedure. In the test trials, a prime word was presented for two seconds, during which time the participant was asked to read it aloud to confirm that the prime word had been correctly recognized. The target word fragment was then presented and the participant was asked to complete it orally. After fifteen seconds, the next prime word was presented, and the same process continued until the last word pair of primes + targets had been presented. Thus, the stimulus onset asynchrony (SOA) between the prime and target words was two seconds, with no inter-stimulus interval (ISI). The same (pseudo-random) order was used for all participants, that is, thirty pairs appeared randomly with the restriction that similar semantic relationships (e.g. 'laugh'–'funny' and 'play'–'amusing') did not appear in successive trials.

Results

Percentages of correctly completed word fragments following semantically related and semantically unrelated primes are shown for both groups in Figure 8.2. In both groups, performance for the related items was much better than that for the unrelated items. Relationship (unrelated, related) × Group (autism, comparison) repeated-measures analysis of variance (ANOVA) revealed a significant main effect of Relationship ($F = 244.0$, $df = 1$, 34, $p < 0.0001$), but neither the main effect of Group ($F = 2.6$, $df = 1$, 34) nor the Relationship × Group interaction ($F = 1.2$, $df = 1$, 34) was significant, indicating that both groups showed similar semantic priming effects.

Discussion

The priming task used in this study examined the associative organization of verbal material in semantic memory. The results of Study 2 replicated those of a previous study of individuals with HFA (Toichi & Kamio, 2001). The findings are also similar to a conceptual priming task by Gardiner, Bowler & Grice (2003). These results suggest that the

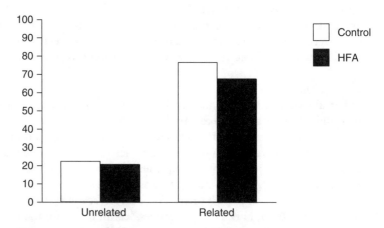

Figure 8.2 Correct completion (%) of unrelated and related word fragments. HFA: participants with high-functioning autism

associative organization of concepts underlying simple common words is unimpaired in individuals with autism spectrum disorders. Unimpaired semantic organization has been suggested in studies using word fluency tasks in which participants are asked to generate words in association with a given semantic category (such as 'animal' or 'vehicle') (e.g. Boucher, 1988); also in a card-sorting task using semantic categories (Tager-Flusberg, 1985a, b) and a Stroop task (Bryson, 1983; Eskes, Bryson & McCormick, 1990). However, a few studies have reported impaired semantic abilities even in individuals with high-functioning autism. In those studies, participants with HFA showed less categorical clustering (Minshew & Goldstein, 1993) or less contextual organization (Fein *et al.*, 1996) than ability-matched comparison groups. These last two studies, however, employed tasks that involved explicit memory components. Such discrepancy in the results suggests that people with HFA may have problems in the relationship between semantic and episodic memory, rather than the structure of semantic knowledge. Study 3 addressed this issue.

Study 3

Semantic processing, or the use of semantic knowledge in encoding words, facilitates recall better than 'shallow' (phonological or perceptual) processing. This phenomenon is known as the levels-of-processing effect (Craik & Tulving, 1975). The phenomenon is robust, and has been confirmed in first- and second-grade children (Geis & Hall, 1976, 1978; Owings & Baumeister, 1979) as well as in healthy adults, and even in patients with amnesia (Cermak & Reale, 1978; Cermak, 1979).

The levels-of-processing effect is important in that it provides evidence concerning the relationship between semantic and episodic memory. It is significant, therefore, that a previous study by the author (Toichi & Kamio, 2002) found reduced levels-of-processing effects in young people with autism whose average IQ was around 80. Study 3, reported here, investigated the relationship between episodic memory and semantic memory in adults with HFA using the levels-of-processing task used in the earlier study, which was in turn based on a task originally developed by Craik and Tulving (1975).

Methods

Materials

A word list was developed from a pool of common words. Thirty nouns were drawn from the list as targets to be studied. A set of questions about each target was also prepared. There were three 'levels' of questions for

Table 8.1. *Graphic, phonological and semantic questions used in*
Study 3 levels-of-processing task

Level	Target: *gyu-u-nyu-u* ('milk') in the Katakana character
Graphic	
: Yes	Is the word written in the Katakana character?
: No	Is the word written in the Hirakana character?
Phonological	
: Yes	Is the pronunciation similar to *shu-u-nyu-u* ('income') ?
: No	Is the pronunciation similar to *tsu-ku-e* ('table') ?
Semantic	
: Yes	Is it a drink?
: No	Is it metal?

each target: graphic, phonological and semantic (see Table 8.1). Graphic
questions concerned the type of character (Katakana or Hiragana, both
syllabaries for writing Japanese) in which a target word was written.
Phonological and semantic questions concerned the pronunciation and
meaning of a target word, respectively. The words used in phonological
questions were closely similar in pronunciation to the targets (such as
'attitude' and 'altitude'), inducing an intensive phonological encoding.
There were two answer types ('yes' and 'no') for each level of questioning,
producing six (3 levels × 2 answer types) different questions for each
target. Six lists, each consisting of 30 questions, were developed by pairing
each of the 30 targets with one question from each of the six alternative
questions. Of the 30 questions about the targets to be learned, 10 questions
were graphic, 10 phonological, and the remaining 10 were semantic. Half
the questions in each set of 10 were the 'yes' type, and half the 'no' type.

Three word lists were prepared for the recognition test, each containing
30 targets and 60 distractors. The three lists each contained the same 90
words printed on one side of a sheet of paper; however, their arrangement
differed.

In addition to the materials to be used at study, as described above, six
further target-question pairs were prepared, to be presented before (3
pairs) and after (3 pairs) the 30 pairs on which the participants would be
tested. The target words used in these additional target-question pairs did
not appear in the recognition test, eliminating possible primacy and
recency effects in recognition performance.

Procedure

Participants were tested individually. As explained above, there were six
different lists of question-target pairs as well as three kinds of answer

sheet, producing 18 (6 learning × 3 test) experimental conditions. One of the 18 conditions was assigned to each participant, so that the task conditions for the 24 participants differed in each group. In the learning phase, participants first saw a question presented on a computer display for eight seconds, followed by the presentation of a target word for two seconds. Participants were then asked to answer 'yes' or 'no' within five seconds following target presentation. The same procedure was repeated until the last item without a break. During this phase, participants did not know that a recognition test would follow. Immediately after the learning phase, a recognition list was given to participants, and they were asked to choose 30 words that they judged as 'old' within a five-minute period.

Results

The percentages of target words recognized at each level of processing (as determined by the question type), and for each group, are shown in Figure 8.3.

Error rates for the graphic, phonological and semantic questions were small in both groups: 0.0%, 0.0% and 0.5% in the experimental group, and 0.0%, 0.0% and 0.0% in the comparison group, respectively. There was no apparent trade-off between the recognition and accuracy of answers.

Preliminary analyses using Group × Level × Answer Type ANOVA did not reveal a significant main effect of the Answer Type, nor did the

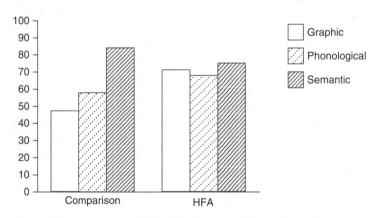

Figure 8.3 Correct recognition (%) of targets (nouns) due to three levels (graphic, phonological, semantic) of processing. HFA: participants with high-functioning autism

Answer Type interact with any other variables. Therefore, the Answer Type factor was omitted from the following analyses.

Group × Level repeated-measures ANOVA on correct recognition revealed a significant main effect of Level (F = 18.6, p < 0.0001, df = 1, 34), but the main effect of Group was not significant (F = 3.6, p = 0.07, df = 2, 68). Group × Level interaction was highly significant (F = 10.7, p < 0.0001, df = 2, 68), indicating a difference in the effect of Level between the two groups. Post hoc comparisons (Fisher's PLSD) revealed a significant difference in recognition between graphic and phonological processing (p = 0.03), and between semantic and phonological processing (p = 0.0001) in the comparison group, indicating the levels-of-processing effect in this group. Unlike the comparison group, there were no significant differences between any two of the three levels in the autism group, indicating the absence of the levels-of-processing effect. When comparisons were made between groups, the autism group performed better than the control group at the graphic level (p < 0.0001), but the two groups did not differ significantly in performance at the semantic or phonological level.

Discussion

In this study, the comparison group showed the levels-of-processing effect as expected, but the autism group did not. This result is consistent with that of the previous study (Toichi & Kamio, 2002) in which participants were those with lower-functioning autism. Whilst memory performance due to graphic processing was significantly better in the autism group than in the comparison group, the two groups did not differ significantly in memory performance due to semantic processing. Superior memory due to graphic processing may be related to an excellent perceptual memory, which has been well documented since the earliest description of autism (Kanner, 1943).

A review of the literature on the levels-of-processing effects shows that the effect has been confirmed not only in healthy adults but also in school-age children (Geis & Hall, 1976, 1978; Owings & Baumeister, 1979). A reduced effect was reported only in children below 10 years old (Lindberg, 1980; Naito, 1990; Weiss, Robinson & Hastie, 1977). In very young children, the development of semantic memory is immature (Ackerman, 1987; see Chi & Ceci, 1987 for a review), and such participants find it difficult to describe to-be-remembered words based on their semantic memory. The participants with autism in this study, on the other hand, were young adults with no intellectual disability. Moreover, the findings of Study 2, reported above, as well as evidence from previous studies suggesting that the organization of semantic knowledge is intact in individuals with autism (e.g. Tager-Flusberg, 1985a, b), make it unlikely that the lack of a levels-of-processing effect in the present study can be attributed to abnormal conceptual or semantic knowledge.

Nevertheless, an impaired relationship between semantic and episodic memory has been repeatedly reported in studies that examined the phenomenon of 'organization' (Fein et al., 1996; O'Connor & Hermelin, 1967; Ramondo & Milech, 1984; Wolff & Barlow, 1979) or semantic clustering in free recall (Hermelin & Frith, 1971; Tager-Flusberg, 1991). In these studies, a semantic relationship between items failed to facilitate LTM for these items.

There are other phenomena that suggest interdependence between episodic memory and semantic memory, such as the influence of word meaning on LTM (Lindberg, 1980; Paivio & Csapo, 1969) and the phenomenon of 'false memory' (Deese, 1959; Roediger & McDermott, 1995). A recent study of individuals with HFA reported a decrease in false memory for lure items that had not been presented (Beversdorf, 2000). The study used a word list prepared to induce false memory (e.g. *bed, rest, night, dream,* etc. all of which are related to the anticipated false memory of *sleep*). In other words, the presented words were expected to induce false memory for the lure items by a semantic relationship between items. Better discrimination of semantically related false items also suggests a decrease in the influence of semantic memory on episodic memory. These findings appear to be in line with the lack of levels-of-processing effect found in this study. Interestingly, however, a second study that examined false memory using a similar task reported no significant difference between people with Asperger syndrome and comparison groups (Bowler et al., 2000). The inconsistency might derive from differences in cognitive characteristics between HFA and Asperger syndrome. A study that examined false memory for sentences (Kamio & Toichi, 2007) also found differences in the integration of semantic information between subgroups of pervasive developmental disorder. Therefore, it seems important to keep in mind a possible difference between subtypes of pervasive developmental disorders when assessing relations between episodic and semantic memory.

Study 4

It has been hypothesized that 'autonoetic consciousness', or the subjective feeling of remembering, may be a critical component of episodic memory (Tulving, 1985; see also Chapter 9, this volume). Theoretically, autonoetic consciousness seems to be part of the conscious awareness of one's own state of mind, that is, a kind of self-awareness.

There are several lines of evidence indicating impaired self-awareness in autism. In a mirror-rouge test, for example, children with autism were less aware of, or more indifferent to, their reflected image (showing rouge on their nose) than age- and ability-matched comparison groups (Dawson & McKissick, 1984; Ferrari & Matthews, 1983). In addition to these behavioural findings, a study which examined autism children's descriptions of themselves suggested reduced self-awareness in terms of social context (Lee & Hobson, 1998). In addition, memory studies reported that individuals with autism performed worse than ability-matched comparison participants in remembering events or activities with which they had been involved (Boucher, 1981a; Boucher & Lewis, 1989; Klein, Chan & Loftus, 1999; Millward *et al.*, 2000). Finally, a study that directly addressed the issue of autonoetic consciousness using memory tasks reported evidence of reduced autonoetic consciousness in individuals with Asperger syndrome (Bowler, Gardiner & Grice, 2000). Thus, both the clinical and psychological findings suggest reduced self-awareness in autism.

The purpose of Study 4 was to examine self-awareness in adults with high-functioning autism using a modified levels-of-processing task. As explained in the introduction to Study 3, in typically developing older children and healthy adults the semantic processing of verbal materials facilitates episodic memory more than 'shallow' (phonological or perceptual) processing (the levels-of-processing effect). Words processed in a self-related manner are remembered even better than those processed in a general semantic context, the 'self-reference effect' (Rogers, Kuiper & Kirker, 1977). For example, the word '*smart*' is remembered better after the question 'Does the word describe you?' than after the question 'Is the meaning of the word similar to *intelligent*?' The self-reference effect has been attributed in part to effective elaboration in encoding due to the highly organized structure of the concept of self, and in part to the facilitation of compatible strategies at the time of retrieval due to the high accessibility of the self-concept (Rogers, Rogers & Kuiper, 1979; Wells, Hoffman & Enzle, 1984). Therefore, the self-reference effect is considered to reflect the organization of the concept of self in semantic memory. If individuals with autism grow up with little self-awareness, then they will not develop a highly organized concept of self, resulting in a reduction or lack of the self-reference effect.

In the modified levels-of-processing task used in Study 4, based on a task used by Rogers, Kuiper and Kirker (1977), the three levels of questioning consisted of phonological, semantic and self-referential questions. Thus, the self-referential questions replaced the graphical questions (see Table 8.2) used in Study 3. Two other modifications were made. First, personality-trait adjectives were used in place of the common nouns used in Study 3. Second, the phonological questions used in this study were expected to induce less effective phonological encoding than in the Study 3 task. This modification was introduced with the aim of eliciting a levels-of-processing effect between the phonological and semantic level. This is important because if there is no levels-of-processing effect between these two levels, then it is difficult to determine whether a potential lack of the self-reference effect is attributable to a self-awareness problem or a lack of levels-of-processing effects in general.

Methods

Materials

A word list was developed from verbal materials collected from spontaneous language used by high-functioning adolescents with and without autism who did not participate in the main part of this study. Ninety adjectives were chosen, 30 of which were used as targets to be studied, with the remaining 60 used as distractors in a recognition test. The adjectives were all common words among Japanese adolescents and adults. There was no significant difference in word frequency between the targets and distractors. The phonological questions in this study were all of the form 'Does the word rhyme with – ?', and were intended to induce less effective encoding than the questions used in Study 3 that required more thorough phonological analyses. Questions at the self-referential level were intended to elicit the processing of targets in a self-related manner.

Table 8.2. *Phonological, semantic and self-referential questions used in Study 4 levels-of-processing task*

Level	Target: *shin-setsu* ('kind')
Phonological	
: Yes	Does the word rhyme with *men-setsu* ('interview')?
: No	Does the word rhyme with *kei-kaku* ('plan')?
Semantic	
: Yes	Is the meaning of the word similar to *yasashi-i* ('tender') ?
: No	Is the meaning of the word similar to *tsumeta-i* ('cold') ?
Self-referential	
: Yes or No	Does the word describe you?

Procedure

The task followed the same procedure as that used in Study 3.

Results

The percentages of target words recognized at each level of processing (as determined by the question type), and for each group, are shown in Figure 8.4. In the learning phase, participants in both groups answered most of the phonological and semantic questions correctly. The rates of incorrect answers to phonological and semantic questions were 0.0% and 1.1% in the comparison group, and 0.0% and 0.0% in the autism group, respectively. The average proportion of 'yes' responses to the self-referent questions was 52.8% and 48.9% in the autism and comparison groups, with no significant difference between groups (t(34) = 1.47, p = 0.15; unpaired t-test, two-tailed).

In the test phase, each participant chose exactly 30 words, as instructed. There was no trade-off between performances for the recognition and accuracy of answers in the learning phase. Preliminary analyses using Group (autism, control) × Level (phonological, semantic, self-referent) × Answer type (yes, no) ANOVA revealed that the Answer did not interact with any other variable. This factor was therefore omitted from the following analyses.

Group ×Level repeated-measures ANOVA yielded a significant main effect of Level (F = 40.0, df = 2, 68, p < 0.0001) and a significant Group × Level interaction (F = 6.2, df = 2, 68, p = 0.003). Post hoc comparisons

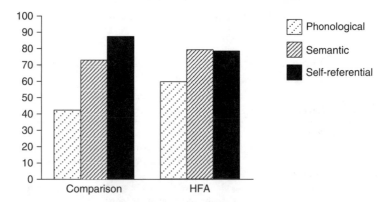

Figure 8.4 Correct recognition (%) of targets (adjectives) due to three levels (phonological, semantic, self-referential) of processing. HFA: participants with high-functioning autism

(Fisher's PLSD) revealed a significant difference in performance for recognition between phonological and semantic processing in both groups ($p < 0.0001$ for both groups). This indicates that both groups showed a levels-of-processing effect. However, a significant difference between semantic and self-referent processing (i.e. self-reference effects) was found in the comparison group ($p = 0.005$), but not in the autism group ($p = 0.67$). Between-group comparisons showed that recognition resulting from phonological processing was better in the autism group than in the comparison group ($p = 0.0006$); otherwise, the two groups did not differ significantly.

Discussion

The results of Study 4 differed from those of Study 3 in that the autism as well as the comparison group showed levels-of-processing effects between phonological and semantic processing. This was probably because the phonological question used in Study 4 induced less effective encoding than the question used in Study 3, depressing the facilitative effect of phonological encoding, especially in the autism group, allowing a levels-of-processing effect to emerge. Nevertheless, the results of Study 4 resembled those of Study 3 in that there was no between-group difference in the facilitative effect of semantic processing.

A self-reference effect was found in the comparison group, but not the autism group, indicating that the participants with autism did not have facilitative effects of self-awareness on episodic memory. A plausible explanation of this finding is that individuals with autism may not develop a highly organized concept of self, and therefore description in a self-referential manner does not facilitate episodic memory (relative to general semantic processing). The result suggests a reduction or lack of self-awareness in autism, an issue which is discussed more fully in Chapter 9, this volume.

Summary

Study 1 confirmed generally unimpaired performance for free recall in the autism group, as expected from the findings of recent studies on high-functioning autism. However, the nature of the verbal materials influenced memory performance in the comparison group, but not in the participants with autism. Although Study 2 suggested unimpaired semantic knowledge (in terms of the semantic relations between words), Study 3 seemed to indicate impairment in the relationship between semantic and episodic memory. Study 3 also found superior memory due to visual processing in participants with autism. Finally, Study 4 suggested a lack of self-awareness in autism, which is consistent with suggestions that people with autism lack the autonoetic awareness that is generally considered to be the hallmark of episodic memory.

The above findings may help to explain some of the unique characteristics of memory in autism. First, the excellent rote memory that has been repeatedly documented in clinical reports may be partly due to superior memory resulting from nonsemantic perceptual (graphic or phonological) processing (as found in Studies 3 and 4). Second, verbal episodic memory may be (slightly in most cases) impaired in high-functioning autism when the materials to be remembered have rich semantic cues (such as high-frequency concrete words) (as seen in Study 1). Such words facilitate effective semantic encoding in typically developing people, but not in people with autism (as shown in Study 3). Third, it is likely that the decreased memory of self-performed events is related to reduced autonoetic consciousness, as suggested by a lack of the self-reference effect. Thus, part of the riddle of autism memory appears to have been clarified in this series of studies.

A number of other characteristics of autism memory remain to be explained. For example, it is difficult to account for the specifically enhanced memory of particular individuals, such memory as for proper names or dates, based on the findings of this study. One possibility is that people with autism can encode such materials much more effectively than typically developing people because of the autism-specific organization of semantic memory. It seems likely that there is a unique way of organizing the lexicon and concepts in individuals with autism based on their unique interest in nonsocial, often perceptual or physical/mechanical traits of the external world. The excellent calendric calculations often seen even in autism children with mental retardation suggest that mechanical processing is their usual way of organizing materials. In autism, ordinary semantic processing might not result in deep elaboration at encoding; instead, mathematical or rule-based processing would result in more effective encoding. This may explain why people with autism are good at remembering such things as timetables and bus numbers. A study by Heavey, Pring and Hermelin (1999; see also Chapter 11, this volume) that tested eight participants with savant syndrome (seven with autism) for calendric calculation reported that they showed excellent memory for dates, particularly those of the period for which immediate calendric calculation was possible. The finding is in line with the above view.

Another issue to be explained may be the role of self-awareness in memory in people with autism. There is converging evidence for a close relationship between impaired episodic memory and reduced autonoetic consciousness in autism, as described in Study 4. On the other hand, clinical findings in people with autism, such as a lack of infantile amnesia (i.e. good memory for experienced events during infancy), seem to challenge the present formulation of episodic memory based primarily on autonoetic consciousness. A study by Naito (2003) that examined relationships between memory and cognitive development suggests an independence of memory from social awareness in small children. The relative role of autonoetic consciousness might differ between children and adults, and between people with autism and those without autism. Research on memory function in autism seems to provide cues to clarify a mechanism of human memory.

References

Ackerman, B. P. (1987). Descriptions: a model of nonstrategic memory development. In H. W. Reese (ed.), *Advances in child development and behavior*, pp. 143–183. New York: Academic Press.

American Psychiatric Association (1994). *Diagnostic and statistical manual of mental disorders*, 4th edn (DSM-IV). Washington, DC: American Psychiatric Association.

Baddeley, A. D. (1999). *Essentials of human memory*. Hore: Psychology Press.

Bennetto, L., Pennington, B. F. & Rogers, S. J. (1996). Intact and impaired memory function in autism. *Child Development, 67,* 1816–1835.

Beversdorf, D. Q., Anderson, J. M., Manning, S. E. *et al.* (1998). The effect of semantic and emotional context on written recall for verbal language in high functioning adults with autism spectrum disorder. *Journal of Neurology, Neurosurgery, and Psychiatry, 65,* 685–692.

Beversdorf, D. Q., Smith, B. W., Crucian, G. P., Anderson, J. M., Keillor, J. M., Barrett, A. M., Hughes, J. D., Felopulos, G. J., Bauman, M. L., Nadeau, S. E. & Heilman, K. M. (2000). Increased discrimination of 'false memories' in autism spectrum disorder. *Proceedings of the National Academy of Sciences of the United States of America, 97,* 8734–8737.

Boucher, J. & Warrington, E. K. (1976). Memory deficits in early infantile autism: some similarities to the amnesic syndrome. *British Journal of Psychology, 67,* 73–87.

Boucher, J. (1978). Echoic memory capacity in autistic children. *Journal of Child Psychology and Psychiatry, 19,* 161–166.

(1981a). Immediate free recall in early childhood autism: another point of behavioural similarity with the amnesic syndrome. *British Journal of Psychology, 72,* 211–215.

(1981b). Memory for recent events in autistic children. *Journal of Autism and Developmental Disorders, 11,* 293–301.

(1988). Word fluency in high-functioning autistic children. *Journal of Autism and Developmental Disorders, 18,* 637–645.

Boucher, J. & Lewis, V. (1989). Memory impairments and communication in relatively able autistic children. *Journal of Child Psychology and Psychiatry*, *30*, 99–122.

Bowler, D. M., Gardiner, J. M. & Grice, S. J. (2000). Episodic memory and remembering in adults with Asperger Syndrome. *Journal of Autism and Developmental Disorders*, *30*, 295–304.

Bowler, D. M., Gardiner, J. M., Grice, S. J. & Saavalainen, P. (2000). Memory illusions: false recall and recognition in high-functioning adults with autism. *Journal of Abnormal Psychology*, *109*, 663–672.

Bowler, D. M., Matthews, N. J. & Gardiner, J. M. (1997). Asperger's syndrome and memory: similarity to autism but not amnesia. *Neuropsychologia*, *35*, 65–70.

Bryson, S. (1983). Interference effects in autistic children: evidence for the comprehension of single stimuli. *Journal of Abnormal Psychology*, *92*, 250–254.

Cermak, L. S. (1979). Amnesic patients' level of processing. In L. S Cermak & F. I. M. Craik (eds.), *Levels of processing in human memory*, pp. 119–139. Hillsdale, NJ: Erlbaum.

Cermak, L. S. & Reale, L. (1978). Depth of processing and retention of words by alcoholic Korsakoff patients. *Journal of Experimental Psychology: Human Learning and Memory*, *4*, 165–174.

Chi, M. T. H. & Ceci, S. J. (1987). Content knowledge: its role, representation, and restructuring in memory development. In H. W. Reese (ed.), *Advances in child development and behavior*, pp. 91–142. New York: Academic Press.

Clayton, N. S. & Dickinson, A. (1998). Episodic-like memory during cache recovery by scrub jays. *Nature*, *395*, 272–274.

Collins, A. M. & Loftus, E. F. (1975). A spreading-activation theory of romantic processing. *Psychological Review*, *82*, 407–428.

Craik, F. I. M. (1971). Age differences in recognition memory. *Quarterly Journal of Experimental Psychology*, *23*, 316–323.

Craik, F. I. M. & Tulving, E. (1975). Depth of processing and the retention of words in episodic memory. *Journal of Experimental Psychology: General*, *104*, 268–294.

Dawson, G. & McKissick, F. C. (1984). Self-recognition in autistic children. *Journal of Autism and Developmental Disorders*, *14*, 383–394.

Deese, J. (1959). On the prediction of occurrence of particular verbal intrusions in immediate recall. *Journal of Experimental Psychology*, *58*, 17–22.

Eskes, G. B., Bryson, S. E. & McCormick, T. A. (1990). Comprehension of concrete and abstract words in autistic children. *Journal of Autism and Developmental Disorders*, *20*, 61–73.

Fein, D., Dunn, M., Allen, D. A. *et al.* (1996). Language and neuropsychological findings. In I. Rapin (ed.), *Clinics in developmental medicine. Preschool children with inadequate communication: developmental language disorder, autism, low IQ*, pp. 123–154. London: MacKeith Press.

Ferrari, M. & Matthews, W. S. (1983). Self-recognition deficits in autism: syndrome specific or general developmental delay? *Journal of Autism and Developmental Disorders*, *13*, 317–324.

Gardiner, J. M., Bowler, D. M. & Grice, S. J. (2003). Perceptual and conceptual priming in autism: an extension and replication. *Journal of Autism and Developmental Disorders, 33,* 259–269.

Geis, M. F. & Hall, D. M. (1976). Encoding and incidental memory in children. *Journal of Experimental Child Psychology, 22,* 58–66.

(1978). Encoding and congruity in children's incidental memory. *Child Development, 49,* 857–861.

Heavey, L., Pring, L. & Hermelin, B. (1999). A date to remember: the nature of memory in savant calendrical calculators. *Psychological Medicine, 29,* 145–160.

Hermelin, B. & Frith, U. (1971). Psychological studies of childhood autism: can autistic children make sense of what they see and hear? *Journal of Special Education, 5,* 107–117.

Kamio, Y. & Toichi M. (2007). Memory illusion in high-functioning autism and Asperger's disorder. *Journal of Autism and Developmental Disorders, 37,* 867–876.

Kanner, L. (1943). Autistic disturbances of affective contact. *Nervous Child, 2,* 217–250.

Klein, S. B., Chan, R. L. & Loftus, J. (1999). Independence of episodic and semantic self-knowledge: the case of autism. *Social Cognition, 17,* 413–436.

Lee, A. & Hobson, R. P. (1998). On developing self-concepts: a controlled study of children and adolescents with autism. *Journal of Child Psychology and Psychiatry, 39,* 1131–1144.

Lindberg, M. A. (1980). Is knowledge base development a necessary and sufficient condition for memory development? *Journal of Experimental Child Psychology, 30,* 401–410.

Millward, C., Powell, S., Messer, D. *et al.* (2000). Recall for self and other in autism: children's memory for events experienced by themselves and their peers. *Journal of Autism and Developmental Disorders, 30,* 15–28.

Minshew, N. J. & Goldstein, G. (1993). Is autism an amnesic disorder? Evidence from the California Verbal Learning Test. *Neuropsychology, 7,* 209–216.

Minshew, N. J., Goldstein, G., Muenz, L. R. *et al.* (1992). Neuropsychological functioning in nonmentally retarded autistic individuals. *Journal of Clinical and Experimental Neuropsychology, 14,* 749–761.

Naito, M. (1990). Repetition priming in children and adults: age-related dissociation between implicit and explicit memory. *Journal of Experimental Child Psychology, 50,* 462–484.

(2003). The relationship between theory of mind and episodic memory: evidence for the development of autonoetic consciousness. *Journal of Experimental Child Psychology, 85,* 312–336.

Neeley, J. H. (1977). Semantic priming and retrieval from lexical memory: roles of inhibitionless spreading activation and limited-capacity attention. *Journal of Experimental Psychology: General, 106,* 226–254.

O'Connor, N. & Hermelin, B. (1967). Auditory and visual memory in autistic and normal children. *Journal of Mental Deficiency Research, 11,* 126–131.

Owings, R. A. & Baumeister, A. A. (1979). Levels of processing, encoding strategies, and memory development. *Journal of Experimental Child Psychology, 28,* 100–118.

Paivio, A. & Csapo, K. (1969). Concrete image and verbal memory codes. *Journal of Experimental Psychology*, *80*, 279–285.

Posner, M. I. & Snyder, C. R. R. (1975). Attention and cognitive control. In R. L. Solso (ed.), *Information processing and cognition: the Layola symposium*, pp. 55–85. Hillsdale, NJ: Erlbaum.

Ramondo, N. & Milech, D. (1984). The nature and specificity of the language coding deficit in autistic children. *British Journal of Psychology*, *75*, 95–103.

Renner, P., Klinger, L. G. & Klinger, M. R. (2000). Implicit and explicit memory in autism: is autism an amnesic disorder? *Journal of Autism and Developmental Disorders*, *30*, 3–14.

Roediger III, H. L. & McDermott, K. B. (1995). Creating false memories: remembering words not presented in lists. *Journal of Experimental Psychology: Learning, Memory and Cognition*, *21*, 803–814.

Rogers, T. B., Kuiper, N. A. & Kirker, W. S. (1977). Self-reference and the encoding of personal information. *Journal of Personality and Social Psychology*, *35*, 677–688.

Rogers, T. B., Rogers, P. J. & Kuiper, N. A. (1979). Evidence for the self as a cognitive prototype: the 'false alarm effect'. *Personality and Social Psychology Bulletin*, *5*, 53–56.

Schopler, E., Reichler, J. R. & Renner, R. B. (1986). *The Childhood Autism Rating Scale (CARS)*. New York: Irvington.

Shinagawa, F., Kobayashi, S., Fujita, K. & Maegawa, H. (1990). *Japanese Wechsler Adult Intelligence Scale (Revised)*. Tokyo: Nihon-Bunka-Kagaku-sha.

Summers, J. A. & Craik, F. I. M. (1994). The effects of subject-performed tasks on the memory performance of verbal autistic children. *Journal of Autism and Developmental Disorders*, *24*, 773–783.

Tager-Flusberg, H. (1985a). The conceptual basis for referential word meaning in children with autism. *Child Development*, *56*, 1167–1178.

(1985b). Basic level and superordinate level categorization by autistic, mentally retarded, and normal children. *Journal of Experimental Child Psychology*, *40*, 450–469.

(1991). Semantic processing in the free recall of autistic children: further evidence for a cognitive deficit. *British Journal of Developmental Psychology*, *9*, 417–430.

Toichi, M. & Kamio, Y. (2001). Verbal association for simple common words in high-functioning autism. *Journal of Autism and Developmental Disorders*, *31*, 483–490.

(2002). Long-term memory and levels-of-processing in autism. *Neuropsychologia*, *40*, 964–969.

(2003). Long-term memory in high-functioning autism: controversy on episodic memory in autism reconsidered. *Journal of Autism and Developmental Disorders*, *33*, 151–161.

Tulving, E. (1985). Memory and consciousness. *Canadian Psychologist*, *26*, 1–12.

Weiss, S. L, Robinson, G. & Hastie, R. (1977). The relationship of depth of processing to free recall in second and fourth graders. *Developmental Psychology*, *13*, 525–526.

Wells, G. L., Hoffman, C. & Enzle, M. E. (1984). Self- versus other-referent processing at encoding and retrieval. *Personality and Social Psychology Bulletin, 121*, 331–354.

Wolff, S. & Barlow, A. (1979). Schizoid personality in childhood: a comparative study of schizoid, autistic and normal children. *Journal of Child Psychology and Psychiatry, 20*, 29–46.

9   Episodic memory and autonoetic consciousness in autistic spectrum disorders: the roles of self-awareness, representational abilities and temporal cognition

Sophie Lind and Dermot Bowler

Introduction

According to Schacter and Tulving (1994), human memory is subserved by a number of mind–brain systems including the episodic and semantic systems (see Gardiner, this volume, Chapter 1). The episodic system encodes and retrieves personally experienced event memories, which consist of complex collections of features including spatial, temporal and contextual information. Conversely, the semantic system is largely responsible for factual memory and general knowledge. These memories are not generally associated with spatial, temporal or contextual information. Crucially, retrieval from each system is associated with a distinct form of conscious awareness: episodic retrieval – or 'remembering' – involves autonoetic (self-knowing) consciousness, whereas semantic retrieval – or 'knowing' – involves noetic consciousness. Thus, semantic retrieval might involve, for example, bringing a known fact to mind, whereas episodic retrieval might involve remembering the particular episode during which that fact was learned. The episodic system underlies the capacity for 'mental time travel' (Suddendorf & Corballis, 1997; Wheeler, Stuss & Tulving, 1997) – either mentally projecting oneself into the past to *re-experience* an event or mentally 'projecting oneself into the future to *pre-experience* [italics added] an event' (Atance & O'Neill, 2005, p. 127).

Individuals with an autistic spectrum disorder (ASD) generally perform well on tasks that require semantic (or other) memory processes, but perform poorly on tasks that demand the support of the episodic system (see this volume, Chapters 12, 14 and 17; also Ben Shalom, 2003; Bennetto, Pennington & Rogers, 1996; Minshew & Goldstein, 2001). This chapter aims to establish the reasons for this impairment in episodic remembering. The main thrust of our argument is to suggest that auto-noetic consciousness is attenuated in people with an ASD. Before considering possible explanations, however, the prerequisites for the development of episodic memory (EM) in typical individuals will be considered. These prerequisites will be used as a framework for exploring the causes of the EM impairment in autism.

Prerequisites of episodic memory in typical development

In typical development, EM is not fully functional until at least 4;0 years of age. Although infants, toddlers and young preschoolers show impressive memory retention, such achievements are likely to be manifestations of other memory systems (Cowan, 1997). The relatively late emergence of EM is likely to be due to the fact that young children cannot yet experience autonoetic consciousness. Wheeler, Stuss and Tulving (1997) define autonoetic consciousness as the ability to mentally represent and become aware of subjective experiences in the past, present and future. It enables the kind of mental time travel that characterizes episodic remembering. This form of consciousness is thought to depend upon a number of interrelated cognitive abilities including having a concept of self, representational abilities that include a capacity for metarepresentation, and certain achievements in the domain of temporal cognition. Until each of these elements is in place, children cannot become autonoetically conscious. We will begin our discussion by considering the typical developmental paths of these three likely prerequisites.

Development of the self

The intuitive assumption that we each possess some kind of unitary core self – something akin to a soul – has given way, in psychology at least, to theories proposing various delineations of the self. For example, the most widely accepted distinction is between the self as the subject of experience – the '*I*' – and the self as the object of experience – the '*me*' (James, 1890). However, Neisser (1988) has developed a more elaborate taxonomy, claiming that there are five forms of self-awareness: ecological, interpersonal, conceptual, private and temporally extended self-awareness. Ecological and interpersonal self-awareness are perceptually based and early developing, together constituting implicit self-awareness (corresponding to James' notion of the 'I'). The former entails awareness of the body in relation to the physical environment, whereas the latter entails awareness of the self in relation to others in the social environment. Conceptual, private and temporally extended self-awareness are later maturing and representationally based, underpinning explicit self-awareness (the 'me'). Conceptual self-awareness occurs when the self becomes the object rather than merely the subject of thought. It entails having a concept of 'me' comprising a set of beliefs about the self. Private self-awareness refers to explicit, conceptual awareness of aspects of the self not accessible to others (e.g. awareness of internal mental states). Finally, temporally extended self-awareness is also conceptual but involves an additional temporal dimension, thereby endowing individuals with a sense of continuity in personal identity through time. These various types of self-awareness are likely to be interrelated/interdependent in that, for example, implicit forms of self-awareness serve as a foundation for explicit self-awareness. Nevertheless, each of these dimensions follows its own ontogenetic trajectory evolving throughout development, particularly during early childhood, as outlined next.

Implicit self-awareness: the ecological and interpersonal selves
A considerable amount of evidence suggests that infants are endowed with rudimentary ecological and interpersonal self-awareness soon after birth (Rochat, 1995). For instance, 24-hour-old neonates show significantly more rooting responses (orienting towards perioral cheek stimulation) when they receive external stimulation from an experimenter's hand than when they are 'self-stimulated' by the experimenter moving the infant's own hand to their cheek (Rochat & Hespos, 1997). Such selective responsiveness demonstrates self/nonself-discrimination and, therefore, a degree of ecological self-awareness. That newborns will learn to suck on a pacifier at a specific rate in order to see or hear a pleasant stimulus such as a picture or their mother's voice (e.g. DeCasper & Fifer, 1980; Siqueland & DeLucia, 1969) shows that they can also exert intentional control over their behaviour, revealing that they have a sense of 'agency' – a critical hallmark of the ecological self (Gibson, 1995; Neisser, 1995). Agency involves implicitly distinguishing between self-caused and environmentally caused changes in perceptual experience. It involves perceiving oneself as the centre of control of one's own action-generated experiences and recognizing one's responsibility for particular changes in perceptual experience (Russell, 1996). Interpersonal self-awareness is clearly evident among 2-month-olds. Infants of this age readily engage in 'protoconversations' with their caregivers (Murray & Trevarthen, 1985) – mutually regulated, coordinated interactions involving turn-taking and imitation of vocal, facial and gestural expressions (Trevarthen & Aitken, 2001) – that show clear awareness of the self in relation to another. That babies exert intentional control in these social exchanges indicates a clear sense of agency in the interpersonal domain also.

Explicit self-awareness: the conceptual, private and temporally extended selves

Conceptual self-awareness

Only in the second year of life do children become reflexively – conceptually – self-aware. A number of concurrent developments, including the emergence of self-conscious emotions, personal pronoun use and a set of explicit beliefs about the self, are considered to be expressions of conceptual self-awareness. However, mirror self-recognition (MSR) is widely regarded as the litmus test of conceptual self-awareness.

In the classic form of the MSR paradigm (Amsterdam, 1972), a familiar adult surreptitiously marks the child's face with brightly coloured pigment under the pretence of wiping their face clean. The experimenter then assesses the child's response to their reflection. Touching the mark is generally thought to indicate the presence of a self-concept and indeed it would appear to imply at least a basic conceptual knowledge of one's typical facial appearance (but, for alternative explanations, see Hobson, 1990; Loveland, 1986, 1993; Mitchell, 1993, 1997). Studies reliably show the mean age of success in this task to be 18 months (Anderson, 1983; Courage, Edison & Howe, 2004; Lewis & Ramsey, 2004). Blushing, shy smiling, gaze aversion and preening are taken to be expressions of embarrassment and pride, both of which are examples of self-conscious emotions. Even the earliest studies of MSR noted these reactions among 21- to 24-month-olds when they were confronted with their reflections (Amsterdam, 1972). Unlike earlier emerging basic emotions, such as fear and joy, self-conscious emotions involve cognitive support and necessarily involve a self-concept, since they are emotions *about* the self (Lewis *et al.*, 1989; Lewis, 1994; Tracy & Robins, 2004). They involve self-evaluative processes whereby one's representation of self is compared to a socially defined standard. Thus, in the case of pride, one has exceeded accepted standards and in the case of embarrassment, one has violated those standards.

The use of personal pronouns to refer to the self is the least controversial marker of conceptual self-awareness. For example, using the terms 'my' and 'mine' to denote ownership implies a concept of self. Moreover, appropriate use of the terms 'me' and 'you' signifies a sophisticated explicit differentiation of self and other, suggesting that the child represents self and other as distinct individuals. Only individuals who make such an explicit distinction can use the terms correctly because, unlike proper names, their meanings shift according to who is speaking – the speaker is always 'I' or 'me' and the listener is always 'you' (Bates, 1990). For example, if a parent and child were to look into a mirror together, the parent would say 'that's you' whilst pointing to the child's reflection, not 'that's me', and yet by 22 to 24 months toddlers can correctly label their own mirror image as 'me' (Lewis & Ramsey, 2004; Courage, Edison & Howe, 2004). Thus, when toddlers begin using these terms, one can confidently infer that they have a self-concept to which they are referring.

Overall, the available evidence suggests that explicit self-awareness in the form of the conceptual self is first apparent in typically developing children between 15 and 24 months. However, the conceptual self undergoes considerable elaboration over time. Its development involves the gradual acquisition of a set of beliefs about the self, knowledge of personal characteristics, features and traits (e.g. Neisser, 1997). In its earliest stages, the self-concept consists mainly of beliefs about physical traits and abilities (e.g. 'I have brown hair'; 'I can skip'), only later extending to psychological and social traits (e.g. 'I'm shy'; 'I have lots of friends') (Damon & Hart, 1988). Thus, ecologically grounded elements of conceptual self-awareness are earlier to develop than interpersonally grounded elements.

The private self

Private self-awareness emerges somewhat later than basic conceptual self-awareness. It involves conceptual awareness of private experiences – of one's own mental life. It thus relies on 'theory of mind' (ToM), which is defined as the conceptual system that underlies the ability to impute mental states to self or other (Perner, 2000). Children come to appreciate mental states such as desires, intentions and beliefs between the ages of about 3 and 5 years, and their ability to attribute these states to self and other appears to develop in parallel (Gopnik & Meltzoff, 1994). Thus, the development of a ToM endows the child with the kind of introspective self-knowledge that characterizes private self-awareness, allowing them to go beyond simply *having* private experiences to include the additional awareness *that* they have them.

The temporally extended self

Temporally extended self-awareness also emerges at around 4 years. It involves awareness of the relations between present, past and future states of self. It is essentially awareness of one's place in, and continued existence through, time and appears to depend upon the capacity for autonoetic consciousness (Moore & Lemmon, 2001). Povinelli, Landau and Perilloux (1996) developed a task to investigate the development of this form of self-awareness. They introduced a temporal component into the traditional MSR test to create the *delayed self-recognition* (DSR) paradigm. Experimenter and child were filmed playing a game in which the child was praised by being patted on the head. Whilst praising the child, the experimenter covertly placed a large sticker on top of their head. After a delay of three minutes, the pair watched the recording and the child's response was assessed. The test is designed to establish whether the child understands the causal relation between this 'past self' represented on the television screen and the 'present self' who is watching the recording. Reaching for the sticker is taken as evidence for a temporally extended concept of self (but, for alternative explanations, see Suddendorf, 1999; Zelazo, Sommerville & Nichols, 1999). Most 4-year-olds, but few 3-year-olds, can locate the sticker on their head (Lemmon & Moore, 2001; Povinelli, Landau & Perilloux, 1996; Povinelli & Simon, 1998; Suddendorf, 1999; Zelazo, Sommerville & Nichols, 1999).

The role of self-awareness in episodic memory development
We will now address the question of how these developments in self-awareness relate to the emergence of EM. A number of researchers have argued for a causal link between self-awareness and EM, agreeing that *explicit* self-awareness must be involved, since autonoetic awareness necessitates directing attention onto a mental representation of the self. However, there is controversy over the *level* of explicit self-awareness required. Howe and Courage (1993) have claimed that the emergence of conceptual self-awareness, as indexed by MSR, is the critical developmental precursor for remembering personally experienced events. However, it can be argued that the MSR task does not capture the kind of self-awareness involved in autonoetic remembering.

Wheeler, Stuss and Tulving (1997, p. 335) suggest that 'autonoetic consciousness affords individuals the possibility to apprehend their subjective experiences throughout time and perceive the present moment as both a continuation of their past and a prelude to their future'. Firstly, the ability to 'apprehend subjective experiences' seems to imply private self-awareness, since it involves focusing attention directly on private experiences. The quote also focuses on the temporality of autonoetic consciousness. This is also highlighted in a second quote in which it is argued that episodic retrieval involves the understanding that 'the self doing the [re] experiencing now is the same self that did it originally' (Wheeler, Stuss & Tulving, 1997, p. 349). This seems to require a concept of self that is extended in time and is represented as such. Thus, autonoetic awareness would seem to involve elements of both private and temporally extended self-awareness. It does not seem likely that these high-level forms of self-awareness are necessary for MSR.

Evidence that EM depends upon private self-awareness is provided by studies showing relationships between performance on ToM tasks and EM tasks (Naito, 2003; Perner, Kloo & Gornick, in press). For example, Perner and Ruffman (1995) found a correlation between free recall, which is thought to rely primarily on the episodic system, and ToM tests measuring understanding of own knowledge states. The likely role of temporally extended self-awareness is supported by studies showing relationships between DSR and EM. Welch-Ross (2001) found that children who demonstrated DSR showed significantly greater episodic recall in mother–child conversations about past events than children who did not show DSR. Similarly, Lemmon and Moore (2001) found a significant correlation between DSR and an EM measure, which involved remembering the temporal order of events in a sticker finding game.

The development of representational abilities

We turn now to the second of the likely developmental prerequisites of EM. Changes in representational abilities are relevant not only in terms of their direct role in the development of autonoetic consciousness and EM but also in terms of the developments in self-awareness that were described above. According to Perner's (1991) representational theory of mind, prior to 18 months of age infants are limited to primary representations which faithfully model the currently perceived state of affairs. Representational skills post 18 months, however, reach a new level of sophistication, with an emerging capacity for secondary representation which allows the child to hold in mind multiple, even contradictory, representations of the world which can be differentiated from and compared to a primary representation of reality.

It has been suggested that conceptual self-awareness relies upon this capacity for secondary representation (Asendorpf, Warkentin & Baudonnière, 1996; Perner, 1991; Suddendorf & Whiten, 2001). Thus, in the case of mirror self-recognition, the 18-month-old is able to hold in mind a stable representation of their typical facial appearance (no mark) and compare it to a veridical, primary representation of their currently perceived reflected image (marked). The infant must recognize the discrepancy between these two representations and use this information to initiate appropriate behaviour – i.e. trying to remove the mark. Prior to the transition from primary to secondary representation, perceptions of self are in a state of constant flux, and self-representations are largely online. At this stage, stable characteristics cannot be attributed to the self and, therefore, there can be no enduring concept of self. Primary representations, although sufficient for ecological and interpersonal self-awareness, are not adequate for conceptual self-awareness.

Developments in representational skill also directly affect the capacity for autonoetic awareness. Autonoetic awareness involves focusing attention on one's own mental states. This capacity for thinking about thoughts – or ToM – involves the ability to metarepresent, i.e. to represent representations as representations (Perner, 1991). EM retrieval involves the explicit understanding that what is being brought to mind is a *mental representation* of a past experience. The memory is identified *as a memory*. Without metarepresentation there is no awareness of the propositional attitude (e.g. 'I remember that') assumed in relation to the information held in mind. It is metarepresentation that underlies the distinction between noetic and autonoetic awareness. Thus, without metarepresentation, memories would involve (semantic) knowing rather than (episodic) remembering, as shown below in (i) and (ii) respectively.

(i) I went to the shop and bought milk.
(ii) [I remember that] I went to the shop and bought milk

A number of authors have argued for the role of metarepresentation in EM development (Nelson & Fivush, 2004; Perner, 2000, 2001; Perner & Ruffman, 1995; Welch-Ross, 1995, 2001). Temporally extended self-awareness may also rely upon metarepresentation because it involves understanding present, past and possible future self-representations *as* (alternative) representations of the same temporally extended coherent self (Perner, 2001; Povinelli, 1995; Povinelli & Simon, 1998).

The development of temporal cognition

Certain developments in temporal cognition are also thought to be prerequisites of EM because, unlike semantic memories, episodic memories involve explicitly thinking about the past. More specifically, EM involves representing remembered events as specific past events that occurred at particular times (McCormack & Hoerl, 2001). For this, events need to be understood as unique and unrepeatable. This clearly distinguishes episodic memories from the generalized script-like memories that dominate in early childhood.

McCormack and Hoerl (2001) suggest that EM relies on 'temporal perspective taking' abilities, which, in turn, rely upon having a concept of time that incorporates both 'nonperspectival' and 'perspectival' temporal frameworks. According to their theory, nonperspectival temporal frameworks are conceptual structures that represent the relationships between events located at different points in time, whereas perspectival temporal frameworks represent the temporal location of events in relation to one's own temporal location. Infants of less than 1 year can imitate novel event sequences in the correct order (Bauer, 1997), thereby showing that they represent the temporal order of event sequences – they have a nonperspectival temporal framework. That children comprehend and use tense correctly to describe past and anticipated future events by the time they are 2;6 years old (e.g. Weist, 1989) suggests that by this age they have at least a rudimentary perspectival temporal framework. It is not, however, until around 4 years of age that children can engage in the kind of temporal perspective taking that McCormack and Hoerl argue is fundamental to EM. That is, the ability to imagine events and their relations to each other from a different temporal perspective whilst monitoring the relation between one's present temporal point of view and the one generated in imagination or recalled from memory. This is only possible once metarepresentational ability has developed, because it crucially depends upon understanding that one's current perspective is just one of many possible perspectives. One must not only occupy (in imagination) different temporal perspectives but also explicitly conceive of them *as* temporal perspectives.

Autonoetic remembering also seems to require an understanding of temporal–causal relationships. Although fairly young children have a basic understanding of causality (e.g. Bullock & Gelman, 1979), it is not until around 4 years of age that they realize that more recently occurring events are likely to bear a more direct causal relation to present circumstances than events located in the more distant past (Povinelli *et al.*, 1999). Povinelli *et al.* (1999) suggest that 3-year-olds have difficulty comprehending the 'causal arrow of time' – i.e. conceiving of time as a sequence of chronologically ordered, causally related episodes – and that this may be related to changes in self-concept. Indeed, children's ability to make temporal–causal inferences dramatically improves between the ages of 3 and 5 years (McCormack & Hoerl, 2005). Povinelli and colleagues suggest that, without an appreciation of the causal arrow of time as well as a capacity for metarepresentation, a child cannot understand the causal relation between present, past and future states of self, and thus cannot entertain a temporally extended representation of self or experience autonoetic consciousness.

How might diminished episodic memory in autism be explained?

We now return to the question of why EM is attenuated in people with ASDs. Evidence relating to the development of self-awareness, representational ability and temporal cognition in autism is reviewed, building on material presented in the three main sections of the first part of the chapter. From our review of the evidence, it is concluded that impairments across all three prerequisites for EM contribute to impaired autonoetic consciousness and hence impaired EM in autism.

Impaired self-awareness in people with autism?

The ecological and interpersonal self

Russell (1996) has suggested that autism involves impairments in self-awareness at the most primitive – ecological – level, hypothesizing a fundamental impairment in self-monitoring and, hence, an impaired sense of agency. However, studies have shown that children with ASDs do have awareness of their own agency in the physical/ecological domain. Russell and Hill (2001) and Williams and Happé (in preparation), for example, found that children with autism were capable of identifying which of a number of moving dots displayed on a computer screen, one of which they were able to move with the computer's mouse, was under their control. More generally, individuals with ASDs (who do not have comorbid diagnoses of dyspraxia) have few difficulties in engaging with the physical world, suggesting they are aware of their bodies in relation to the physical environment and that ecological self-awareness is largely intact.

By contrast, individuals with ASDs appear to be less aware of themselves in relation to other people. Many characteristics of autism suggest that interpersonal self-awareness is severely impaired (e.g. Hobson, 1990, 1993; Loveland, 1993; Neisser, 1988; Tomasello, 1995). In typical development, interpersonal self-awareness is obtained through early social interaction, imitation, turn-taking and so on. However, because social interaction among children with ASDs is so impoverished, they cannot acquire the usual wealth of self-relevant information available through such experiences. Some children with autism show indifference to other people, treating them as objects rather than as beings with whom one can meaningfully and contingently interact. Even in less severe cases, interactions tend to be stereotyped and lacking in reciprocity, according to the *Diagnostic and Statistical Manual of Mental Disorders*, 4th edition (DSM-IV; American Psychiatric Association, 1994). The difficulty may be with monitoring self in relation to other in order to coordinate action. Perhaps a specific problem of 'interpersonal agency'?

The conceptual self

There is clear evidence that children with autism do develop an explicit concept of self, albeit one that is somewhat developmentally delayed. What is striking, however, about the self-concepts of these children is their markedly atypical quality. Given that early implicit self-awareness is thought to serve as a foundation for later explicit forms of self-awareness, it is no surprise that interpersonally, but not ecologically, grounded components of explicit self-awareness are impaired in autism. So, for example, MSR is relatively intact, whereas self-conscious emotion, pronoun use, and beliefs about the self are all atypical, as outlined below. Children with autism are capable of *mirror self-recognition* at the appropriate mental age (Dawson & McKissick, 1984; Ferrari & Matthews, 1983; Neuman & Hill, 1978; Spiker & Ricks, 1984). However, successful performance on the task is not evidence of *intact* conceptual self-awareness. It merely suggests that these individuals have conceptual self-knowledge of their typical facial appearance – they have mental representations of what they look like. It is worth noting here that the fact that MSR is relatively unimpaired in children with autism, whereas EM is impaired, weakens Howe and Courage's (1993) claim that MSR marks the critical cognitive change underlying EM.

The interpersonally grounded component of conceptual self-awareness has been explored in studies of children's conscious awareness of themselves in social situations. In particular, the experience of *self-conscious emotion* is clearly interpersonally grounded. Factors such as personal responsibility, normative standards, and the role of an audience, have been identified as important for the experience of these emotions (Capps, Yirmiya & Sigman, 1992). None of the MSR studies carried out with children with ASDs reported the kind of self-conscious affective reactions that occur among typically developing children in this test. More generally, it seems that individuals with autism are less likely to spontaneously experience these emotions (see Faran & Ben Shalom, this volume, Chapter 5). They do not show the characteristic changes in facial expression, posture or gestures that are associated with these emotional states (Kasari, Chamberlain & Bauminger, 2001). For example, although they experience pleasure, they are less likely to experience pride, in response to a personal achievement (Kasari *et al.*, 1993). It is possible, however, that the problem here lies not with conceptual self-awareness but, rather, with lack of awareness of the presence of others or lack of awareness of social standards. It has also been reported that they are less likely to empathize with others (Sigman *et al.*, 1992). This is important because the capacity for empathy entails an understanding that self is like other, whilst also representing self and other as distinct individuals. Reduced empathizing capacity may, therefore, reflect an impaired concept of self, at least at an emotional level.

There is also an autism-specific deficit in another of the established behavioural markers of conceptual self-awareness: *personal pronoun use*. Since Kanner's (1943) seminal paper, it has been widely acknowledged that individuals with autism tend to have difficulty using personal pronouns such as 'I', 'you' and 'me'. In young children with autism, pronoun reversal errors are relatively common (Lee, Hobson & Chiat, 1994; Tager-Flusberg, 1989). Indeed, the problem exists over and above any general language impairment, and is so prevalent that it is used as a diagnostic criterion for autism (Le Couteur, Lord & Rutter, 2003). Typical patterns of difficulty include treating pronouns as if they were proper names attached to a fixed referent – saying, for example, 'You want a drink' in order to request a drink for themselves. Other characteristic difficulties include substituting third-person pronouns such as 'he' or 'she' or proper names for first-person pronouns (Jordan, 1989). Using third-person labels in this way circumvents the problem of shifting referents involved in pronoun use. Appropriate pronoun use is clearly an interpersonally grounded facet of conceptual self-awareness since it requires an understanding of self in relation to others.

Lee and Hobson (1998) assessed conceptual self-knowledge using Damon and Hart's (1988) self-understanding interview to compare the *beliefs about the self* of a group of children and adolescents with autism to those of a matched comparison group. Their results fit the emerging pattern, in that ecologically grounded conceptual self-knowledge was intact but interpersonally grounded conceptual self-knowledge was impaired. Specifically, participants with autism produced significantly more, but qualitatively similar, descriptions of their physical and active characteristics, relative to the comparison group. Self-descriptive statements of psychological and social characteristics, on the other hand, differed qualitatively from those of comparison children and, in the latter instance, quantitatively, in that they produced significantly fewer descriptions that fell into the social category.

The private self

Autism clearly entails a serious impairment in private self-awareness. This may be regarded as a specific manifestation of the ToM impairment associated with autism. Individuals with ASDs have difficulty not only with understanding others' mental states but also with understanding their own. For example, children with autism have equal difficulty attributing knowledge or ignorance to self or other depending upon whether that person has had informational access to that knowledge (e.g. through seeing or being told about a piece of information) (Kazak, Collis & Lewis, 1997; Perner et al., 1989). Furthermore, they find it difficult to distinguish their own intended from unintended actions. In particular, when their unintended actions have a desirable outcome they show a tendency to claim that their action was, in fact, deliberate (Philips, Baron-Cohen & Rutter, 1998; however, Russell & Hill, 2001, failed to replicate this finding). This suggests an impairment of introspective awareness – difficulty with conceptualizing their own mental processes.

These problems appear to extend to the emotional domain also. Again, individuals with autism are not only impaired in identifying emotions in others but also in processing their own emotional states. In a recent study, Hill, Berthoz and Frith (2004) asked adult participants to complete a questionnaire assessing own emotion processing. They found that, compared to a typically developing comparison group, participants with high-functioning autism reported greater difficulties in identifying and describing their feelings and showed a greater propensity for externally oriented thinking. Similarly, Ben Shalom *et al.* (2006) reported that children with ASDs showed normal physiological emotional reactions, as measured by galvanic skin response, but impaired ability to report these emotions. Thus, impaired private self-awareness is evident in adults as well as children with ASDs.

Frith and Happé (1999) suggest that those high-functioning individuals who do develop some introspective awareness (many individuals produce elaborate autobiographical accounts) have done so through a 'slow and painstaking learning process' (Frith & Happé, 1999, p. 2), developing a qualitatively different kind of self-consciousness. In a study of three adults with Asperger syndrome, Hurlburt, Happé and Frith (1994) did, indeed, find that self-reported inner experiences differed markedly from those reported by typically developing individuals. Specifically, participants with Asperger syndrome reported thoughts that were concrete and factually based comprising mainly visual images. Most intriguingly, they did not report any form of inner speech and tended not to report emotions or bodily sensations. This suggests that private self-awareness, like conceptual self-awareness, is qualitatively different in individuals with ASDs.

The temporally extended self

In a recent study of delayed self-recognition, Lind and Bowler (in preparation) found that children with ASDs tended to remove the stickers which had been covertly placed on their heads by the experimenter only when asked explicitly to do so. By contrast, comparison children tended to remove the sticker without direct prompting. These results are suggestive of impaired temporally extended self-awareness. There is also indirect evidence of such an impairment. Young typically developing children who fail DSR, tend to label past self-images such as photographs and video recordings using their own name, rather than saying 'me' (Povinelli, Landau & Perilloux, 1996). Taking a third-person stance, by using a proper name, may well indicate an inability to identify with the depicted image (past self-representation), which may require a sense of personal continuity through time. Indeed, it is at least possible that those children who labelled the image using their proper name were not recognizing the videos/photographs as themselves but, rather, showing a simple learned association between 'that face' and 'that name'. Lind and Bowler (in preparation) found that participants with ASD were significantly more likely than comparison participants to label their own video image using their proper name. Lee, Hobson and Chiat (1994) also found that, in contrast to comparison children, even fairly verbally able children with autism showed this same propensity to use proper names in a photograph naming task. This observation is suggestive of an impairment, or delay in the development of, a temporally extended self in children with autism.

To summarize, let us once again consider how Neisser's (1988) five kinds of self-awareness, as described in the section on the development of self in typical children, manifest themselves in people with autism. The evidence reviewed earlier in the chapter suggests that although ecological self-awareness is probably intact, interpersonal self-awareness is not. Conceptual self-awareness is also atypical, as is evident from, amongst other things, abnormal pronoun use, self-conscious emotion and the formation of beliefs about the self that have social connotations. If autonoetic consciousness depends upon explicit self-awareness, it can be inferred that anything that disrupts this development may potentially impact upon EM. Impairments in conceptual, private and temporally extended self-awareness are likely to contribute directly to the EM impairment in autism. Impairments in interpersonal self-awareness may have indirect effects through altering the development of explicit self-awareness.

The claim that impaired sense of self contributes to EM impairments in autism is consistent with the fact that individuals with ASDs have particular difficulties when memory tasks demand a high degree of self-involvement (e.g. Millward et al., 2000; Russell & Jarrold, 1999; see also Toichi, this volume, Chapter 8). However, it is clear that EM depends upon more than self-awareness. As explained above it requires certain (related) representational and temporal-cognitive skills. This is discussed below.

Impaired representational abilities?

The same underlying difficulty in ToM/metarepresentation that leads to impairments in private self-awareness is also likely to impact upon the capacity of people with ASDs to experience autonoetic consciousness. Consequently, much of the evidence reported in the section on private self-awareness in autism is relevant here. Impaired performance on ToM tasks is usually interpreted as the result of difficulty with metarepresentation – with conceptualizing mental states. Metarepresentational problems would mean that individuals with autism would not be aware of their own propositional attitudes to the information in their own minds. Thus, memories could not be identified *as* memories and, therefore, could not be consciously reflected upon as memories. This might explain why recall in autism seems to be dominated by knowing rather than remembering (Bowler, Gardiner & Grice, 2000; Bowler, Gardiner & Gaigg, 2007).

An impairment of temporal cognition?

As mentioned above, mental time travel requires past- or future-oriented thinking. Problems with these forms of cognition may well contribute to the observed impairments. Both clinical and anecdotal accounts suggest that people with autism have a 'poor intuitive sense of time' (Boucher, 2001, p. 111). It is notable, also, that cognitive problems in autism include difficulty in both thinking backwards (episodic remembering) and thinking forwards (planning) through time (e.g. Bowler, Gardiner & Grice, 2000; Ozonoff, Pennington & Rogers, 1991).

Very little work directly assessing temporal cognition in autism has been reported. Recently, however, Boucher *et al.* (2007) found that children and adolescents with ASDs were impaired relative to a matched comparison group on a number of tests designed to assess the ability to use temporal concepts in thinking and reasoning. Of particular note was the fact that the experimental group had significantly more difficulties with both past- and future-oriented think-ing. So, for example, one of the tests involved presenting the children with a picture of a seaside scene and asking them to describe what was happening. Participants with autism were less likely to describe possible antecedents or consequents of the currently depicted state of affairs. Unlike comparison children, who produced descriptions such as 'That man's lying on the mat – he'll get sunburned if he's not careful', children with autism tended to describe the scene primarily in terms of the present moment, producing descriptions such as 'There's a person surfing. And someone sunbathing.' These problems with past- and future-oriented thinking were not related to performance on a battery of tests of theory of mind, suggesting that difficulties with temporal cognition – particularly the ability to make temporal-causal inferences – could contribute to EM impairments independently of difficulties associated with impaired metarepresentation. What we do not yet know, however, is whether individuals with autism can form and coordinate perspectival and nonperspectival temporal frameworks. If this ability were to be impaired then it may well contribute to EM impairments.

Summary

Experimental evidence shows that individuals with autism have diminished EM and the self-involved, time-related experiences of autonoetic awareness that accompany this kind of remembering. The aim of this chapter was to establish the cause, or causes, of this impairment. There are a number of possible explanations, as is evident from a review of the prerequisites for the development of EM in typically developing children. These include the normal development of self-awareness. It has been claimed, for example, that the development of a self-concept indexed by successful mirror self-recognition is the critical prerequisite for EM. Related to the development of self are changes in representational abilities, from primary to secondary representations, to metarepresentation. A third prerequisite for the development of EM is an ability to think and reason about time. Impaired metarepresentation is often considered to offer a sufficient explanation of impaired EM in autism. Whilst accepting that diminished ability to conceive of one's own mental states could impact on EM in various ways, an explanation in terms of impaired metarepresentational ability may be too strong in view of the evidence that there is some residual self-awareness in relation to memory in this population. Moreover, there is some evidence of impaired temporal cognition in people with ASDs, occurring independently of any impairment of metarepresentational abilities. Impaired temporal cognition is consistent with our suggestion that people with ASDs have an impoverished concept of the temporally extended self. We also present evidence that the development of self is abnormal in people with autism at the foundational stage of an implicit interpersonal self, and argue that this has secondary effects on the acquisition of an explicit self-concept. What remains to be explained is how evolving conceptions of self and of events strung out in time are related, and how they interact with other areas of psychological functioning.

Acknowledgements

The authors would like to thank the Economic and Social Research Council, the Medical Research Council, the Wellcome Trust and the Department of Psychology, City University, for financial support in the preparation of this chapter.

References

American Psychiatric Association (1994). *Diagnostic and statistical manual of mental disorders*, 4th edn (DSM-IV). Washington, DC: American Psychiatric Association.

Amsterdam, B. (1972). Mirror self-image reactions before age two. *Developmental Psychobiology*, 5, 297–305.

Anderson, J. R. (1983). The development of self-recognition: a review. *Developmental Psychobiology*, 17, 35–49.

Asendorpf, J. B., Warkentin, V. & Baudonnière, P. M. (1996). Self-awareness and other awareness II: mirror self-recognition, social contingency awareness, and synchronic imitation. *Developmental Psychology*, 32, 313–321.

Atance, C. M. & O'Neill, D. (2005). The emergence of episodic future thinking in humans. *Learning and Motivation*, 36, 126–144.

Bates, E. (1990). Language about me and you: pronominal reference and the emerging concept of self. In D. C. Cicchetti & M. Beeghly (eds.), *The self in transition: infancy to childhood*, pp. 165–182. Chicago: University of Chicago Press.

Bauer, P. J. (1997). Development of memory in early childhood. In N. Cowan (ed.), *The development of memory in childhood*, pp. 83–111. Hove: Psychology Press.

Ben Shalom, D. (2003). Memory in autism: review and synthesis. *Cortex*, 39, 1129–1138.

Ben Shalom, D., Mostofsky, S. H., Hazlett, R. L., Goldberg, M. C., Landa, R. J., Faran, Y., McLeod, D. F. & Hoehn-Saric, R. (2006). Normal physiological emotions but differences in expression of conscious feelings in children with high-functioning autism. *Journal of Autism and Developmental Disorders*, 36, 395–400.

Bennetto, L., Pennington, B. & Rogers, S. J. (1996). Intact and impaired memory functions in autism. *Child Development*, 67, 1816–1835.

Boucher, J. (2001). 'Lost in a sea of time': time parsing and autism. In C. Hoerl & T. McCormack (eds.), *Time and memory: issues in philosophy and psychology*, pp. 111–135. Oxford: Clarendon Press.

Boucher, J., Pons, F., Lind, S. & Williams, D. (2007). Temporal cognition in children with autistic spectrum disorders: tests of diachronic perspective taking. *Journal of Autism and Developmental Disorders*, 37, 1413–1429.

Bowler, D., Gardiner, J. & Grice, S. (2000). Episodic memory and remembering in adults with Asperger syndrome. *Journal of Autism and Developmental Disorders*, 30, 295–304.

Bowler, D. M., Gardiner, J. M. & Gaigg, S. B. (2007). Factors affecting conscious awareness in the recollective experience of adults with Asperger's syndrome. *Consciousness and Cognition*, 16, 124–143.

Bullock, M. & Gelman, R. (1979). Preschool children's assumptions about cause and effect: temporal ordering. *Child Development*, 50, 89–96.

Capps, L., Yirmiya, N. & Sigman, M. (1992). Understanding of simple and complex emotions in non-retarded children with autism. *Journal of Child Psychology and Psychiatry and Allied Disciplines*, 33, 1169–1182.

Courage, M. L., Edison, S. C. & Howe, M. L. (2004). Variability in the early development of visual self-recognition. *Infant Behaviour and Development*, 27, 509–532.

Cowan, N. (ed.) (1997). *The development of memory in childhood*. Hove: Psychology Press.

Damon, W. & Hart, D. (1988). *Self-understanding in childhood and adolescence.* New York: Cambridge University Press.

Dawson, G. & McKissick, F. C. (1984). Self-recognition in autistic children. *Journal of Autism and Developmental Disorders, 14,* 383–394.

DeCaspar, A. J. & Fifer, W. P. (1980). On human bonding: newborns prefer their mother's voices. *Science, 208,* 1174–1176.

Ferrari, M. & Matthews, W. S. (1983). Self-recognition deficits in autism: syndrome-specific or general developmental delay? *Journal of Autism and Developmental Disorders, 13,* 317–324.

Frith, U. & Happé, F. (1999). Theory of mind and self-consciousness: what is it like to be autistic? *Mind and Language, 14,* 1–22.

Gibson, E. J. (1995). Are we automata? In P. Rochat (ed.), *The self in infancy: theory and research,* pp. 3–15. Amsterdam: Elsevier/North Holland.

Gopnick, A. & Meltzoff, A. N. (1994). Minds, bodies, and persons: young children's understanding of the self and other as reflected in imitation and theory of mind research. In S. T. Parker, R. W. Mitchell & M. L. Boccia (eds.), *Self-awareness in animals and humans,* pp. 166–186. New York: Cambridge University Press.

Happé, F. (2003). Theory of mind and the self. *Annals of the New York Academy of Sciences, 1001,* 134–144.

Hill, E., Berthoz, S. & Frith, U. (2004). Brief report: cognitive processing of own emotions in individuals with autistic spectrum disorder and in their relatives. *Journal of Autism and Developmental Disorders, 34,* 229–235.

Hobson, R. P. (1990). On the origins of self and the case of autism. *Development and Psychopathology, 2,* 163–181.

  (1993). Through feeling and sight to self and symbol. In U. Neisser (ed.), *The perceived self: ecological and interpersonal sources of self-knowledge,* pp. 254–279. Cambridge: Cambridge University Press.

Howe, M. L. & Courage, M. L. (1993). On resolving the enigma of infantile amnesia. *Psychological Bulletin, 113,* 305–326.

Howe, M. L., Courage, M. L. & Edison, S. C. (2003). When autobiographical memory begins. *Developmental Review, 23,* 471–494.

Hurlburt, R. T., Happé, F. & Frith, U. (1994). Sampling the form of inner experience in three adults with Asperger syndrome. *Psychological Medicine, 24,* 385–395.

James, W. (1890). *The principles of psychology.* New York: Holt.

Jordan, R. R. (1989). An experimental comparison of the understanding and use of speaker-addressee personal pronouns in autistic children. *British Journal of Disorders of Communication, 24,* 169–172.

Kanner, L. (1943). Autistic disturbances of affective contact. *Nervous Child, 2,* 217–250.

Kasari, C., Chamberlain, G. & Bauminger, N. (2001). Social emotions and social relationships: can children with autism compensate? In J. A. Burack & T. Charman (eds.), *The development of autism: perspectives from theory and research,* pp. 309–323. Mahwah, NJ: Erlbaum.

Kasari, C., Sigman, M. D., Baumgartner, P. & Stipek, D. J. (1993). Pride and mastery in children with autism. *Journal of Child Psychology and Psychiatry, 34,* 353–362.

Kazak, S., Collis, G. M. & Lewis, V. (1997). Can young people with autism refer to knowledge states? Evidence from their understanding of 'know' and 'guess'. *Journal of Child Psychology and Psychiatry, 38,* 1001–1009.

Le Couteur, A., Lord, C. & Rutter, M. (2003). *Autism diagnostic interview–revised.* Los Angeles, CA: Western Psychological Services.

Lee, A. & Hobson, R. P. (1998). On developing self-concepts: a controlled study of children and adolescents with autism. *Journal of Child Psychology and Psychiatry, 39,* 1131–1144.

Lee, A., Hobson, R. P. & Chiat, S. (1994). I, you, me, and autism: an experimental study. *Journal of Autism and Developmental Disorders, 24,* 155–176.

Lemmon, K. & Moore, C. (2001). Binding the self in time. In C. Moore & K. Lemmon (eds.), *The self in time: developmental perspectives,* pp. 163–179. Hillsdale, NJ: Erlbaum.

Lewis, M. (1994). Myself and me. In S. T. Parker, R. W. Mitchell & M. L. Boccia (eds.), *Self-awareness in animals and humans,* pp. 20–34. New York: Cambridge University Press.

Lewis, M. & Ramsey, D. (2004). Development of self-recognition, personal pronoun use, and pretend play during the 2nd year. *Child Development, 75,* 1821–1831.

Lewis, M., Sullivan, M. W., Stanger, C. & Weiss, M. (1989). Self development and self-conscious emotion. *Child Development, 60,* 146–156.

Lind, S. E. & Bowler, D. M. (in preparation). Delayed self-recognition in autism spectrum disorder: evidence for impaired temporally extended self-awareness.

Loveland, K. A. (1986). Discovering the affordances of a reflective surface. *Developmental Review, 6,* 1–24.

    (1993). Autism, affordances, and the self. In U. Neisser (ed.), *The perceived self: ecological and interpersonal sources of self-knowledge,* pp. 237–253. Cambridge: Cambridge University Press.

McCormack, T. & Hoerl, C. (2001). The child in time: temporal concepts and self-consciousness in the development of episodic memory. In C. Moore & K. Lemmon (eds.), *The self in time: developmental perspectives,* pp. 203–227. Hillsdale, NJ: Erlbaum.

    (2005). Children's reasoning about the causal significance of the temporal order of events. *Developmental Psychology, 41,* 54–63.

Millward, C., Powell, S., Messer, D. & Jordan, R. (2000). Recall for self and other in autism: children's memory for events experienced by themselves and their peers. *Journal of Autism and Developmental Disorders, 30,* 15–28.

Minshew, N. J. & Goldstein, G. (2001). The pattern of intact and impaired memory functions in autism. *Journal of Child Psychology and Psychiatry, 42,* 1095–1101.

Mitchell, R. W. (1993). Mental models of mirror self-recognition: two theories. *New Ideas in Psychology, 11,* 295–325.

    (1997). Kinesthetic-visual matching and the self-concept as explanations of mirror-self-recognition. *Journal for the Theory of Social Behaviour, 27,* 17–39.

Moore, C. & Lemmon, K. (eds.) (2001). *The self in time: developmental perspectives.* Hillsdale, NJ: Erlbaum.

Murray, L. & Trevarthen, C. (1985). Emotional regulation of interactions between 2-month-olds and their mothers. In T. M. Field & N. A. Fox (eds.), *Social perception in infants,* pp. 177–197. Norwood, NJ: Ablex.

Naito, M. (2003). The relationship between theory of mind and episodic memory: evidence for the development of autonoetic consciousness. *Journal of Experimental Child Psychology, 85,* 312–336.

Neisser, U. (1988). Five kinds of self-knowledge. *Philosophical Psychology, 1,* 35–59.

    (1995). Criteria for an ecological self. In P. Rochat (ed.), *The self in infancy: theory and research,* pp. 17–34. Amsterdam: Elsevier/North Holland.

    (1997). Concepts and self-concepts. In U. Neisser & D. A. Jopling (eds.), *The conceptual self in context: culture, experience and self-understanding,* pp. 3–12. New York: Cambridge University Press.

Nelson, K. & Fivush, R. (2004). The emergence of autobiographical memory: a social cultural developmental theory. *Psychological Review, 111,* 486–511.

Neuman, C. J. & Hill, S. D. (1978). Self-recognition and stimulus preference in autistic children. *Developmental Psychobiology, 11,* 571–578.

Ozonoff, S., Pennington, B. & Rogers, S. (1991). Executive function deficits in high-functioning autistic individuals: relationship to theory of mind. *Journal of Child Psychology and Psychiatry, 32,* 1081–1105.

Perner, J. (1991). *Understanding the Representational Mind.* Cambridge, MA: MIT Press.

    (2000). Memory and theory of mind. In E. Tulving & F. I. M. Craik (eds.), *The Oxford handbook of memory,* pp. 297–312. Oxford: Oxford University Press.

    (2001). Episodic memory: essential distinctions and developmental implications. In C. Moore & K. Lemmon (eds.), *The self in time: developmental perspectives,* pp. 181–202. Hillsdale, NJ: Erlbaum.

Perner, J., Frith, U., Leslie, A. M. & Leekam, S. R. (1989). Explorations of the autistic child's theory of mind: knowledge, belief, and communication. *Child Development, 60,* 689–700.

Perner, J., Kloo, D. & Gornick, E. (in press). Episodic memory development: theory of mind is part of re-experiencing experienced events. *Infant and Child Development.*

Perner, J. & Ruffman, T. (1995). Episodic memory and autonoetic consciousness: developmental evidence and a theory of childhood amnesia. *Journal of Experimental Child Psychology, 59,* 516–548.

Philips, W., Baron-Cohen, S. & Rutter, M. (1998). Understanding intention in normal development and autism. *British Journal of Developmental Psychology, 16,* 337–348.

Povinelli, D. J. (1995). The unduplicated self. In P. Rochat (ed.), *The self in infancy: theory and research,* pp. 161–191. Amsterdam: Elsevier/North Holland.

Povinelli, D. J., Landau, K. R. & Perilloux, H. K. (1996). Self-recognition in young children using delayed versus live feedback: evidence of a developmental asynchrony. *Child Development, 67,* 1540–1554.

Povinelli, D. J., Landry, A. M., Theall, L. A., Clark, B. R. & Castille, C. M. (1999). Development of young children's understanding that the recent past is causally bound to the present. *Developmental Psychology, 35,* 1426–1439.

Povinelli, D. J. & Simon, B. B. (1998). Young children's understanding of briefly versus extremely delayed images of self: emergence of the autobiographical stance. *Developmental Psychology, 34,* 188–194.

Rochat, P. (ed.) (1995). *The self in infancy: theory and research.* Amsterdam: Elsevier/North Holland.

Rochat, P. & Hespos, S. J. (1997). Differential rooting response by neonates: evidence for an early sense of self. *Early Development and Parenting, 6,* 105–112.

Russell, J. (1996). *Agency: its role in mental development.* Hove: Erlbaum.

Russell, J. & Hill, E. L. (2001). Action monitoring and intention reporting in children with autism. *Journal of Child Psychology and Psychiatry, 42,* 317–328.

Russell, J. & Jarrold, C. (1999). Memory for actions in children with autism: self versus other. *Cognitive Neuropsychiatry, 4,* 303–331.

Schacter, D. L. & Tulving, E. (1994). What are the memory systems of 1994? In D. L. Schacter & E. Tulving (eds.), *Memory systems 1994,* pp. 1–38. Cambridge, MA: MIT Press.

Sigman, M. D., Kasari, C., Kwon, J. H. & Yirmiya, N. (1992). Responses to negative emotions of others by autistic, mentally retarded, and normal children. *Child Development, 63,* 786–807.

Siqueland, E. R. & DeLucia, C. A. (1969). Visual reinforcement of nonnutritive sucking in human infants. *Science, 165,* 1144–1146.

Spiker, D. & Ricks, M. (1984). Visual self-recognition in autistic children: developmental relationships. *Child Development, 55,* 214–225.

Suddendorf, T. (1999). Children's understanding of the relation between delayed video representation and current reality: a test for self-awareness? *Journal of Experimental Child Psychology, 72,* 157–176.

Suddendorf, T. & Corballis, M. C. (1997). Mental time travel and the evolution of the human mind. *Genetic, Social, and General Psychology Monographs, 123,* 133–167.

Suddendorf, T. & Whiten, A. (2001). Mental evolution and development: evidence for secondary representation in children, great apes, and other animals. *Psychological Bulletin, 127,* 629–650.

Tager-Flusberg, H. (1989). An analysis of discourse ability and internal state lexicons in a longitudinal study of autistic children. Paper presented at the Biennial Meeting of the Society for Research in Child Development, Kansas City, April 1989.

Tomasello, M. (1995). Understanding the self as a social agent. In P. Rochat (ed.), *The self in infancy: theory and research,* pp. 449–460. Amsterdam: Elsevier/North Holland.

Tracy, J. L. & Robins, R. W. (2004). Putting the self into self-conscious emotions: a theoretical model. *Psychological Inquiry, 15,* 103–125.

Trevarthen, C. & Aitken, K. J. (2001). Infant intersubjectivity: research, theory, and clinical applications. *Journal of Child Psychology and Psychiatry, 42,* 3–48.

Weist, R. M. (1989). Time concepts in language and thought: filling the Piagetian void from two to five years. In I. Levin & D. Zakay (eds.), *Time and human cognition: a lifespan perspective*, pp. 63–118. Amsterdam: North Holland.

Welch-Ross, M. K. (1995). An integrative model of the development of autobiographical memory. *Developmental Review, 15*, 338–365.

(2001). Personalizing the temporally extended self: evaluative self-awareness and the development of autobiographical memory. In C. Moore & K. Lemmon (eds.), *The self in time: developmental perspectives*, pp. 97–120. Hillsdale, NJ: Erlbaum.

Wheeler, M., Stuss, D. & Tulving, E. (1997). Towards a theory of episodic memory: the frontal lobes and autonoetic consciousness. *Psychological Bulletin, 121*, 331–354.

Williams, D. & Happé, F. (in preparation). Unimpaired awareness of agency in autism spectrum disorder.

Zelazo, P. D., Sommerville, J. A. & Nichols, S. (1999). Age-related changes in children's use of external representations. *Developmental Psychology, 35*, 1059–1071.

10 Impairments in social memory in autism? Evidence from behaviour and neuroimaging

Sara Jane Webb

Introduction

Memory has been described as both a weakness and strength in individuals with autism spectrum disorders (ASDs). This conflict reflects the complexity and diversity of definitions of memory: much of human development involves memory functions, and these functions may differ on both the underlying neural circuitry and the type of encoding, storage and retrieval mechanisms needed. Everyday memory tasks for children include explicit recall and use of factual information (e.g. What is the capital of Washington State?), improved behaviour during repeated motor actions (e.g. riding a bike), or generalization of an event into a schema (e.g. ordering lunch at *any* restaurant). Whilst impairments in the medial temporal lobe have been proposed to play a role in autism (e.g. Bachevalier, 1994; Dawson *et al.*, 2003; DeLong, 1992; and also Bachevalier, this volume, Chapter 2, Mayes & Boucher, this volume, Chapter 3), they represent but one of a number of phenotypes that are related to autism. Further, comorbid conditions such as impulsivity, anxiety, hyper- and hypo-sensory responses, fine motor impairments, oculomotor abnormalities, and seizure disorders found in subsets of children may further impair cognitive function and specifically memory.

Autism is defined by impairments in the areas of social interaction and communication and marked by the presence of a restricted repertoire of behavioural activities and interest. Impairments can be seen in the decreased use of nonverbal behaviours to regulate social and communicative interactions, a lack of understanding of social conventions, an absence of spontaneous enjoyment of others and of emotional reciprocity, impaired awareness of others, inflexible behaviours and preoccupations, and a narrowed range of interests. Whilst these descriptions only highlight some of the behaviours in autism, the core feature of the disorder involves anomalies in attention to and use of social information. These behaviours are juxtaposed with examples of memory as an area of potential sparing. For example, some children with ASDs demonstrate memory abilities that far exceed performance expectations based on mental age. Despite the presence of preserved or even exceptional memory abilities, these behaviours often seem limited or domain specific.

The goal of this chapter is to address the question of whether or not individuals with ASDs have memory impairments that are specific to social stimuli. To this end, the first section will review what is known about memory for faces, voices and emotion in individuals with autism. The second section will examine the neural basis of memory for familiar items. And lastly, current hypotheses suggesting that memory impairments are the consequence of impairments in the medial temporal lobe, or of impairments of perception and encoding, attention, social motivation or expertise will be explored.

Social memory and behaviour

Face processing and memory

One of the early descriptions of autism highlighted the affected individual's indifference towards the faces of others (Kanner, 1943). This failure to attend to others, to look at faces, may be one of the earliest indicators of autism (Werner et al., 2000). Evidence suggests that human infants are biased to attend to face-like stimuli, with rapid development over the first year in the skills associated with encoding, differentiating and forming memories for faces (for reviews see de Haan, Humphreys & Johnson, 2002; Nelson, 2001). The maturation of face processing skills extends through late childhood and early adolescence (e.g. Aylward et al., 2005; Carey & Diamond, 1977; Taylor et al., 1999). During recognition of familiar faces, young children (5 to 6 years of age) rely more on outer face features such as hair or ears, while 9- to 10-year-old children mostly use internal features (Campbell & Tuck, 1995). Around the same time children begin to rely less on irrelevant paraphernalia to recognize unfamiliar faces (Flin, 1985) but are still less efficient at using spatial relations or second-order relations (Mondloch et al., 2004). Both featural and configural encoding are important to face recognition (Flin, 1985; Collishaw & Hole, 2000). There is consensus that by adulthood configural processing is critical for recognition, as performance declines when faces are inverted (e.g. Farah, Tanaka & Drain, 1995).

Both face processing and face memory have received extensive study both in terms of typical developmental processes as well as in individuals with autism. To assess face processing, a discrimination task or a matching task is often used. In these types of tasks, the example and the test stimuli are presented simultaneously such that real-time comparative processes can occur. Importantly, the participant does not need to form a representation, store it and recall it for use later. Studies of face processing in autism have shown that by middle childhood, children with ASDs perform worse than peers matched for mental age and chronological age on a number of tasks including tests of face discrimination (Tantam *et al.*, 1989), lip reading, gender and gaze discrimination (Deruelle *et al.*, 2004; but see Gepner, de Gelder & de Schonen, 1996) and face–voice matching (Boucher, Lewis & Collis, 1998).

Face memory involves recognition of familiar faces as well as learning and memory for new faces. Boucher, Lewis and Collis (1998) asked children with autism and comparison children matched for verbal and chronological age to identify pictures of faces as either those of individuals working at their own school, or 'at another school' (i.e. individuals unfamiliar to the child). Children with autism correctly identified fewer faces than the comparison participants, and performance on this task was correlated with performance on a familiar face–voice matching task. Of note, 3 out of 19 children with an ASD, and 7 out of the 20 comparison children performed at ceiling. On the other end of performance, 4 out of the 19 children with an ASD performed below the lowest score of the comparison group. This range demonstrates considerable variability in performance. One potential source of variability may be symptom severity. In a large sample of children with ASDs, Klin *et al.* (1999) found that children with autism but not children with PDD-NOS (pervasive developmental disorder – not otherwise specified) performed worse than nonverbal mental-age-matched comparison children and verbal mental-age-matched comparison children on a test of face memory, although there were no differences between groups on a test of spatial memory.

Face memory vs other stimulus memory

To determine relative deficits in social memory, social and nonsocial memory tasks must be equivalent so that differences in performance cannot be accounted for by a secondary characteristic of the stimuli or by differences in the task structure. At the perceptual level, differences in stimulation of lower-level sensory systems can lead to differences in perception and attention. At the task level, differences in the number of items the participant is asked to remember or in the delay period could result in performance differences between groups. In this section, the focus will be on experiments that utilize the same task structure but employ different types of stimuli.

For children with typical development (TD), memory is better for faces compared to nonface visual stimuli (Hauck *et al.*, 1998). By contrast, children with autism do not show superior memory for faces as compared to nonface stimuli: two studies have shown that children with autism perform comparably on face and nonface tasks (Hauck *et al.*, 1998; Serra *et al.*, 2003), and another study showed that they perform worse on a face memory as compared with a nonface memory task (Boucher & Lewis, 1992). Furthermore, in all three of these studies, the children with ASDs performed worse than comparison children on the face memory task.

Memory for faces may not, however, be the only aspect of face processing that is impaired. In their study, Boucher and Lewis (1992) also investigated face vs nonface discrimination ability, and found that although the children with ASDs were not impaired in face discrimination compared with a developmentally delayed matched comparison group, they were worse at discriminating between faces than they were at discriminating between buildings, a discrepancy which did not occur in the comparison group. The authors concluded that impaired performance on the face recognition task could not be accounted for by impairments in face discrimination or attention. In another study in which face and nonface discrimination ability was assessed, children and adolescents with Asperger Syndrome (AS) performed worse on tasks involving matching of faces *and* geometric forms in contrast to a comparison group (Davies *et al.*, 1994).

In an older sample, adults with ASDs performed worse than comparison groups matched for chronological age and verbal IQ on a test of face memory; their performance on the face memory test was also significantly worse than their performance on a test of memory for buildings (Blair *et al.*, 2002). Further, the adults with autism performed better on tests of memory for nonanimate living items (leaves) than for either animate living items (cats, horses) or nonliving animate items (motorbikes). Comparison participants showed no difference in memory for leaves, cats, horses or motorbikes and there were no differences between the autism group and the comparison group matched for verbal mental age on these tests (Blair *et al.*, 2002).

Memory for features of faces

Impaired performance on face tasks compared to tasks using nonface stimuli begs the question of whether or not individuals with ASDs are utilizing a less efficient strategy when forming memories for faces. There is general consensus that mature face encoding and discrimination utilizes both holistic and configural processing strategies (e.g. Diamond & Carey, 1986; Farah, Tanaka & Drain, 1995); and holistic and configural processing strategies are found in children with typical development between 4 and 16 years of age (Flin, 1985; Freire & Lee, 2001; Tanaka *et al.*, 1998). One source of evidence leading to this conclusion is the fact that TD children generally show superior performance for upright compared to inverted faces (e.g. Itier & Taylor, 2004; Joseph & Tanaka, 2003; Sangrigoli & de Schonen, 2004), and inversion is thought to disrupt holistic and configural processing and result in reliance on feature-based strategies. Comparisons between the processing of upright and inverted faces is one of the methods that has been used to investigate face encoding in individuals with autism. A second method for examining encoding strategies in people with autism has been to look at memory and performance when facial information is obscured or absent, such as when only the lower half of the face is presented. This allows a direct test of what information is necessary or sufficient to make correct memory decisions. The results of studies using both these methods are summarized below.

On tasks using upright and inverted faces as stimuli, children with ASDs have either demonstrated equivalent performance (Valentine, 1988; Langdell, 1978) or, in one study, superior ability to process inverted faces, in contrast to comparison participants (Hobson, Ouston & Lee, 1988). In another study (Joseph & Tanaka, 2003), children with ASDs showed an upright advantage (increased recognition accuracy) when whole face recognition depended on the mouth region. When face recognition depended on the eye region, however, recognition scores did not differ for upright faces vs inverted faces. Thus, children with ASDs were affected by inversion and could use holistic strategies, but this was dependent on the part of the face that was needed to make the recognition judgement.

Children with autism may also be attending to different areas of the face. Although children with ASDs could recognize the faces of classmates, Langdell (1978) found that they were less able to judge identity using the eye region or upper part of the face, suggesting differential attention strategies. Children with ASDs have also been reported to show better performance when recognizing isolated facial features and partially obscured faces than typical children (Hobson, Ouston & Lee, 1988; Tantam *et al.*, 1989). However, Wilson, Pascalis and Blades (2006) found that children with ASDs did not differ from children with developmental delay on identifying familiar faces in a forced choice recognition paradigm based on whether the information included the full face, the inner face, or only the outer face area. These results, taken together, suggest that children with ASDs rely on different information from the face and/or different processing strategies to perform face memory tasks. The degree to which this is specific to ASD is unclear and the deficits underlying these impairments are unknown. One possibility is that comparison children with developmental delay may also have social deficits; thus deficits in social ability, not the specific diagnosis, may be related to alternative processing strategies.

Memory for voices

People are not only identifiable by their faces but by their voices. Boucher, Lewis and Collis (1998) found that children with autism were impaired in matching the voices and faces of familiar people and in recognizing the voices of familiar people in contrast to comparison participants matched on verbal mental age. Of note, 5 children were unable to perform the test – 3 children did not complete training and 2 children were unwilling to finish testing. These same children were able to meet criteria for training and were able to successfully complete all test trials on the familiar face test. One interpretation is that the children had more difficulty on memory for voices compared to faces. However, in a more recent study, the same authors (Boucher, Lewis & Collis, 2000) found that 9-year-old children with autism performed similarly to comparison participants with specific language impairment on familiar voice–face matching, sound–object matching, familiar voice recognition and unfamiliar voice discrimination tasks.

Emotion memory

Emotion memory tasks often differ from face memory tasks in that the experiments rely on identifying or categorizing the stimuli as matching a prototype or stored representation. For example, the individual must utilize a visual stored representation of a facial expression to make a decision about the match between the stored representation and the test exemplar. Tasks that use faces depicting emotion have produced mixed results, but in general suggest difficulty in matching (Braverman et al., 1989; Celani, Battacchi & Arcidiacono, 1999; Hobson, 1986a, b), categorizing (Gepner, de Gelder & de Schonen, 1996) and recognition of facial expressions (Gepner, de Schonen & Buttin, 1994). However, it has been suggested that when children are matched on verbal mental age, differences in performance on emotion perception tasks disappear (Ozonoff, Pennington & Rogers, 1990). Identification of higher order 'belief based' emotion but not basic emotions from pictures of the eyes is impaired in adults with autism and Asperger syndrome (Baron-Cohen, et al., 1997). Using a more complex task, Grossman et al. (2000) found that children with Asperger syndrome did not demonstrate deficits in recognition of basic emotions, but showed impairment when the verbal labels were mismatched to the emotion expression. (See Faran and Ben Shalom, this volume, Chapter 5, for a fuller discussion of emotion recognition.)

Summary: social memory and behaviour

From these sets of studies, several conclusions can be drawn. First, face memory is *at least* relatively impaired in individuals with autism. In the seven studies of face memory reviewed (Blair *et al.*, 2002; Boucher & Lewis, 1992; Boucher, Lewis & Collis, 1998; Davies *et al.*, 1994; Hauck *et al.*, 1998; Klin *et al.*, 1999; Serra *et al.*, 2003), individuals with autism performed worse than comparison participants on the face memory task. It is more difficult to draw a firm conclusion about the relation between performance on face memory versus memory for nonface stimuli given the differences in task structure and participant characteristics across the various studies. However, it appears that face memory seems to be more difficult for people with ASDs than memory for other types of visual stimuli. Given the uneven profile of overall memory abilities in people with autism, and specifically their deficits in spatial memory (e.g. Williams, Goldstein & Minshew, 2006), contrast tasks should be chosen with care. A third tentative conclusion is that children with ASDs are relatively less impaired and may even be advantaged on tests that involve attention towards the mouth region. Finally, the age of the child and the severity of their autism may influence the degree of impairment of memory for social stimuli. This is a common caveat in the field of developmental disabilities; better descriptions of participant criteria will help to inform comparisons across studies.

Social memory and neuroimaging

Face and object memory

It has been shown that infants and young typically developing children exhibit event-related potential (ERP) differences when processing familiar (parent, favourite toy) versus unfamiliar faces and objects by 4 months of age, and that this pattern changes with age (e.g. Carver *et al.*, 2003; de Haan & Nelson, 1999; Webb, Long & Nelson, 2005). In a study with 3- to 4-year-old children, Dawson *et al.* (2002) found that TD children and children with developmental delay (DD) showed differential ERPs to the unfamiliar face as compared to their mother's face, and to an unfamiliar object compared to a favourite object, at the posterior P400 component and the frontal Nc (TD) or the Slow Wave (DD). Children with ASDs failed to show differential ERPs to their mother's face versus an unfamiliar face at either component but did show differential ERPs to a favourite versus an unfamiliar toy at the P400 and Nc. These results suggest a specific impairment in memory for faces but not objects in young children with ASD. Of note, the results of the children with ASD during the object memory task were more similar to the results from the TD group; that is, memory was demonstrated at the same components, suggesting similar memory process as comparison participants matched for chronological age but not those matched for mental and chronological age (the DD group).

While ERPs are sensitive to the temporal dynamics of neural processes, functional magnetic resonance imaging (fMRI) is sensitive to anatomical or spatial dynamics of neural processes (via measurement of blood flow). fMRI studies of older individuals with ASDs suggest that whilst familiarity may activate the expected neural circuits, unfamiliar face processing may not do so. Specifically, Schultz et al. (2000) found that when high-functioning adolescents and adults with autism and Asperger syndrome were viewing unfamiliar faces, they had significantly more activation in the inferior temporal gyrus and less activation in the right fusiform gyrus than comparison participants. The authors concluded that individuals with ASDs were using nonface areas to accomplish face perception. However, a study by Pierce et al. (2004) showed that when adults with ASD viewed familiar faces, they showed greater, rather than less, fusiform activation. Moreover, the overall neural circuitry activated whilst processing familiar faces was similar to that activated by comparison participants, although more limited in range.

The authors proposed that increased fusiform activation to familiar faces may reflect enhanced attention and motivation. Consistent with this interpretation, a case study by Grelotti et al. (2005) found fusiform and amygdala activation during discrimination of Digimon characters in a child with autism who had a 'special interest' in Digimon. The response to Digimon characters was greater than to other nonexpertise categories and to unfamiliar faces. Taken together, these reports suggest that a failure to activate the fusiform to unfamiliar faces (Schultz et al., 2000; also Pierce et al., 2005) is not due to basic abnormalities in the structure of the fusiform but may reflect the type of information that is being processed.

The results from studies utilizing ERP and fMRI provide complementary information about the nature of social memory in autism. First, the ERP results suggest that memory for faces is abnormal in young children with ASD, children with ASDs failing to show differentiation of the two stimuli at the memory-related components analysed (Nc, P400 and Slow

Wave). In contrast, the fMRI results suggest that the processing of faces approaches the normal pattern *if* the faces are already familiar to the participant. Thus, the adults with autism were able to recruit more typical regional resources within the inferior temporal lobe during viewing of familiar faces. Although age differences in the samples are likely to be a large contributor to the differences in results, future research will need to examine the ERP components that reflect encoding of faces during viewing of familiar stimuli. If processing of familiar faces activates more typical spatial sources, then it is possible this may also result in more typical temporal processes. Second, given that the proposed generator of the Nc (in infancy) is the prefrontal cortex (Reynolds & Richards, 2005), future fMRI studies would benefit from examining the role of the frontal cortex during familiar and unfamiliar processing. Of note, these studies highlight the lack of information about the neural basis of the formation and retrieval of new social memories in individuals with autism.

Accounting for performance on tests of social memory in autism

Social memory may be particularly vulnerable to impairment as social items and events may be more complex and less predictable than non-social items and events, involving relational processing and an extensive 'social neural network' in the brain. This suggests that there are numerous potential primary and intermediary processes that could result in an impairment in social memory. The next section focuses on the current theories that attempt to account for these impairments.

Memory and the medial temporal lobe

Variability in functioning in autism may be accounted for by differences in the extent of medial temporal lobe dysfunction (see Bachevalier, this volume, Chapter 2; Barth, Fein & Waterhouse, 1995; Dawson, 1996; Waterhouse, Fein & Modahl, 1996). In animal models, monkeys with lesions of the hippocampus and the amygdala show more severe memory and social impairments than those with amygdala lesions alone (Bachevalier, 1994). Dawson and colleagues found that performance by children with autism on a delayed match to sample task was correlated with the severity of autism symptoms (Dawson *et al.*, 1998). Furthermore, in 3- to 4-year-old children with ASDs, performance on medial temporal lobe / ventromedial prefrontal cortex tasks was strongly associated with joint attention (Dawson *et al.*, 2002), a core early feature of the disorder. Individuals with lower-functioning autism are more likely to show memory impairments related to the medial temporal lobe (Ameli *et al.*, 1988; Boucher & Warrington, 1976; Rumsey & Hamburger, 1988) whereas individuals with HFA are less likely to show such deficits (Barth, Fein & Waterhouse, 1995). It is unclear if these results reflect differential memory impairments based on functioning, or if higher-functioning individuals may have more compensatory strategies.

The medial temporal lobe and hippocampal system specifically is important for memory functions including memory for context, source memory and deferred imitation. Such memory skills are vital to forming representations of social events. One proposal suggests that the hippocampal system is involved in the binding of features, items or events into a cohesive memory (Cohen & Eichenbaum, 1993; Cohen *et al.*, 1999; see also DeLong, this volume, Chapter 6). An impairment in feature binding might explain some of the impairments in autism such as the profile of weak central coherence (Frith, 1989).

A number of other proposed functions of the hippocampus are central to both social and non-social memory: encoding of novel scenes (Stern *et al.*, 1996), allocentric or observer-independent representations (Burges *et al.*, 2001), recalling semantically encoded words (Nyberg *et al.*, 1996), forming face–name associations (Kapur *et al.*, 1995), and associations between items (Henke *et al.*, 1997). The role of the medial temporal lobe and hippocampus in autistic symptomology cannot be discounted, as is clear from the focus on possible medial temporal lobe and hippocampal involvement in several chapters in the present book (see in particular Chapters 2, 3, 6 and 14).

Perception and encoding

Functional memory performance cannot occur if images or events are not fully encoded. Disruptions in the encoding phase could provide degraded, distorted or partial information to the system, resulting in an altered memory trace or in stored information that does not allow the individual to perform the task as a typical individual might. There are multiple hypotheses as to how social information may be encoded improperly.

First, Brock *et al.* (2002) as well as our group (Dawson, Webb & McPartland, 2005) have proposed that many characteristic impairments in autism may arise due to a failure of perceptual/temporal binding. The failure to integrate information into a meaningful whole (weak central coherence – Frith, 1989) may result from a failure to integrate information at a 'higher level' (Brock *et al.*, 2002). At the centre of this proposal is the question of how information about local details can be combined to describe coherent objects or complex scenes. To form a coherent object, any given neuron in the visual system must 'carry' information about how effective the stimulus is in activating the neuronal receptive field as well as cell assemblies (Shadlen & Movshon, 1999). The temporal binding hypothesis (Milner, 1974; von der Malsburg, 1981) states that neurons that respond to the same object are tagged by their temporal correlation during firing. If temporal binding fails to occur, then information about local details will not be combined (feature binding) and coherent representations of objects and events will not be formed. This can have downstream consequences for the use of information by other systems.

A second possibility is that there is an early onset, higher-order perceptual/cognitive deficit that prevents the infant with autism from extracting perceptually relevant information from faces such as would be utilized in category and prototype formation (Gastgeb, Strauss & Minshew, 2006; Klinger & Dawson, 2001; Strauss, 2004). Individuals with autism have difficulty finding the 'odd face' in a set of photographs regardless of whether this reflects an odd expression or identity (Tantam *et al.*, 1989). Further, Weeks and Hobson (1987) found that individuals with ASDs sorted photos by hats rather than facial expression. These two studies suggest that individuals with autism use an atypical set of criteria for categorizing faces. The failure to form prototypes or the formation of atypical prototypes has direct implications for representational processes. For example, emotional expressions are abstracted from exposure to multiple identities displaying similar facial movement under a given social context. If there is a failure to extract the relevant features and configuration of a given expression or if the wrong features are used, the prototype will either fail to develop or would be incorrect. When the child needed to use that stored representation to make a decision about a new person expressing an emotion (e.g. is *this* person angry?), the information would not be available and the child would not be able to respond appropriately.

Lastly, these deficits might reflect dysfunctions in higher-order visual processing circuits. These could include dysfunction of the specific neural mechanism that supports face processing, such as the fusiform gyrus, or disruptions in the use of high and low spatial frequency information. High-functioning adolescents and adults with autism and Asperger syndrome had significantly less activation in the right fusiform gyrus during the processing of unfamiliar faces than comparison participants (e.g. Schultz *et al.*, 2000). While memory for faces as measured by ERPs shows disrupted memory processing, impairments in early stage processing of faces also exist. The N170 component is an ERP component measured at posterior temporal sensors that is greater and faster to face stimuli than to other visual categories (Bentin *et al.*, 1996); the N170 is thought to be generated by areas identified as face-processing regions (e.g. Rossion *et al.*, 2003). In contrast to comparison participants, individuals with high-functioning ASD exhibited slower N170 latencies to faces than to control stimuli (McPartland *et al.*, 2004). In 3- to 4-year-old children with ASDs, the developmental N170 was also found to be delayed. Children with TD exhibited a faster developmental N170 to faces than to objects. In contrast, children with ASDs showed the opposite pattern – faster responses to objects than to faces (Webb *et al.*, 2006). Both of these reports provide evidence that early structural encoding of faces is disrupted in ASDs and is characterized by slower speed of information processing.

Deruelle *et al.* (2004) suggest that the feature-based processing strategies used by individuals with autism may result from over reliance on high spatial frequency information. Facial image information arises from two types of information: high spatial frequency information, which carries information about features, and low spatial frequency information, which carries configural information (Costen, Parker & Craw, 1994). Using either high or low pass filtered images, Deruelle *et al.* (2004) found that children with autism made facial identity judgements based on high spatial frequency information, whereas comparison children used low spatial frequency information. This would account for differences in performance based on configural versus featural information and impairments found in perception of coherent motion (Milne *et al.*, 2002; Spencer *et al.*, 2000), biological motion (Blake *et al.*, 2003), and dynamic facial expressions of emotions (Gepner, Deruelle & Grynfeltt, 2001; Gepner & Mestre, 2002).

Proposed deficits in perception and encoding cover a wide range of visual abilities and may suggest impairments in higher-level visual cortex processes or in the use of this information to form veridical representations. These types of impairments would not be limited to social stimuli but to any type of category formation if prototype formation was impaired, including stimuli that utilized low spatial frequency information, stimuli that were dynamic, or stimuli that required feature binding to be perceived coherently.

Attention

Several studies have suggested that individuals with autism process faces using abnormal strategies. Attention may be implicated in two important ways: the amount of attention and the direction of attention. Hermelin and O'Connor (1967) found that individuals with autism had shorter visual fixations to both faces and nonsocial stimuli. Of note, Boucher and Lewis (1992) found longer fixations in the autism group to be associated with better performance on a face recognition task. Studies of visual attention to faces have indicated that individuals with autism exhibit reduced attention to the core features of the face, such as the eyes and nose, relative to typical individuals (Klin *et al.*, 2002; Pelphrey *et al.*, 2002; Trepagnier, Sebrechts & Peterson, 2002). However, when viewing emotionally expressive faces, children with ASDs exhibit more typical patterns of visual attention, fixating more on the eyes and mouth than other parts of the face (van der Geest *et al.*, 2002).

Deficits in attention may reflect the task requirements. First, during realistic, complex viewing situations such as during a movie scene, Klin *et al.* (2002) found that high-functioning adults with autism looked more to the mouths than the eyes of characters. Comparison participants spent twice as much time on the eye region than the autism group, and percentage of fixation on the eye region was predictive of group member-ship. However, in the autism group, percentage of time fixating on the mouth was predictive of social competence, with higher percentages of time focusing on the mouth reflecting higher social competence. Second, during viewing of static facial images and particularly when a task involves matching or memory, fixation to the eye region may be similar to that displayed by typical individuals (Sterling *et al.*, 2005). This may reflect either an explicit strategy based on feedback or a featural processing style. For example, Hadjikhani *et al.* (2004) found that directed attention to the presence of a cross hair in the centre of the face during viewing resulted in relatively typical fusiform activation in adults with autism.

The behavioural characteristic of 'eye avoidance' is well known in autism. In addition, publicity over research results that highlight failure to look at the eyes has created an impact among parents and therapists. Anecdotally, in a recent study, several adult subjects with autism com-mented on the fact that they knew they should look at the eye region. Whilst individuals may explicitly modulate their attention, failure to scan the internal triangle of the face may lead to a lack of information integra-tion and reflect the use of a modified featural strategy. If face memory relies both on featural and configural processing, then successful strat-egies may require fixation on informative features and sampling of the internal configuration.

Social motivation

According to the social motivation hypothesis, face-processing deficits result from a primary deficit in social motivation (Dawson *et al.*, 2005;

Grelotti *et al.*, 2002; Schultz, 2005). The notion that individuals with autism lack social motivation is based partly on clinical observation: diagnostic criteria for autism include 'a lack of spontaneous seeking to share enjoyment, interests, or achievements with other people' and 'lack of social or emotional reciprocity' (DSM-IV; American Psychiatric Association, 1994, p. 70). If a child is not motivated to attend to social stimuli in the environment, this results in reduced attention to faces as well as to all other social stimuli such as the human voice, hand gestures, biological motion and emotion expressions. Decreased attention could result in a lack of expertise, failure to develop configural processing, and/or disrupted prototype formation. From this, the brain would lack the expected information to correctly organize cortical circuitry and would result in atypical regional specialization and inefficiency in information processing (Dawson, Webb & McPartland, 2005). The origin of the motivational impairments may be related to difficulty in forming representations of the reward value of social stimuli in the reward system per se (Schultz, 1998) or the ability to form representations of others as 'like me' (Decety & Sommerville, 2003; Meltzoff & Brooks, 2001).

Expertise

Lack of expertise is one likely consequence of impaired social motivation. However, it could arise in other ways, and may be considered in its own right as a possible explanation of social memory impairments. Visual expertise in other domains results in a number of changes in attention and memory. Many of the characteristics used to define expertise processing are those that are found in face processing: recognition of an item at the subordinate level as quickly as at the basic level (Tanaka, Curran & Sheinberg, 2005); sensitivity to configural processing (Gauthier *et al.*, 1998); or activation of the fusiform face area (Gauthier *et al.*, 2000). Facial expertise is probably both an experience-expectant and experience-dependent learning process. Our experience with faces reflects a normal expected environment in which the individual attends to the faces in his/her environment as well as being dependent on the attribution of the face as meaningful or relevant to the individual.

Familiarity may also represent a type of expertise. Children are able to show adult-like performance (naming) when the stimulus materials (faces of cartoon characters) or the semantic classifications (European or American origin) are familiar (Rahman, Sommer & Olada, 2004). Further, expertise items and familiar faces evoke fusiform activation in individuals with autism (Grelotti *et al.*, 2005; Pierce *et al.*, 2004). Importantly, experience can be influenced through therapeutic training. Faja and colleagues (Faja *et al.*, 2004) found that individuals with ASDs, when given specific training on how to view faces, improved their sensitivity to configural information.

Summary

Are memory impairments in autism pervasive or are they related to the type of information that the child needs to remember? The work cited in this chapter provides evidence of impaired performance in individuals with autism across the age spectrum on tasks involving face and voice memory both for newly learned items as well as for familiar stimuli. In most tasks using direct comparisons between social and nonsocial stimuli, individuals with autism performed worse than comparison participants on tasks using social stimuli. However, it remains difficult to identify the specific source of the impairment. Several hypotheses have been suggested including deficits in the medial temporal lobe memory system *per se*, perceptual and encoding deficits, attention abnormalities, fundamental impairments in social motivation, or failure to develop expertise. Importantly, these hypotheses are not mutually exclusive. It is possible that memory impairments may represent a variable phenotype in autism that, when combined with abnormalities in the visual processing circuit or social motivation, create a specific impairment in memory for faces. Similarly, difficulties in identifying familiar voices may reflect another set of specific interactions. Addressing each individual hypothesis as well as the potential for complex interactions will provide important information for both defining the phenotype of autism as well as suggesting strategies for intervention.

Acknowledgement

The writing of this article was funded by a grant from Cure Autism Now. Support was also provided by a programme project Grant U19HD35465 from the National Institute of Child Health and Human Development and the National Institute on Deafness and Communication Disability, which is part of the Collaborative Program of Excellence in Autism, and by a centre Grant U54MH066399 from the National Institute of Mental Health, which is part of the National Institutes of Health STAART Centers Program. The author gratefully acknowledges the contribution of Geraldine Dawson, Mike Murias, Jill Boucher, Dermot Bowler and the UW Autism Center Research Program Staff.

References

Ameli, R., Courchesne, E., Lincoln, A., Kaufman, A. S. & Grillon, C. (1998). Visual memory processes in high-functioning individuals with autism. *Journal of Autism and Developmental Disorders, 18,* 601–615.

American Psychiatric Association (1994). *Diagnostic and statistical manual of mental disorders,* 4th edn (DSM-IV). Washington, DC: American Psychiatric Association.

Aylward, E. H., Park, J. E., Field, K. M., Parsons, A. C., Richards, T. L., Cramer, S. C. & Meltzoff, A. N. (2005). Brain activation during face perception: evidence of a developmental change. *Journal of Cognitive Neuroscience, 17,* 308–319.

Bachevalier, J. (1994). Medial temporal lobe structures and autism: a review of clinical and experimental findings. *Neuropsychologia, 32,* 627–648.

Baron-Cohen, S., Jolliffe, T., Mortimore, C. & Robertson, M. (1997). Another advanced test of theory of mind: evidence from very high functioning adults with autism or Asperger syndrome. *Journal of Child Psychology and Psychiatry, 38,* 813–822.

Barth, C., Fein, D. & Waterhouse, L. (1995). Delayed match-to-sample performance in autistic children. *Developmental Neuropsychology, 11,* 53–69.

Bennetto, L., Pennington, B. F. & Rogers, S. J. (1996). Intact and impaired memory functions in autism. *Child Development, 67,* 1816–1835.

Bentin, S., Allison, T., Puce, A., Perez, E. & McCarthy, G. (1996). Electrophysiological studies of face perception in humans. *Journal of Cognitive Neuroscience, 8,* 551–565.

Blair, R. J., Frith, U., Smith, N., Abell, F. & Cipolotti, L. (2002). Fractionation of visual memory: agency detection and its impairment in autism. *Neuropsychologia, 40,* 108–118.

Blake, R., Turner, L. M., Smoski, M. J., Pozdol, S. L. & Stone, W. L. (2003). Visual recognition of biological motion is impaired in children with autism. *Psychological Science 14,* 151–157.

Boucher, J. & Lewis, V. (1992). Unfamiliar face recognition in relatively able autistic children. *Journal of Child Psychology and Psychiatry, 33,* 843–859.

Boucher, J. & Warrington, E. K. (1976). Memory deficits in early infantile autism: some similarities to the amnesic syndrome. *British Journal of Psychology, 67,* 73–87.

Boucher, J., Lewis, V. & Collis, G. (1998). Familiar face and voice matching and recognition in children with autism. *Journal of Child Psychology and Psychiatry, 39,* 171–181.

Boucher, J., Lewis, V. & Collis, G. M. (2000). Voice processing abilities in children with autism, children with specific language impairments, and young typically developing children. *Journal of Child Psychology and Psychiatry, 41,* 847–857.

Braverman, M., Fein, D., Lucci, D. & Waterhouse, L. (1989). Affect comprehension in children with pervasive developmental disorders. *Journal of Autism and Developmental Disorders, 19*(2), 301–316.

Brock, J., Brown, C. C., Boucher, J. & Rippon, G. (2002). The temporal binding deficit hypothesis of autism. *Developmental Psychopathology 14,* 209–224.

Burgess, N., Maguire, E. A., Spiers, H. J. & O'Keefe, J. (2001). A temporoparietal and prefrontal network for retrieving the spatial context of lifelike events. *Neuroimage, 14*, 439–453.

Campbell, R. & Tuck, M. (1995). Children's recognition of inner and outer face-features of famous faces. *Perception, 24*, 451–456.

Carey, S. & Diamond, R. (1977). From piecemeal to configurational representation of faces. *Science, 195*, 312–314.

Carver, L. J., Dawson, G., Panagiotides, H., Meltzoff, A. N., McPartland, J., Gray, J. & Munson, J. (2003). Age-related differences in neural correlates of face recognition during the toddler and preschool years. *Developmental Psychobiology, 42*, 148–159.

Celani, G., Battacchi, M. W. & Arcidiacono, L. (1999). The understanding of the emotional meaning of facial expressions in people with autism. *Journal of Autism and Developmental Disorders, 29*, 57–66.

Cohen, N. & Eichenbaum, H. (1993). *Memory, amnesia, and the hippocampal system*. Cambridge, MA: MIT Press.

Cohen, N., Ryan, J., Hunt, C., Romine, L., Wszalek, T. & Nash, C (1999). Hippocampal system and declarative (relational) memory: summarizing the data from functional neuroimaging studies. *Hippocampus, 9*, 83–98.

Collishaw, S. M. & Hole, G. J. (2000). Featural and configurational processes in the recognition of faces of different familiarity. *Perception, 29*, 893–909.

Costen, N., Parker, D. M. & Craw, I. (1994). Spatial content and spatial quantisation effects in face recognition. *Perception, 23*(2), 129–46.

Davies, S., Bishop, D., Manstead, A. S. & Tantam, D. (1994). Face perception in children with autism and Asperger's syndrome. *Journal of Child Psychology and Psychiatry, 35*, 1033–1057.

Dawson, G. (1996). Neuropsychology in autism: a report on the state of the science. *Journal of Autism and Developmental Disorders, 26*, 179–184.

Dawson, G., Carver, L., Meltzoff, A., Panagiotides, H., McPartland, J. & Webb, S. (2002). Neural correlates of face and object recognition in young children with autism spectrum disorder, developmental delay, and typical development. *Child Development, 73*, 700–717.

Dawson, G., Meltzoff, A. N., Osterling, J., Rinaldi, J. & Brown, E. (1998). Children with autism fail to orient to naturally occurring social stimuli. *Journal of Autism and Developmental Disorders, 28*(6), 479–85.

Dawson, G., Webb, S. J. & McPartland, J. (2005). Understanding the nature of face processing impairments in autism: insights from behavioral and electrophysiological studies. *Developmental Neuropsychology, 27*, 403–424.

Dawson, G., Webb S. J., Schellenberg, G., Dager, S., Friedman, S., Aylward, E. & Richards, T. (2003). Defining the phenotype of autism: genetic, brain and behavioral perspectives. *Development and Psychopathology, 14*, 581–611.

de Haan, M., Humphreys, K. & Johnson, M. H. (2002). Developing a brain specialized for face perception: a converging methods approach. *Developmental Psychobiology, 40*, 200–212.

de Haan, M. & Nelson, C. A. (1999). Brain activity differentiates face and object processing in 6-month-old infants. *Developmental Psychology, 35*, 1113–1121.

Decety, J. & Sommerville, J. A. (2003). Shared representations between self and other: A social cognitive neuroscience view. *Trends in Cognitive Science*, 7, 527–533.

DeLong, G. (1992). Autism, amnesia, hippocampus, and learning. *Neuroscience and Biobehavioral Reviews*, 16, 63–70.

Deruelle, C., Rondan, C., Gepner, B. & Tardif, C. (2004). Spatial frequency and face processing in children with autism and Asperger syndrome. *Journal of Autism and Developmental Disorders*, 34, 199–210.

Diamond, A. & Carey, S. (1986). Why faces are and are not special: an effect of expertise. *Journal of Experimental Psychology: General*, 115, 107–117.

Faja, S., Aylward, E., Bernier, R., Bloomquist, M. & Dawson, G. (2004). Face processing in autism: is there plasticity in brain activation? International Meeting for Autism Research, Sacramento, CA, May 2004.

Farah, M., Tanaka, J. W. & Drain, H. M. (1995). What causes the face inversion effect? *Journal of Experimental Psychology: Human Perception and Performance*, 21, 628–634.

Flin, R. H. (1985). Development of face recognition: an encoding switch? *British Journal of Psychology*, 76, 123–134.

Freire, A. & Lee, K. (2001). Face recognition in 4- to 7-year-olds: processing of configural, featural, and paraphernalia information. *Journal of Experimental Child Psychology*, 80, 347–371.

Frith, U. (1989). *Autism: explaining the enigma*. Oxford: Blackwell.

Gastgeb, H., Strauss, M. & Minshew, N. (2006). Do individuals with autism process categories differently? The effect of typicality and development. *Child Development*, 77, 1717–1729.

Gauthier, I., Skudlarski, P., Gore, J. C. & Anderson, A. W. (2000). Expertise for cars and birds recruits brain areas involved in face recognition. *Nature Neuroscience*, 3, 191–197.

Gauthier, I., Williams, P., Tarr, M. J. & Tanaka, J. (1998). Training 'greeble' experts: a framework for studying expert object recognition processes. *Vision Research*, 38, 2401–2428.

Gepner, B., de Gelder, B. & de Schonen, S. (1996). Face processing in autistics: evidence for a generalised deficit? *Child Neuropsychology*, 2, 123–139.

Gepner, B., Deruelle, C. & Grynfeltt, S. (2001). Motion and emotion: a novel approach to the study of face processing by young autistic children. *Journal of Autism and Developmental Disorders*, 31, 37–45.

Gepner, B., de Schonen, S. & Buttin, C. (1994). Face processing in young autistic children. *Infant Behavior and Development*, 17, 661.

Gepner, B. & Mestre, D. (2002). Rapid visual motion integration deficit in autism. *Trends in Cognitive Science*, 6, 455.

Grelotti, D., Gauthier, I. & Schultz, R. (2002). Social interest and the development of cortical face specialization: what autism teaches us about face processing. *Developmental Psychobiology*, 40, 213–225.

Grelotti, D., Klin, A., Gauthier, I., Skudlarski, P., Cohen, D., Gore, J., Volkmar, F. & Schultz, R. (2005). fMRI activation of the fusiform gyrus and amygdala to cartoon characters but not to faces in a boy with autism. *Neuropsychologia*, 43, 373–385.

Grossman, J. B., Klin, A., Carter, A. S. & Volkmar, F. R. (2000).Verbal bias in recognition of facial emotions in children with Asperger syndrome. *Journal of Child Psychology and Psychiatry, 41*, 369–379.

Hadjikhani, N., Chabris, C., Joseph, R., Clark, J., McGrath, L., Aharon, I., Feczko, E., Tager-Flusberg, H. & Harris, G. (2004). Early visual cortex organization in autism: an fMRI study. *Neuroreport: For Rapid Communication of Neuroscience Research, 15*, 267–270.

Hauck, M., Fein, D., Maltby, N., Waterhouse, L. & Feinstein, C. (1998). Memory for faces in children with autism. *Child Neuropsychology, 4*, 187–198.

Henke, K., Buck, A., Weber, B. & Wieser, H. G. (1997). Human hippocampus establishes associations in memory. *Hippocampus, 7*, 249–256.

Hermelin, B. & O'Connor, N. (1967). Remembering of words by psychotic and subnormal children. *British Journal of Psychology, 58*, 213–218.

Hobson, R. (1986a). The autistic child's appraisal of expressions of emotion: a further study. *Journal of Child Psychology and Psychiatry, 27*, 671–680.

(1986b). The autistic child's appraisal of expressions of emotion. *Journal of Child Psychology and Psychiatry, 27*, 321–342.

Hobson, R., Ouston, J. & Lee, A. (1988). What's in a face? The case of autism. *British Journal of Psychology, 79*, 441–453.

Itier, R. J. & Taylor, M. J. (2004). Face recognition memory and configural processing: a developmental ERP study using upright, inverted, and contrast-reversed faces. *Journal of Cognitive Neuroscience 16*, 487–502.

Joseph, R. M. & Tanaka, J. (2003). Holistic and part-based face recognition in children with autism. *Journal of Child Psychology and Psychiatry, 44*, 529–542.

Kanner, L. (1943). Autistic disturbances of affective contact. *Nervous Child, 2*, 217–250.

Kapur, N., Friston, K. J., Young, A., Frith, C. D. & Frackowiak, R. S. (1995). Activation of human hippocampal formation during memory for faces: a PET study. *Cortex, 31*, 99–108.

Klin, A., Jones, W., Schultz, R., Volkmar, F. & Cohen, D. (2002). Visual fixation patterns during viewing of naturalistic social situations as predictors of social competence in individuals with autism. *Archives of General Psychiatry, 59*, 809–816.

Klin, A., Sparrow, S. S., de Bildt, A., Cicchetti, D. V., Cohen, D. J. & Volkmar, F. R. (1999). A normed study of face recognition in autism and related disorders. *Journal of Autism and Developmental Disorders, 29*, 499–508.

Klinger, L. & Dawson, G. (2001). Prototype formation in autism. *Developmental Psychopathology, 13*, 111–124.

Langdell, T. (1978). Recognition of faces: an approach to the study of autism. *Journal of Child Psychology, Psychiatry and Allied Disciplines, 19*, 255–268.

McPartland, J., Dawson, G., Webb, S. J., Carver, L. & Panagiotides, H. (2004). Event-related brain potentials reveal anomalies in temporal processing of faces in autism spectrum disorder. *Journal of Child Psychology and Psychiatry, 45*, 1235–1245.

Meltzoff, A. N. & Brooks, R. (2001). 'Like me' as a building block for understanding other's minds: bodily acts, attention, and intention. In Malle, B. F. (ed.), *Intentions and intentionality: foundations for social cognition*, pp. 171–192. Cambridge, MA: MIT Press.

Milne, E., Swettenham, J., Hansen, P., Campbell, R., Jeffries, H. & Plaisted, K. (2002). High motion coherence thresholds in children with autism. *Journal of Child Psychology and Psychiatry, 43,* 255–263.

Milner, P. (1974). A model for visual shape recognition. *Psychological Review, 81,* 521–535.

Mondloch, C. J., Dobson, K. S., Parsons, J. & Maurer, D. (2004). Why 8-year-olds cannot tell the difference between Steve Martin and Paul Newman: factors contributing to the slow development of sensitivity to the spacing of facial features. *Journal of Experimental Child Psychology, 89,* 159–181.

Nelson, C. (2001). The development and neural bases of face recognition. *Infant and Child Development, 10,* 3–18.

Nyberg, L., McIntosh, A. R., Houle, S., Nilsson, L. G. & Tulving, E. (1996). Activation of medial temporal structures during episodic memory retrieval. *Nature, 380*(6576), 715–717.

Ozonoff, S., Pennington, B. F. & Rogers, S. J. (1990). Are there emotion perception deficits in young autistic children? *Journal of Child Psychology and Psychiatry, 31* (3), 343–61.

Pelphrey, K. A., Sasson, N. J., Reznick, J. S., Paul, G., Goldman, B. D. & Piven, J. (2002). Visual scanning of faces in autism. *Journal of Autism and Developmental Disorders, 32,* 249–261.

Pierce, K., Haist, F., Sedaghat, F. & Courchesne, E. (2004). The brain response to personally familiar faces in autism: findings of fusiform activity and beyond. *Brain, 127,* 2703–2716.

Pierce, K., Muller, R. A., Ambrose, J., Allen, G. & Courchesne, E. (2005). Face processing occurs outside the fusiform 'face area' in autism: evidence from functional MRI. *Brain, 124,* 2059–2073.

Rahman, R., Sommer, W. & Olada, E. (2004). I recognize your face, but I can't remember your name: a question of expertise? *Quarterly Journal of Experimental Psychology A., 57,* 819–834.

Reynolds, G. D. & Richards, J. E. (2005). Familiarization, attention, and recognition memory in infancy: an event-related potential and cortical source localization study. *Developmental Psychology, 41,* 598–615.

Rossion, B., Joyce, C. A., Cottrell, G. W. & Tarr, M. J. (2003). Early lateralization and orientation tuning for face, word, and object processing in the visual cortex. *Neuroimage, 20,* 1609–1624.

Rumsey, J. M. & Hamburger, S. D. (1988). Neuropsychological findings in high-functioning men with infantile autism, residual state. *Journal of Clinical Experimental Neuropsychology, 10,* 201–221.

Sangrigoli, S. & de Schonen, S. (2004). Effect of visual experience on face processing: a developmental study of inversion and non-native effects. *Developmental Science, 7,* 74–87.

Schultz, W. (1998). Predictive reward signal of dopamine neurons. *Journal of Neurophysiology, 80,* 1–27

Schultz, R. T. (2005). Developmental deficits in social perception in autism: the role of the amygdala and fusiform face area. *International Journal of Developmental Neuroscience, 23* (2–3), 125–141.

Schultz, R. T., Gauthier, I., Klin, A., Fulbright, R., Anderson, A., Volkmar, F., Skudlarski, P., Lacadie, C., Cohen, D. & Gore, J. (2000). Abnormal ventral temporal cortical activity during face discrimination among individuals with autism and Asperger syndrome. *Archives of General Psychiatry, 57,* 331–340.

Serra, M., Althaus, M., de Sonneville, L. M. J., Stant, A. D., Jackson, A. E. & Minderaa, R. B. (2003). Face recognition in children with a pervasive developmental disorder not otherwise specified. *Journal of Autism and Developmental Disorders, 33,* 303–317.

Shadlen, M. N. & Movshon, J. A. (1999). Synchrony unbound: a critical evaluation of the temporal binding hypothesis. *Neuron, 24,* 67–77, 111–125.

Spencer, J., O'Brien, J., Riggs, K., Braddick, O., Atkinson, J. & Wattam-Bell, J. (2000). Motion processing in autism: evidence for a dorsal stream deficiency. *Neuroreport, 21,* 2765–2767.

Sterling, L., Dawson, G., Panagiotides, H. & Webb, S. J. (2005). Attentional patterns of familiar face processing in individuals with autism. International Meeting for Autism Research, Boston, MA, May 2005.

Stern, C. E., Corkin, S., Gonzalez, R. G., Guimaraes, A. R., Baker, J. R., Jennings, P. J., Carr, C. A., Sugiura, R. M., Vedantham, V. & Rosen, B. R. (1996). The hippocampal formation participates in novel picture encoding: evidence from functional magnetic resonance imaging. *Proceedings of the National Academy of Science USA, 93,* 8660–8665.

Strauss, M. (2004). Facial expertise: the perception and recognition of faces by infants, preschoolers, and adults with autism. In current research and hypotheses about the face processing abilities of individuals with autism. Paper presented at the International Meeting for Autism Research. Sacramento, CA.

Tanaka, J., Kay, J., Grinnell, E., Stansfield, B. & Szechter, L. (1998). Face recognition in young children: when the whole is greater than the sum of its parts. *Visual Cognition, 5,* 479–496.

Tanaka, J., Curran, T., & Sheinberg, D. L. (2005). The training and transfer of real-world perceptual expertise. *Psychological Science, 16,* 145–151.

Tantam, D., Monaghan, L., Nicholson, H. & Stirling, J. (1989). Autistic children's ability to interpret faces: a research note. *Journal of Child Psychology and Psychiatry, 30,* 623–630.

Taylor, M., McCarthy, G., Saliba, E. & Degiovanni, E. (1999). ERP evidence of developmental changes in processing of faces. *Clinical Neurophysiology, 110,* 910–915.

Trepagnier, C., Sebrechts, M. & Peterson, R. (2002). Atypical face gaze in autism. *Cyberpsychology & Behavior, 5,* 213–217.

Valentine, T. (1988). Upside-down faces: a review of the effect of inversion upon face recognition. *British Journal of Psychology, 79,* 471–491.

van der Geest, J. N., Kemner, C., Verbaten, M. N. & van Engeland, H. (2002). Gaze behavior of children with pervasive developmental disorder toward human faces: a fixation time study. *Journal of Child Psychology and Psychiatry*, *43*, 669–678.

von der Malsburg, C. (1981). The correlation theory of brain function (internal report 81–2). Göttingen: Max Planck Institute for Biophysical Chemistry.

Waterhouse, L., Fein, D. & Modahl, C. (1996). Neurofunctional mechanisms in autism. *Psychological Review*, *103*, 457–489.

Webb, S. J., Dawson, G., Bernier, R. & Panagiotides, H. (2006). Evidence of atypical face processing in young children with autism. *Journal of Autism and Developmental Disorders*, *36*, 881–890.

Webb, S. J., Long, J. & Nelson, C. A. (2005). A longitudinal investigation of visual event-related potentials in the first year of life. *Developmental Science*, *8*, 605–616.

Weeks, S. J., Hobson, R. P. (1987). The salience of facial expression for autistic children. *Journal of Child Psychology and Psychiatry*, *28*, 137–151.

Werner, E., Dawson, G., Osterling, J. & Dinno, N. (2000). Brief report: recognition of autism spectrum disorder before one year of age: a retrospective study based on home video tapes. *Journal of Autism and Developmental Disorders*, *30*, 157–162.

Williams, D. L., Goldstein, G. & Minshew, N. J. (2006). The profile of memory function in children with autism. *Neuropsychology*, *20*, 21–29.

Wilson, R., Pascalis, O. & Blades, M. (2006). Familiar face recognition in children with autism: the differential use of inner and outer face parts. *Journal of Autism and Developmental Disorders*, *37*(2), 314–320.

11 Memory characteristics in individuals with savant skills

Linda Pring

Introduction

In this chapter it is argued that memory performance provides a coherent picture of savant abilities, even though the talents displayed make different demands on memory and learning. The chapter opens with an introduction to savant talent, to issues in relation to domain-specificity and modularity, as well as the role of practice and implicit memory. These topics have been picked out because of their relevance to memory and also because of associations with autism. Three sections then follow which focus on savant memory performance amongst numerical and calendar calculators, musicians and artists, where the evidence from empirical studies is placed in the context of the issues raised in the Introduction. Finally, a theoretical interpretation is presented which, it is argued, provides a convincing account of the development of savant abilities.

Savant talent

Savants are often individuals of low general intelligence who nonetheless show outstanding capacity in a specific and often restricted domain, such as musical ability (e.g. Miller, 1989; Sloboda, Hermelin & O'Connor, 1985; Young & Nettlebeck, 1994), linguistic ability (Dowker, Hermelin & Pring, 1996; Smith & Tsimpli, 1991), calendar calculation (giving the correct day of the week that corresponds to a particular date) (Heavey, Pring & Hermelin, 1999), arithmetical calculation (Anderson, O'Connor & Hermelin, 1999), or drawing ability (e.g. Pring & Hermelin, 1997; Selfe, 1977). The majority of savants have a diagnosis of autism or Asperger syndrome, or show significant autistic-like features, together sometimes referred to as autistic spectrum disorders (ASDs). Approximately 9.8 per cent of individuals with autism exhibit special skills in comparison with individuals matched for mental age (Rimland, 1978), but it is rare for people with ASDs to display talent which is exceptional by the standard of cultural norms in the general population. The association between autism and talent has been related to obsessional preoccupations in the restricted area of interest (Hermelin & O'Connor, 1991), to visual impairment (Miller, 1989; Pring & Tadic, 2005; Treffert, 1989), to practice (Howe, Davidson & Sloboda, 1998) and, in particular, to the characteristic cognitive style of information processing found in autism (Frith, 1989; Happé, 1999; Pring, Hermelin & Heavey, 1995).

An uneven intelligence profile is typically found in autism, which is characterized by unexpectedly high scores in tests that require local rather than global, contextual or Gestalt information processing. Thus, although autism is a disorder characterized by impairment, certain cognitive–perceptual strengths are also present (Happé, 1999). According to Frith's weak central coherence theory (Frith, 1989), individuals with autism have difficulty drawing together information in order to construct higher-level meaning in context. Thus in their performance, especially perceptual performance, we see cognitive strategies characterized as weak coherence underlying exceptional skills. Indeed, this may play a significant role in predisposing certain individuals to develop their talents to savant level. Furthermore the adoption of these strategies, such as inhibiting the effects of context and focusing attention on details rather than on wholes, may extend beyond autism to help explain some of the psychological characteristics seen in high-achieving talented individuals drawn from the typical population, such as artists or mathematicians (Hermelin, 2001; Pring, Hermelin & Heavey, 1995).

Individuals displaying exceptional talent, including savants, may pose a challenge to many theories of intelligence, since their performance cannot be understood in terms of conventional intelligence tests and must be considered at least partially independent of general intellectual ability. Theoretical advances have instead turned to a consideration of domain-specific and domain-general processes as a way of understanding high-level expertise and the expression of talent.

Modularity and domain-specificity

From a psychological perspective, some would argue that there are more similarities between artists and scientists than differences between them (Root-Bernstein & Root-Bernstein, 2004). It can be argued that the skills needed to express talents are rather similar whatever the domain. The inventor, for example, may be someone who has 'intrinsic motivation towards work ... a problem-finding vision and a problem-solving focus' (Henderson, 2004, p. 120). On the other hand experimental studies of the component skills involved in talented performance have favoured the notion that talent and creativity is best considered from a 'domain-specific' viewpoint (e.g. Amabile, 1996; O'Connor & Hermelin, 1988). Winner (2000) argues that talents are unlearned, domain-specific traits that may be developed in favourable circumstances, but that cannot be manufactured. Others have defined talent as the *potential* for exceptional performance (Detterman, 1993; Feldman & Katzi, 1998) and as such it is more difficult to measure than ability and skill.

With regard to studies with savants, a number have shown that there is a difference between individuals with savant talents in drawing and painting when compared with individuals with a similar diagnosis of autism but no special drawing skills. For example the 'talented' group were significantly faster and more accurate at the Block Design test (Wechsler, 1992) and also at finding hidden or embedded figures from a display that contained either abstract visual patterns or representational pictures (Pring, Hermelin & Heavey, 1995; Ryder, 2003). Perhaps it is not so surprising that individuals with a talent for drawing, whether savant or not, might indeed have superior skills in domain-specific, i.e. visuo-perceptual, tasks (Getzels & Csikszentmihalyi, 1976; Ryder, Pring & Hermelin, 2002).

Such findings can fit well with Fodor's theory of modularity (Fodor, 1983), but can also be understood within a more interactive vision within the developmental neoconstructivist approach suggested by Karmiloff-Smith (2004) where certain brain-based subsystems, or modules, can be informationally encapsulated – in other words they are specific and independent, not only of each other but of general information processing capacity too. This could explain how individuals with low cognitive skills and poor performance on some intelligence tests might still display talent in a restricted domain (O'Connor & Hermelin, 1988). The definition of the term 'modules' has been loose and an appeal to more narrowly defined modules, referred to as 'micro-domains' (Karmiloff-Smith, 1992), such as poetry writing, numbers, music or painting, may be a more appropriate level of description in the context of savant talent.

Practice and implicit memory

The question of the development of talent in the context of autism remains uncertain. The influence of hormonal imbalance has been cited as a potential factor (Treffert, 2000), and genetic and other biological factors have also been considered, though sometimes rejected (Howe, Davidson & Sloboda, 1998). For example, reports of children with autism who display musical or number talents shared with other nonautistic members of their close family have led to the suggestion that talent is independently heritable. However, some have argued that the concept of talent itself is unhelpful in understanding exceptional performance and that the consequences of extensive practice have far greater explanatory power since, through practice alone, talents or skills may be developed and manifested (Ericsson & Faivre, 1988; Howe, 1991; Howe, Davidson & Sloboda, 1998). Certainly the development of talent has been associated with exceptional interest in, and preoccupation with, the subject domain (Ericcson 2003; Weissberg, 1999), such as is likely to sustain high practice levels. Moreover, in the present context it must be significant that individuals with autism typically display repetitive and obsessional interests. Hermelin and O'Connor (1991) referred to the high degree of obsessional traits in the personalities of the autistic savants they studied, even in relation to a comparison group of individuals with autism. Practice with the subject matter then may be something that comes easily both to individuals with high motivational levels and interest (Howe, Davidson & Sloboda, 1998) and to individuals with autism.

Certainly, long-term memory schemas built up on the back of practice can help to structure knowledge. This can have the consequence of freeing up limited resources as well as allowing individuals to capitalize on expectancies. There is, however, a problem in the use of the term 'practice', since it sidesteps issues concerning the nature of the mechanisms which might be used by savants to establish knowledge in long-term memory (LTM), the LTM knowledge structures that may underlie performance, and the retrieval structures which might be involved. Regarding the issue of retrieval from LTM, the model described by Ericsson & Kintsch (1995) referring to structures that are very complex and can activate both representational and action-based procedures, can be helpful in understanding expert performance. Regarding the mechanisms which might be active in savants' knowledge acquisition, however, there is a specific problem in that practice implies the use of explicitly determined cognitive strategies, whereas in the case of savants, reports seem to describe implicit processes based on simple exposure to the material as the basis for learning in LTM. Yet the explicit or implicit nature of the learning is often not given a great deal of emphasis (e.g. in Gobet's 1997 computational model). Moreover Trehub and Schellenberg (1998) refer to a three-factor model of high ability, arguing that none of the factors of explicit goal setting, evaluation or feedback are evident in savant activity.

Some researchers have appealed to 'rote' memory in connection with savant performance. Miller (1999) in the context of music, for example, identifies three core characteristics of rote memory: that it results in a high-fidelity representation of the original information, involves little reorganisation, and is primarily concerned with the physical aspects of the stimuli resulting in an inflexible and domain-specific output. Horwitz and his colleagues (e.g. Horwitz *et al.*, 1965) also seek to explain the performance of the outstanding calendar and numerical calculating abilities of the twins John and Michael in this way (see Sacks, 1985). However, recent evidence based on group studies, has shown that the information typically involved in the process of number or date calculation, graphic reproduction or musical performance is far from 'undigested' or 'inflexible', as the term rote memory implies, but is instead reliant on highly organized, flexible knowledge structures, capable of being used for generative and creative output (Heavey, Pring & Hermelin, 1999; Hermelin & O'Connor, 1986; Pring & Hermelin, 2002).

Especially important then, in the context of savant performance, is the likelihood that practice or exposure may afford the potential for implicit learning. In his model of learning (ACT*/ACT-R) Anderson (e.g. 1990) argues for a process of proceduralization that transforms declarative knowledge (explicitly represented) to an 'automated form' – an implicit knowledge system. Anderson's view of thinking and learning is complex, but essentially he argues that expertise is best understood as being based on a knowledge system which is developed piecemeal, dependent on the accrual and tuning of small units, which can be combined to produce complex cognition. Whereas explicit learning is subject to individual differences, implicit learning shows little variation as a function of age or intelligence. There is evidence to suggest that implicit learning is particularly suited to the acquisition of complex skills such as language (Reber, 1992). Reber (1989) for example, found that individuals were able to choose whether strings of words conformed to an artificial grammar, without being able to verbalize the rules for that decision process explicitly. Implicit learning of material can build up a complex but organized knowledge network, independent of cognitively mediated explicit processing of material. However, we still need to learn more about the mechanisms of this nondeclarative long-term memory (Bitan & Karni, 2004; Squire & Zola, 1996). Moreover it is a challenge to find a way of measuring the acquisition of, or indeed memory for, talent-related material in savant syndrome.

The following sections provide some descriptions and discussion of displays of savant skills and empirical studies of memory capacity and performance.

Savant abilities in different domains

Number and calendar calculators

Although very rare in occurrence, the outstanding performance of savant calculators, especially number calculators, has attracted much interest and been described in the literature (e.g. Heavey, 2003; Smith, 1983). Louis Fleury, for example, was described by Critchley (1979, p. 78) as a 'blind, intractable, destructive imbecile', whose calculation skills included multidigit multiplication and division, squaring, square and cubed roots, and algebra. In an average of four seconds, he could give the square root of any number running into four figures and in only six seconds the cube root of any number into six figures. Prime number calculation is also a skill that arithmetic calculators display. HP, a 31-year-old male with a diagnosis of autism (described by Heavey, 1997) could identify five-digit primes with ease; and Michael, also with a diagnosis of autism, with a nonverbal intelligence quotient (IQ) equivalent on the Raven's Progressive Matrices Test – Revised (Raven, 1998) to 128, but an unscorable test performance on the Peabody Picture Vocabulary Test (Dunn & Dunn, 1981), was able to generate prime numbers and recognize four- or five-digit primes taking about fifty seconds to generate them, and about eleven seconds to accurately identify them (Anderson, O'Connor & Hermelin, 1999; Hermelin & O'Connor, 1990). Often the speed of calculation has been emphasized but at other times it is the prodigious memory involved that has attracted attention. For example, when Jedediah Buxton (1702–72) was given a numerical problem to solve, after five hours of mental calculation (it seems without any written aide memoire), he asked in which direction the line of 28 numbers comprising the answer should be read!

In terms of LTM, a complex hierarchical associative network of number concepts and related numerical material may characterize the knowledge of these savants. How is this acquired? All ten savants described by Heavey (1997) show many autistic tendencies and are likely to fall within the spectrum of autistic disorders, with seven out of ten having a diagnosis of autism. The attention to detail observed in people with autism (see above) is likely to help focus on the basic information whether it is number factors or, for calendrical calculators, day, month or year attributes (see below). In addition, there is ready access to the material: a new date occurs every day and counting is a simple, cognitively undemanding numerical operation. The acquisition process builds in, through repeated association, the regularities apparent in the material. The network of complex associations and internal relationships among numbers can allow emergent properties to be accessed. Arithmetical solutions and shortcuts or rules may be integrated into the network. Such reasoning has been outlined by Heavey (2003) and explains both factorization and prime number recognition and generation.

Individuals with savant arithmetical ability are rare. However, such individuals often also have the ability to calendar calculate and there are many similarities in both the acquisition and operation involved in these skills, although the ability to calendar calculate may also occur in isolation. Calendar calculation refers to the ability to rapidly supply the day of the week of a given date, with some savants able to perform calculations spanning thousands of years (e.g. Horwitz *et al.*, 1965) or taking between 1.5 and 10 seconds to accurately identify the day of the week for dates such as 1 April 1850, 22 June 1979 or 15 December 1964 (Heavey, 1997).

The calendar conforms to certain regularities such as the 28-year rule, where in the Gregorian calendar the day–date configuration repeats itself every 28 years; or the corresponding month rule, where certain month pairs share the same day–date structure within a given year. A number of studies have reported evidence for calendar knowledge being represented within a structured knowledge network (Ho, Tang & Ho, 1991; O'Connor & Hermelin, 1986; Young & Nettlebeck, 1994). Thus speed of calculation is facilitated in certain predictable formulations such as in dates falling in years with identical structures.

To test these conjectures empirically, Heavey, Pring and Hermelin (1999) systematically investigated memory function in a group of savant calendar calculators and a group of age-, ability- and diagnosis-matched participants without savant ability. Their study showed that the savants did not have unusually increased memory capacity with respect to *general* short- and long-term memory as measured by digit span or recall of words from a list. They did, however, show clear recall superiority for calendrical material *in the absence of the calculation process*. This suggests that the calculators must encode date information unusually effectively, rather than having increased memory capacity. Furthermore, in another study reported by Heavey *et al.* (1999), calculation facilitated memory retrieval suggesting that, as in language studies (e.g. Slamecka & Graf, 1978), active processing produces more accessible memories compared with passive learning conditions.

For the savants, with their characteristic poor verbal performance, it seems that the structure of their calendar information provides more cues for memory retrieval than perhaps even semantic knowledge. Tager-Flusberg (1991) tested the organization of semantic knowledge in a group of participants with autism. She found that their recall was not

Table 11.1. *Same-day and different-day examples presented to participants*

List 1: 1988 (Leap)	List 2: 1989
15 February 1988 (Monday)	11 July 1989 (Tuesday)
7 November 1988 (Monday)	4 March 1989 (Saturday)
24 October 1988 (Monday)	20 December 1989 (Wednesday)
18 July 1988 (Monday)	13 April 1989 (Thursday)
List 3: 1991	List 4: 1992 (Leap)
10 October 1991 (Thursday)	8 May 1992 (Friday)
27 June 1991 (Thursday)	19 October 1992 (Monday)
7 March 1991 (Thursday)	26 January 1992 (Sunday)
25 April 1991 (Thursday)	11 November 1992 (Wednesday)

enhanced by presenting a list of semantically related words (animal names) when compared with semantically unrelated words. Furthermore, the performance of the group with autism was not attributable to an encoding deficit; the participants were able to use semantic cues to facilitate word retrieval. This suggests that these word items are stored in a semantically related format in LTM, but these pre-existing links and associations are not activated in order to facilitate retrieval (see Toichi, this volume, Chapter 8, and Bowler & Gaigg, this volume, Chapter 17).

In a series of related investigations (Reidy & Pring, in preparation), we tested the knowledge organization of our group of savant calculators $(n = 8)$[1] by exploring their memory performance using the same paradigm as that of Tager-Flusberg (1991) but replacing semantically related and unrelated lists with specially constructed lists of dates. Examples are given in Table 11.1. Although the participants did not calculate the day of the week for the given dates (e.g. 10 October 1991), in the lists we showed them the dates presented either *shared* the day of the week (List 1 and List 3), or the dates referred to *different* days of the week (List 2 and List 4). In this way it was possible to discover whether sharing a day makes a list more memorable, presumably because it is coded in that way in LTM. Thus in the memory task the savants were presented (visually and auditorally) with blocks of individual dates taken from the lists, and asked to recall them later. They were advised not to try and calculate the day but only to try and remember the dates.

[1] The savant participants are described in Heavey, Pring and Hermelin (1999).

The results showed that our group of savant calculators recalled significantly more dates that shared the same day of the week (5.9 out of a maximum of 8) than dates from the list where the days came from different parts of the week (3.9), and furthermore a near significant advantage for leap years (5.1) when compared to nonleap years (4.5). This evidence shows that their memory performance is sensitive to the structure of the calendar material and reflects the organization of the material. Individuals with autism (and savant calculating skills) are not incapable of displaying complex structural knowledge regularities in memory performance; it is simply that this emerges in a domain of expertise (e.g. numerical or date material) rather than in the semantic/conceptual knowledge system.[2]

Musical savants

Music is typically highly regular and rigidly structured (Justus & Bharucha, 2001). By constructing, storing and recalling the use of the rules and patterns that govern music, musicians are able to build up cognitive representations of musical structure and thus process musical information more effectively than nonmusicians (Sloboda, 1985). These musical cognitive representations arise from probabilistic associations or rules learned implicitly whilst attending to music (Zatorre, 2003), and it follows that its structure conforms to the musical tradition or format to which the musician has most regularly been exposed (Justus & Bharucha, 2001; Peretz & Hyde, 2003; Sloboda, 1985).

In terms of musical ability, savant skills have at times been considered comparable to those of professional musicians, including the ability to transpose music across keys, render imitations of specific musical styles, distinguish constituent tones from chords, and to have an exceptional memory for music (Hermelin, O'Connor & Lee, 1987; Miller, 1989; Sloboda, Hermelin & O'Connor, 1985). Several studies of musical memory have suggested that the knowledge that musical savants have acquired is structurally based in that it embodies an associative network modelling musical grammar. In line with this, musical savants' errors in memory tasks tend to be structure-preserving. Precise intervallic relationships may not be remembered but overall pitch contours are (Sloboda, Hermelin & O'Connor, 1985). Furthermore, their structural knowledge influences memory performance so that they experience difficulty memorizing

---

[2] A complete description of this and related studies can be found in Heavey (1997) and in Reidy (nee Heavey) & Pring (in preparation).

music written in unfamiliar as opposed to familiar styles (Sloboda Hermelin & O'Connor, 1985; Young & Nettlebeck, 1995).

It is likely that such exceptional skills result from outstanding absolute pitch (AP) abilities (Heaton, Hermelin & Pring, 1998; Miller, 1989; Treffert, 2000). Absolute pitch is the ability to recognize, label and remember pitch information without reference to an external standard. It is extremely rare: only 1 in 10,000 in the normal Western population possesses AP (Takeuchi & Hulse, 1993) and the acquisition of AP is automatic and unconscious and likened to the acquisition of language (Deutsch, Henthorn & Dolson, 2004). Early musical exposure or instruction can influence its development (Takeuchi & Hulse, 1993; Levitin, 1994) but it is not a necessary component of musical ability or talent, and many professional musicians do not possess it (though it was possessed by Bach, Beethoven and Mozart). By contrast, *all* cases of musical savants described in the literature do possess absolute pitch. Heaton, Hermelin and Pring (1998) highlighted the incipient AP abilities in children with autism and the musical abilities of an autistic child with exceptional AP abilities (Heaton, Pring & Hermelin, 1999), arguing that these abilities are dependent on, or linked with, weak coherence. Children with profound visual impairments also appear to show a potential to develop absolute pitch ability (Ockelford, 1988) and certainly have excellent pitch memory (Pring & Painter, 2002). Hamilton, Pascual-Leone and Schlaug (2004) reported a very much higher than expected prevalence amongst blind musicians, and the relationship between autism and blindness has recently been discussed in relation to musical talent (see Pring, 2005). More research is needed to understand the relationship between AP, visual impairment and musical processing. The ability to hold in memory individual pitches independently, and the development of musical knowledge and the memory system supporting the performance of musical savants are clearly intimately related.

Although studies of musical savants make it clear that pitch memory and pitch reproduction are exceptional, the limits of such abilities have not often been the focus of experimental study. Recently, Ockelford and Pring (2005) measured the limits of the capacity of DP, a musical savant, from the viewpoint of both learning and memory. DP is a young man who suffered from retinopathy of prematurity and has been totally blind from birth; additionally he also has a diagnosis of autism and severe learning difficulties. In a longitudinal study (Ockelford & Pring, 2006) we asked DP to learn a specially composed piece of blues music over an eighteen-month period. His output, which was monitored in the learning phase bi-weekly and in the memory phase every three months, reflected fascinating additions and transpositions of the musical material, creative elements and the use of schematized representations.

To understand DP's basic capacities in terms of perception and learning however, we explored the limits of his perceptual/memory skills in relation to his ability to process pitch clusters and chords. One exacting measure of absolute pitch is based on the outstanding capacity of some possessors of AP to identify the pitches of individual notes in complex note clusters (chords). This is difficult to do not least because the material seems to be highly coalescent and presents a gestalt, which, by definition, is hard to break down into its constituent elements. Our investigation compared chord-disaggregation performance in DP and nonsavant musician SE, both with at least the basic attributes of absolute pitch. DP is an exceptional musician who knows from memory literally thousands of piano pieces ranging in style from classical, through jazz and the blues to contemporary popular music. He performs regularly in the UK and abroad. SE is comparable in age to DP and is also a jazz musician with absolute pitch. At the time at which the research was being carried out he was studying for a degree in music from Kings College, University of London. The task DP and SE were asked to perform involved the reproduction of chords[3] varying in size from four to nine notes, played on an electronic keyboard. The two participants heard (only once) twenty different examples of chords from each level of difficulty (i.e. 120 chords). A 'hear and play' paradigm was used, and the number of notes correctly reproduced was the measure of accuracy.

In the literature there are no accounts of chord disaggregation that go beyond the use of four notes, and deconstructing chords is an extremely rare skill (Huron, 2001). DP's performance was truly exceptional but unfortunately we had not realized that we would need two sets of hands if we were to find DP's limit in terms of accuracy! Figure 1 shows DP's results in comparison with those of SE, who himself performed extremely well, indicating very good absolute pitch abilities.

There are problems with what would constitute chance performance in such a study, since as chords have more and more notes in them, given the physical limits on what can be performed with eight fingers and two thumbs, guessing the notes that are present becomes an ever more profitable strategy. Nevertheless the results are striking. DP is nearly 97 per

---

[3] The pitch range was restricted from the C below middle C to the G two-and-a-half octaves higher. Chords were largely 'tonal' and 'tertian' in nature: that is, conforming to the pitch frameworks of the major and minor scales with the possibility of chromatic alterations, all of which are ultimately definable as concatenations of thirds. Some comprised clusters of notes (series of tones and semitones, e.g. E flat, F sharp, G, A flat, B flat) that lay beyond the confines of Western tonality.

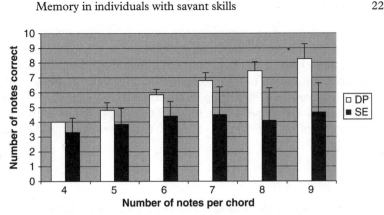

Figure 11.1 Figure displaying performance (DP: musical savant; SE: AP-matched control musician) on a disaggregation task

cent accurate overall. Moreover, his responses invariably followed the stimuli almost immediately (informally measured as between 400 and 1000 ms). It is not likely that such a rapid response is consciously mediated, and DP does not have the verbal skills to provide any potential insights into the process he uses to attain such high levels of performance. Nevertheless, DP shows evidence of an exceptionally detailed perceptual representation derived from the sensory stimulus and one that affords an immediate translation into fingering. It is hard to say if this should be considered a reflection of long-term memory knowledge representations or an episodically based short-term memory capacity for domain-specific material. DP's performance is so exceptional that it is effectively at ceiling, making it hard to say whether or not his performance would (at the limits) have similar characteristics to SE's performance. Analysis of SE's performance revealed that in playing a note cluster: (a) the top notes followed by the bottom notes were more accurate than the 'inner' notes; (b) notes corresponding to the black keys on a piano were correctly reproduced less often than white notes; and (c) intervallic size predicted accuracy (a cluster of notes a semitone apart was more difficult than for notes each a third apart). This suggests that the notes are retained in a sequence with flanker interference effects explaining the relatively accurate end-note accuracy. For DP it might be that there would be no note position effects indicating his 'direct' access to the individual notes, perceived and retained independently.

The importance of the motor aspect of DP's skills needs to be considered in more depth and it would be interesting to ask how far it is possible to measure DPs abilities without the 'playing' component. In studies of savant artists for example, exceptional performance often relies on measures based on drawing output, but not exclusively. There are examples where authors have tried to differentiate cognitive/perceptual mechanisms from the motor output components (Hermelin & Pring, 1998; Mottron & Belleville, 1993; Pring, Hermelin & Heavey, 1995). Informal descriptions of DP suggest that his musical processing is represented independently of his fingering, but it is hard to see how this could be tested empirically.

Savant artists

A number of explanations of savant artistic ability have focused on the outstanding memory often shown (Hill, 1975; LaFontaine, 1974). Selfe (1977) and Sacks (1985) have both highlighted the capacity of savant artists to produce visually correct, complex artistic outputs, in some cases several months after seeing the initial image. Selfe provided one of the best-known descriptions of this ability in her reports of child artist, Nadia (Selfe, 1977). Diagnosed with autism when she was 6 years old, Nadia possessed no expressive language skills and poor comprehension. However, at the age of 3 and a half years she developed an amazing capacity to draw. This drawing ability apparently arose spontaneously, omitting the scribbling stage of normal children's drawing development, and she went straight on to drawing very sophisticated images, mainly of animals but also including people, trains and other objects. She was also able to add and omit details and to draw images that were rotations from the original viewpoint. In addition, her drawings displayed linear perspective, foreshortening, occlusion and proportioning, all without any sort of training, although these features are not usually apparent in artistic output until much later in life.

The visual knowledge and understanding that must underlie the ability to portray linear perspective, to take into account size constancy, and to use perspective knowledge to achieve rotational transformations as Nadia did, are not well understood. Professional artists typically find these drawing techniques difficult or impossible to execute, even with training. Yet Nadia is not alone amongst artistic savants to display such exceptional drawing skill. It has been shown that adolescents with autism have a unique ability to draw accurate ellipses representing circle projections, demonstrating a facility with the use of perspective (Ropar & Mitchell, 2002). EC, an exceptional draughtsman showing exactly the same abilities as Nadia, was described by Mottron and Belleville in a series of studies (e.g. 1993). Stephen Wiltshire (e.g. as described by Pring & Hermelin, 1997), who seems exceptional in his mastery of drawing spatial relationships, could also use linear perspective and take into account size constancy, albeit to a lesser extent. One may speculate that these individuals have implicitly learnt the geometry of spatial relationships and other computations necessary for such procedural memory and output to operate so effectively.

In the case of Nadia and EC, additional similarities associated with exceptional drawing style were also noted. Neither seems to have made mistakes or used an eraser even when producing highly complex drawings of unusual views. EC can draw perfect lines, circles and ellipses. Both draw without regard to the edge of the paper, 'the drawings stop at the end of the sheet, irrespective of the outline of the configuration in the real world. It is not rare to find a half-complete object or person missing an essential part' (Mottron & Belleville, 1993, p. 287), and this feature of drawing has been documented amongst other savant artists (Ryder, 2003). The sense that the image has been reproduced on a piecemeal basis, without regard to the holistic impression, is hard to miss in such drawing behaviour and seems to support the weak perceptual coherence theory described in connection with the cognitive style seen in autism.

Hermelin and Pring (1998) explored the use of two particular pictorial devices in a group of nine savant artists and nine gifted children of normal intellectual ability and advanced drawing skill. These devices were linear perspective, and size and shape constancy as dealt with in pictorial form. The pictorial rules of linear perspective were developed in fifteenth-century Italy and were derived from geometrical laws. They include the notion that lines that run parallel in the three-dimensional world must converge in a picture and must meet eventually in a vanishing point. According to Gombrich (1988) this feature has dominated Western art until the early twentieth century. Constancy refers to the way the brain creates a stable perceptual world by seeming to be immune to changes in the retinal image. A man walking towards the distance does not lose identity, and – however small the retinal image – is not viewed as 'a boy', though the computed size might suggest that. It is as well to remember that an artist can retain the absolute size of the image in a drawing, safe in the knowledge that the viewer will apply constancy as much for a painting or drawing as s/he does for the 3D world it depicts.

Young children do not spontaneously use linear perspective or draw far away objects smaller than those that are near (Freeman & Cox, 1985). They, along with many artistically naïve adults, fail to properly implement these pictorial drawing devices. This is true not only for drawing but also in dealing with model constructions. Hermelin and Pring (1998) tested gifted child artists and artistic savants on a pair of tasks, the first of which involved drawing cars or planes at various distances from the viewer along a road or a runway; and in the second part of which the participants had to select models of cars or planes of varying proportions and place them within a road or runway represented by bricks. Both groups could implement size and shape constancy in their drawings, unlike normally developing children. Significantly, though, while the gifted children could transfer their understanding to a model construction task, the artistic savants failed to do so, their performance seeming to be restricted specifically to drawing.

Similarly, O'Connor and Hermelin (1987) reported a study with a group of savant artists and an IQ-matched nongifted comparison group. They presented participants with a variety of simple memory tasks, involving both recognition and reproduction of concrete and abstract drawn shapes. The performance of the savants was comparable to that of the IQ- matched comparison group on a short-term memory-matching task, but superior when the task involved a drawn response, such as reproduction of a complex figure from memory. The results, therefore, show that while superior visual memory can be indexed with a drawn response, visual recognition memory in savant artists is no better than that of nongifted, IQ-matched participants. Indeed, Mottron and Belleville (1993) report the same pattern in relation to EC. This again then implicates some implicit mechanisms involving procedural or LTM components in savant performance, rather than basic short-term memory capacity.

A theoretical model of savant abilities

The recent model of *Enhanced Perceptual Functioning* in autism (Mottron *et al.*, 2006) advances the ideas encapsulated in weak perceptual coherence and provides a convincing account of the development of savant abilities. Recent evidence from neuroimaging studies in autism provides support for this model by suggesting ways for neural circuitry to differ both in top-down processing and in the progression of sensory analysis. Thus, Frith (2003) observes that over a wide variety of tasks early sensory processing areas of the brain are activated normally or even *over*-activated in individuals with autism, whilst later processing areas are under-activated. The greater volume in brain size seen in autism may occur because of a lack of neuronal pruning. Frith speculates that sensory processing may be exceptional and higher-level processing under-represented (e.g. in the failure to show activation of the fusiform gyrus in face processing).

Thus, perceptual enhancement leading to unique and potentially more detailed percepts might result. Such differential circuitry would impact not only on behaviour at the perceptual level, but also on the resultant memory representations. This would be in line with the autism advantage seen in perspective drawing (Ropar & Mitchell, 2002) where higher-order knowledge can have an interfering rather than an advantageous effect. It is also consistent with musical perception in individuals with autistic spectrum disorder in whom pitch memory is characterized as retaining uniquely specified individual percepts/representations (see above, in relation to musical savants). If the unusual binding processes and neuronal circuitry indicated in autistic spectrum disorders (with the associated limitations to higher-order specialization and increased sensory processing) are confirmed, clearly it could explain why savants build up *differently structured* memory stores that are accurate in perceptual terms and may mediate different styles of learning and behaviour.

Summary

Talent is an elusive concept. However, there appears to be sound evidence that both savants and experts share important qualities. Implicit (unconscious) learning and the organization of proceduralized knowledge play an important part in the manifestation and development of savant talent. However, it would be inappropriate to consider the knowledge and memory systems underlying such expertise as rigid. There is evidence that savant performance includes a level of flexibility and creativity in art (Hermelin *et al.* 1999), music (Hermelin, O'Connor & Lee, 1987) and number (Pring & Hermelin, 2002), suggesting that the description of savant memory as 'rote' would be inappropriate. The particularly detailed way of thinking and processing of perceptual material in individuals with autism, plus their restricted and specific interests, may predispose them to build up complex knowledge structures in LTM. This may help to explain the existence of superior mnemonic abilities in many of the musical savants, calendrical or arithmetical calculators, and savant linguists described in the literature. It is harder to understand the basis of savant artistic talent. However, it may be related to the unique perceptual skills and consequent LTM organization of visuo-spatial knowledge. It is suggested that Mottron *et al.*'s theoretical model of Enhanced Perceptual Functioning provides a convincing account of the acquisition of savant abilities, and that recent evidence from neuroimaging studies of individuals with autism is consistent with this model.

Acknowledgements

Many thanks go to Dr Lisa Reidy and Dr Nicola Ryder for allowing me to include work from their PhD theses and to Katherine Woolf for her contribution with musical savants.

References

Amabile, T. M. (1996). *Creativity in context.* Boulder, CO: Westview.

Anderson, J. R. (1990). *The adaptive character of thought.* Hillsdale, NJ: Erlbaum.

Anderson, M., O'Connor, N. & Hermelin, B. (1999). A specific calculating ability. *Intelligence, 26*(4), 383–403.

Bitan, T. & Karni, A. (2004). Procedural and declarative knowledge of word recognition and letter decoding in reading and spelling. *Cognitive Brain Research, 19*(3), 229–243.

Critchley, M. (1979). *The divine banquet of the brain.* New York: Raven Press.

Detterman, D. K. (1993). Discussion. In G. R. Bock & K. Ackrille (eds.), *Ciba Foundation Symposium 178: the origins and development of high ability,* pp. 22–43. New York: Wiley.

Deutsch, D., Henthorn, T. & Dolson, M. (2004). Absolute pitch, speech and tone language: some experiments and a proposed framework. *Music Perception, 21*(3), 339–356.

Dowker, A., Hermelin, B. & Pring, L. (1996). A savant poet. *Psychological Medicine, 26,* 913–934.

Dunn, L. M. & Dunn, L. (1981). *Peabody Picture Vocabulary Test – revised.* Circle Pines, MN: American Guidance Service.

Ericsson, K. A. (2003). Exceptional memorizers: made, not born. *Trends in Cognitive Sciences, 7,* 233–235.

Ericsson, K. A. & Faivre, I. A. (1988). What's exceptional about exceptional abilities? In I. K. Obler & D. Fein (eds.), *The exceptional brain: neuropsychology of talent and special abilities,* pp. 436–473. New York: Guilford Press.

Ericsson, K. A., Krampe, R. & Tesch-Römer, C. (1993). The role of deliberate practice in the acquisition of expert performance. *Psychological Review, 100,* 363–406.

Ericsson, K. A. & Kintsch, W. (1995). Long-term working memory. *Psychological Review, 102,* 211–245.

Feldman, D. H. & Katzir, T. (1998). Natural talents: an argument for extremes. *Behavioral and Brain Sciences, 21,* 414–415.

Fodor, J. A. (1983). *Modularity of mind.* Cambridge, MA: MIT Press.

Freeman, N. H. & Cox, M. V. (1985). *Visual order: the nature of development of pictorial representation.* Cambridge: Cambridge University Press.

Frith, C. (2003). What do imaging studies tell us about the neural basis of autism? *Autism: neural basis and treatment possibilities; Novartis Foundations Symposium, 251,* 149–176.

Frith, U. (1989). *Autism: explaining the enigma.* Oxford: Blackwell.

Getzels, J. W. & Csikszentmihalyi, M. (1976). *The creative vision: a longitudinal study of problem finding in art.* New York: Wiley.

Gobet, F. (1993). A computer model of chess expertise. *Proceedings of the 15th Annual Meeting of the Cognitive Science Society*, 463–468.

Gombrich, E. H. (1988). *Art and illusion: a study in the psychology of pictorial representation*. London: Phaidon Press.

Hamilton, R. H., Pascual-Leone, A. & Schlaug, G. (2004). Absolute pitch in blind musicians. *Neuroreport*, *15*(5), 803–806.

Happé, F. G. E. (1999). Autism: cognitive deficit or cognitive style? *Trends in Cognitive Science*, *3*, 216–222.

Heaton, P., Hermelin, B. & Pring, L. (1998). Autism and pitch processing: a precursor for savant ability? *Music Perception*, *15*, 291–305.

Heaton, P., Pring, L. & Hermelin, B. (1999). A pseudo-savant: a case of exceptional musical splinter skills. *Neurocase*, *5*, 503–509.

Heavey, L. (1997). Memory in the calendar calculating savant. Unpublished PhD thesis, University of London.

(2003). Arithmetical savants. In A. Dowker and A. J. Baroody (eds.), *The development of arithmetic concepts and skills: constructing adaptive expertise*, pp. 409–433. Mahwah, NJ: Erlbaum.

Heavey, L., Pring, L. & Hermelin, B. (1999). A date to remember: the nature of memory in savant calendrical calculators. *Psychological Medicine*, *29*, 145–160.

Henderson, S. J. (2004). Inventors: the ordinary genius next door. In R. J. Sternberg, E. L. Grigorenko & J. L. Singer (eds.), *Creativity*, p. 120. Washington, DC: American Psychological Association.

Hermelin, B. (2001). *Bright splinters of the mind*. London: Jessica Kingsley.

Hermelin, B. & O'Connor, N. (1986). Idiot savant calendrical calculators: rules and regularities. *Psychological Medicine*, *16*, 885–893.

(1990). Factors and primes: a specific numerical ability. *Psychological Medicine*, *20*, 163–169.

(1991). Talents and preoccupations in idiots–savants. *Psychological Medicine*, *21*, 959–964.

Hermelin, B., O'Connor, N. & Lee, S. (1987). Musical inventiveness of five idiots–savants. *Psychological Medicine*, *17*, 685–694.

Hermelin, B. & Pring, L. (1998). The pictorial context dependency of savant artists: a research note. *Perceptual and Motor Skills*, *87*, 995–1001.

Hermelin, B. & Pring, L., with Buhler, M., Wolff, S. & Heaton, P. (1999). A visually impaired savant artist: interacting perceptual and memory representations. *Journal of Child Psychiatry and Psychology*, *7*, 1129–1139.

Hill, A. L. (1975). An investigation of calendar calculating by an idiot savant. *American Journal of Psychiatry*, *132*, 557–560.

Ho, E. D. F., Tsang, A. K. T. & Ho, D. Y. F. (1991). An investigation of the calendar calculation ability of a Chinese calendar savant. *Journal of Autism and Developmental Disorders*, *21*, 315–327.

Horwitz, W. A., Kestenbaum, C., Person, E. & Jarvik, L. (1965). Identical twin – 'idiot savants' – calendar calculators. *American Journal of Psychiatry*, *121*, 1075–1079.

Howe, M. J. A. (1989). *Fragments of genius: the strange feats of idiots savants*. London: Routledge.

Howe, M. J. A. (1991). *The origins of exceptional ability*. London: Routledge.

Howe, M. J. A., Davidson, J. W. & Sloboda, J. A. (1998). Innate talents: reality or myth? *Behavioral and Brain Sciences, 21*, 399–342.

Huron, D. (2001). Absolute pitch. *Music Perception, 19*, 45–54.

Justus, T. & Bharucha, J. (2001). Modularity in musical processing: the automacity of harmonic priming. *Journal of Experimental Psychology: Human Perception and Performance, 27*, 1000–1011.

Karmiloff-Smith, A. (2007). Atypical epigenesis. *Developmental Science, 10*, 84–88.

LaFontaine, L. (1974). Divergent abilities in the idiot savant. PhD thesis, Boston University.

Lehmann, A. C. (1997). Acquisition of expertise in music: efficiency of deliberate practice as a moderating variable in accounting for sub-expert performance. In J. A. Sloboda & I. Deliege (eds.), *Perception and cognition of music*. Mahwah, NJ: Erlbaum.

Levitin, D. J. (1994). Absolute memory for musical pitch: evidence from the production of learned memories. *Perception & Psychophysics, 56*, 414–423.

Miller, L. K. (1989). *Musical savants: exceptional skill in the mentally retarded*. Hillsdale, NJ: Erlbaum.

Miller, L. (1999). The savant syndrome: intellectual impairment and exceptional skill. *Psychological Bulletin, 125*, 31–46.

Mottron, L. & Belleville, S. (1993). A study of perceptual analysis in a high-level autistic subject with exceptional graphic abilities. *Brain and Cognition, 23*, 279–309.

(1995). Perspective production in a savant autistic draughtsman. *Psychological Medicine, 25*, 639–648.

Mottron, L., Dawson, M., Soulières, I., Hubert, B. & Burack, J. A. (2006). Enhanced perceptual functioning in autism: an update, and eight principles of autistic perception. *Journal of Autism and Developmental Disorders, 36*, 27–34.

Norris, D. (1990). How to build a connectionist idiot (savant). *Cognition 35*, 277–291.

O'Connor, N. & Hermelin, B. (1987). Visual memory and motor programmes: their use by idiot–savant artists and controls. *British Journal of Psychology, 78*, 307–323.

(1988). Low intelligence and special abilities. *Journal of Child Psychology and Psychiatry, 29*, 391–396.

(1989). The memory structure of autistic idiot–savant mnemonists. *British Journal of Psychology, 80*, 97–111.

Ockelford, A. (1988). Some observations concerning the musical education of blind children and those with additional handicaps. Paper presented at the 32nd Conference of the Society for Research in Psychology of Music and Music Education (now SEMPRE) at the University of Reading.

Ockelford, A. & Pring, L. (2005). Learning and creativity in a prodigious musical savant. Edited summaries selected from the Proceedings of the International

Conference of the Royal National Institute for the Blind held in London April 2005, *International Congress Series, 1282,* 903–907.

(2006). Learning and creativity in a musical savant. Paper presented at the 4th Mary Kitzinger International Conference on Visual Impairment, Kingston University, July 2006.

Peretz, I. & Hyde, K. L. (2003). What is specific to music processing? Insights from congenital amusia. *Trends in Cognitive Science, 7,* 362–367.

Pring, L. (2005). Savant syndrome. *Developmental Medicine and Child Neurology, 47*(7), 500–503.

Pring, L. & Hermelin, B. (1997). Native savant talent and acquired skill. *Autism, 1,* 199–214.

(2002). Numbers and letters: exploring an autistic savant's unpractised ability. *Neurocase, 8,* 330–337.

Pring, L., Hermelin, B. & Heavey, L. (1995). Savants, segments, art and autism. *Journal of Child Psychology and Psychiatry, 36,* 1065–1076.

Pring, L. & Painter, J. (2002). Recollective experience in the visually impaired: the role of sensory and conceptual processing. *British Journal of Visual Impairment and Blindness, 20,* 24–32.

Pring, L. & Tadic, V. (2005). More than meets the eye: blindness, autism and talent. In L. Pring (ed.), *Autism and blindness: research and reflections,* p. 66. London and Philadelphia: Whurr.

Raven, J. C. (1998). *Raven's standard progressive matrices test.* San Antonio, TX: Harcourt.

Reber, A. S. (1989). Implicit learning and tacit knowledge. *Journal of Experimental Psychology: General, 118,* 219–235.

(1992). The cognitive unconscious: an evolutionary perspective. *Consciousness & Cognition, 1,* 93–113.

Rimland, B. (1978). Inside the mind of the autistic savant. *Psychology Today, 12*(3), 69–80.

Root-Bernstein, R. & Root-Bernstein, M. (2004). Artistic scientists and scientific artists: the link between polymathy and creativity. In R. J. Sternberg, E. L. Grigorenko & J. L. Singer (eds.), *Creativity,* pp. 127–151. Washington, DC: American Psychological Association.

Ropar, D. & Mitchell, P. (2002). Shape constancy in autism: the role of prior knowledge and perspective cues. *Journal of Child Psychology and Psychiatry, 43*(5), pp. 647–654.

Ryder, N. (2003). The creative and generative capacity of savant artists with autism. Unpublished PhD thesis, University of London.

Ryder, N., Pring, L. & Hermelin, B. (2002). Lack of coherence and divergent thinking: two sides of the same coin in artistic talent? *Current Psychology, 21,* 168–175.

Sacks, O. (1985). *The man who mistook his wife for a hat.* London: Duckworth.

Selfe, L. (1977). *Nadia: a case of extraordinary drawing ability in an autistic child.* London: Academic Press.

Shah, A. & Frith, U. (1993). Why do autistic individuals show superior performance on the Block Design task? *Journal of Child Psychology and Psychiatry, 34,* 1351–1364.

Slamecka, N. J. & Graf, P. (1978). The generation effect: delineation of a phenomenon. *Journal of Experimental Psychology: Human Learning and Memory*, *4*, 592–604.

Sloboda, J. A. (1985). *The musical mind: the cognitive psychology of music*. Oxford: Oxford University Press.

Sloboda, J. A., Hermelin, B. & O'Connor, N. (1985). An exceptional musical memory. *Music Perception*, *3*, 155–170.

Smith, S. B. (1983). *The great mental calculators*. New York: Columbia University Press.

Smith, N. & Tsimpli, I. (1991). Linguistic modularity? A case study of a 'savant' linguist. *Lingua*, *84*, 315–351.

Snyder, A., Mitchell, D. & Bossomaier, J. (2004). Concept formation: 'Object' attributes dynamically inhibited from conscious awareness. *Journal of Integrative Neuroscience*, *3*(1), 31–46.

Squire, L. R. & Zola, S. M. (1996). The structure and function of declarative and nondeclarative memory systems. *Proceedings of the National Academy of Sciences, USA*, *93*, 13515–13522.

Tager-Flusberg, H. (1991). Semantic processing in the free recall of autistic children: further evidence for a cognitive deficit. *British Journal of Developmental Psychology*, *9*, 417–430.

Takeuchi, A. H. & Hulse, S. H. (1993). Absolute pitch. *Psychological Bulletin, 113*, 345–361.

Treffert, D. A. (1989). *Extraordinary people: understanding 'idiot-savants'*. New York: Bantam.

    (2000). Savant syndrome. In A. E. Kazdin (ed.), *Encyclopedia of psychology*, vol. 7, pp. 144–148. London: Cambridge University Press.

Trehub, S. E. & Schellenberg, E. G. (1998). Cultural determinism is no better than biological determinism. *Brain and Behavioural Sciences*, *21*, 427–428.

Wechsler, D. (1992). *Wechsler Intelligence Scale for Children*, 3rd UK edn. London: Psychological Corporation.

Weisberg, R. W. (1999). Creativity and knowledge: a challenge to theories. In R. J. Sternberg (ed.), *Handbook of creativity*, pp. 226–250. New York: Cambridge University Press.

Winner, E. (2000). Giftedness: current theory and research. *Current Directions in Psychological Science*, *9*, 153–156.

Young, R. L. & Nettelbeck, T. (1994). The 'intelligence' of calendrical calculators. *American Journal on Mental Retardation*, *99*, 186–200.

    (1995). The abilities of a musical savant and his family. *Journal of Autism and Developmental Disorders*, *25*, 231–248.

Zatorre, R. J. (2003). Absolute pitch: a model for understanding the influence of genes and development on neural and cognitive function. *Nature Neuroscience*, *6*, 692–695.

12   Working memory and immediate memory in autism spectrum disorders

Marie Poirier and Jonathan S. Martin

Introduction

This chapter provides a brief overview of research on short-term and working memory function in autism.[1] Our discussion first considers some of the general findings relating to memory performance in autism and then turns to the case of storage over the short term. The more complex case of working memory tasks where both processing and maintenance are necessary is then discussed.

Autism and memory

Early studies of people with autism described them as having good rote memory but impairments of higher-order memory functions requiring more elaborate processing or organization of materials (Hermelin & O'Connor, 1970). With the development of memory theory, research into the spared and impaired memory functions of individuals with autism has generated a more comprehensive, and more complex, picture.

Some studies have identified mnemonic abilities that are in the normal range. First, there is evidence that priming is unaffected in autism, at least in higher-functioning individuals (HFA; e.g. Bowler, Matthews & Gardiner, 1997). Another area of strength is cued recall, which appears preserved even in individuals with low-functioning autism (LFA; Boucher & Lewis, 1989; Boucher & Warrington, 1976; Tager-Flusberg, 1991). Recognition memory also seems to be in the normal range for relatively able autistic groups (Barth, Fein & Waterhouse, 1995; Minshew *et al.*, 1992; Minshew *et al.*, 1994); however, there is evidence of a deficit in those with global cognitive impairment (e.g. Boucher & Warrington, 1976). More recent studies suggest that this view of preserved recognition

---

[1] Here, the expressions short-term and immediate memory are used interchangeably and in a theoretically neutral sense; both are taken to mean memory for the very recent past (i.e. a few seconds).

memory in HFA needs to be qualified. Bowler, Gardiner and Grice (2000) and Bowler *et al.* (2000) have shown that despite similar levels of overall recognition, individuals with Asperger syndrome, relative to a comparison group, produce fewer 'remember' responses and more 'know' responses, reflecting different kinds of conscious awareness associated with memory.

In contrast to the above list of preserved functions, a number of memory impairments are associated with autism. Difficulties with the free recall of supra-span lists have been reported with a variety of materials; however, semantic features or associations within the lists may be a critical factor in this finding (see Chapter 4, this volume; Boucher & Warrington, 1976; Bowler, Matthews & Gardiner, 1997; Bowler *et al.*, 2000; Hermelin & O'Connor, 1967; Volkmar *et al.*, 1996).

Another area where impairments have been reported is source memory. Source memory refers to remembering the context elements surrounding a specific event or item. Bennetto, Pennington and Rogers (1996) tested a group of high-functioning children and adolescents with autism. Participants had to remember one of two previously presented lists while ignoring the items from the other. The findings indicated that participants with autism made almost eight times as many intrusion errors (reporting items from the to-be-ignored list) as did the group without autism, in line with the suggestion that source memory is impaired in the former group.

Boucher (2001) offered an interesting interpretation of these results. As suggested by Farrant, Blades and Boucher (1998), she noted that the errors reported in the Bennetto, Pennington and Rogers (1996) study could be the result of time-based discrimination difficulties: problems organizing memory representations along the time dimension would make it more difficult to determine which list a given item was taken from. Accordingly, Farrant and colleagues reported no source memory impairment when the source discrimination did not call upon the time dimension. In their study, participants were required to indicate which speaker had uttered a particular word during the study phase.

The two aforementioned studies suggest that participants with autism may have time-based discrimination difficulties without any significant source memory deficits in other domains. Bowler, Gardiner and Berthollier (2004) have nevertheless shown that, under certain circumstances at least, individuals with HFA have a source memory impairment. They noted that the Bennetto, Pennington and Rogers (1996) and the Farrant, Blades and Boucher (1998) studies differed not only in terms of the degree of reliance on time-based discrimination: whereas Bennetto and colleagues made use of a recall task, Farrant and colleagues used a cued recall procedure. Bowler, Gardiner and Berthollier (2004) reasoned that this difference could potentially explain the inconsistencies in the results of the two studies. They used a source memory task and manipulated the amount of support available at the point of recall. To-be-remembered words were presented in a variety of contexts and this was followed by a recognition phase. The critical conditions were introduced following this recognition memory test. If participants indicated they recognized a word, they were asked about the specifics of the presentation modality in one of two ways. In the supported condition, they had to choose from a series of options presented on a computer screen, whereas in the unsupported condition they simply had to attempt to recall the presentation condition associated with the recognized word at study. The participants with autism showed a source memory deficit in the recall condition but not in the cue-supported condition. Bowler and colleagues suggested that this agrees with the task-support hypothesis, a proposal similar to one developed by Craik (see Craik & Anderson, 1999). The latter argued that the memory changes seen in normal ageing are characterized by an increasing reliance on external sources to support recall, a reliance correlated with age-related frontal impairment (Craik *et al.*, 1990). Hence, there might be some relationship between the causes of memory deficits seen in ageing and in autism (Bowler, Gardiner & Berthollier, 2004).

Autism and short-term memory: the hypotheses

With respect to short-term memory, one can argue that many current theoretical views lead us to expect short-term memory impairments in autism.

First, let us consider the temporal processing deficit proposal put forward by Boucher (2001). This proposal implies that people with autism will have problems with memory for *when* events occurred because this type of information requires appropriate processing and retrieval of temporal–contextual information. As the tasks most frequently used to test short-term memory involve remembering a sequence of stimuli *in their order of presentation*, some degree of impairment could be expected. If items must be recalled in order, their temporal or order relationships must be encoded and retrievable. In effect, a number of current computational models of short-term memory rely on the encoding of an internal timing-context signal in order to predict and describe performance on short-term memory tasks (e.g. Brown, Preece & Hume, 2000; Burgess & Hitch, 1996). Accordingly, Boucher (2001) notes that it is somewhat surprising that memory span is unimpaired in able people with autism.

A similar but more general idea is that individuals with autism do not encode contextual/relational information in the same manner or to the same degree as neurotypical individuals (see Chapters 6, 10, 14 and 17 of this volume for various instantiations of this general idea). Again, this can be seen as predicting retrieval difficulties when correct performance involves recalling items in order; almost without exception, recent formal models of memory for order have suggested an important role for contextual and/or relational information (Brown, Neath & Chater, 2000).

A further proposal put forward to account for memory difficulties in autism is the task-support hypothesis. The latter suggests an analysis of memory function in autism where recall is impaired as well as memory for the contextual and personally experienced dimensions of events. The hypothesis is associated with the idea that memory problems in autism are attributable to difficulties at retrieval more than to problems during initial processing (Bowler, Gardiner & Berthollier, 2004). It predicts that the difference between individuals with autism and comparison groups will be much reduced when there is structured external support for retrieval. As many immediate memory tasks do not provide the type of support thought to eliminate these performance discrepancies, group differences would be expected.

The task-support hypothesis suggests a parallel between the cognitive impairments seen in normal ageing and those seen in autism. Interestingly, in normal ageing, there is a clear impairment of short-term recall (Salthouse, 1991). Maylor, Vousden and Brown (1999) conducted a detailed examination of short-term memory for serial order in ageing. They confirmed the previously reported decrement in the performance of older adults, modelling their data with a time-based computational model of memory. Based on an analogy between ageing and autism, both groups should show a deficit in ordered short-term recall.

Finally, another similarity between ageing and autism is worth noting as the results summarized below support the suggestion. Boucher (2001) has pointed out that some of the memory difficulties of individuals with autism, especially in the high-functioning range, become apparent when task difficulty is increased. She notes for example that the immediate free recall of lists in the span range shows no impairment but that slightly more difficult versions of the same task do. This is reminiscent of many of the findings in the study of normal ageing where interactions between task difficulty and an effect of age are frequently reported: while no age effect is found with an easy version of a given task, a clear age effect emerges when a more difficult version is used (Craik & Anderson, 1999).

Autism and short-term memory: the data

When it comes to memory for the immediate past, the most frequent view states that short-term memory is unimpaired in individuals with autism or – in the case of individuals with intellectual deficits – that it is commensurate with their other cognitive skills (Bennetto, Pennington & Rogers, 1996; Boucher, 2001). However, our review of the data suggests that this conclusion may have been premature.

In relation to immediate memory in autism, the most frequently cited paper is probably the chapter by Hermelin and O'Connor (1970). In this work, the authors summarize the work on immediate memory and conclude that verbal memory span appears intact in autistic children. This analysis has had considerable influence on the view adopted generally in the field.

Here we wish to revisit briefly the studies discussed by Hermelin and O'Connor (1970) as well as a few others that helped establish this influential view. First, it is important to bear in mind that when arguing for intact short-term memory functioning in autism, one is arguing for a null effect. Hence, it is necessary to show that a reasonable effort was made to test for a positive effect (Frick, 1995). With the benefit of hindsight, we would suggest that this may not be the case and that, in fact, there is evidence to indicate that immediate memory – at least for verbal material – is impaired in autism.

There is a group of well-known studies that reported null effects when comparing the immediate memory performance of participants with autism to that of various comparison groups. This includes the seminal studies by Hermelin and O'Connor (1967), O'Connor and Hermelin (1965) as well as an ingenious study by Boucher (1978). Although the paper by Hermelin and O'Connor (1967) and the one by Boucher present a number of interesting findings, their samples of participants were equated on their digit spans before their immediate memory for verbal material was tested. Currently, all models of immediate memory assume that both digit span and the immediate serial recall of verbal material call upon the same cognitive mechanisms. Simply put, if autism and comparison samples are equated on digit span, then the absence of a difference when testing memory span for words is what would be expected.

Regarding the study by O'Connor and Hermelin (1965), a short-term recognition task was used, rather than a memory span or serial recall procedure. Participants were presented with a line drawing of a square, taken from a set of two; two or three seconds later both of the squares used in the task were presented and the participant had to point to the one used on the current trial. This is a very simple two-alternative forced-choice recognition task; as standard recognition performance is often in the normal range for individuals with autism it is perhaps not surprising that the autism group was not impaired in this instance. This is also what would be predicted on the basis of the task-support hypothesis.

Other studies have equated participants on a number of variables such as mental age, scores on standardized vocabulary tests, or other standard measures that did not include memory span. One such study was conducted by O'Connor and Hermelin (1967) to examine the effect of organization and serial position on the immediate memory of children with autism. Their results showed a disadvantage for the autism group in the serial recall of verbal information. Conversely, the disadvantage was not reproduced when pictures were used instead of words. However, the list-length went from six and eight in the case of words to only four in the case of pictures. The latter may have been associated with ceiling effects, especially since the mean span of the participants was four pictures. In another study, Hermelin and O'Connor (1975) compared the span and supra-span scores of individuals with autism (described as HFA in this study – but diagnostic criteria have changed since), as well as neurotypical and deaf participants. As they were interested in the effect of presentation conditions more than in immediate memory *per se*, they matched the participants on the basis of their digit spans. Not surprisingly, they did not find overall differences in the serial recall of span or supra-span lists of digits. However, in the more difficult backward recall condition, a detailed analysis of supra-span performance showed a significant disadvantage for the autism group. This agrees well with the aforementioned hypothesis suggesting that in more able participants with autism, there may be an interaction between immediate memory performance and task difficulty.

In summary, the idea of intact immediate memory in autism is based on a number of early studies. However, a close look at this work in the light of current thinking on immediate memory leads to the suggestion that there may well be an immediate memory deficit in autism.

Generally speaking, some of the methodological characteristics of early studies also limit their reliability somewhat. For example, in these studies, span-type tasks are often used to measure short-term memory, a choice that is perhaps not ideal. If any significant proportion of the participants with autism shows a pattern of deficits similar to that seen in healthy elderly people, then the deficit may only be apparent when supra-span lists or a more difficult test is utilized. Also, as span tasks are usually terminated when participants start to make mistakes, the tasks can have reduced sensitivity; this may not readily allow the detection of the group-by-difficulty *interaction* that the above hypothesis would predict.

Finally, in most of the older studies where span or immediate memory was examined, a small number of trials were used, often between three and six. In recent studies of short-term memory, the number of trials considered reasonable is between twelve and twenty. This number of trials is especially important if one is dealing with populations where there is significant variability within and between participants.

Martin *et al.* (2006) reported an investigation comparing participants with Asperger syndrome (AS)[2] and matched comparison participants. However, they were careful not to match participants on memory span. For example when matching for intelligence, they used pro-rata scores that excluded the memory span subtest of the Wechsler Adult Intelligence Scale (WAIS) (Wechsler, 2002). Participants were given sixteen trials of immediate serial recall of lists of seven digits. The results showed a significant 15 per cent disadvantage for the AS group (mean $= 0.64$) relative to the comparison group (mean $= 0.79$). This finding hence coincides with the analyses above but of course requires replication. Martin *et al.* (2006) also examined the immediate serial recall of words in individuals with AS. The words used only appeared once within the test, which is not the case in tests using digits. Results showed that individuals with AS had a performance deficit relative to the matched comparison group and that this was attributable to their memory for the order in which the to-be-recalled items appeared.

As mentioned above, these findings are in line with a number of theoretical proposals put forward in the field. An alternative suggestion is that individuals with autism do not use effortful rehearsal or more elaborate encoding strategies to the same degree as comparison participants; this would hinder the recall but not the recognition in short-term memory tasks (see Smith and Gardiner, this volume, Chapter 13, for a discussion of the use of rehearsal by people with ASDs). We are currently conducting a number of further studies in order to establish and understand these results better.

Working memory

Working memory has been defined as 'a limited capacity system allowing the temporary storage and manipulation of information necessary for such complex tasks as comprehension, learning and reasoning'

---

[2] All individuals with Asperger syndrome were diagnosed by experienced clinicians, and met DSM-IV (American Psychiatric Association, 1994) or ICD-10 (World Health Organization, 1993) criteria for Asperger syndrome excluding the requirement for an absence of clinically significant developmental problems of language.

(Baddeley, 2000). Working memory tasks typically involve the online maintenance and processing of information. The best-known general model of these processes is the Working Memory model (Baddeley, 1986, 2000; Baddeley & Hitch, 1974), although it is not always referred to when discussing working memory in autism.

In the autism literature, working memory is often considered as an executive function, a term used to classify a range of cognitive processes that are involved in the planning and guiding of complicated procedures. Zelazo and Müller (2002) suggest that it is an ill-defined but useful concept referring to a cluster of cognitive abilities that bear a 'family resemblance'. These processes are generally agreed to include inhibition, mental flexibility (or set-shifting), planning and working memory (generally defined).

Executive functions are strongly associated with the frontal lobes, and in particular the prefrontal cortex. Patients with acquired frontal lobe damage typically show impaired performance on tests of executive function, and similar deficits have been demonstrated in a range of developmental disorders where congenital lesions to the frontal lobes are suspected. These disorders include autism, attention deficit disorder, obsessive compulsive disorder, Tourette's syndrome, phenylketonuria and schizophrenia (Hill, 2004). There is strong evidence to suggest that individuals with autism have performance deficits in a range of executive tests. Functions that have shown impairments include set-shifting (e.g. Ozonoff & Jensen, 1999), planning (e.g. Bennetto, Pennington & Rogers, 1996), working memory (e.g. Bennetto, Pennington & Rogers, 1996), and working memory and inhibitory control (Hughes & Russell, 1993). This pattern of performance has led some researchers to propose an account of autism where symptoms are explained in terms of an executive function deficit. However, this view has been controversial (see Hill, 2004).

Whilst the occurrence of deficits in some executive tasks is well established, evidence for impairment on working memory tests in people with autism is less robust, some studies demonstrating poorer performance in autism, and others finding equivalent performance to matched participants without autism. As Joseph *et al.* (2005) point out, this is perhaps surprising since the cognitive processes supported by working memory (as it is typically conceived) are thought to be required in the tests of executive function that participants with autism are consistently impaired on. For example, in a planning task such as the Tower of London, the participant must generate, maintain and update actions in working memory (Joseph *et al.*, 2005; Shallice, 1982). The apparent reliance of this task upon working memory would perhaps predict a more consistent finding of working memory difficulties than has been demonstrated in the studies reviewed next.

Studies of working memory in autism

Bennetto, Pennington and Rogers (1996) examined memory perform-ance in autism using a variety of different tests. They compared a group of 11- to 25-year-olds with autism, with full-scale IQs of at least 69, with a matched group of participants who had a variety of learning disorders without autism (primarily dyslexia). The tests used in the study included two verbal working memory tasks: sentence span (participants had to complete the last words in a set of sentences, and then later recall these words sequentially) and counting span (participants had to count the number of dots presented on a set of cards, and then recall them sequen-tially). The autism group were found to be impaired on both the working memory tasks and on tests of temporal order memory, source memory and free recall. This pattern of memory performance led Bennetto and colleagues to draw a comparison with the performance shown by patients with frontal lobe damage. Pennington *et al.* (1997) interpreted these findings as evidence that executive dysfunction in autism is caused by a severe working memory deficit which affects both the planning of behav-iour and the acquisition and use of concepts.

A different conclusion was reached by Russell, Jarrold and Henry (1996) when they compared working memory performance between a group of children with autism and a clinical and nonclinical comparison group. The clinical group consisted of children with moderate learning difficulties (MLD), while the other group contained age-matched typi-cally developing children. Three different capacity tasks were used: a dot counting task, a sentence span task, and an odd-man-out task. All three tasks required the concurrent storage of information whilst carrying out a related cognitive task. For example, in the case of the dot counting task, participants had to count dots on presented cards while also remem-bering the totals of previously presented cards. Russell and colleagues found that the autism group were not impaired on the working memory tests when compared to the MLD comparison group, although both these groups were impaired in relation to the normally developing com-parison group. Whilst these results suggest that the children with autism had a working memory impairment, a difference between the autism and MLD group would be expected if working memory was a core deficit in autism (i.e. if it played a causal role in the specific symptoms of autism). Russell and colleagues suggest that working memory deficits may accompany many different types of neurological impairment, but are not fundamental in causing autistic symptoms.

However, some studies have questioned whether working memory deficits are present in autism at all. Ozonoff and Strayer (2001) tested a group of high-functioning children and adolescents with autism, comparing their performance with a clinical comparison group diagnosed with Tourette's syndrome and a typically developing comparison group. The study used three computer-based tests: a running memory task (where participants had to say whether a presented shape matched a shape presented either one or two trials back); a spatial-memory span task (in which participants had to report the location of a shape presented in a previous trial); and a box search task (where participants had to search a series of boxes, without returning to a box they had already searched). No differences were found between the autism group and either of the two comparison groups, leading the authors to conclude that working memory is not an impaired executive function in autism. This was also the conclusion of Geurts *et al.* (2004) who assessed executive and nonexecutive test performance in children with HFA and children with attention deficit and hyperactivity disorder. They used the self-ordered pointing task (which is very similar to the box search task used by Ozonoff and Strayer) in order to measure working memory performance. In this test the participant is required to view an array of 6, 8, 10 or 12 abstract and difficult-to-verbalize designs which change position from trial to trial. The task is to point to a different item on each trial. Although differences between the groups were found on other executive tests, such as the Tower of London, no difference in performance was found between the groups on the self-ordered pointing task. This study provides further evidence to support the claim that working memory is intact in autism.

It may be possible to reconcile the conflicting findings reviewed above by applying a task-support analysis. It is tempting to conclude that the tasks where no group effect is reported tend to provide a much higher level of support at retrieval than the tasks that produced a reliable performance deficit. Some support for this suggestion is presented below.

Using a variant of the self-ordered pointing test, Joseph *et al.* (2005) demonstrated that when items can be verbally encoded, children with autism show a deficit when compared to children without autism. Joseph *et al.* tested performance on a nonspatial self-ordered pointing task in children with normal IQ scores. The task had two versions: a verbal version, in which the stimuli were pictures of concrete, single-syllable, nameable objects, and a nonverbal version, in which the stimuli were abstract designs that were difficult to name or encode verbally. The task required the children to point to one object from an array of 4, 6, 9 or 12 items, and then point to a different item on each succeeding trial. The experimental group was found to perform as well as the comparison group on the nonverbal version of the task, but performed less well on the verbal version. This suggests that in the verbal condition, the experimental group was failing to use the opportunity to verbally encode and rehearse items in working memory. This interpretation is consistent with the work of Russell, Jarrold and Hood (1999) who have suggested that difficulties using inner speech to regulate behaviour may partly underlie the autistic executive deficits that have been reported in many studies. Recent work by Whitehouse, Maybery and Durkin (2006) also shows that children with autism experience difficulties in tasks that are thought to rely on verbal rehearsal (see also Smith & Gardiner, this volume, Chapter 13).

A study by Hughes (1996) found that children with autism performed significantly less well than matched children without autism on the Luria (1961) hand game. This test requires participants to make a fist when the experimenter points a finger, and vice versa. Importantly, this executive test requires the participant to maintain an arbitrary task rule (to respond with the opposite gesture to the experimenter) in working memory in order to override a prepotent response (to respond with the same gesture). In a similar vein, Joseph, McGrath and Tager-Flusberg (2005) investigated executive working memory performance in relation to language ability. Using the Knock–Tap test (a task analogous to the Luria hand game), children with autism were found to be impaired when compared to matched participants. Another working memory and inhibition task was also used, the day–night task, which required children to respond to cards with a picture representing the night by saying 'day', and to cards with a picture representing the day by saying 'night'. On this test, no differences were found between the autism and comparison group, replicating a finding first reported by Russell, Jarrold and Hood (1999). While this may appear to contradict other findings, Russell and colleagues argue that the requirement to respond verbally in this task effectively prevents the use of inner speech in order to rehearse task rules. This means that the advantage that the comparison group would otherwise derive by using inner speech is not possible in this context. However, whether this level of verbal output is sufficient to prevent rehearsal is debateable. Both these studies lend some support to Russell and colleagues' hypothesis that executive deficits in autism may be the result of a difficulty in using inner speech to regulate behaviour. According to Russell (1997), it is the combination of a prepotent response and the need to maintain a rule in working memory that causes difficulties for people with autism, not simply the use of working memory. Russell concludes that a working memory deficit is unlikely to be fundamental to autism.

While Russell's (1997) theory can account for many of the seemingly contradictory findings from studies of executive performance, recent research has suggested that people with autism may also have difficulties with tests of spatial working memory. Although some studies have found no evidence for spatial working memory impairments in autism (e.g. Ozonoff & Strayer, 2001), such deficits have now been observed both in adults and in children with autism. Minshew, Luna and Sweeney (1999) assessed a group of adolescents and adults with HFA. They found poorer spatial working memory performance relative to a comparison group when using the oculomotor delayed response paradigm, a task which measures the ability to make a saccadic eye movement to the location of a target previously presented in the periphery. This finding was supported by Morris *et al.* (1999) who examined spatial working memory in adults with Asperger syndrome (the participants met ICD-10 criteria, but without the requirement for language delay) and two groups with frontal and temporal lobe excisions, respectively. Using the executive golf task, a computerized test in which participants have to predict (by pointing on the screen) which hole a golfer will putt their ball into, they found that the participants with AS were impaired relative to typical adults, and their performance was comparable to that of patients with frontal lobe lesions. Further evidence of impaired performance was also reported by Williams *et al.* (2005) who assessed verbal and spatial working memory performance in children, adolescents and adults with HFA. They found a dissociation between performance on the verbal task (which was normal) and the spatial task, on which the autistic group was impaired. Goldberg *et al.* (2005) assessed the performance of children with higher-functioning autism on a range of executive tests. Using the Spatial Working Memory test, they found that the autistic group performed significantly worse than the comparison group. This finding was also supported by Williams, Goldstein and Minshew (2006) who tested children with HFA on the finger windows task, which requires the child to remember the sequence in which an experimenter pokes a pen through a series of holes on a card (see Williams, Minshew & Goldstein, this volume, Chapter 7).

These studies provide evidence that people with autism may be impaired on spatial working memory tasks. This is especially compelling since the difficulties have been demonstrated in both child and adult groups with higher-functioning autism. Williams *et al.* (2005) suggest that the discrepancy found between their results and those of Ozonoff and Strayer (who found intact performance on a spatial memory span task) might be because the items used in that study could be verbalized, allowing participants to rehearse them in order to support performance. However, this interpretation is not supported by the findings of Joseph *et al.* (2005) who found evidence that autistic children failed to use verbal mediation on a self-ordered pointing task.

There is currently little theoretical explanation for the deficits that have been found using spatial working memory tasks, and it is unclear how they relate to other areas of functioning. One problem with comparing verbal and spatial working memory tasks is that it is not easy to equate their relative difficulty level (Williams, Goldstein & Minshew, 2006). It is important to ascertain whether the poorer performance shown by individuals with autism is due to a specific memory difficulty, or caused by other factors inherent in the design of these types of memory task. By definition, spatial memory tasks involve more complex visual attention demands than verbal tasks. It is well established that individuals with autism tend to be biased in their attention towards local rather than global properties, a factor that must be considered when designing appropriate tasks. It is also often the case that spatial memory tasks are less prescriptive in terms of attention than verbal tasks, since an action is not usually required until after the presentation of the sequence (such as in the finger windows task) whereas in typical verbal tasks items are read or counted before the test stage. Because the task is less prescriptive, it is possible that participants with autism may not be attending to the task in the same way as other participants, a factor which may lead to poorer performance. Further research investigating spatial working memory is clearly needed.

Processing load effects

While theoretical accounts of working memory in autism have tended to be related to performance on executive tests, Minshew and Goldstein (1998) have suggested an alternative. They view autism as an information-processing disorder that has a pronounced effect upon complex information processing (Williams, Goldstein & Minshew, 2006; also this volume, Chapter 7). As information processing becomes more complex, working memory resources become increasingly stretched. These authors argue that memory problems occur because of inadequate context facilitation and the reduced availability of concepts and schemas (Williams, Goldstein & Minshew, 2006). Echoing suggestions put forward in the literature on short-term recall, the proposal is that impairments should become apparent, and increase, as cognitive load increases. Minshew and Goldstein (2001) tested performance on a maze-learning task in which the number of choice point elements in the maze was manipulated. While both groups took a similar number of trials to learn the 6-choice-point maze, the autism group required significantly more trials to learn mazes with 10 and 14 choice points. A similar pattern in performance was reported by Joseph *et al.* (2005) using their verbal version of the self-ordered pointing task. When the working memory load was low (i.e. 6 items or fewer), autistic and comparison groups were equivalent, with differences appearing and increasing as the load increased. Joseph *et al.* suggested that some studies may not have found deficits in working memory performance in people with autism because differences may not be apparent at low processing loads.

While there is accumulating evidence to support this account of memory performance in autism, there are a few issues that require further attention. First, the concept of information-processing complexity is hard to define precisely. Without a more explicit definition, it could prove difficult to adequately predict and explain the pattern of performance seen in autism. It is also not clear how an information complexity approach can explain the pattern of impaired performance on tests of spatial memory, unless it is assumed that such tasks represent greater information-processing complexity. However, the results reported to date are promising and this may be a valuable direction for future research – especially if a more explicit model is proposed.

Summary and conclusions

Research investigating working memory in autism has yielded less than consistent findings. Nevertheless, several studies have reported that both children and adults who are on the autism spectrum show poorer performance on tests of spatial working memory than matched comparison groups (e.g. Williams *et al.*, 2005). Currently there is little theoretical explanation for this deficit.

There has also been evidence that autistic impairment on working memory tasks may emerge and increase as task complexity increases (e.g. Joseph *et al.*, 2005). These findings have led some researchers to suggest that autism is a disorder of complex information processing (e.g. Williams, Goldstein & Minshew, 2006) that leads to difficulties as the complexity of a given task increases. While this proposal is not yet clearly enough defined to allow unambiguous empirical predictions, it has received support from several different studies and suggests that previous null findings may require re-examination. It is possible that past research has not used sufficiently demanding tasks for group differences to emerge.

In our opinion, this brief examination of short-term memory and working memory in autism clearly indicates that a considerable amount of work is needed in order to determine the nature of any short-term storage or working memory deficits in autism. Among the factors repeatedly found to help make sense of discrepancies and produce clearer patterns of findings two stand out: task support at the point of memory retrieval and task difficulty and information-processing complexity.

Current findings suggest that impairments of verbal short-term memory are more likely than previously thought. Moreover, the data also clearly suggest that spatial working memory is impaired in autism. The picture is less clear when in comes to verbal working memory. However, the work in this area has perhaps suffered because of reliance on under-specified and changing definitions of processes and tasks. Further research where factors such as task support, processing complexity or task difficulty are more carefully taken into account could perhaps go a long way in clarifying the empirical picture. Finally, referring more systematically to current models of immediate and working memory (Baddeley, 1986, 2000; Brown, Neath & Chater, 2000) could prove helpful in guiding research.

Acknowledgements

The authors would like to thank the Economic and Social Research Council for financial support during the preparation of this chapter.

References

American Psychiatric Association (1994). *Diagnostic and Statistical manual of mental disorders*, 4th edn (DSM-IV). Washington, DC: American Psychiatric Association.

Baddeley, A. D. & Hitch, G. J. (1974). Working memory. In G. Bower (ed.), *The psychology of learning and motivation*, vol. 8, pp. 47–90. San Diego, CA: Academic Press.

Baddeley, A. (1986). *Working memory*. Oxford: Clarendon Press.

Baddeley, A. D. (2000). The episodic buffer: a new component of working memory? *Trends in Cognitive Science*, 4, 417–423.

Barth, C., Fein, D. & Waterhouse, L. (1995). Delayed match-to-sample performance in autistic children. *Developmental Neuropsychology*, 11, 53–56.

Bennetto, L., Pennington, B. & Rogers, S. (1996). Intact and impaired memory functions in autism. *Child Development*, 67, 1816–1835.

Boucher, J. (1978). Echoic memory capacity in autistic children. *Journal of Child Psychology and Psychiatry*, 19, 161–166.

(2001). Lost in a sea of time: time parsing and autism. In C. Hoerl & T. McCormack (eds.), *Time and memory: issues in philosophy and psychology*, pp. 111–135. Oxford: Oxford University Press.

Boucher, J. & Lewis, V. (1989). Memory impairments and communication in relatively able autistic children. *Journal of Child Psychology and Psychiatry, 30*, 99–122.

Boucher, J. & Warrington, E. (1976). Memory deficits in early infantile autism: some similarities to the amnesic syndrome. *British Journal of Psychology, 67*, 73–87.

Bowler, D. M., Gardiner, J. M. & Berthollier, N. (2004). Source memory in adolescents and adults with Asperger's syndrome. *Journal of Autism and Developmental Disorders, 34*, 533–542.

Bowler, D. M., Gardiner, J. M. & Grice, S. (2000). Episodic memory and remembering in adults with Asperger's syndrome. *Journal of Autism and Developmental Disorders, 30*, 295–304.

Bowler, D. M., Gardiner, J. M., Grice, S. & Saavalainen, P. (2000). Memory illusions: false recall and recognition in adults with Asperger's Syndrome. *Journal of Abnormal Psychology, 109*, 663–672.

Bowler, D. M., Matthews, N. J. & Gardiner, J. M. (1997). Asperger's syndrome and memory: similarity to autism but not amnesia. *Neuropsychologia, 35*, 65–70.

Brown, G. D. A., Neath, I. & Chater, N. (2000). SIMPLE: a local distinctiveness model of scale-invariant memory and perceptual identification. Manuscript submitted for publication.

Brown, G. D. A., Preece, T. & Hulme, C. (2000). Oscillator-based memory for serial order. *Psychological Review, 107*, 127–181.

Burgess, N. & Hitch, G. (1996). A connectionist model of STM for serial order. In S. Gathercole (ed.), *Models of short-term memory*, pp. 51–71. Hove: Psychology Press.

Craik, F. I. M. & Anderson, N. D. (1999). Applying cognitive research to problems of aging. In D. Gopher & A. Koriat (eds.), *Attention and Performance XVII*, pp. 583–615. Mahwah, NJ: Erlbaum.

Craik, F. I. M., Morris, L. W., Morris, R. G. & Loewen, E. R. (1990). Relations between source amnesia and frontal lobe functioning in older adults. *Psychology and Ageing, 5*, 148–151.

Farrant, A., Blades, M. & Boucher, J. (1998). Source monitoring by children with autism. *Journal of Autism and Developmental Disorders, 28*, 43–50.

Frick, R. W. (1995). Accepting the null hypothesis. *Memory and Cognition, 23*, 132–138.

Geurts, H. M., Verte, S., Oosterlaan, J., Roeyers, H. & Sergeant, J. A. (2004). How specific are executive functioning deficits in attention deficit disorder and autism? *Journal of Child Psychology and Psychiatry, 45*, 836–854.

Goldberg, M. C., Mostofsky, S. H., Cutting, L. E., Mahone, E. M., Astor, B. C., Denckla, M. B. & Landa, R. J. (2005). Subtle executive impairment in children with autism and children with ADHD. *Journal of Autism and Developmental Disorders, 3*, 279–293.

Hermelin, B. & O'Connor, N. (1967). Remembering of words by psychotic and subnormal children. *British Journal of Psychology, 58*, 213–218.

(1970). *Psychological experiments with autistic children*. Oxford: Pergamon Press.

(1975). The recall of digits by normal deaf and autistic children. *British Journal of Psychology*, *66*, 203–209.

Hill, E. L. (2004). Evaluating the theory of executive dysfunction in autism. *Developmental Review*, *24*, 189–233.

Hughes, C. (1996). Control of action and thought: normal development and dysfunction in autism: a research note. *Journal of Child Psychology and Psychiatry*, *37*, 229–236.

Hughes, C. H. & Russell, J. (1993). Autistic children's difficulties with mental disengagement from an object: its implications for theories of Autism. *Developmental Psychology*, *29*, 498–510.

Joseph, R. M., McGrath, L. & Tager-Flusberg, H. (2005). Executive dysfunction and its relationship to language impairment in school-age children with autism. *Developmental Neuropsychology*, *27*, 361–378.

Joseph, R. M., Steele, S., Meyer, E. & Tager-Flusberg, H. (2005). Self-ordered pointing in children with autism: failure to use verbal mediation in the service of working memory? *Neuropsychologia*, *43*, 1400–1411.

Luria, A. R. (1961). *The role of speech in the regulation of normal and abnormal behavior*. Oxford: Pergamon Press.

Martin, J. S., Poirier, M., Bowler, D. M. & Gaigg, S. B. (2006). Short-term serial recall in individuals with Asperger's syndrome. Poster presented at the International Meeting for Autism Research, Montreal.

Maylor, E. A., Vousden, J. I. & Brown, G. D. A. (1999). Adult age differences in short-term memory for serial order: data and a model. *Psychology and Aging* *14*, 572–594.

Minshew, N. J. & Goldstein, G. (1998). Autism as a disorder of complex information processing. *Mental Retardation and Developmental Disabilities Research Reviews*, *4*, 129–136.

(2001). The pattern of intact and impaired memory functions in autism. *Journal of Child Psychology and Psychiatry*, *7*, 1095–1101.

Minshew, N. J., Goldstein, G., Muenz, L. R. & Payton, J. B. (1992). Neuropsychological functioning in non mentally retarded autistic individuals. *Journal of Clinical and Experimental Neuropsychology*, *14*, 749–761.

Minshew, N. J., Goldstein, G., Taylor, H. G. & Siegel, D. J. (1994). Academic achievement in high functioning autistic individuals. *Journal of Clinical & Experimental Neuropsychology*, *16*, 261–270.

Minshew, N. J., Luna, B. & Sweeney, J. A. (1999). Oculomotor evidence for neocortical systems but not cerebellar dysfunction in autism. *Neurology*, *52*, 917–922.

Morris, R. G., Rowe, A., Fox, N., Feigenbaum, J. D., Miotto, E. C. & Howlin, P. (1999). Spatial working memory in Asperger's syndrome and in patients with focal frontal and temporal lobe lesions. *Brain and Cognition*, *41*, 9–26.

O'Connor, N. & Hermelin, B. (1965). Visual analogies of verbal operations. *Language and Speech*, *8*, 197–207.

(1967). Auditory and visual memory in autistic and normal children. *Journal of Mental Deficiency Research*, *11*, 126–131.

Ozonoff, S. & Jensen, J. (1999). Specific executive function profiles in three neurodevelopmental disorders. *Journal of Autism and Developmental Disorders*, *29*, 171–177.

Ozonoff, S. & Strayer, D. L. (2001). Further evidence of intact working memory in autism. *Journal of Autism and Developmental Disorders*, *31*, 257–263.

Pennington, B. F., Rogers, S. J., Bennetto, L., Griffith, E. M., Reed, D. T. & Shyu, V. (1997). Validity tests of the executive dysfunction hypothesis of autism. In J. Russell (ed.), *Autism as an executive disorder*, pp. 143–178. Oxford: Oxford University Press.

Russell, J. (1997). How executive disorders can bring about an inadequate 'theory of mind'. In J. Russell (ed.), *Autism as an executive disorder*, pp. 256–304. Oxford: Oxford University Press.

Russell, J., Jarrold, C. & Henry, L. (1996). Working memory in children with autism and with moderate learning difficulties. *Journal of Child Psychology and Psychiatry*, *37*, 673–686.

Russell, J., Jarrold, C. & Hood, B. (1999). Two intact executive capacities in children with autism: implications for the core executive dysfunctions in the disorder. *Journal of Autism and Developmental Disorders*, *29*, 103–112.

Salthouse, T. A. (1991). *Theoretical perspectives on cognitive aging.* Hillsdale, NJ: Erlbaum.

Shallice, T. (1982). Specific impairments of planning. *Philosophical Transactions of the Royal Society of London 3*, *298*, 199–209.

Tager-Flusberg, H. (1991). Semantic processing in the free recall of autistic children: further evidence for a cognitive deficit. *British Journal of Developmental Psychology*, *9*, 417–430.

Volkmar, F. R., Klin, A., Schultz, R., Brown, R., Marans, W. D., Sparrow, S. & Cohen, D. J. (1996). Asperger's syndrome. *Journal of the American Academy of Child and Adolescent Psychiatry*, *35*, 118–123.

Wechsler, D. (2002). *The Wechsler Adult Intelligence Scale*, 3rd edn. San Antonio, TX: Psychological Corporation.

Whitehouse, A. J. O., Maybery, M. T. & Durkin, K. (2006). Inner speech impairments in autism. *Journal of Child Psychology and Psychiatry*, *47*, 857–865.

Williams, D. L., Goldstein, G., Carpenter, P. A. & Minshew, N. J. (2005). Verbal and spatial working memory in autism. *Journal of Autism and Developmental Disorders*, *35*, 747–756.

Williams, D. L., Goldstein, G. & Minshew, N. J. (2006). The profile of memory function in children with autism. *Neuropsychology*, *20*, 21–29.

World Health Organization (1993). *International classification of diseases*, 10th edn (ICD-10). Geneva: WHO.

Zelazo, P. D. & Müller, U. (2002). Executive functions in typical and atypical development. In U. Goswami (ed.), *Handbook of childhood cognitive development*, pp. 445–469. Oxford: Blackwell.

13 Rehearsal and directed forgetting in adults with Asperger syndrome

Brenda J. Smith and John M. Gardiner

Introduction

Episodic memory impairments in individuals with autistic spectrum disorders (ASDs) are quite selective and can be interpreted in terms of both retrieval and encoding impairments. For example, whilst recall of test items without specific cues (free recall) is often impaired in children with autism in relation to comparison groups, performance is relatively unimpaired when appropriate retrieval cues are provided at the test stage of the procedure (Boucher & Lewis, 1989; Boucher & Warrington, 1976; Tager-Flusberg, 1991). Bowler, Matthews and Gardiner (1997) found that adults with Asperger syndrome (AS), defined as high-functioning individuals on the autistic spectrum that met the *International Classification of Diseases*, 10th edition (ICD-10; World Health Organization, 1993) criteria for AS excluding the language criteria, were also unimpaired in cued-recall in comparison to typical adults. Impaired free recall and intact cued recall is consistent with a retrieval deficit and Bowler and colleagues proposed a 'task support hypothesis', in which they suggested that many of the mild memory impairments found in individuals with ASDs would be alleviated with appropriate support, particularly at retrieval.

Free recall is not always impaired in individuals with ASDs. For example, whilst children with low-functioning autism (LFA) were unimpaired in their recall of unstructured word-strings presented in the form of sentences, in relation to comparison samples, they were impaired in their recall of grammatically correct, structured sentences (Hermelin & O'Connor, 1967). Children with autism and adults with a diagnosis of AS according to ICD-10 criteria have also been shown to be impaired in their recall of lists of words that are semantically related, but not words that are drawn from different semantic categories (Bowler, Matthews & Gardiner, 1997; Tager-Flusberg, 1991). These findings demonstrate that individuals with ASDs appear to be less able than comparison groups to use the structure or context of material to aid recall. Indeed, other researchers have found that individuals with autism are less effective at organizing material to improve recall, suggesting an organizational deficit (Minshew & Goldstein, 2001; Minshew *et al.*, 1992). An organizational deficit implicates differences in encoding strategies in episodic memory tasks, and the way in which an item is encoded has a direct impact upon the successful retrieval of that item (see Gardiner, this volume, Chapter 1).

Indeed, other recent findings in relation to memory performance in adults with ASDs have been explained in terms of encoding strategies. For example, a group of adults with AS (according to ICD-10 criteria) showed a deficit in their recall of related items presented in lists, and were more likely to recall related but unpresented items than a sample of typical adults (Bowler *et al.*, 2000). Using the converging associates paradigm originally devised by Deese (1959), Bowler *et al.* (2000) found that, following the presentation of lists of related words (e.g. *bed, rest, dream, tired*) that were also highly associated with a critical unpresented word (e.g. *sleep*), both participant groups were as likely to recall the critical lure, replicating the usual findings of a tendency to experience the illusion of having seen the critical, unstudied item. However, the adults with AS incorrectly recalled significantly more previously unpresented words (noncritical illusions) than the comparison group (though see Beversdorf *et al.*, 2000). Bowler *et al.* (2000) suggested that the findings of impaired recall of related words, together with a greater tendency to recall more unstudied items, are consistent with the AS group being aware of the relationship between the studied words, but forming less effective associative links between the studied items at encoding.

The main purpose of this chapter is to describe experiments in which we compared the encoding strategies of a group of adults with an ICD-10-based diagnosis of AS with those of a sample of typical adults (Smith, Gardiner & Bowler, 2007). More specifically, we investigated rehearsal processes at encoding both by measuring rehearsal directly, using an overt rehearsal technique, and by manipulating rehearsal by instructions given at study. We first review some previous evidence suggestive of possible differences in rehearsal style in adults with high-functioning autism (HFA).[1] Second, we review some evidence of developmental shifts in the employment of encoding strategies in typically developing (TD) children, as well as children with autism, in order to consider possible

---

[1] Here we conform to the preferred usage of 'HFA' in this book, to refer to individuals with the triad of impairments in the absence of clinically significant language or intellectual deficits, regardless of whether or not they have received a diagnosis of Asperger syndrome.

implications for adults with ASDs. We go on to consider how our findings, which show that there are some differences in rehearsal style, relate to the organizational deficit and task support hypotheses.

Rehearsal strategies in free recall and recognition

Craik and Lockhart (1972) distinguished between two encoding strategies, which have become known as maintenance rehearsal and elaborative rehearsal. Maintenance rehearsal can be defined as simply holding information in mind, or repeating information in a rote fashion, but at a consistently shallow level. Elaborative rehearsal can be defined as creating associative links between studied items or prior knowledge either in a cumulative fashion, or with the use of mental representations or imagery, resulting in a deeper memory trace. The degree of elaboration at the encoding stage is positively correlated with the likelihood of free recall, whereas maintenance rehearsal sometimes increases recognition and is less effective in relation to free recall (Craik & Tulving, 1975; Geiselman & Bjork, 1980; Greene, 1987; Rundus, 1977).

Words that are concrete and high in imagery and meaningfulness are, by their nature, easier to encode elaborately than abstract words that are low in imagery and meaningfulness. This finding has been termed the concrete noun effect (Paivio, Yuille & Madigan, 1968). After replicating the concrete noun effect with concrete and abstract Japanese words in a sample of typical adults, Toichi and Kamio (2003) found that a sample of individuals with HFA displayed lower recall of concrete nouns, but not abstract nouns, than the comparison group. One potential explanation for the reduced concrete noun effect is an encoding deficit hypothesis, in that individuals with HFA might be less likely to encode such words as elaboratively as comparison groups. Moreover, such an encoding deficit might also explain the additional benefit from retrieval cues evidenced by individuals with ASDs discussed previously (Boucher & Lewis, 1989; Boucher & Warrington, 1976; Bowler, Matthews & Gardiner, 1997; Tager-Flusberg, 1991), since the additional support at retrieval might compensate for shallower memory traces at encoding.

The 'levels-of-processing' framework (see Gardiner, this volume, Chapter 1) established that, in typical adults, semantic encoding (focusing on meaning) is the most effective way to enhance recall, followed by phonological encoding (focusing on sound), whilst graphic encoding (focusing on visual appearance) is the least effective (Craik & Tulving, 1975). Mottron, Morasse and Belleville (2001) manipulated the encoding strategies of adolescents and adults with HFA and typical individuals for words presented in a matrix. At study, participants were asked to point to each word in the matrix, following an indication by the experimenter. The experimenter drew attention to each word, either by naming it (no cue), or indicating the beginning letters (phonological cue), or indicating the semantic category of the word (semantic cue). Both groups recalled more of the semantically encoded words in a subsequent free recall task, and there were no significant differences between groups in recall of any cue type. Participants were then given a cued recall task for the unrecalled words and the type of cues at recall either related to the phonological or semantic aspects of the words. The additional cues at recall had a different effect on each group in that the comparison group still displayed a statistical advantage for the semantically cued words, whereas this advantage was not evident in the individuals with ASDs. The phonological cues at recall were equally as effective as the semantic cues for the latter group, which Mottron Morasse and Belleville (2001) interpreted as indicating a low-level, phonological encoding bias in individuals with ASDs.

Toichi and Kamio (2002) presented adults with HFA and typical adults with Japanese words along with questions at the study stage encouraging attendance to similarly structured hierarchical levels of processing (e.g. is the word written in Katakana/Hirakana character?/ Is the pronunciation similar to —?/ Is it a drink?). A subsequent recognition test showed that, although overall recognition rates were similar between the two groups, there was a reduced levels-of-processing effect in participants with HFA in comparison to typical adults. Unlike the comparison participants, there were no significant differences between the three encoding types (graphic, phonological and semantic) and the individuals with HFA recognized significantly more graphically encoded words than the comparison group.

Toichi and Kamio (2002) concluded that these findings are consistent with a superior rote memory in the sample of individuals with HFA, which may indicate that these individuals engaged in more item-by-item or rote rehearsal than the control group and less associative or elaborative rehearsal. Before describing our own studies that addressed this question, however, we first review some developmental evidence in relation to the natural course of development of rehearsal strategies and to successful training techniques used in TD children and children with autism.

The development of elaborative rehearsal

Developmental research has indicated that TD children adopt increasingly sophisticated encoding strategies in memory tasks. For example, Kunzinger (1985) used an overt rehearsal technique, originally devised by Rundus and Atkinson (1970), in a longitudinal study in which children were asked to try and learn items by repeating them out loud at a mean age of 7;5 years and then again at 9;5 years. Prior to the testing session, the children were made aware of two rehearsal strategies; repeating one word at a time (maintenance rehearsal) and repeating more than one word at a time, either in a cumulative fashion in the order in which the words were presented, or a more mixed fashion (elaborative rehearsal). They were allowed a few practice sessions so that they could adopt their preferred strategy prior to the test. Following Rundus and Atkinson (1970), the words rehearsed within each inter-stimulus interval were termed a 'rehearsal set' (RS) and the number of *different* words (ignoring repetitions) rehearsed within a set determined RS size. The extent of elaborative rehearsal was therefore reflected in the RS size. There was more elaborative rehearsal evident in the older children compared to the younger children, and the degree of elaboration was also shown to correlate significantly with improved long-term memory (LTM) recall.

Ornstein *et al.* (1985) had also found evidence for the use of more elaborative rehearsal in children with a mean age of 12;4 years in comparison to children with a mean age of 8;1 years using a similar rehearsal strategy training and overt rehearsal technique. However, the younger children were able to successfully engage in more elaborative rehearsal when the items remained visible after they had been displayed, in comparison to them being covered after their initial presentation. Whilst this additional task support did not improve the recall of the older children, recall did improve for the younger group.

The ability to categorize or group a subset of stimuli according to a particular criterion (e.g. a semantic category) is also relevant to the development of elaborative rehearsal. Hock, Park and Bjorklund (1998) assessed the recall of words presented on cards by two groups of children with mean ages of 8;2 and 10;3 years, respectively. On the basis of their recall scores, children were then placed in either a 'high-recall' or 'low-recall' group, and the learning strategies of the high- and low-recall groups were compared. All the children were found to adopt a strategy of trying to sort the cards into meaningful groups prior to rehearsing them out loud. However, the recall success depended on the temporal deployment of these strategies, with the high-recall children employing the grouping strategy earlier than the low-recall children. Hock, Park and Bjorkland (1998) suggested that the children with lower recall displayed what they termed a 'utilization deficit', as similar strategies were employed by the latter group, but only later during study and hence less successfully. They suggested that this may have been due to the later development, or maturation, of relevant cognitive mechanisms.

Justice (1985) linked the development of more effective encoding strategies in children to a potential shift from more effortful to more automatic application of them. Groups of children with mean ages of 7;7, 9;9 and 11;8 years, respectively, watched videotaped examples of someone 'grouping' (categorizing), 'repeating' (rehearsing), 'naming' and 'looking' at sets of pictures that could be semantically categorized. The children were also asked to recall a different set of pictures and category clustering was measured. These two tasks were alternated, so that half the children saw the videotape first and half the children took part in the memory study first. Metamemory (awareness that categorizing was the best strategy) improved with age, as did recall. The middle age-group only showed awareness of the best strategy when they saw the video before the memory task, which Justice (1985) interpreted as evidence of a developmental shift in strategic awareness and the move to an automatic application of that strategy, as demonstrated by the older children.

Research investigating the rehearsal strategies of children with ASDs is limited, but there is some evidence that the memory strategies of these children may mirror those of young TD children. Children with LFA engaged in less oral rehearsal (Hermelin & O'Connor, 1975) and were less likely to display a spontaneous use of memory strategies (Bock, 1994) than comparison samples. However, Tager-Flusberg (1985) found that children with autism with a mean age of 10;5 years could categorize items as well as comparison samples, regardless of the level of prototypicality of the items. Together with the evidence of a deficit in recall of semantically related material by children with autism mentioned earlier (Tager-Flusberg, 1991), these findings indicate an awareness of the semantic relationship between study items, but a failure to spontaneously use this information to aid recall.

Bock (1994) found that a small sample of children with LFA aged between 12;8 and 16;0 years could be effectively taught sorting strategies (grouping items according to a colour, or shape), and that this strategy could not only be maintained but generalized to other tasks involving similar strategies. More recently, Goldstein and Bebko (2005) success-fully trained a small sample of children with ASDs with an average age of 10;4 years and with relatively high IQ scores to use slightly more sophis-ticated grouping and rehearsal strategies to improve their recall of pic-tures of objects. These children also demonstrated the ability to transfer these skills to other tasks.

The evidence from the studies engaging TD children in overt rehearsal indicate that this technique is a useful one in revealing differences in rehearsal style, particularly with respect to elaborative rehearsal. The provision of task support at study through training and instructions has also shown to be effective with both TD children and children with autism. This latter finding is consistent with a 'utilization deficit' (Hock, Park & Bjorkland, 1998), in indicating an ability to adopt appropriate encoding strategies with guidance but a failure to do so spontaneously.

In the light of these findings we (Smith, Gardiner & Bowler, 2007) decided to investigate rehearsal strategies in a sample of adults with a diagnosis of AS (according to ICD-10 criteria), compared with typical adults individually matched for age and IQ. We investigated whether the adults with AS would spontaneously display less elaborative rehearsal and more maintenance rehearsal in comparison with typical adults and whether any encoding deficit would be reduced following appropriate training.

Overt rehearsal and free recall

We first tested participants' free recall without any instructions regarding rehearsal strategies, to compare the natural rehearsal strategies of both groups. Participants were simply made aware that both the order and number of words rehearsed was unrestricted within the time constraints (presentation rate of five seconds per word), but that they should repeat the words out loud in a way that would help them remember as many words from each list as possible. As previous experiments have indicated lower recall of semantically related (categorized) words, but not unrelated words, relative to comparison groups (Bowler, Matthews & Gardiner, 1997), these two types of lists were included to attempt to replicate these findings. A list of phonologically related (rhyming) words was also included, to see if the deficit in recall of related items is general and extends to phonologically related words. Alternatively, if there is a low-level, phonological encoding bias (Mottron, Morasse & Belleville, 2001) one might expect no deficit, or even enhanced recall of rhyming words. Participants recalled words from two lists of each type, to increase the number of observations.

Analysis of the recall data showed that the group of individuals with AS recalled significantly fewer words from the list of categorized nouns and also from the list of rhyming words than did the comparison group. However, recall of the words from the unrelated lists was similar for both participant groups. These findings support the organizational deficit hypothesis (Minshew et al., 1992) by showing that the failure to aid recall by establishing links between studied items (relational deficit) is not just evident in semantically related material, but extends to phonologically related material. They provide no support for a phonological encoding bias.

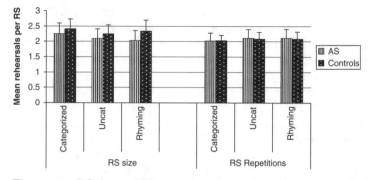

Figure 13.1 RS size and RS repetitions for adults with AS and typical adults

As training sessions for the children with autism had proved relatively successful in earlier studies (Bock, 1994; Goldstein & Bebko, 2005), participants in our study were then given brief training sessions prior to a second testing session with similar lists. During training, they were made explicitly aware of the relations between the words in the categorized and rhyming lists to encourage more elaborative rehearsal techniques. They were also instructed in the use of an imagery mnemonic for the categorized and noncategorized words, as this has proved a successful method of improving recall and encouraging relational processing in adults (Bower, 1972; Marschark & Hunt, 1989). Following training, the recall of the adults with AS was still impaired, relative to that of the comparison participants. This finding differed from the evidence of successful strategy training in children with ASDs (Bock, 1994; Goldstein & Bebko, 2005). Moreover, the results failed to provide further evidence of the task support hypothesis (Bowler, Matthews & Gardiner, 1997), although the support in this case was provided at study and not at test (see Smith, Gardiner & Bowler, 2007 for further discussion of free recall data).

The rehearsal data, with which we are mainly concerned here, were then analysed in terms of RS size, to reflect the degree of elaborative rehearsal, and in terms of RS repetitions, to reflect the degree of maintenance rehearsal. RS size was calculated in the same way as that described for Kunzinger (1985). RS repetitions were calculated as the number of times the presented word was repeated within each RS. The rehearsal data shown in Figure 13.1 are for the lists prior to training and so reflect the natural rehearsal styles of the two participant groups. It was predicted that if the adults with AS engage in less elaborative rehearsal and more maintenance rehearsal than is usual, then their rehearsal data might show smaller RS size (reflecting less elaboration), and greater RS repetitions (reflecting more maintenance rehearsal), than the comparison group. The bars on the left of Figure 13.1 illustrate the average RS size for each group and are consistently smaller for the AS group than the comparison group for each type of word list. In contrast, the bars on the right of Figure 13.1, which illustrate the average number of RS repetitions, are equal, or slightly higher for the AS group than the comparison group. These data reveal trends in the expected directions of less elaboration and slightly more maintenance rehearsal for the AS participants. These trends in rehearsal, however, did not differ statistically between the two groups.

As with the recall data, the training in our studies did not result in the expected outcome. Rather than increasing the RS size for the AS participants, the only significant impact of the training on the rehearsal data was a very small reduction in RS size for both participant groups.

Toichi and Kamio (2003) found that a free recall deficit in a population of individuals with HFA was apparent at primacy (the first few words in the list), rather than recency (the last few words in the list), a finding previously reported by Boucher (1981) in children with LFA. To see if a similar pattern was evident in our sample of adults with AS, scores were calculated for the recall of words according to each serial position of the list from all three kinds of list prior to training (in order to maximize the numbers of observations, even though recall in adults with AS was not impaired in all lists). The mean recall for each serial position (max 6) was then calculated for each participant group and these are shown in Figure 13.2. The number of times each word was rehearsed during each study trial was then calculated, again according to the original serial position of the word and the corresponding means for each participant group are shown in Figure 13.3. There is no maximum score for these data as rehearsal was unrestricted apart from the time limitations. To portray the underlying trends more clearly, these serial position curves were smoothed by averaging over each 3 successive data points except the first and the last.

Figure 13.2 shows that the deficit in recall for the AS group is not evident at recency but is quite consistent across the other serial positions, most notably at primacy, and the deficits for the middle and primacy items were statistically significant and consistent with previous findings (Boucher, 1981; Toichi & Kamio, 2003). As primacy is linked to long-term memory (LTM) recall and recency to short-term memory (STM) recall (Atkinson & Shiffrin, 1968; Waugh & Norman, 1965), these findings show that, as expected, any encoding deficit is limited to LTM. The data in Figure 13.3 indicate that both participant groups rehearsed the words from the beginning of the list more times than the middle or

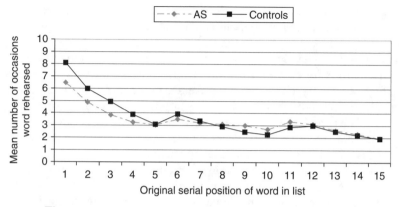

Figure 13.2 Mean recall of words for each serial position in the lists for adults with AS and typical adults

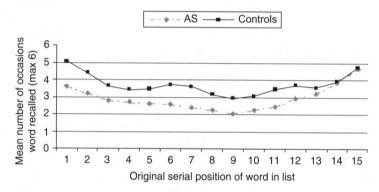

Figure 13.3 Mean number of rehearsals of words for each serial position in the lists for adults with AS and typical adults

the end. This is what one would expect, given that there would have been more opportunity to repeat words that were seen earlier, rather than later in the lists. However, the average rehearsal of primacy items is slightly lower for the adults with AS than it is for the typical adults. These trends were numerical only, but indicate that the AS participants were rehearsing the words at the beginning of the list fewer times on average than the comparison group. The words from the recency portion of the list were rehearsed a similar number of times, on average, in both groups.

These data suggest a potential, if weak, link between rehearsal style and recall. It may be that, whilst the overt rehearsal technique has been shown to be quite successful at identifying different strategies in children

(Kunzinger, 1985; Ornstein *et al.*, 1985), potential differences in rehearsal style in adults with AS may be more subtle and less easily identified with this method. It may also be that any such differences in rehearsal might have more effect in recognition tests than in recall, and might be more readily observed by a stronger, but covert, manipulation of rehearsal, as obtained by the use of a directed forgetting paradigm.

Directed forgetting and recognition

Directed forgetting is an effective way of manipulating rehearsal strategies. Using this technique, participants are shown material and subsequently cued to either learn or forget it, either in an item-by item or a list-by-list technique (see Basden & Basden, 1996). At test, participants are unexpectedly asked either to recall or to recognize items that were previously presented, *regardless* of whether the items were to-be-learned (TBL), or to-be-forgotten (TBF). In the item-by-item method (which is of most concern for this chapter), participants only engage in active learning strategies for TBL words and not for TBF words, so the type of cue (learn or forget) respectively increases, or decreases, the degree of elaborative rehearsal engaged in by the participants. Typical adults generally recall, or recognize, significantly more TBL words than TBF words. This has been termed the 'directed-forgetting effect' (Woodward, Bjork & Jongeward, 1973).

Following Woodward, Bjork and Jongeward (1973), Gardiner, Gawlick and Richardson-Klavehn (1994) found that the degree of elaboration could be further manipulated by altering the timing of the cue. Whilst the overall presentation rate of the items remained at 7 seconds per item, the cue was either shown immediately following the test word or delayed by 5 seconds. The 5-second delay before the cue was given results in the participants having to hold the word in their mind for longer, thus engaging in more maintenance rehearsal and reducing the time available for elaborative rehearsal. Presenting the cue immediately after the word enables participants to engage in more elaborative rehearsal and reduces the amount of maintenance rehearsal.

Gardiner, Gawlick and Richardson-Klavehn (1994) then tested recognition memory for all the words, using the remember–know paradigm (Tulving, 1985). In this paradigm, Remember (R) responses reflect autonoetic awareness and Know (K) responses reflect noetic awareness, which respectively reflect retrieval from episodic and semantic memory (see Gardiner, this volume, Chapter 1). Conscious recollection in the sense of bringing back to mind something that the participant thought at the time that they saw the word in the study list is indicated by an R response. A strong feeling that the word had appeared on the study list because it seems familiar, but without the additional recollection of anything thought about at that time, is indicated by a K response. Gardiner and colleagues found that the short cue delay resulted in greater R responses (thus that they were enhanced by elaborative rehearsal) and that the long cue delay resulted in greater K responses (thus that they were enhanced by maintenance rehearsal).

Adults with AS have previously shown reduced R responses in comparison to typical adults, thus demonstrating reduced autonoetic awareness and providing further evidence of a mild episodic memory impairment (Bowler, Gardiner & Gaigg, 2007; Bowler, Gardiner & Grice, 2000; Bowler *et al.*, 2000). In our study we aimed to replicate this finding and link it directly with rehearsal in the directed forgetting paradigm. If adults with AS engage in less elaborative rehearsal than typical adults, one would expect a reduced directed forgetting effect, with reduced recognition evident for TBL but not for TBF words. Moreover, this reduced effect should be evident in R responses and not in K responses. Given that the potential for elaboration is maximized when the cue appears after a short delay, this finding might be even stronger after a short cue delay than a long cue delay.

A group of adults with a diagnosis of AS, according to ICD-10 criteria, and a group of typical adults individually matched with the AS participants for age and IQ participated in the experiment. The study list words were all concrete nouns, in order to replicate the reduced concrete noun effect reported by Toichi and Kamio (2003). Half of the words were followed by a cue to learn and half of the words by a cue to forget, distribution of cue type being randomized. The timing of the cue was also manipulated, so that half of the cues appeared immediately after the words and half appeared after a delay of 5 seconds. Cue delay was counterbalanced and blocked by list half. After a short break, participants were given instructions on the R/K procedure. As in previous studies (e.g. Bowler, Gardiner & Grice, 2000), R and K were referred to in the instructions for the participants as Type A and Type B memory, respectively, to avoid confusion between the specific meaning of R (Remember) and K (Know) in this paradigm with their meaning of the whole words in everyday usage.

The proportions of correctly recognized words in the directed-forgetting recognition experiment are shown in Figures 13.4 and 13.5 for long and short cue delay respectively. (False alarm rates to unstudied words were similarly low in each group.) Directly comparing the learn and forget columns shows the directed forgetting effect for each group. As the difference between these two columns is greater for the comparison group than for the adults with AS, this demonstrates a reduced directed

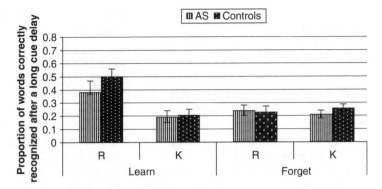

Figure 13.4 Proportion of words correctly recognized according to instruction, divided between R and K responses for adults with AS and typical adults in the long cue delay condition

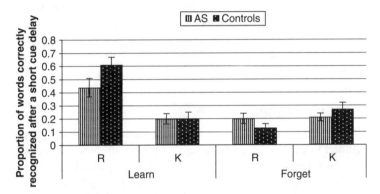

Figure 13.5 Proportion of words correctly recognized according to instruction, divided between R and K responses for adults with AS and typical adults in the short cue delay condition

forgetting effect for the AS sample. Both figures show that performance between the two groups differs for TBL words only. As individuals only actively engage in learning words TBL, rather than TBF, this supports the contention that memory impairments in adults with AS are more likely to occur when effortful learning strategies are being employed.

Comparison of the R/K columns in the two figures indicates that lower recognition scores overall in the AS group reflect fewer R responses relative to the comparison group. As R responses are enhanced by elaborative rehearsal (Gardiner, Gawlick & Richardson-Klavehn, 1994), these data support the hypothesis that adults with AS engage in less elaborative rehearsal than comparison participants. Comparison between Figures 13.4 and 13.5 reveals that the recognition of TBL words is better in the short cue delay condition compared to the long cue delay condition in both groups. This is to be expected, as the potential to elaborate is greater when the cue appears sooner, rather than later. However, whilst the directed forgetting effect is fairly stable in the R responses for the AS participants for both long and short cued-delayed words, the short cue delay resulted in an increased directed forgetting effect in R responses for the comparison group (indicated by the greater difference between learn and forget columns in Figure 13.5 compared to Figure 13.4). Consequently, whilst increasing the potential for elaboration is effectively utilized by the comparison group, the AS group did not appear to use the additional rehearsal time to its full advantage.

The most striking feature of the results shown in Figures 13.4 and 13.5 is that it is only in the R responses for the TBL words that there is any substantial difference in the performance of the two groups. This difference is entirely consistent with the hypothesis of an encoding deficit in elaborative rehearsal and, in contrast with the results of our previous study, this time the experimental conclusions were supported statistically.

Concluding remarks

The results of the overt rehearsal and directed forgetting experiments outlined in this chapter help to elucidate our understanding of encoding processes in individuals with ASDs. For the overt rehearsal experiment, there was a trend in the RS data towards slightly reduced RS size and slightly more RS repetitions for the adults with AS in relation to typical comparison participants. The serial position analyses of these data indicated that the adults with AS rehearsed the words at the beginning of the list fewer times, on average, than the adults without AS, which is also indicative of reduced elaboration. The deficit at primacy for the recall as well as for the rehearsal data is suggestive of a connection between rehearsal style and the mild impairment in recall. Consequently, the findings of the first study provide at least some tentative support for differences in rehearsal style in this population.

Stronger support for this hypothesis was provided by the results of the directed forgetting recognition experiment. Concrete nouns were selected for this experiment because of their elaborative qualities and the deficit in recognition for the AS group was most evident when the potential for elaboration was greatest, that is, for TBL words with a short cue delay. The fact that the deficit was apparent in R responses and not K suggests that this deficit is specific to elaborative rehearsal and not maintenance rehearsal, which provides further support for the previous finding of a deficit in episodic memory, as assessed by remember responses, in this population (Bowler, Gardiner & Grice, 2000; Bowler, Gardiner & Gaigg, 2007). These results may also help to explain why performance is improved for individuals with ASDs when support is provided at test, if one assumes that good retrieval cues can compensate for shallower encoding (Boucher & Lewis, 1989; Boucher & Warrington, 1976; Bowler, Matthews & Gardiner, 1997; Bowler, Gardiner & Berthollier, 2004; Tager-Flusberg, 1991).

Together, our findings suggest that the tendency for children with autism not to spontaneously engage fully in the most effective encoding strategies (Bock, 1994) may continue into adulthood. Developmental evidence links effective recall to the combined strategies of grouping and rehearsal, which appear to become more effective and automatic with age (Hock, Park & Bjorkland, 1998; Justice, 1985; Kunzinger, 1985). The results of our studies indicate that these strategies may be less effective and automatic in adults with AS in comparison to typical adults. An inability to fully deploy the most effective strategies would fit with a more general theory of an organizational deficit within individuals with ASDs (Minshew et al., 1992; Minshew & Goldstein, 2001). There was a slight tendency for greater maintenance rehearsal (Toichi & Kamio, 2002) in the overt rehearsal study, but not in the directed forgetting study, where greater maintenance rehearsal should have increased the proportions of K responses (Gardiner, Gawlick & Richardson-Klavehn, 1994; see too Bowler, Gardiner & Grice, 2000). There was no evidence of a bias towards phonological encoding in our study, but unlike Mottron, Morasse and Belleville (2001), we did not provide phonological retrieval cues.

Attempts at training children with autism to use more effective learning strategies appear to have been quite successful (Bock, 1994; Goldstein & Bebko, 2005). Our attempt at training adults with AS to engage in more elaborative techniques in the free-recall task failed to bring their recall performance to that of the comparison group, or to significantly increase the degree of overt elaborative rehearsal they engaged in. This might be because the training sessions we employed with the adults were relatively brief and involved more complex strategies, compared with those in studies with children. As support at test has been shown to compensate for memory impairments in adults with ASDs so that they match the performance of typical adults (e.g. Bowler, Gardiner & Berthollier, 2004), the quest to find mnemonic strategies that will successfully improve recall of contextual material in high-functioning individuals with ASDs is important, not least because of its potential application in educational and work environments.

Summary

In this chapter, we described experiments in which we compared the encoding strategies of a group of adults with a diagnosis of AS, according to ICD-10 criteria, with a sample of typical adults. More specifically, we investigated rehearsal processes at encoding both by measuring rehearsal directly, using an overt rehearsal technique, and by manipulating rehearsal by means of instructions given at study. We discussed the findings of these studies in relation to evidence of the development of rehearsal strategies in TD children and children with autism to consider possible parallels with adults with ASDs. We went on to consider how our findings, which show that there are some differences in rehearsal style, relate to the organizational deficit and task support hypotheses.

Acknowledgements

The work reported in this chapter forms part of a PhD thesis of the University of Sussex. The research of the first author is supported by Studentship Grant PTA-030-2002-01037 from the Economic and Social Research Council and the second author's research is funded by a Grant GO401413 from the Medical Research Council held jointly with Dermot Bowler, who is principal investigator. We are grateful for their support. We would like to thank Dermot Bowler for his collaboration in the studies described in this chapter, and Sebastian Gaigg for his support with regard to co-ordinating appointments with participants. We would also like to thank all those who kindly volunteered to take part in this research.

References

Atkinson, R. C. & Shiffrin, R. M. (1968). Human memory: a proposed system and its control process. In K. W. Spence & J. T. Spence (eds.), *The psychology of learning and motivation: advances in research and theory*, vol. 2, pp. 89–195. New York: Academic Press.

Basden, B. H. & Basden, D. R. (1996). Directed forgetting: further comparisons of the item and list methods. *Memory*, 4, 633–653.

Beversdorf, D. Q., Smith, B. W., Crucian, G., Anderson, J. M., Keillor, J., Barrett, A., Hughes, J., Felopulos, G. I., Bauman, M. L., Nadeau, S. E. & Heilman, K. M. (2000). Increased discrimination of 'false memories' in autism spectrum disorder. *Proceedings of the National Academy of Sciences of the United States of America*, 97, 8734–8737.

Bock, M. A. (1994). Acquisition, maintenance, and generalization of a categorization strategy by children with autism. *Journal of Autism and Developmental Disorders*, *24*, 39–51.

Boucher, J. (1981). Immediate free recall in early childhood autism: another point of behavioural similarity with the amnesic syndrome. *British Journal of Psychology*, *72*, 211–215.

Boucher, J. & Lewis, V. (1989). Memory impairments and communication in relatively able autistic children. *Journal of Child Psychology and Psychiatry*, *30*, 99–122.

Boucher, J. & Warrington, E. (1976). Memory deficits in early infantile autism: some similarities to the amnesic syndrome. *British Journal of Psychology 67*, 73–87.

Bower, G. H. (1972). Mental imagery and associative learning. In L. W. Gregg (ed.), *Cognition in learning and memory*, pp. 51–88. New York: Wiley.

Bowler, D. M., Gardiner, J. M. & Berthollier, N. (2004). Source memory in adolescents and adults with Asperger's Syndrome. *Journal of Autism and Developmental Disorders 34*, 533–542.

Bowler, D. M., Gardiner, J. M. & Gaigg, S. B. (2007). Factors affecting conscious awareness in the recollective experience of adults with Asperger's Syndrome. *Consciousness and Cognition*, *16*, 124–143.

Bowler, D. M., Gardiner, J. M. & Grice, S. (2000). Episodic memory and remembering in adults with Asperger Syndrome. *Journal of Autism and Developmental Disorders*, *30* (4), 295–304.

Bowler, D. M., Gardiner, J. M., Grice, S. & Saavalainen, P. (2000). Memory illusions: false recall and recognition in adults with Asperger's Syndrome. *Journal of Abnormal Psychology*, *109*, 663–672.

Bowler, D. M., Matthews, N. J. & Gardiner, J. M. (1997). Asperger's Syndrome and memory: similarity to autism but not amnesia. *Neuropsychologia 35*, 65–70.

Craik, F. I. M. & Lockhart, R. (1972). Levels of Processing: a framework for memory research. *Journal of Verbal Learning and Verbal Behavior*, *2*, 671–684.

Craik, F. I. M. & Tulving, E. (1975). Depth of processing and the retention of words in episodic memory. *Journal of Experimental Psychology: General*, *104*, 268–294.

Deese, J. (1959). On the prediction of occurrence of particular verbal intrusions in immediate recall. *Journal of Experimental Psychology*, *58*, 17–22.

Frith, U. (1989). *Autism: explaining the enigma*. Oxford: Blackwell.

Frith, U. & Snowling, M. (1983). Reading for meaning and reading for sound in autistic and dyslexic children. *Journal of Developmental Psychology*, *1*, 329–342.

Gardiner, J. M., Gawlick, B. & Richardson-Klavehn, A. (1994). Maintenance rehearsal affects knowing, not remembering; elaborative rehearsal affects remembering, not knowing. *Psychonomic Bulletin & Review*, *1*, 107–110.

Geiselman, R. E. & Bjork, R. A. (1980). Primary versus secondary rehearsal in imagined voices: differential effects on recognition. *Cognitive Psychology*, *12*, 188–205.

Goldstein, G. & Bebko, J. (2005). Memory strategy training and children with autism spectrum disorders. Poster presented at International Meeting for Autism Research (IMFAR), May, 2005.

Greene, R. L. (1987). Effects of maintenance rehearsal on human memory. *Psychological Bulletin, 102*, 403–413.

Happé, F. (1999). Autism: cognitive deficit or cognitive style? *Trends in Cognitive Sciences, 3*, 216–222.

Hermelin, B. & O'Connor, N. (1967). Remembering of words by psychotic and subnormal children. *British Journal of Psychology, 58*, 213–218.

Hermelin, B. M. & O'Connor, N. (1975). Seeing, speaking and ordering. In N. O'Connor (ed.), *Language, cognitive deficits and retardation.* London: Butterworth.

Hill, E. L. & Frith, U. (2003). Understanding autism: insights from mind and brain. *Philosophical Transactions of the Royal Society. London, B 358*, 281–289.

Hock, H. S., Park, C. L. & Bjorklund, D. F. (1998). Temporal organization in children's strategy formation. *Journal of Experimental Child Psychology, 70*, 187–206.

Justice, E. M. (1985). Categorization as a preferred memory strategy: developmental changes during elementary school. *Developmental Psychology, 21*, 1105–1110.

Kunzinger, E. L. (1985). A short-term longitudinal study of memorial development during early grade school. *Developmental Psychology, 21*, 642–646.

Marschark, M. & Hunt, R. R. (1989). A re-examination of the role of imagery in learning and memory. *Journal of Experimental Psychology: Learning, Memory and Cognition, 15*, 710–720.

Minshew, N. J. & Goldstein, G. (2001). The pattern of intact and impaired memory functions in autism. *Journal of Child Psychology and Psychiatry, 42*, 1095–1101.

Minshew, N. J., Goldstein, G., Muenz, L. R. & Payton, J. B. (1992). Neuropsychological functioning in nonmentally retarded autistic individuals. *Journal of Clinical and Experimental Neuropsychology, 14*, 749–761.

Mottron, L., Morasse, K. & Belleville, S. (2001). A study of memory functioning in individuals with autism. *Journal of Child Psychology and Psychiatry, 42*, 253–260.

Ornstein, P. A., Medlin, R. G., Stone, B. P. & Naus, M. J. (1985). Retrieving for rehearsal: an analysis of active rehearsal in children's memory. *Developmental Psychology, 21*, 633–641.

Paivio, A., Yuille, J. C. & Madigan, S. A. (1968). Concreteness, imagery, and meaningfulness values for 925 nouns. *Journal of Experimental Psychology Monograph Supplement, 76*, 1–25.

Rundus, D. (1977). Maintenance rehearsal and single-level processing. *Journal of Verbal Learning and Verbal Behavior 16*, 665–681.

Rundus, D. & Atkinson, R. (1970). Rehearsal processes in free recall: a procedure for direct observation. *Journal of Verbal Learning and Verbal Behavior, 9*, 99–105.

Smith, B. J., Gardiner, J. M. & Bowler, D. M. (2007). Deficits in free recall persist in Asperger's syndrome despite training in the use of list-appropriate learning strategies. *Journal of Autism and Developmental Disorders, 37*, 445–454.

(under review). Directed forgetting in adults with Asperger's syndrome.

Tager-Flusberg, H. (1985). Basic level and superordinate level categorization by autistic, mentally retarded, and normal children. *Journal of Experimental Child Psychology*, *40*, 450–469.

(1991). Semantic processing in the free recall of autistic children: further evidence for a cognitive deficit. *British Journal of Developmental Psychology*, *9*, 417–430.

Toichi, M. & Kamio, Y. (2002). Long-term memory and levels-of-processing in autism. *Neuropsychologia*, *40*, 964–969.

(2003). Long-term memory in high-functioning autism: controversy on episodic memory in autism reconsidered. *Journal of Autism and Developmental Disorders*, *33*, 151–161.

Tulving, E. (1985). Memory and consciousness. *Canadian Psychologist*, *26*, 1–12.

Waugh, N. C. & Norman, D. A. (1965). Primary memory. *Psychological Review*, *72*. 89–104.

Woodward, A. E., Bjork, R. A. & Jongeward, R. H. (1973). Recall and recognition as a function of primary rehearsal. *Journal of Verbal Learning & Verbal Behavior*, *12*, 608–617.

World Health Organization (1993). *International classification of diseases*, 10th edn (ICD-10). Geneva: WHO.

14   Memory, language and intellectual ability in low-functioning autism

Jill Boucher, Andrew Mayes and Sally Bigham

Introduction

Over the last two decades most psychological and neuropsychological research into autism has focused on individuals with Asperger syndrome or high-functioning autism (HFA),[1] rather than on individuals with low-functioning autism (LFA) or what is termed autistic disorder in the *Diagnostic and Statistical Manual of Mental Disorders*, 4th edition (DSM-IV; American Psychiatric Association, 1994). The core symptoms of autism, namely impairments of social interaction, communication and behavioural flexibility, are more likely to occur in pure form in people with HFA than people with LFA, and it makes sense, therefore, to focus on HFA to improve understanding of the core impairments.

A consequence of this strategy, however, has been a relative neglect of the impairments of language and intellectual ability that distinguish LFA from HFA. This is regrettable for both practical and theoretical reasons. From a practical point of view the combined effects of cognitive and linguistic impairments with autism are devastating for individuals themselves, and for their families and carers. Better understanding of the additional impairments is needed to provide optimal interventions and care. From a theoretical point of view, familial and genetic studies indicate that vulnerability to language impairment is related to vulnerability to autism (e.g. Bolton *et al.*, 1994; Piven & Palmer, 1997; Folstein *et al.*, 1999; Tomblin, Hafeman & O'Brien, 2003; Bartlett *et al.*, 2004). Understanding the bases of the language impairment in LFA should therefore contribute to understanding autism as a whole.

There is, however, no corresponding evidence of intellectual impairment in families that include someone with autism, and it is often

[1] 'High-functioning autism' is used here to refer to individuals with the triad of autism-diagnostic impairments whose current levels of cognitive functioning and language are normal. Thus the term includes people with 'Asperger syndrome'. This usage is adopted because to date there is no clear evidence that Asperger syndrome is a discrete disorder.

assumed that intellectual disability (ID) co-occurs with autism for reasons unconnected with autism itself. However, this assumption leaves unexplained why autism and ID are so strongly associated, as pointed out by Bailey, Phillips and Rutter (1996). These authors also noted that verbal intelligence, but not nonverbal intelligence, shows a substantial association with the severity of autism symptomology and with familial loading (Bolton *et al.*, 1994), and suggested that attempts to explain the association between autism and ID should focus on verbal abilities.

In this chapter we pursue Bailey *et al.*'s suggestion by developing the hypothesis outlined towards the end of Mayes and Boucher, this volume, Chapter 3, that a pervasive impairment of declarative memory is a critical cause of both the language impairment and the impairment of verbal intelligence (and hence overall intellectual disability) in people with low-functioning autism. This hypothesis builds on suggestions by Bachevalier (1994; also this volume, Chapter 2) and Bauman and Kemper (2004), and is consistent with the model of autism proposed in Boucher *et al.* (2005; see also Ben Shalom, 2003; Faran and Ben Shalom, this volume, Chapter 5). According to this model, the socio-emotional impairments of autism are associated with the disruption of co-ordinated activity between amygdala and prefrontal structures, and the additional language and learning impairments in LFA are associated with a disruption of co-ordinated hippocampal–parahippocampal and prefrontal activity. The relative sparing of procedural memory, and the resulting over-dependence on its use, can help to explain some of the repetitive behaviours diagnostic of autism – a suggestion also made by Bauman and Kemper (2004).

The chapter is in three main sections. The first section covers what has to be explained in terms of the typical profiles of linguistic and intellectual abilities in individuals with LFA. In the second main section we present our hypothesis, and suggest how it may explain the linguistic and intel-lectual ability profiles described, finishing with a short review of evidence relating to declarative memory in LFA. In the third main section we consider other explanations of the language and intellectual impairments in LFA, and suggest how our hypothesis may relate to these theories. The chapter concludes with a short summary.

What has to be explained

The linguistic profile is considered first, because we argue that declarative memory impairment affects language acquisition in the first instance, and intellectual ability secondarily.

The typical language profile in people with low-functioning autism

Language profiles in individuals with LFA are diverse. This diversity has numerous causes, including the fact that the profile varies with the severity of the language impairment; that the profile changes with age (Rapin & Dunn, 2003); and that the incidence of comorbid conditions including hearing loss, dyspraxia, and specific language impairment (SLI) is higher in people with autistic spectrum disorders (ASDs) than in the general population (Rapin, 1996; Kjelgaard & Tager-Flusberg, 2001).

Despite the diversity of language profiles at the level of individuals, a typical profile emerges from group studies (see Lord & Paul, 1997, for a detailed review). This profile is described next, features of the profile being enumerated in the order in which they will be discussed in the section headed 'Explaining the language impairment in low-functioning autism', later in the chapter.

1. The severity of the language impairment in lower-functioning autism ranges from mild to profound, and a high proportion of individuals never acquire language, or acquire at most a few words or signs used communicatively.[2] Individuals with no language, or negligible communicative language, may be described as having nonverbal LFA (NV-LFA). Correspondingly, those with some useful language may be described as having verbal LFA (V-LFA).

2. Language comprehension in people with V-LFA is invariably impaired: no instances of expressive language impairment in the absence of comprehension impairment have been found in large-scale studies (Rapin & Dunn, 2003). The universal comprehension impairment reflects a problem in relating linguistic symbols to an underlying knowledge-base. Thus, in an early review of studies of language in LFA, Fay and Schuler (1980) described word learning as consisting of 'the assignment of concrete labels rather than rule-linked conceptual units .... Memorised words denote but fail to connote' (p. 84). Similarly, in their review of language in autism, Lord and Paul (1997, p. 212) comment on the 'limited ability to integrate linguistic input with real-world knowledge'.

3. The language impairment in V-LFA is amodal: spoken, signed and written language are all affected, although there may be minor differences in the facility with which language can be acquired in one or

---

[2] As the diagnosis of able individuals with ASDs increases, it becomes harder to put a figure on the proportion of individuals with no language. At one time a figure of 50 per cent would have been accepted, but that decreases with the extension of the diagnostic capsule upwards.

other modality (especially where some comorbid condition such as hearing loss is present).

4. Phonology (sometimes referred to as articulation) and grammar (sometimes referred to as syntax) in people with V-LFA are less reliably and persistently impaired than semantics.[3] Early studies of verbal children of school age suggested that phonology and grammar were appropriate for mental age (Bartolucci et al., 1976; Boucher, 1976; Tager-Flusberg, 1981). Recent studies that include preschool children suggest that clinically significant phonological and grammatical abnormalities are commonly present in younger children but tend to resolve, especially in the more able, whereas difficulties in the processing of meaning persist (Rapin & Dunn, 2003; see also Kjelgaard & Tager-Flusberg, 2001).

5. There is a tendency to reproduce rote-learned chunks of grammatically well-formed language in echolalic and formulaic language (Kanner, 1946; Prizant, 1983a; Dobbinson, Perkins & Boucher, 2003). The use of echolalic and formulaic language can give the impression that expressive language is superior to comprehension, masking a paucity of productive expressive language (Dobbinson, 2000).

6. Finally, expressive language in V-LFA is characterized not only by echolalic utterances and excessive formulaicity, but also by the use of idiosyncratic words or phrases, and neologisms (Kanner, 1946; Volden & Lord, 1991). There are also problems with deictic terms, especially personal pronouns (Lee, Hobson & Chiat, 1994).

The intellectual ability profile in people with low-functioning autism

As in the case of language profiles, individual intelligence test profiles in LFA show considerable variation.[4] This is not surprising given the multifactorial nature of intelligence (Mackintosh, 1998); the profile also changes with age (Mayes & Calhoun, 2003a). Across groups, however, an LFA-specific profile emerges. The profile is first described utilizing the distinction between verbal and nonverbal intelligence as exemplified in the Wechsler intelligence scales (Wechsler, 1974, 1981). This is followed

---

[3] Pragmatics is always impaired in individuals with ASDs, even those who are high functioning. However, pragmatics relates to the use of language, and is more to do with communication than with structural language (which is a means of communication), which is why the pragmatic impairment is not discussed here.

[4] Intelligence theory and testing are not, of course, the only framework that can be used for examining intellectual abilities, but they provide the most useful framework for present purposes – not least because of the availability of research data based on standardized measures.

Table 14.1. *Summary of findings from studies using the Wechsler intelligence tests (adapted from Siegel, Minshew & Goldstein, 1996, with permission)*

	Age status of participants	FSIQ	VQ	PQ	VQ < PQ difference
Ohta, 1987	Children[*]	72	65	85	20
Wassing, 1965	Children[*]	71	59	88	29
Lincoln et al., 1988	Children[*]	69	60	84	24
Allen et al., 1991	Children[*]	68	57	85	28
Bartak et al. 1975	Children[*]	67	NR (<67)	97	>30
Narita & Koga, 1987	NR	66	61	78	17

FSIQ = Full-Scale Intelligence Quotient; VQ = Verbal Quotient; PQ = Performance Quotient
NR = not reported
[*]Pre-adolescent

by a short section utilizing the distinction between fluid and crystallized intelligence (Horn & Cattell, 1966; Cattell, 1971).

Profile based on the verbal–nonverbal distinction

Bailey *et al.* are not the only authors who have noted that overall intellectual disability in LFA owes more to a decline in verbal intelligence than a decline in nonverbal intelligence (see for example Rumsey, 1992; Lincoln, Allen & Kilman, 1995; Siegel, Minshew & Goldstein, 1996; Lord & Paul, 1997; however, see Mayes & Calhoun, 2003b for some contrary evidence). Evidence in support of this suggestion is summarized in Table 14.1, which shows findings from studies using versions of the Wechsler intelligence scales to assess Verbal and Performance (nonverbal) abilities in individuals whose Full-Scale IQ is below 75.

Notably, the discrepancy between verbal and nonverbal intelligence in low-ability individuals with autism does not extend to high-functioning individuals, in whom no consistent pattern of verbal or nonverbal superiority occurs (Minshew, Turner & Goldstein, 2005).

More detailed examination of the intelligence test profiles of groups of individuals with verbal LFA assessed using the Wechsler scales shows the following. Of the six Verbal subtests, the Comprehension subtest is least well performed, with performance on the Information, Vocabulary, Arithmetic and Similarities subtests also low in relation to Full-Scale IQ, leaving performance on the Digit Span subtest constituting a relative peak of ability, though not necessarily within the normal range (Lincoln, Allen & Kilman, 1995; Siegel, Minshew & Goldstein, 1996). Performance across the five Performance (nonverbal) subtests is also uneven, with scores on the Picture Arrangement subtest and the Digit Symbol (adult version) or Coding (children's version) subtest consistently lower than those on the Block Design, Picture Completion and Object Assembly subtests (Lincoln, Allen & Kilman, 1995; Siegel, Minshew & Goldstein, 1996).

Notably, individuals with high-functioning autism differ from groups with V-LFA in their Verbal subtest profile, performing well on the Information, Vocabulary, Arithmetic and Similarities subtests (although performing less well on the Comprehension subtest) (Klin et al., 2000; Minshew, Taylor & Goldstein, 2005). Performance on Digit Span does not emerge as a peak ability in individuals with HFA because they perform well on most of the other Verbal subtests. Notably, also, individuals with high-functioning autism do not differ from groups with V-LFA in their Performance (nonverbal) subtest profile, although achieving higher scores than low-functioning individuals.

Individuals with nonverbal LFA, who are not testable on formal scales, may be profoundly and pervasively mentally impaired. However, some individuals with NV-LFA are well oriented within familiar environments, with daily living skills that are superior to either their social or their communication abilities (Carter et al., 1998; Kraijer, 2000). It may be inferred that these individuals have acquired at least some implicit, pre-verbal knowledge of basic-level categories: they put on shoes, open doors, turn on taps, eat with spoons, etc. These mute, or nearly mute, individuals also have some relatively spared nonverbal abilities, generally to do with fitting and assembly skills (DeMyer, 1976).

Profile based on the fluid–crystallized intelligence distinction

A widely accepted distinction made in the literature on intelligence is that between fluid and crystallized intelligence (Horn & Cattell, 1966; Cattell, 1971). Fluid intelligence reflects the ability to solve novel problems not dependent on acquired knowledge, and may be thought of as corresponding to a general reasoning factor 'g', reflecting genetic potential. Crystallized intelligence, on the other hand, corresponds to acquired knowledge and is more dependent on verbal ability, experiential opportunities and education.

Individuals with V-LFA tend to perform better on Raven's Matrices (Raven, Court & Raven, 1986), which is generally considered to reflect fluid intelligence, than they do on the Comprehension, Information, Similarities, Arithmetic and Vocabulary subtests of the Wechsler tests, all of which reflect verbally mediated, crystallized intelligence (Dawson et al., 2007). This suggests that fluid intelligence is generally less impaired than crystallized intelligence in people with V-LFA. The relative sparing of fluid intelligence is also suggested by the finding that speed of processing (widely considered to correlate with 'g') is not significantly impaired in lower-functioning individuals with autism (Scheuffgen *et al.*, 2000).

Pervasive declarative memory impairment as an explanation of language impairment and intellectual disability in low-functioning autism

The hypothesis

We hypothesize that the language and intellectual ability profiles of individuals with low-functioning autism, outlined above, derive in large part from impairments of long-term declarative memory. This hypothesis was introduced in Mayes and Boucher (this volume, Chapter 3) in terms of combined impairments of recollection and familiarity, affecting recall and recognition of both personally experienced events and impersonal facts. In that chapter we briefly presented neurobiological evidence consistent with this hypothesis. Here we flesh out the hypothesis, and review the behavioural evidence relating to it. First, however, we briefly recapitulate the distinction between declarative and nondeclarative, or procedural, memory.

The distinction between declarative and nondeclarative memory

Memory that is accompanied by a conscious feeling of memory is generally described as declarative, or explicit. Memory not so accompanied is generally described as nondeclarative, or implicit. Memory for personally experienced events (episodic memory) and memory for factual information (semantic memory) are generally accompanied by a conscious feeling of memory, and may therefore be described as declarative. By contrast, the heterogeneous kinds of learning covered by procedural memory (see this volume, Gardiner, Chapter 1, and Mayes & Boucher, Chapter 3) are not usually accompanied by a conscious feeling of memory, and may be described as nondeclarative, or implicit.[5]

---

[5] The distinctions between declarative and nondeclarative, explicit and implicit, are not clear cut. Memories that we actually use often comprise differently weighted mixtures of declarative and nondeclarative memory with feelings of memory correspondingly varying in strength.

Explaining the language profile

Key features of the language profile in people with LFA as described earlier in the chapter are considered in turn, and explained in terms of the hypothesis.

1. According to the hypothesis, the complete or near-complete absence of language in people with nonverbal LFA results from a total loss, or near total loss, of declarative memory, comparable to that seen in severe forms of adult-acquired global amnesia as described in Chapter 3. The language impairment in people with verbal LFA is hypothesized to result largely from diminished, but not total loss of, declarative memory ability, with procedural memory and immediate memory relatively intact.

2. The universal impairment of comprehension and meaning in V-LFA is hypothesized to result from impaired access to memory for preverbal categorical knowledge of the world. Access to such information is required for the acquisition of fully meaningful linguistic symbols. For example, the typically developing infant or young child who hears the word *dog* spoken in the presence of an actual dog, or picture of a dog, sees the dog in front of her, accesses her memory for information relating to the category of 'dogs-in-general', and learns that *dog* refers to (this particular dog and) dogs-in-general (see Figure 14.1a). A child who is unable to access her categorical knowledge of 'dogs-in-general' will hear the word *dog*, and learn only that *dog* refers to this particular dog (see Figure 14.1b).

Figure 14.1a Learning that a word refers to a particular referent and to the category to which the referent belongs

Figure 14.1b Learning to label a particular referent

Thus, single-word naming of basic-level categories (whether by spoken word or manual sign) *can* proceed in the absence of declarative memory. However, the linguistic symbols that are acquired will tend to operate like proper names with fixed meanings rather than with rich, flexible and generalizable meanings. An impairment of declarative memory would therefore cause early word learning to have the character of 'the assignment of concrete labels rather than rule-linked conceptual units', as noted by Fay and Schuler (1980) in their early review. An impairment of declarative memory would also cause precisely the 'limited ability to integrate linguistic input with real-world knowledge' noted by Lord and Paul (1997, p. 212). Moreover, recent work by Preissler (2006) confirms that children with autism tend to make the kind of symbol–referent association (underlying denotation), rather than the normal symbol–reference association (underlying connotation), as illustrated in Figures 14.1b and 14.1a, respectively. Lord and Paul's comment that linguistic *input* – i.e. heard speech, seen manual signs or seen written language – fails to connect with real-world knowledge, highlights the problems of comprehension that would result from the limited and inflexible meanings that words have for individuals with V-LFA. Thus, impaired comprehension can be traced back to the declarative memory impairment underlying the acquisition of linguistic meaning.

It seems likely that those categories and concepts that are normally acquired via language – for example, superordinate terms or abstract words – would be cumulatively affected both by the overall delay in language acquisition, but also by the limited meaning of such linguistic symbols as have been acquired. There is some evidence which might suggest that acquisition of superordinate terms, at least, is not impaired (e.g. Tager-Flusberg, 1985a, b; Boucher, 1988). However, these studies compared participant groups matched for verbal mental age using a vocabulary comprehension test that included both basic-level and superordinate-level items, biasing towards negative findings.

3. A pervasive declarative memory impairment will affect language acquisition in all modalities, as outlined in the previous paragraph.

4. In contrast to the effect of declarative memory impairment on the acquisition of linguistic meaning, the sparing of procedural memory in people with V-LFA will leave the acquisition of phonology and grammar relatively intact. This is because the items and combinatorial rules of phonology and grammar are learned unconsciously (Ullman, 2004) – we only gain explicit access to this knowledge if we study linguistics. However, the development of grammar will not be completely spared, because it is partly dependent on linguistic meaning, via the process sometimes referred to as semantic bootstrapping. For this reason, the acquisition of grammatical items and rules will be most affected in younger or less able individuals with V-LFA, whose lexical development is most impoverished.

5. Spared procedural memory and spared immediate memory will also enable the individual with declarative memory impairment to acquire perceptual representations of chunks of heard speech or seen writing. According to Ullman's (2004) 'see-saw' effect, such selectively spared abilities will be utilized to an unusual extent to compensate for diminished declarative memory. The phonologically and grammatically correct language reproduced will give the impression that expressive language is superior to comprehension, masking the impairment of truly productive expressive language.

6. Use of idiosyncratic language and impaired understanding and use of deictic terms can be explained mainly in terms of the social impairments of people with ASDs, and specifically by a lack of understanding of other minds (see below), rather than by our hypothesis. However, spared associative learning of the kind that is included within the set of procedural memory abilities (Mayes and Boucher, this volume, Chapter 3) may contribute to the tendency to use idiosyncratic terms (cf. Kanner's, 1946, well-known anecdote about an individual's use of 'Don't throw the dog off the balcony' to mean 'No').

Explaining the intellectual ability profile

Verbal versus nonverbal abilities

The lower scores of individuals with verbal LFA on Verbal as opposed to Performance (nonverbal) subtests of the Wechsler scales can be understood in terms of the effect that a partial impairment of declarative memory, combined with spared procedural and immediate memory, would have on the performance of individual subtests.

In particular, those subtests most likely to be adversely affected by declarative memory impairment are all in the Verbal group, namely: the Comprehension, Information, Vocabulary, Arithmetic and Similarities subtests, all of which are heavily dependent on linguistic knowledge *per se*, on language-mediated learning, and to a greater or lesser extent on the ability to access factual knowledge from semantic memory. At the same time, most of those subtests least likely to be affected by declarative memory impairment are in the Performance group, namely Block Design, Picture Completion, and Object Assembly – all subtests probing perceptual and constructive visuo-spatial abilities, with limited reliance on language, verbal mediation, or access to factual knowledge in semantic memory. This, we argue, is sufficient to explain the pattern of VQ < PQ observed in individuals with low-functioning autism (see Table 14.1).

Of the remaining subtests, performance on the Digit Span Verbal subtest is – according to the hypothesis – relatively spared because it tests immediate memory, with minimal dependence on either language or long-term declarative memory. Relatively poor performance on the Picture Arrangement and Digit Symbol/Coding nonverbal subtests may be explained in terms of their partial dependence on language mediation and on declarative memory (for events, in the case of Picture Arrangement; for the symbols/codes provided in the case of Digit Symbol/Coding). The fact that the VQ < PQ discrepancy reliably occurs in groups of individuals with V-LFA, despite the relatively good performance on Digit Span and the relatively poor performances on Picture Arrangement and Digit Symbol/Coding, underlines the extent to which the contrasting performances on the other Verbal and Performance subtests drives VQ and PQ apart.

It is important to stress that we are not claiming that declarative memory impairments are the sole cause of impaired performance on certain intelligence subtests in lower-functioning individuals with ASDs. In terms of the hypothesis, individuals with HFA perform well on most of the Verbal subtests precisely because they do not have diminished declarative memory leading to the impairments of language and semantic memory that affect lower-functioning individuals. However, individuals with HFA, as well as those with LFA, perform consistently less well on the Comprehension subtest than on other Verbal subtests; and less well on Picture Arrangement and Digit Symbol/Coding than on other Performance subtests (Siegel, Minshew & Goldstein, 1996; Minshew, Turner & Goldstein, 2005). This suggests that other, autism-specific impairments are depressing performance on these particular tests. In the case of Comprehension, which assesses understanding and knowledge of social situations and conventions, autism-related social impairments are clearly contributory. In the case of Picture Arrangement and Digit Symbol/Coding, impaired episodic memory (which affects individuals across the spectrum) may be a contributory factor. Impaired sequential processing may also be involved – a possibility that is discussed towards the end of the chapter.

Finally, the fact that not all those individuals who have nonverbal LFA are profoundly intellectually impaired is of particular relevance to the hypothesis. According to the hypothesis, these individuals have total, or near total loss of declarative memory, leaving procedural memory at least relatively intact. Nondeclarative, procedural forms of memory are sufficient for the acquisition of categorical knowledge based on sensory-perceptual experience, as is evident from observation of preverbal typically developing infants. Implicit learning would therefore proceed in these individuals, including the acquisition of basic-level categorical knowledge, and some daily living skills and routines. Similarly, visuo-spatial abilities, including certain fitting and assembly skills of the kinds assessed in formal intelligence tests would be relatively spared, leading to the uneven patterns of ability that have been observed (Carter et al., 1998; DeMyer, 1976; Kraijer, 2000). By contrast, those individuals with NV-LFA who are profoundly and pervasively mentally impaired are hypothesized to have total or near total loss of both declarative and procedural memory, probably associated with extensive bilateral medial temporal lobe dysgenesis or damage (DeLong & Heinz, 1997) as well as other structural brain abnormalities.

The fluid versus crystallized intelligence distinction

The discrepancy between relatively spared performance on tasks mainly dependent on fluid intelligence, as opposed to impaired performance on tasks that are largely dependent on language and other acquired knowledge, can be explained in terms of the problems of language acquisition and of access to memory for factual or episodic information entailed by a pervasive impairment of declarative memory. Specifically, impaired declarative memory will have negative effects on measures of crystallized intelligence which, by definition, assess abilities that are dependent on language and acquired knowledge. Assuming that the declarative memory impairment is selective, general reasoning ability need not be affected, leaving performance on measures of fluid intelligence, such as Raven's Matrices, relatively spared (Dawson *et al.*, 2007). Speed of processing would also be unaffected, as has been observed by Scheuffgen *et al.* (2000).

Evidence relating to the hypothesis

A pervasive impairment of long term declarative memory would be manifested in impaired performance on tests of delayed free recall and recognition extending across memory for factual information as well as memory for personally experienced episodes. Consistent with the tendency to focus on people with high-functioning autism or Asperger syndrome in recent neuropsychological research, there have been relatively few studies of memory in lower-functioning autism over the last two decades. The results of early studies and a few that are more recent are summarized next.

Free recall in people with LFA has generally been found to be either impaired or anomalous. Impairments have been shown for recall of meaningful verbal material (e.g. O'Connor & Hermelin, 1967; Hermelin & O'Connor, 1967; Fyffe & Prior, 1978; Tager-Flusberg, 1991), and also events (Boucher, 1981a; Boucher & Lewis, 1989; Millward *et al.*, 2000). Anomalies have been demonstrated in tests of the recall of unrelated words, where recency effects tend to make a greater than normal contribution to overall performance (Boucher, 1978, 1981b; Fyffe & Prior, 1978). Free recall impairments and anomalies in people with LFA are unsurprising, given the evidence of impaired recollection and associated impairments of episodic memory in people with HFA, as documented in other chapters in this book.

The more critical test of our hypothesis concerns the predictions that (a) recognition memory will be impaired; and (b) impaired recognition will relate to levels of conceptual, lexical and factual knowledge, including performance on specific verbal intelligence subtests.

Regarding prediction (a), there is some evidence suggestive of impaired recognition memory in people with LFA. However, the evidence is sparse and inconclusive. For example, Boucher and Warrington (1976), using a picture recognition task with a mixed-ability group, noted wide variation in the scores of the children with autism, although there was no overall group impairment. These authors suggested that the lower-functioning children in their study, but not the higher-functioning children, may have had a recognition impairment. In another early study, Ameli *et al.* (1988) reported impaired recognition of nonmeaningful, but not meaningful, visual stimuli in a mixed-ability group; however, the control group was not matched for verbal ability in this study. Summers and Craik (1994) reported impaired word recognition; and Barth, Fein and Waterhouse

(1995) reported visual recognition impairment, although the impairment was not evident when differences in nonverbal ability were partialled out. Dawson *et al.* (1998, 2001) showed impaired performance on a test of delayed nonmatching to sample, but interpreted this finding in terms of impaired reward-association mechanisms, rather than as a recognition impairment *per se*.

Regarding prediction (b), there are no published studies assessing relations between recognition and conceptual-lexical and factual knowledge in LFA. In a recent study (Boucher *et al.*, 2007) we set out to obtain additional data concerning recognition abilities in individuals with LFA, and to test the prediction that recognition relates to conceptual and lexical abilities in this group, but not in comparison groups. This study is briefly described next.

The aim of the study was to test predictions (a) and (b) as outlined above. A group of teenagers with V-LFA was compared with a young, ability-matched group of typically developing (TD) children, a group of children with HFA matched with the TD group for age, and an age- and language-ability-matched group of teenagers with intellectual disability (ID) without autism. To test the prediction that recognition memory will be uniquely impaired in individuals with LFA, we administered two visual recognition tasks, using nonmeaningful materials. To test the prediction that recognition will correlate with conceptual-lexical knowledge in individuals with LFA, but not in other groups, we gave the participants four tests assessing access to, and explicit use of, conceptual and lexical knowledge. We used analyses of covariance, controlling for differences in nonverbal abilities, to compare recognition memory in the four groups, and also to compare conceptual-lexical knowledge in the four groups. Bivariate correlation tests were used to assess relations between recognition and conceptual-lexical knowledge in each of the four groups.

The results of the study were in line with the predictions in so far as recognition was more impaired in the LFA group than in the other three groups, though only consistently significantly impaired relative to the TD group. There was, in addition, a strong positive correlation between recognition scores and scores on measures of conceptual and linguistic knowledge in the LFA group, but not in the TD or ID groups, although there was a trend towards positive correlation in the HFA group.

Summary

In sum, firm evidence of a pervasive declarative memory impairment in LFA, affecting recognition as well as recall, is currently lacking, although the weight of the evidence is positive. Regarding the prediction that recognition and conceptual-linguistic knowledge will be related in people with the profile of autism-related language impairments, the evidence from our recent study supports the prediction, and is hard to explain except in terms of the hypothesis.

Other suggested explanations of language (and intellectual) impairments in low-functioning autism

It is certain that more than one causal factor contributes to structural language impairments in LFA, even before considering the additional effects of comorbid conditions which modify linguistic profiles in individuals and subgroups. It is therefore important to set our own theory into the context of other major theories, and to consider how other theories may relate to our own.

Several explanations of the language impairment in LFA have been proposed in the past, a few of which share with our own hypothesis the potential to explain the intellectual impairment, also, although this is rarely emphasized. In this section, the theories presented all relate primarily to the language impairment. Where they may have some potential to explain intellectual disabilities, this is mentioned.

Mindblindness

Mindblindness (Baron-Cohen, 1995) resulting from reduced empathy (Baron-Cohen, 2005) cannot but affect the way in which language as a shared conventional symbol system is acquired by people with ASDs (Hobson, 1993; Bloom, 2000). In particular, impaired mindreading would contribute to abnormal lexical development, given that typically developing children routinely infer the speaker's intention when forming an association between a novel object or action and a novel word – something that children with autism do not generally do (Baron-Cohen, Baldwin & Crowson, 1997; Preissler & Carey, 2005). It can be assumed, therefore, that mindblindness contributes to the abnormalities of lexical development that are so marked in people with LFA and which remain in subtle form in higher-functioning individuals (Happé, 1994). Mindblindness can also explain the problems that younger and less able individuals have in understanding and using deictic terms – i.e. terms whose meaning depends on the identity of the speaker ('you'/'me'), or the speaker's location ('here'/'there').

However, as pointed out by Bloom (2000), mindblindness cannot offer a sufficient explanation of language impairment in LFA because individuals with HFA/Asperger syndrome have impaired joint attention and theory of mind but nevertheless develop clinically normal language. As Bloom argues, there must be other routes into language that people with HFA are able to utilize, but which are unavailable to people with LFA. According to the declarative memory hypothesis, the critical difference is that people with HFA, unlike people with LFA, have normal access to implicitly acquired knowledge-of-the world, and are therefore able to acquire a predominantly normal word-meaning system (as illustrated in Figure 14.1a).

Impaired symbol formation and use; impaired ability to form semantic categories

An early suggestion of 'asymbolia' (Ricks & Wing, 1975) is broadly compatible with the declarative memory hypothesis, so long as asymbolia is interpreted as a description of individuals with NV-LFA, with anomalous symbol formation characterizing V-LFA. Another, somewhat similar, early theory was that individuals with 'Kanner's syndrome' / 'early infantile autism' have impaired ability to form semantic categories which are integrated into an underlying conceptual system (Menyuk, 1978; Fay & Schuler, 1980; Tager-Flusberg, 1981). This theory is also compatible with our hypothesis, if understood as a difficulty in forming *explicit* semantic categories that fully connote *implicit* conceptual knowledge. Both these early theories have some potential to explain the intellectual impairments, as well as the language impairments, in LFA.

Specific language impairments

The early theory that specific language impairments (SLI) contribute to low-functioning autism (Churchill, 1972) has been reinvigorated by recent studies showing that the commonalities between SLI and language impairments in autism are more frequent (Rapin & Dunn, 2003) and more fine-grained (Kjelgaard & Tager-Flusberg, 2001; Roberts, Rice & Tager-Flusberg, 2004) than was previously thought. These findings pose challenges for understanding the relationship between autism and specific language impairments (SLIs) at all levels of causal analysis. However, we concur with Bishop (2004) and with Botting and Conti-Ramsden (2003) who conceptualize the relation between SLI and language impairment in autism in terms of a continuum of language-related impairments, features of which can occur in the various subtypes of SLI and also in association with autism, as a result of shared genetic risk factors. According to this view, SLI cannot by itself explain the language impairment in LFA, although the two conditions share some linguistic features, and mixed forms of autism and SLI can occur at all levels of ability (Bartak, Rutter & Cox, 1975; Kjelgaard & Tager-Flusberg, 2001).

Impairments of sequencing and segmenting

Impaired sequencing has been suggested as a cause of language impairment and IQ troughs in LFA (Lincoln, Allen & Kilman, 1995; see also Tanguay, 1984). Sequencing is generally identified with the processing of transient or successive inputs such as heard speech, or seen sign language, that occur through time; and also with analytic as opposed to holistic processing. The suggestion of impaired analysis of transient or successive inputs is implicit in the impaired segmenting hypothesis proposed by Prizant (1983b) as an explanation of language impairment in LFA (see also Boucher, 2000).

Consistency between the explanations of language and intellectual impairments in LFA in terms of impaired declarative memory and in terms of impaired sequencing and segmenting may be achieved by building on insights into psychological processes underlying autism, some of which are presented in this book. Specifically, it was early suggested (Frith, 1989) that weak central coherence in autism might result from abnormalities of integrative neural binding. This hypothesis was argued for in greater detail by Brock *et al.* (2002), who suggested that whereas activity in local neural networks functions normally, the synchronization, or binding together, of activity across networks may be dysfunctional in autism. The notion of impaired binding as a contributory cause of various aspects of the behavioural abnormalities in autism is now increasingly invoked, including as an explanation of the declarative memory impairments and anomalies that occur in HFA/Asperger syndrome (e.g. in this volume: DeLong, Chapter 6; Webb, Chapter 10; and Bowler & Gaigg, Chapter 17). If, as seems intuitively likely, the synchronization of neural activity across disparate local networks is dependent on the same oscillatory or cyclic mechanisms that subserve the temporal analysis of transient inputs, then the memory impairments emphasized in this and other chapters in this book, and the sequencing–segmenting impairments noted by others, can be seen as having the same root cause.

Other explanatory theories

Ullman's (2004) model of the prerequisites for language acquisition is relevant to our hypothesis, in that he argues that lexical development is dependent on declarative memory, whereas phonological and grammatical development are dependent on procedural memory. Ullman proposes, albeit very briefly, that procedural memory impairment underlies language impairment in autism (also in SLI). This proposal appears to be based on a limited knowledge of the language profile in autism. However, his model may be important for an understanding of the relationship between autism and SLI.

Baron-Cohen (2006) has recently argued that an excessive tendency to systemize could cause, or contribute to, the language impairment in LFA and also the intellectual impairment. This theory has not been well developed, and cannot therefore be meaningfully assessed. However, in seeking a common explanation for the language and intellectual impairments together, Baron-Cohen is, as we are, following the precept of Bailey *et al.* referred to at the outset of this chapter, and this is to be welcomed.

Summary

Little attempt has been made to explain why language impairment and intellectual disability occur together in people with low-functioning autism, and this is regrettable for both practical and theoretical reasons. In this chapter we present behavioural arguments and evidence supporting the hypothesis that both the language impairment and the ID derive in part from a pervasive impairment of declarative memory, affecting memory for factual information as well as personally experienced events, and manifested in impairments of recognition as well as recall. We describe the profiles of language ability and disability, and of intellectual ability and disability, most characteristic of people with LFA, and argue that diminished declarative memory, leaving procedural memory and immediate memory unimpaired, can explain the profiles seen in groups of individuals with V-LFA; whereas total, or near total, loss of declarative memory, leaving procedural and immediate memory relatively intact in some but not all individuals, can explain the profiles associated with NV-LFA. We present evidence, including some from a recent study of our own, which provides some support for the hypothesis, although more investigation is needed. Finally, we consider alternative or additional explanations of the language impairment in LFA, and suggest how our own theory relates to other possible causal factors.

Acknowledgement

The empirical work reported in this chapter was supported by a grant from the Economic and Social Research Council.

References

Allen, M., Lincoln, A. & Kaufman, A. (1991). Sequential and simultaneous processing abilities of high-functioning autistic and language-impaired children. *Journal of Autism and Developmental Disorders*, *21*, 483–502.

Ameli, R., Courchesne, E., Lincoln, A., Kaufman, A. & Grillon, C. (1988). Visual memory processes in high functioning individuals with autism. *Journal of Autism and Developmental Disorders*, *18*, 601–615.

American Psychiatric Association (APA) (1994). *Diagnostic and statistical manual of mental disorders*, 4th edn (DSM-IV). Washington, DC: American Psychiatric Association.

Bachevalier, J. (1994). Medial temporal lobe structures and autism: a review of clinical and experimental findings. *Neuropsychologia*, *32*, 627–648.

Bailey, A., Phillips, W. & Rutter, M. (1996). Autism: towards an integration of clinical, genetic, neuropsychological, and neurobiological perspectives. *Journal of Child Psychology and Psychiatry*, *37*, 89–126.

Baron-Cohen, S. (1995). *Mindblindness*. London: MIT Press.

  (2005). The empathising system: a revision of the 1994 model of the mind-reading system. In B. Ellis & D. Bjorkland (eds.), *Origins of the social mind*, pp. 468–492. New York: Guilford Press.

  (2006). Two new theories of autism: hyper-systemising and assortative mating. *Archives of Diseases of Childhood*, *91*, 2–5.

Baron-Cohen, S., Baldwin, D. & Crowson, M. (1997). Do children with autism use the speaker's direction of gaze strategy to crack the code of language? *Child Development*, *68*, 48–57.

Bartak, L., Rutter, M. & Cox, A. (1975). A comparative study of infantile autism and specific developmental receptive language disorder: I. The children. *British Journal of Psychiatry*, *126*, 127–145.

Barth, C., Fein, D. & Waterhouse, L. (1995). Delayed match-to-sample performance in autistic children. *Developmental Neuropsychology*, *11*, 53–69.

Bartlett, C., Flax, J., Logue, M., Brett, J., Smith, D., Vieland, V., Tallal, P. & Brzustowicz, L. (2004). Examination of potential overlap in autism and language loci on chromosomes 2, 7, and 13 in two independent samples ascertained for specific language impairment. *Human Heredity*, *57*, 10–20.

Bartolucci, G., Pierce, S., Streiner, D. & Tolkin-Eppel, P. (1976). Phonological investigation of verbal autistic and mentally retarded subjects. *Journal of Autism and Childhood Schizophrenia*, *6*, 303–315.

Bauman, M. L. & Kemper, T. L. (2004). Structural brain anatomy in autism: what is the evidence? In M. L. Bauman & T. L. Kemper (eds.), *The neurobiology of autism*, pp. 119–145. Baltimore: Johns Hopkins Press.

Ben Shalom, D. (2003). Memory in autism: review and synthesis. *Cortex 39*: 1129–1138.

Bishop, D. V. M. (2004). Autism and specific language impairment: categorical distinction or continuum? In G. Bock & J. Goode (series eds.), *Autism: neural bases and treatment possibilities*, pp. 213–226. London: Novartis Foundation.

Bloom, P. (2000). *How children learn the meaning of words*. Cambridge, MA: MIT Press.

Bolton, P., Macdonald, H., Pickles, Crowson, M., Bailey, A. & Rutter, M. (1994). A case-control family history study of autism. *Journal of Child Psychology and Psychiatry*, *35*, 877–900.

Botting, N. & Conti-Ramsden, G. (2003). Autism, primary pragmatic difficulties, and specific language impairment: can we distinguish them using psycholinguistic markers? *Developmental Medicine and Child Neurology*, *45*, 515–524.

Boucher, J. (1976). Articulation in early childhood autism. *Journal of Autism and Childhood Schizophrenia*, *6*, 297–302.

(1978). Echoic memory capacity in autistic children. *Journal of Child Psychology and Psychiatry*, *19*, 161–166.

(1981a). Memory for recent events in autistic children. *Journal of Autism and Developmental Disorders*, *11*, 293–301.

(1981b). Immediate free recall in early childhood autism: another point of behavioural similarity with the amnesic syndrome. *British Journal of Psychology*, *72*, 211–215.

(1988). Word fluency in high-functioning autistic children. *Journal of Autism and Developmental Disorders*, *18*, 637–647.

(2000). Time parsing, normal language acquisition, and language-related developmental disorders. In M. Perkins & S. Howard (eds.), *New directions in language development and disorders*, 13–23. London: Kluwer Academic/ Plenum Publishers.

Boucher, J., Bigham, S., Mayes, A. & Musket, T. (2007). Recognition and language in low-functioning autism. *Journal of Autism and Developmental Disorders*. epub ahead of print.

Boucher, J., Cowell, P., Howard, M., Broks, P., Farrant, A., Roberts, N. & Mayes, A. (2005). A combined clinical neuropsychological and neuroanatomical study of adults with high-functioning autism. *Cognitive Neuropsychiatry*, *10*, 165–214.

Boucher, J. & Lewis, V. (1989). Memory impairments and communication in relatively able autistic children. *Journal of Child Psychology and Psychiatry*, *30*, 99–122.

Boucher, J. & Warrington, E. K. (1976). Memory deficits in early infantile autism: some similarities to the amnesic syndrome. *British Journal of Psychology*, *67*, 73–87.

Brock, J., Brown, C. C., Boucher, J. & Rippon, G. (2002). The temporal binding deficit hypothesis of autism. *Development and Psychopathology*, *14*, 209–224.

Carter, A. S., Volkmar, F., Sparrow, S., Wang, J-J., Lord, C., Dawson, G., Fombonne, E., Loveland, K., Mesibov, G. & Schopler, E. (1998). The Vineland Adaptive Behaviour Scales: supplementary norms for individuals with autism. *Journal of Autism and Developmental Disorders*, *28*, 287–302.

Cattell, R. B. (1971). *Abilities: their structure, growth and action*. Boston: Houghton Mifflin.

Churchill, D. (1972). The relation of infantile autism and early childhood schizophrenia to developmental language disorders of childhood. *Journal of Autism and Childhood Schizophrenia*, *2*, 182–197.

Dawson, G., Meltzoff, A., Osterling, J. & Rinaldi, J. (1998). Neuropsychological correlates of early autistic symptoms. *Child Development*, *69*, 1247–1482.

Dawson, G., Osterling, J., Rinaldi, J., Carver, L. & McPartland, J. (2001). Recognition and stimulus-reward association: indirect support for the role of ventromedial prefrontal dysfunction in autism. *Journal of Autism and Developmental Disorders, 31,* 337–341.

Dawson, M., Soulières, I., Gernsbacher, M.-A. & Mottron, L. (2007). The level and nature of autistic intelligence. *Psychological Science, 18,* 657–662.

DeLong, R. & Heinz, E. R. (1997). The syndrome of early-life bilateral hippocampal sclerosis. *Annals of Neurology, 43,* 11–17.

DeMyer, M. K. (1976). Intellectual disabilities of autistic children. In L.Wing (ed.), *Early childhood autism,* pp. 169–193. Oxford: Pergamon Press.

Dobbinson, S. (2000). Repetitiveness and productivity in the language of adults with autism. Unpublished PhD thesis, University of Sheffield.

Dobbinson, S., Perkins, M. & Boucher, J. (2003). The interactional significance of formulas in autistic language. *Clinical Linguistics and Phonetics, 17,* 299–307.

Fay, W. & Schuler, A. L. (1980). *Emerging language in autistic children.* London: Edward Arnold.

Folstein, S., Santangelo, S., Gilman, S., Piven, J., Landa R., Lainhart, J., Hein, J. & Wzorek, M. (1999). Predictors of cognitive test patterns in autism families. *Journal of Child Psychology and Psychiatry, 38,* 667–683.

Frith, U. (1989). *Autism: explaining the enigma.* Oxford: Blackwell.

Fyffe, C. & Prior, M. (1978). Evidence for language recoding in autistic, retarded and normal children. *British Journal of Psychology, 69,* 393–402.

Happé, F. (1994). *Autism: an introduction to psychological theory.* London: UCL Press.

Hermelin, B. & O'Connor, N. (1967). Remembering of words by psychotic and normal children. *British Journal of Psychology, 68,* 213–218.

Hobson, R. P. (1993). *Autism and the development of mind.* Hove: Erlbaum.

Horn, J. & Cattell, R. (1966). Refinement and test of the theory of fluid and crystalised general intelligences. *Journal of Educational Psychology, 57,* 253–270.

Kanner, L. (1946). Irrelevant and metaphorical language in early infantile autism. *American Journal of Psychiatry, 103,* 242–246.

Kjelgaard, M. & Tager-Flusberg, H. (2001). An investigation of language profiles in autism: implications for genetic subgroups. *Language and Cognitive Processes, 16,* 287–308.

Klin, A., Sparrow, S., Marans, W., Carter, A. & Volkmar, F. (2000). Assessment issues in children and adolescents with Asperger syndrome. In A. Klin, F. Volkmar & S. Sparrow (eds.), *Asperger syndrome,* pp. 309–339. New York: Guilford Press.

Kraijer, D. (2000). Review of adaptive behaviour studies in mentally retarded persons with autism/pervasive developmental disorder. *Journal of Autism and Developmental Disorders, 30,* 39–48.

Lee, A., Hobson, R. P. & Chiat, S. (1994). I, you, me, and autism: an experimental study. *Journal of Autism and Developmental Disorders, 24,* 155–176.

Lincoln, A., Allen, M. & Kilman, A. (1995). The assessment and interpretation of intellectual abilities in people with autism. In E. Schopler & G. Mesibov (eds.), *Learning and cognition in autism,* pp. 89–118. New York: Plenum Press.

Lincoln, A., Courchesne, E., Kilman, B., Elmasian, R. & Allen, M. (1988). A study of intellectual abilities in high-functioning people with autism. *Journal of Autism and Developmental Disorders*, 18, 505–523.

Lord, C. & Paul, R. (1997). Language and communication in autism. In D.Cohen & F.Volkmar (eds.), *Autism and pervasive developmental disorders*, 2nd edn, pp. 195–225. New York: Wiley.

Mackintosh, N. (1998). *IQ and human intelligence*. Oxford: Oxford University Press.

Mayes, S. D. & Calhoun, S. (2003a). Ability profiles in children with autism: influence of age and IQ. *Autism*, 7, 65–80.

(2003b). Analysis of WISC-III, Stanford–Binet IV, and Academic Achievement Test scores in children with autism. *Journal of Autism and Developmental Disorders*, 33, 329–342.

Menyuk, P. (1978). Language: what's wrong and why. In M. Rutter and E. Schopler (eds.), *Autism: a reappraisal of concepts and treatment*, pp. 105–116. New York: Plenum Press.

Millward, C., Powell, S., Messer, D. & Jordan, R. (2000). Recall for self and other in autism: children's memory for events experienced by themselves and their peers. *Journal of Autism and Developmental Disorders*, 30, 15–28.

Minshew, N., Turner, C. & Goldstein, G. (2005). The application of short forms of the Wechsler Intelligence Scales in adults and children with high functioning autism. *Journal of Autism and Developmental Disorders*, 35, 45–52.

Narita, T. & Koga, Y. (1987). Neuropsychological assessment of childhood autism. *Advances in Biological Psychiatry*, 16, 156–170.

O'Connor, N. & Hermelin, B. (1967). Auditory and visual memory in autistic and normal children. *Journal of Mental Deficiency Research*, 11, 126–131.

Ohta, M. (1987). Cognitive disorders of infantile autism: a study employing the WISC, spatial relationship conceptualisation, and gesture imitations. *Journal of Autism and Developmental Disorders*, 17, 45–62.

Piven, J. & Palmer, P. (1997). Cognitive deficits in parents from multiple incidence autism families. *Journal of Child Psychology and Psychiatry*, 38, 1011–1021.

Preissler, M. (2006). Symbolic representation of pictures and words in children with autism. Paper presented at the Scottish Autism Research Group seminar series at Glasgow Caledonian University in September 2006.

Preissler, M. A. & Carey, S. (2005). The role of inferences about referential intent in word learning: evidence from autism. *Cognition* 97: B13–B23.

Prizant, B. (1983a). Echolalia in autism: assessment and intervention. *Seminars in speech and language*, 4, 63–77.

(1983b). Language acquisition and communicative behaviour in autism: towards an understanding of the 'whole' of it. *Journal of Speech and Hearing Disorders*, 48, 296–307.

Rapin, I. (1996). *Preschool children with inadequate communication*. London: Mac Keith Press.

Rapin, I. & Dunn, M. (2003). Update on the language disorders of individuals on the autistic spectrum. *Brain and Development*, 25, 166–172.

Raven, J. C., Court, J. & Raven, J. (1986). *Raven's Progressive Matrices*. London: H. K. Lewis.

Ricks, D. & Wing, L. (1975). Language, communication, and the use of symbols in normal and autistic children. *Journal of Autism and Childhood Schizophrenia*, 5, 191–219.

Roberts, J., Rice, M. & Tager-Flusberg, H. (2004). Tense marking in children with autism. *Applied Psycholinguistics*, 25, 429–448.

Rumsey, J. M. (1992). Neuropsychological studies of high-level autism. In E. Schopler & G. Mesibov (eds.), *High functioning individuals with autism*, pp. 41–64. New York: Plenum Press.

Scheuffgen, K., Happé, F., Anderson, M. & Frith, U. (2000). High 'intelligence', low 'IQ'? Speed of processing and measured IQ in children with autism. *Development and Psychopathology*, 12, 83–90.

Siegel, D., Minshew, N. & Goldstein, G. (1996). Wechsler IQ profiles in diagnosis of high-functioning autism. *Journal of Autism and Developmental Disorders*, 26, 389–406.

Summers, J. A. & Craik, F. I. M. (1994). The effects of subject-performed tasks on the memory performance of verbal autistic children. *Journal of Autism and Developmental Disorders*, 24, 773–783.

Tager-Flusberg, H. (1981). On the nature of linguistic functioning in early infantile autism. *Journal of Autism and Developmental Disorders*, 11, 45–56.

(1985a). Basic level and superordinate level categorisation by autistic, mentally retarded, and normal children. *Journal of Experimental Child Psychology*, 40, 450–469.

(1985b). The conceptual basis for referential word meaning in children with autism. *Child Development*, 56, 1167–1178.

(1991). Semantic processing in the free recall of autistic children: further evidence for a cognitive deficit. *British Journal of Developmental Psychology*, 9, 417–430.

Tanguay, P. (1984). Toward a new classification of serious psychopathology in children. *Journal of American Academy of Child Psychiatry*, 23, 374–384.

Tomblin J., Hafeman, L. & O'Brien, M. (2003). Autism and autism risk in siblings of children with specific language impairment. *International Journal of Language and Communication Disorders*, 38, 235–250.

Ullman, M. (2004). Contributions of memory circuits to language. *Cognition 92*, 231–270.

Volden, J. & Lord, C. (1991). Neologisms and idiosyncratic language in autistic speakers. *Journal of Autism and Developmental Disorders*, 21, 109–130.

Wassing, H. (1965). Cognitive functioning in early infantile autism: an examination of four cases by means of the Wechsler intelligence scale for children. *Acta Paedopsychiatrica*, 32, 122–135.

Wechsler, D. (1974). *Wechsler Intelligence Scale for Children – revised manual*. New York: Psychological Corporation.

(1981). *Wechsler Adult Intelligence Scale – revised manual*. New York: Psychological Corporation.

Part IV

Overview

15 Practical implications of memory characteristics in autistic spectrum disorders

Rita R. Jordan

Introduction

Schacter (2003) has given an accessible account of practical memory characteristics in the general population, through an analysis of memory problems – characterized as the seven 'sins' of memory. Memory in autistic spectrum disorders (ASDs) is nontypical; nevertheless, Schacter's analysis provides a useful framework for examining that difference in practical aspects of memory. This chapter will consider practical functioning of memory in people with ASDs, through looking at the evidence of its features and how it differs from typical memory functioning. This evidence comes both from the research literature and also as reported in clinical or autobiographical accounts of individuals.

Everyday memory functioning in autism

Reports of memory functioning in autism often stress memory as a 'preserved ability' or a cognitive strength. A study of 'savant' skills in children with ASDs (Clark, 2005) has shown that all the children studied had savant memory skills either as their sole savant ability (rare) or in addition to others. However, the reported savant memory skills generally represent a narrow range of abilities, largely rote memory skills (Boucher & Lewis, 1989; Jordan, 1999; Kanner, 1943; Wing, 1981). The narrow and rigid nature of these skills provides evidence of memory processes in ASDs that are significantly different from those found in typical development.

Typical human cognitive processing has evolved for efficiency in everyday situations; even problems in processing can be seen as unwanted 'side effects' of a system geared for maximum enhancement of common problem solving in daily life, as Schacter (2003) argues. Processing in people with ASDs is more akin to artificial intelligence and, while that also has advantages, it is not geared to everyday problem solving. Memories are retained in the form that they are laid down, accurately recording the original encoding, and only accessible if the right cues are used. Each item in that memory remains embedded in the context of its original storage and cannot be accessed and applied outside that context.

An intelligent and verbal young woman with autism (and severe dyslexia) likes to attend 'blockbuster' movies such as Harry Potter adventures or the Lord of the Rings cycle. However, her dyslexia means she has not read the texts on which the films are based and she is not able to follow the plot on the screen because it is too fast and fleeting for her to process. When asked questions such as 'What was it about?' her strategy is to repeat the soundtrack of the film – each word and sound – in its entirety. It is an amazing feat of memory but it is completely irrelevant to the purposes of social discourse to which the original question was addressed. Her response is also rigid and, although after prolonged teaching she has learned to stop, her natural response to interruptions is to 're-wind the tape' and start again at the beginning of the film.

This young woman has one alternative strategy for such situations, and that is to focus on a single frame of the film. She has participated in experiments (Klin *et al.*, 2002), observing visual fixation patterns of people with ASDs, while watching a film of complex social and emotional events. When asked what the film was about, she responded 'a doorknob'. It took careful scrutiny of the film to find a shot when (at a moment of acute emotional tension) there is a rather fine brass doorknob also in shot. There is a similar moment in a film of another young man with autism, taken when he was 28, but including reflection on an earlier film of him, taken when he was 7. This young man displayed remarkable memory for facts and was a calendrical calculator. At one point he is asked what the earlier film was about and he, also, responds with a description of one frame in the film: 'It is about me looking through the window with the curtains ... ' Thus, even remarkable skills, as revealed in lengthy rote abilities, are in fact a sign of impaired practical functioning.

Different kinds of memory

Problems in using memory arise not just from inability to abstract the 'gist' of memories, but also from problems of access and control. It is misleading to refer to memory systems or processes as a whole as 'advanced' or 'deficient' in autism, since different aspects of the memory are differentially affected, as outlined below.

Immediate short-term memory (memory span) is generally found to be good in people with ASDs, especially the aspects that are sometimes referred to as 'perceptual representation' (Gardiner, this volume, Chapter 1; but see also Poirier & Martin, this volume, Chapter 12) or 'sensory memory' (Ameli *et al.*, 1988; Barth, Fein & Waterhouse, 1995; Bennetto, Pennington & Rogers, 1996; Boucher, 1978; Hermelin & Frith, 1971). This includes 'echoic memory' (immediate memory of auditory information) and eidetic imaging (often leading to a photographic memory). Procedural (motor) memories for skills (Tulving, 1972; Gardiner, this volume, Chapter 1) also appear to be unaffected, and indeed memories that others might process as semantic schemas (rules for eating in a restaurant, for example) seem to function as procedural memories in people with autism. Thus, in situations where others are more obviously guided by sets of social or cognitive rules (organized into schemas), people with autism appear to use procedural memory, where each step cues the one to follow and this in turn serves as a cue for the next step; the first step needs to be externally cued and the procedure is inflexibly 'as remembered' and not adaptable to the immediate context. This is a hypothesis about the underlying mechanism, which has yet to be tested.

An alternative view of the rigid application of learned schemas is that of Peterson (2002), who sees schema formation in people with ASDs as a rigid process itself and that, once established, the schemas do not adjust to other schemas, simultaneously activated in complex situations, as is typically the case. Even in this explanation, it is not clear whether the difficulty is with adapting the schemas, or that schemas are only activated (or at least attended to) one at a time, so that the possibility of adjustment to other schemas does not arise. As with so many cognitive processes, it is, therefore, hard to isolate memory processes from other co-occurring or related processes, such as attention, on which they may depend.

Semantic memory, as defined by Tulving (1972), is akin to what others describe as 'knowing'; semantic memories are stored in meaning categories, and, according to Tulving, become divorced from the particular circumstances (time, person, place, affect) of their acquisition. This kind of memory has also been found to be relatively intact in higher-functioning individuals with autism (Bowler, Gardiner & Grice, 2000; O'Shea *et al.*, 2005). This can result in a richly developed memory for 'facts', especially in topics of particular interest to the individual. At the same time, there is a problem in spontaneously using meaning in encoding or retrieving memories (Tager-Flusberg, 1991; see also this volume, Chapters 8 and 17). This means that teaching has to move beyond teaching facts and include teaching awareness of their own knowledge and of ways to access these memories (Jordan, 2001; Jordan & Powell, 1991; Powell & Jordan, 1992).

Episodic memories (Gardiner, this volume, Chapter 1) are memories for particular 'events' and involve all the aspects of those events, including the engagement of the self. Such episodic memories necessarily entail an element of source memory, which involves recalling, *inter alia*, the time, place, person and affect associated with the origin of the memory. There is some confusion about how episodic or source memory is affected in people with ASDs. Part of the ambiguity comes from the ways in which such memories are accessed. For example, Bowler, Gardiner and Berthollier (2004) showed that source recall but not source recognition was impaired in individuals with high-functioning autism (HFA).[1] In addition, episodic or source memories are generally recalled spontaneously, alongside retrieval of the experience both that they happened, and that they happened to the individual themselves. In other words, episodic memories are often *personal* episodic memories, part of autobiographical memory (Brewer, 1986). Individuals with ASDs often have extensive semantic autobiographical memories, being able to recite many facts about themselves and their personal history, but there are problems with un-cued personal episodic memories, which require a personal sense of self to search for past experiences. Thus, persons with autism may use semantic information about themselves (e.g. a learnt response to the question 'What did you do in cookery today?') that has nothing to do with the reality of what happened (which would involve personal episodic memory). For example, they may chart in detail the making of a lemon meringue pie, when in fact they had made a meat loaf. This is not lying, and in fact individuals may have no awareness that their response is anything other than appropriate. Powell and Jordan (1993; Jordan & Powell, 1995) have theorized the reasons for these difficulties in terms of problems in developing an 'experiencing self'. There is some empirical support from a study showing that children with ASDs (unlike comparison participants) were more able to recall events they had witnessed happening to others (nonpersonal episodic memory) than events they had personally experienced (Millward *et al.*, 2000). Similarly, Klein, Chan and Loftus (1999) reported the case of a man with autism who could describe himself in psychological terms but could not report instances when he had displayed the traits he described.

It may be that at least some episodic memories that do not involve the personal dimension can be accessed without problems by individuals with autism. The degree to which there is a sense of self or agency involved in episodic memories may depend on whether the process of memorizing is implicit (incidental) or explicit (intentional). So, for example, Blair *et al.* (2002) showed a dissociation in visual memory functioning in

---

[1] The term 'HFA' is used, as in other chapters in this book, to refer to individuals with the triad of impairments in the absence of clinically significant language or intellectual deficits, regardless of whether or not they have received a diagnosis of Asperger syndrome.

participants with ASDs: apart from the expected impairment in face recognition, the experimental group were impaired in recognition of all potential agents (living or mechanical) but superior in recognition of nonagents such as buildings or leaves. This suggests particular problems in encoding goal-directed behaviour. Similarly, Gardiner, Bowler and Grice (2003) showed that adults with Asperger syndrome (AS) were able to remember as well as comparison participants when learning had been incidental (no contextual cues and concentration on readability rather than meaning), but with the intentional memory tasks they exhibited more intrusion errors ('remembering' semantically related words, which were not part of the set to be memorized). This could be interpreted (although this is not done by the authors) as the individuals with AS treating the implicit memories as objective events (nonpersonal episodic memory). The explicit memory tasks, however, would be expected to involve personal episodic memory (i.e. could not readily be processed objectively), so those with AS may have processed these through semantic memory – leading to the semantic intrusions found in recall. This fits with earlier work by these same authors (Bowler, Gardiner & Grice, 2000) where it was found that an AS group showed similar recognition ability to comparison participants but used semantic memory preferentially to episodic memory in recall. The authors point out that personal episodic memory involves autonoetic consciousness, which is a similar concept to that of an 'experiencing self".

In spite of their apparent preference for, and superiority in, semantic over episodic memory, individuals with autism have been shown to have specific difficulties in using semantic information to categorize material for easier recall (Hermelin & O'Connor, 1970; Tager-Flusberg, 1991). There are no problems with cued recall, whatever the nature of the cue (perceptual, phonological, categorical or conceptual) and whether the material to be remembered is visual or auditory (Bowler, Matthews & Gardiner, 1997; Minshew et al., 1992, 1994). Minshew et al. (1994) conclude that the degree of memory impairment found in autism depends on the extent to which spontaneous organization of the material to be remembered is required. Bowler, Matthews & Gardiner (1997) showed, in addition, that individuals with AS did not differ from comparison participants in the number of semantic intrusions in either implicit or explicit conditions of a cued recall task. It is still possible that the two groups used different forms of processing for the implicit tasks, even though both groups were better able to recall words they had just read in the implicit recall conditions and words they had generated in the explicit recall conditions. The explicit recall instructions specifically directed participants to use episodic rather than semantic memory so it appears that memory problems do not always depend on that distinction, outlined above, but on the necessity for spontaneous elaboration of the material to be remembered, as suggested by Minshew, Goldstein and Siegel (1997) (see also Smith & Gardiner, this volume, Chapter 13).

In a recent exploration of source memory in autism, O'Shea *et al.* (2005) shed further light on memory anomalies in children with ASDs. Children in their study performed similarly to typically developing and cognitively matched children with general learning difficulties on a measure of fact recognition (as predicted, since it involves semantic memory) but significantly worse on measures of source memory. However, the problems with source memory were not equal across all sources: the experimental and comparison groups showed similar scores when the source to be remembered involved objects in the room, but the autism group performed significantly worse than the comparison groups when the source involved specific social information (person) or objects physically close to social information (a folder held near the face). This suggests that the memory problems relate to attentional problems in encoding, since individuals with ASDs have been shown to pay greater attention to nonsocial than social information (Klin *et al.*, 2002) and to have particular problems in the encoding of faces (Pierce *et al.*, 2001; also Webb, this volume, Chapter 10).

These findings are open to different interpretations but overall suggest that anomalies of memory performance in people with ASDs may result from differences in attention and the salience of stimuli at encoding, difference in the extent to which initial stimuli are elaborated at encoding, and differences in the ability of individuals with ASDs to spontaneously generate mnemonic strategies at both encoding and recall. It also appears that what may appear as an advanced or 'savant' memory skill may in fact be evidence of failure to engage in those mnemonic strategies that would allow efficient and flexible encoding and retrieval of memories. These mnemonic variables are also important in explaining common memory problems across the normal population. A consideration of common memory problems may therefore suggest how far memory anomalies in autism are essentially exaggerations of common problems or are unique to people with ASDs.

Schacter's (2003) 'seven sins' of memory

Schacter (2003) has analysed practical memory problems commonly observed in everyday life, delineating both the nature of the problem and how such problems arise as a by-product of otherwise useful processing abilities.

(i)   Transience

This is the simple notion that we forget over time. The typical curve of forgetting for the episodic memory of presented nonsense syllables (a steep curve of forgetting at first, followed by a slower rate over time) is modified when the events to be remembered have personal meaning and when there are opportunities to relate the information to other meaningful information and to rehearse in some way. What also happens in normal memory is that the details of the episode are lost over time and what is retained is the gist of the event, which (depending on its distinctiveness) may in turn be gradually subsumed into a semantic memory of that type of event (e.g. what happens at Christmas parties in general, rather than what happened at a particular one). If it is important to retain particular details of a memory, effective memory strategies relate the details to cues (often visual cues) that are either features of the environment in which the memory is to be recalled (e.g. the architectural features of the examination hall) or are elaborated narratives (the more distinctive and bizarre, the better). These are typical mnemonic strategies used in memory training, or by performers exhibiting amazing feats of memory, comparable to that shown by savants with autism.

This is not to suggest that people with autism go through these conscious memory processing strategies, but rather to recognize that many people with ASDs are visual thinkers naturally (Grandin, 1995) and that they may visualize even auditory experiences, making details more likely to be retained than abstracted meaning (the gist). This suggests that input processing in autism differs considerably from that of typical individuals, and that the problems in retaining episodic memories may be the reverse of those found in typical development: specifically, it may be easier to retrieve details than the general meaning of an event. Thus, retrieval will depend on accessing the relevant visual cues but, since the cues are not consciously used in encoding memories, recall is a matter of the chance occurrence of the relevant cues. This can happen in normal processing also, where apparently forgotten information details may be unexpectedly triggered by a cue (smell being particularly potent for this). In typical development this is not the only source of retrieval of source memories: one can 'search' one's memory using the sense of self and memory of one's personal experiences to do so. People with ASDs are more reliant on the provision of cues. This form of memory processing will also have a more general effect on learning since it is the ability to memorize the 'gist' of events that enables us to generalize our learning beyond the initial context of its encoding (McClelland, 1995).

An imbalance between relatively intact verbatim memory and impaired memory for gist will also have effects on other aspects of development. For example, the 'phonological loop' through which memories are retained in working memory for further processing has been found to be essential for learning new vocabulary (Gathercole *et al.*, 1997) and for receptive speech (retaining the start of a sentence while the rest unfolds, so its overall meaning can be processed). Typically developing 2-year-olds have limited immediate memory spans allowing only small numbers of phonemes and morphemes to enter working memory for processing, and this facilitates the relevant mappings between sounds and meanings necessary for the acquisition of vocabulary and also grammar (Eigsti & Bennetto, in preparation). Children with ASDs, however, have relatively well-preserved memory spans and thus provide too many opportunities for error and confusion in mapping – the worst conditions for meaningful language learning

(ii)   Absent-mindedness

As mentioned above, memory strength also depends on the elaboration that occurs in working memory, in typical development usually through imbuing the memory with meaning and significance, but sometimes through the operation of deliberate mnemonic strategies. Schacter (2003) suggests that the common experience of absent-mindedness (when we forget where we put things, why we have come upstairs, appointments, our drive home from work and so on) arises when there has been a failure in the initial encoding, usually because we fail to pay attention to the relevant feature. This may occur because we are distracted by something else, or do something immediately following that prevents elaboration and rehearsal of the memory.

There are two ways in which we can remember past events: recollection (recalling specific details) and familiarity (a vague and general sense of knowing, without specific details). Divided attention at encoding devastates recollection but leaves familiarity intact, a common state with respect to everyday activities that do not usually require full attention to perform. Schacter refers to this as 'amnesia for the automatic' (p. 46). A further instance of absent-mindedness is called 'change blindness' and, as the name suggests, refers to the failure to notice changes in the environment (even when these are dramatic), when attention is highly focused elsewhere. This effect is heightened when the original encoding is generalized, and not focused on details.

It is a common clinical and autobiographical observation that people with ASDs are prone to the kind of absent-mindedness resulting in poor recollection, in spite of their ability often to recall all the details of an event verbatim. Individuals with autism who have prodigious memories for facts in their areas of special interest nevertheless report that they are unable to remember to bring the correct materials to a lesson or to remember the homework they were required to do (Jackson, 2003; Sainsbury, 2000). There has been little research on this issue. However, people with ASDs may have extreme forms of focused attention ('mono-tropic attention': Murray, Lesser & Lawson, 2005) and thus memories for anything outside their narrow window of attention may fail because of encoding failures. In addition, clinical, autobiographical and research reports suggest that far from exhibiting 'change blindness', people with ASDs are extremely sensitive to environmental change. This too may be a function of attention. In the O'Shea *et al.* (2005) study of source memory, the memory for particular sources (details) depended on their original saliency. Social stimuli, and faces in particular, are not salient for people with autism, therefore changes in these sources were not noticed, whereas other changes were registered. In reporting severe bullying by a gang of boys in her youth, a woman with AS explains how she was unable to pick out her assailants later because all she had registered was that they had 'boy-like faces' (Gerland, 1997). This is a reflection of the shallow general processing that people with autism often give to faces: what is not encoded cannot be remembered.

(iii)   Blocking

This is the phenomenon whereby there appears to be a blocking of access to stored semantic information, together with the frustration of feeling that it is 'on the tip of one's tongue' and yet the more one struggles to recall, the harder it seems to be. Circumlocutions are often possible, because the person has access to many semantic details, save the name. Schacter suggests that in blocking, the memory has been encoded and it has not been lost (as in transience) because it will often 'pop' into one's mind at a later time; there is also a cue to recall, since that is what provokes the frustration of not being able to remember.

Proper names are the most common causes of blockages in the general population, especially as one ages. Schacter points out that a name may be represented visually, conceptually and phonologically and the latter (which enables us to recall the name) only occurs after the other two representations have occurred. There is a further complication in lan-guage processing, in the form of the lexical level of representation between the conceptual and the phonological. Burke *et al.* (1991) have a model of lexical representation in which common lexical items are linked directly to all conceptual representations of a name, whereas proper names are only linked to a single individual ('person identity node') who is a part of the conceptual representation of that name and through whom all other conceptual linkages must be made. Thus, there are fewer associations through which the proper name (as a lexical item) may be retrieved than there are for common names. Anomia refers to a condition in which naming is a specific difficulty, in spite of considerable conceptual knowledge about the item or person, and the ability to both recognize the name when displayed and to echo the name, once given.

Some individuals with ASDs appear to have conditions close to anomia, where they exhibit particular word-finding problems. However, there are features related to perceptual and conceptual processing in autism that may complicate the situation further. There are biographical accounts suggesting that thinking is more associative than conceptual in people with autism (De Clercq, 2003; Grandin, 1995; Rosch, 1973). If this were so, people with ASDs would be more prone to block names that were not directly associated with the current cue. For people with an ASD it is often the case that names are attached to parts of objects, or to particular instances of their occurrence (De Clercq, 2003). It is also likely that the capacity to search memory is limited (Jordan & Powell, 1995) and even that the order in which lexical items are retrieved may differ. Van Dalen (1995), a man with autism, describes how his perception of objects proceeds from a visual representation of the parts, then the whole, then the name and only after that the functional concept.

(iv)   Misattribution

This can occur where there is a sense of familiarity ('déjà vu') without the recall of detail or where there are false source/episodic memories. Misattribution can underlie plagiarism, where we misattribute the idea or phrase to ourselves when in fact we have simply read or heard about it (mistaken source memory). Déjà vu seems to result from current experiences stirring up memories of similar (though not identical) past experiences. There is something (as yet poorly understood) about those memories that makes them appear identical to the current experience and this leads to the feeling that this experience has happened before (and that one can predict what will happen next). Other forms of misattribution result in examples of false identification by witnesses. This commonly results from a lack of binding together of all the component parts of a memory experience so that real memories of parts may be inappropriately combined with parts from other events and result in misattribution of sources for a memory.

There are almost no reported instances of déjà vu in autism (but see Boucher, 2007), although that is not to say that they do not occur. If they do not occur that may be because people with ASDs often appear to be less aware of their own feelings (Jordan, 2002) and so may not seek to account for current feelings of familiarity through misattribution of source memories. There is an equal lack of evidence about false identification, at least in relation to witnessing of events. However, given the reluctance of people with autism to 'guess' when events are ambiguous or uncertain, it would not be expected that they would attempt to resolve ambiguity by such misattributions.

However, as shown above, individuals with autism do often have fragmented perceptions and may be less likely than the typically developing to bind their memories together in a coherent whole (see this volume, Chapters 6, 7 and 14). This would then make it possible for different parts of particular events to be misattributed to different sources, or even to be mistaken for categorical memory. As De Clercq (2003, p. 23) demonstrates, it is common for individuals with ASDs to have memories of one aspect of an item (i.e. a source memory) associated with lexical representations of those events (e.g a bicycle remembered not as such – a semantic memory – but as 'a wheels in mud'). De Clercq gives many more instances of episodic memories serving as semantic memories, with associated 'names', in the development of her son with an ASD.

(v)   Suggestibility

This refers to the tendency for individuals to incorporate misleading current or remembered sources (people, media, events, items) into their personal episodic memories. This tendency is triggered by an event (often a cue) in the retrieval process. It is a form of delusion that is not associated with any psychosis, but appears as a relatively common part of normal memory functioning. Suggestibility is seen (and is at its most problematic) where leading questions lead to false testimony in witnesses, false confessions in extreme situations, and 'false memories' of abuse in psychotherapeutic contexts. Even intended noncommittal feedback to the witnesses' statements serves to increase confidence in both real and false memories of events (Wells & Bradfield, 1998). It is particularly prevalent in interviews with children or with people with general learning difficulties, where 'confirming' questions (e.g. *Are you sure . . . ?*) are interpreted as a challenge to their first answer, and an invitation to think again. Suggestibility increases when persons have reasons to mistrust their own actual memories (or perhaps lack of memories) (Schacter, 2003).

So, for example, people with learning difficulties may have learnt to trust authority figures as 'knowing best'.

People with lower-functioning autism may also have experience of relying on others to guide them, but are protected from suggestibility by some of the problems associated with autism. Thus, they are unlikely to pick up on the pragmatic cues that might lead nonautistic individuals to alter their responses to try to match what they think the adult is implying. Nor are they likely to alter their perceptions to take account of more recently acquired information or to take account of other episodic or semantic memories they may have. However, their problems with receptive language and with pragmatics (especially in those with classical autism) may mean that they use the language around them as a cue to what is required. In this way, leading questions may suggest an answer to a question that they have failed to understand and they may then pick up on that suggestion as their answer, whether or not it actually represents what they remember.

When it comes to false memories themselves, it would be expected that the same difficulties with picking up on pragmatic cues and adjusting memories to fit internal (cognitive) and external contexts would protect people with autism from this problem. This seems to be the case, in that memories in autism do not seem to alter over time, but retain the features of when they were established. However, experimental tests of susceptibility to false memories have produced ambiguous results (Beversdorf et al., 2000; Bowler et al., 2000). Clearly more evidence is required to establish the facts, before explanations of presumed differences are sought or practical implications developed.

(vi)   Bias

This occurs when memories alter, not as a result of testing conditions at retrieval or intrusions of other memories, but as a kind of motivated forgetting or distortion of our own past views and actions, as exemplified in our memories. Thus there is a tendency to distort memories of the past either to fit our current views and codes of conduct or to bolster our current state. People tend to attribute consistency to their own behaviour and views over time and to distort memories to fit this consistent view. However, there is also a distorting tendency that exaggerates change in some states over time, in support, for example, of therapy undertaken (and believed in) or in relation to a new direction in life (entering or leaving a marriage or a job).

Hindsight bias is similar in that people come to believe that the outcome of events was inevitable, from what was known before. People then selectively recall memories that support the 'inevitability' of the outcome and ignore (or forget?) contrary indications. Research shows that the motivators for bias are influences from general semantic knowledge and misattributions. The strength of this bias depends in part on the strength of our own egocentric bias, whereby our own memories have far greater potency than reports of others, so that our own 'adjusted' memories also have more credence. Stereotypes are a subset of biased memories in that they are generic descriptions of past experiences used to categorize and thus are semantic rather than episodic memories, i.e. one is unaware of the biased sources of this stereotyped knowledge. Gazzaniga (1998) has also demonstrated from split-brain patients how the left hemisphere of the brain constantly distorts the accurate detailed memories of the right hemisphere to build a consistent view of the world, in line with both general knowledge and stereotypes.

As was seen earlier, people with ASDs do not share the potency of a concept of 'self' as a regulator of their mental life (see Lind & Bowler, this volume, Chapter 9). They are therefore less likely to show egocentric, or other, bias. They are also protected from bias by the failure of their memories to adjust to existing context or to their general semantic knowledge. Thinking (including remembering) is unusually objective in people with ASDs (Jordan & Powell, 1995; Suddendorf & Corballis, 1997) and memories remain both rigid and accurate (in relation to their time of encoding). Such detailed discrimination of the particular should mean that people with autism are not prone to stereotyping in their thinking or memories.

(vii)   Persistence

This is when memories (usually unpleasant) continually intrude on thoughts and the person cannot prevent him/herself from continually ruminating over past mistakes. This not only leads to debilitating regret but also to 'counterfactual' thinking when an alternative course of action, and thus outcome, is dwelt on. Persistence and counterfactual thinking are influenced by evaluations of the self, based on personal episodic memories, which both lead to, and are influenced by, states of depression and stress. Obsessive self-rumination can be deleterious to mental health but talking about one's negative experiences has a beneficial effect.

Unlike many of the other common 'sins' of memory, persistence may be relatively common in autism, although this has not been the subject of direct research. In typical individuals, intrusive memories of personally experienced episodes may be cued by factors such as an emotional state. For example, negative states such as depression and high stress and anxiety may trigger memories of when the person was in that state, so that the memories are also negative. The obsessive nature of autistic thinking, the vulnerability to anxiety, and the inability of people with autism to produce coherent narratives of their experiences (Tager-Flusberg, 1991) and share their emotions and memories with others (Jordan, 2002) combine to suggest that memory persistence may be quite common. Autism-specific therapies are now being developed to help with the depression resulting from the negative effects of such persistent and negative memories.

Summary

People with ASDs share some aspects of memory processing with the general population, but also display significant differences. These differences have some positive effects in that they can lead to remarkable feats of detailed memory for facts and for particular events, that apparently remain unaltered for years. The processes of memorizing in autism also offer considerable (though not perfect) immunity from many of the everyday problems arising from typical processing, identified by Schacter (2003) as the 'Seven sins of memory'.

The significant failures in encoding at input make memories for the gist of events unavailable. However, the ready association of memories with visual cues allows some compensation in extensive recall of accurate details over time, modifying the typical *transience* of memory for event detail. Conversely, these failures in processing at the encoding stage plus attentional biases will make people with ASDs more *absent-minded* for items outside their focus of interest, while attention to detail will lead to a tenacious (and often prodigious) memory in relation to their interests. The same focus on detail will result in fewer associations for each memory (i.e. each event is 'unique') and so more likelihood of memory *blocking*.

There is little empirical research on *misattribution* of memories in people with ASDs, but it is likely that a lack of awareness of their own feelings will reduce the selection of a mistaken source for feelings of the 'familiarity' of events. However, people with autism may be less able to 'bind together' their memories in a co-ordinated way, and unusual forms of processing at this stage leads to the potential for bizarre associations. So, for example, people with autism may attach semantic meaning (and even names) to details of episodic memory, leading to idiosyncratic concepts and labels, increasing susceptibility to misattribution. The evidence on *suggestibility* in autism is also ambiguous. Pragmatic difficulties may lead to errors in processing and attaching meaning but people with ASDs should be less susceptible to conformity to what is expected. However, experimental evidence relating to suggestibility is contradictory and more research is needed. The same applies to *bias* in memory where the style of processing detail in an objective way and out of context should make for less opportunity for biased memories. Once again, this remains to be tested. Finally, clinical accounts of people with ASDs suggest that they are not immune to the effects of *persistent* memories, and may lack appropriate ameliorating strategies such as reflection on emotional states and sharing memories with others. Specific techniques are needed to help those with autism who suffer from depression and anxiety as a result of these persistent negative memories.

Many signs of apparent 'advanced' memory functioning are in fact signs of disability and lead to distinct problems in everyday memory, additional to those identified by Schacter. People with ASDs may display savant memory skills at the expense of efficiently accessed and coherent memories and may need to be taught particular mnemonic strategies to overcome these difficulties, whilst preserving remarkable feats of memory for raising self-esteem. There is a start in cognitive education pro-grammes that address these needs, but their development will depend on teachers and carers recognizing the true state of affairs concerning memory functioning in ASDs.

References

Ameli, R., Courchesne, E., Lincoln, A., Kaufman, A. S. & Grillon, C. (1988). Visual memory processes in high functioning individuals with autism. *Journal of Autism and Developmental Disorders, 18*, 601–615.

Barth, C., Fein, D. & Waterhouse, L. (1995). Delayed match to sample perform-ance in autistic children. *Developmental Neuropsychology, 11*, 53–69.

Bennetto, L., Pennington, B. F. & Rogers, S. L. (1996). Intact and impaired memory functions in autism. *Child Development, 67*, 1816–1835.

Beversdorf, D. Q., Smith, B. W., Crucian, G. P., Anderson, J. M., Keillor, J. M., Barrett, A. M., Hughes, J. D., Felopulos, G. J., Bauman, M. L., Nadeau, S. E. & Heilman, K. M. (2000). Increased discrimination of 'false memories' in autism spectrum disorder. *Proceedings of the National Academy of Sciences, 97*, 8734–8737.

Blackburn, R. (2000). Within and without autism. *Good autism practice, 1*, 12–18.

Blair, R. J. R., Frith, U., Smith, N., Abell, F. & Cipolotti, L. (2002). Fractionation of visual memory: agency detection and its impairment in autism. *Neuropsychologia, 40*, 108–118.

Boucher, J. (1978). Echoic memory capacity in autistic children. *Journal of Child Psychology and Psychiatry, 19*, 161–166.

(2007). Memory and generativity in very high functioning autism: a firsthand account, and an interpretation. *Autism: the International Journal of Research and Practice 11*, 255–264.

Boucher, J & Lewis, V. (1989). Memory impairments and communication in relatively able autistic children. *Journal of Child Psychology and Psychiatry, 30,* 99–122.

Bowler, D. M. Gardiner, J. M. & Berthollier, N. (2004). Source memory in adolescents and adults with Asperger's syndrome *Journal of Autism and Developmental Disorders, 34,* 533–542.

Bowler, D. M., Gardiner, J. M. & Grice, S. (2000). Episodic memory and remembering in adults with Asperger syndrome. *Journal of Autism and Developmental Disorders, 30,* 295–304.

Bowler, D. M., Gardiner, J. M., Grice, S. & Saavalainen, P. (2000). Memory illusions: false recall and recognition in high-functioning adults with autism. *Journal of Abnormal Psychology, 109,* 663–672.

Bowler, D. M., Matthews, N. J. & Gardiner, J. M. (1997). Asperger's syndrome and memory: similarity to autism but not amnesia. *Neuropsychologia, 35,* 65–70.

Brewer, W. F. (1986). What is autobiographical memory? In D. C. Rubin (eds.), *Autobiographical memory,* pp. 25–49. Cambridge: Cambridge University Press.

Bruck, M. & Ceci, S. J. (1999). The suggestibility of children's memory. *Annual Review of Psychology, 50,* 419–39.

Burke, D., MacKay, D. G., Worthley, J. S. & Wade, E. (1991). On the tip of the tongue. What causes word failure in young and older adults? *Journal of Memory and Language, 30,* 237–246.

Clark, T. (2005). Autistic savants: educational strategies for the functional application of savant and splinter skills in children with autism and Asperger's disorder. Paper presented at the Australian Autism Research Symposium 23–24/07/2005, Sydney, Australia: Autism Spectrum.

De Clercq, H. (2003). *Mum, is that a human being or an animal?* Bristol: Lucky Duck Publishing.

Eigsti, I-M. & Bennetto, L. (in preparation). Syntactic abilities and memory functions in young children with autism.

Gardiner, J. M., Bowler, D. M. & Grice, S. J. (2003). Further evidence of preserved priming and impaired recall in adults with Asperger's syndrome. *Journal of Autism and Developmental Disorders, 33,* 259–269.

Gathercole, S. E., Hitch, G. J., Service, E. & Martin, A. J. (1997). Phonological short-term memory and new word learning in children. *Developmental Psychology, 33,* 966–979.

Gazzaniga, M. S. (1998). The split brain revisited. *Scientific American, 279,* 50–55.

Gerland, G. (1997). *A real person.* London: Souvenir Press.

Grandin, T. (1995). How people with autism think. In E. Schopler & G. B. Mesibov (eds.), *Learning and cognition in autism.* New York: Plenum Press.

Griffith, E. M., Pennington, B., Wehner, E. A. & Rogers, S. J. (1999). Executive functions in young children with autism. *Child Development, 70,* 817–832.

Hermelin, B. & Frith, U. (1971). Psychological studies of childhood autism: can autistic children make sense of what they see and hear? *Journal of Special Education, 5,* 107–117.

Hermelin, B. & O'Connor, N. (1970). *Psychological experiments with autistic children.* Oxford: Pergamon Press.

Jackson, L. (2003). *Freaks, geeks and Asperger Syndrome: a user guide to adolescence.* London: Jessica Kingsley.

Jordan, R. (1999). *Autistic spectrum disorders: an introductory handbook for practitioners.* London: David Fulton.

Jordan, R. R. (2001). *Autism with severe learning difficulties.* London: Souvenir Press.

(2002). What's love got to do with it? Making sense of emotions in autism: biology, cognition and treatment. In G. Linfoot (ed.), *Building bridges: papers from Autism Research Conference, Durham 2002.* Sunderland: Autism North.

Jordan, R. R. & Powell, S. D. (1991). Teaching thinking – the case for principles. *European Journal of Special Needs Education,* 6, 112–123.

(1995). *Understanding and teaching children with autism.* Chichester: Wiley.

Kanner, L. (1943). Autistic disturbances of affective contact. *Nervous Child,* 2, 217–250.

Klein, S. B., Chan, R. L. & Loftus, J. (1999). Independence of episodic and semantic self-knowledge: the case from autism. *Social Cognition,* 17, 413–436.

Klin, A., Jones, W., Schultz, R., Volkmar, F. & Cohen, D. (2002). Visual fixation patterns during viewing of naturalistic social situations as predictors of social competence in individuals with autism. *Archives of General Psychiatry,* 59, 809–816.

McClelland, J. L. (1995). Constructive memory and memory distortions: a parallel distributed processing approaching. In D. L. Schacter (ed.), *Memory distortion: how minds, brains, and societies reconstruct the past,* pp. 69–90. Cambridge, MA: Harvard University Press.

Millward, C., Powell, S., Messer, D. & Jordan, R. (2000). Recall for self and other in autism: children's memory for events experienced by themselves and their peers. *Journal of Autism and Developmental Disorders,* 30, 15–28.

Minshew, N. J., Goldstein, G., Muenz, L. R. & Payton, J. B. (1992). Neuropsychological functioning in non-mentally retarded autistic individuals. *Journal of Clinical and Experimental Neuropsychology,* 14, 749–761.

Minshew, N. J., Goldstein, G., Taylor, H. & Siegel, D. J. (1994). Academic achievement in high-functioning autistic individuals. *Journal of Clinical and Experimental Neuropsychology,* 16, 261–270.

Minshew, N. J., Goldstein, G. & Siegel, D. J. (1997). Neuropsychologic functioning in autism: profile of a complex information processing disorder. *Journal of the International Neuropsychological Society,* 3, 303–316.

Morris, R. G., Rowe, A., Fox, N., Feigenbaum, J. D., Miotto, E. C. & Howlin, P. (1999). Spatial working memory in Asperger's syndrome and in patients with focal frontal and temporal lobe lesions. *Brain and Cognition,* 41, 9–26.

Mottron, L., Belleville, S., Stip, E. & Morasse, K. (1998). Atypical memory performance in an autistic savant. *Memory,* 6, 593–607.

Murray, D., Lesser, M. & Lawson, W. (2005). Attention, monotropism and the diagnostic criteria for autism. *Autism: the International Journal of Research and Practice,* 9, 139–156.

O'Shea, A. G., Fein, D. A., Cillessen, H. N., Klin, A. & Schultz, R. T. (2005). Source memory in children with autism spectrum disorders. *Developmental Neuropsychology,* 27, 337–360.

Peterson, D. M. (2002). Mental simulation, dialogical processing and the syndrome of autism. In J. Dokic & J. Proust (eds.), *Simulation and knowledge of action*, pp. 185–197. Amsterdam: John Benjamins.

Pierce, K., Muller, R. A., Ambrose, J., Allen, G. & Courchesne, E. (2001). Face processing occurs outside the fusiform 'face area' in autism: evidence from functional MRI. *Brain, 124,* 2059–2073.

Powell, S. D. & Jordan, R. R. (1992). Remediating the thinking of pupils with autism: principles into practice. *Journal of Autism and Developmental Disorders, 22,* 413–418.

(1993). Being subjective about autistic thinking and learning how to learn. *Educational Psychology, 13,* 359–370.

Rosch, E. (1973). Principles of categorisation. In E. Rosch & B. Lloyd (eds.), *Cognition and categorisation*, pp. 27–48. Hillsdale, NJ: Erlbaum.

Sainsbury, C. (2000). *Martian in the playground.* Bristol: Lucky Duck Publishing.

Schacter, D. (2003). *How the mind forgets and remembers.* London: Souvenir Press.

Suddendorf, T. S. & Corballis, M. C. (1997). Mental time travel and the evolution of the human mind. *Genetic, Social and General Psychology Monographs, 123,* 133–167.

Szelag, E., Kowalska, J., Galkowski, T. & Poppel, E. (2004). Temporal processing deficits in high functioning children with autism. *British Journal of Psychology, 95,* 269–282.

Tager-Flusberg, H. (1991). Semantic processing in the free recall of autistic children: further evidence for a cognitive deficit. *British Journal of Developmental Psychology, 9,* 417–430.

Tulving, E. (1972). Episodic and semantic memory. In E. Tulving & W. Donaldson (eds.), *Organisation of memory*, pp. 381–403. New York: Academic Press.

Van Dalen, J. G. T. (1995). Autism from within. *Link: the Journal of Autism Europe, 17,* 11–12.

Wells, G. L. & Bradfield, A. L. (1998). Good, you identified the suspect: feedback to eyewitnesses distorts their reports of the witnessing experience. *Journal of Applied Psychology, 83,* 360–76.

Wing, L. (1981). Asperger's syndrome: a clinical account. *Psychological Medicine, 11,* 115–129.

16 A different memory: are distinctions drawn from the study of nonautistic memory appropriate to describe memory in autism?

Laurent Mottron, Michelle Dawson and Isabelle Soulières

> What has to be accepted, the given, is – so one could say – *forms of life*.
> L.Wittgenstein, *Philosophical Investigations*, 1955

The statement 'Corgis and basset hounds have ears of different lengths' is meaningful and useful when it comes to recognizing these life forms, but is uninformative about their hearing ability. 'Sharks have longer flippers than whales' also has some kind of meaning, even if the life forms belong to different families, but fails to indicate which one is the better swimmer. However, 'squid have more fingers than humans' is a somewhat misleading statement (squid hardly ever wear gloves, even in cold seas), and it is difficult to find a context where such a statement would be useful. The usefulness of a statement about one form of life using descriptive units relevant to another form of life depends on how members of these families resemble one another, and such a statement is not informative about the consequences of the described difference.   *À la manière de* L. Wittgenstein

Normocentrism and deficit-oriented explanations: ubiquitous problems in neurocognitive research in autism

Cognitive neuroscientists working on autism are looking for an 'uneven cognitive profile' (Happé, 1999) characterizing the specificity of autism compared to typical development and other neurodevelopmental disorders. Similarly and at a finer scale, thirty years of research on memory in autism has resulted in the compilation of a complex profile of 'spared' and 'impaired' areas in memory (see Bowler & Gaigg, this volume, Chapter 17). This profile is based on divergence ('peaks' and 'troughs')

311

of autistic performance from a baseline performance of nonautistics identical in general intelligence. Spared/impaired, peaks/troughs, intact/damaged, and all equivalent descriptions, are products of what we call 'normocentrism'.[1] This is the measurement of autistic cognitive performance relative to performance of nonautistics or typically developing individuals (TDIs), in tasks relevant to systems, concepts, or cognitive loci defined from the study of TDIs.

Criticizing normocentrism at an ethical and methodological level, one of us (MD), an autistic researcher, once said, 'We are not nonautistic people with fragmented excesses and deficits; we are wholly and completely autistic people.'

This chapter develops the idea that normocentric descriptions of autistics[2] as defective nonautistics bias our understanding of autism information processing, and therefore of memory in autism. We begin with a consideration of ethical issues arising from descriptions of different life forms. Then we propose that nonautistic memory subsystems, relations among these subsystems, and their rules of functioning, do not straightforwardly apply to autistics. Three aspects of autistic memory are presented in order to defend our hypothesis: savant memory, surface memory and categorization.

Ethics: how should life forms be described?

The grasping and locomotion system of squid consists of ten tentacles and uses water for propulsion. This system is only awkwardly described by using concepts tailored for humans. A 'humanocentric' description of squid would be that they have 2.5 times more arms and legs than us, that these legs are boneless, and that they move by jumping horizontally under water. Apart from being distinctly unparsimonious, this description would be misleading. It leads to the inference of nails at the end of squid extremities, and to erroneous assumptions re the effect of boneless squid legs on how fast they can swim compared to humans. Fortunately,

---

[1] In reference to 'ethnocentrism', 'the tendency to evaluate other groups according to the values and standards of one's own ethnic group, especially with the conviction that one's own ethnic group is superior to the other groups', *The American Heritage Dictionary of the English Language*, 4th edn (New York: Houghton Mifflin, 2004).

[2] Our respectful use of 'autistic' rather than 'person with autism' arises from the views of autistic people (e.g. see Sinclair, 1999, 'Why I dislike person first language', web.syr.edu/~jisincla/person_first.htm), and parallels the use of 'female' versus 'person with femaleness' and 'lesbian' versus 'person with lesbianism'. Likewise, there is the 'World Association of the Deaf', not the 'World Association of Persons with Deafness'. See the American Psychological Association (2001) 'Guidelines to reduce bias in language', e.g. 'Respect people's preferences; call people what they prefer to be called.'

the strategy scientists use to describe squid does not take the human case as its reference point. Even when squid were first described, scientists were not baffled that cephalopod mollusc tentacles lacked nails; the difference between human and squid life forms is large enough to protect against the comic or tragic consequences of 'humanocentrism'.

However, in a situation where a scientist with an excellent knowledge of fish is confronted with a life form he has not seen before – a squid – he might describe this discovery in reference to fish. He might make statements like 'Squid are disordered fish. They have superior prehensile abilities, but inferior skin resistance', etc. But accepting the emergence of 'tentacles' and other squid-specific concepts, rather than persevering in using fish-oriented concepts, is closer to the idea we have of science. A scientist interested in an accurate description of squid would develop, if they did not exist already, hierarchical taxonomies which, at a general level, use concepts (e.g. limbs) that encompass phenotypic differences among life forms and, at the specific level, are tailored to the described life form. In this chapter, we consider the hypothesis that neuroscientists who describe autistic cognition often behave like fish-experts who refuse to invent a concept for tentacles, and describe squid as impaired fish.

Ethics: the presumed dangers of analogies involving different life forms

Serious concerns and objections are usually raised when an analogy involving different life forms is applied to the situation of describing autistics. The spectre of dehumanization, past and current, is invoked by an assumption that any reference, even via analogy, to a different form of life necessarily means a life that is less than or other than human.

In the case of autism, these ethical qualms can only be described as ironic. Scientists in various fields have proposed that autistics teach us about what is fundamentally and uniquely human – because it is this essence of humanity that autistics lack (Bloom, 2004; Hobson, 2003; Pinker, 2002; Tomasello *et al.*, 2005). We therefore contend that it is the biased description of autism from a nonautistic standpoint that provides the foundation for the unethical dehumanization of autistics (Dawson, 2004a, b). The use of concepts such as 'positive/negative symptoms', 'excesses/deficits', 'spared/impaired', etc., to describe autistic behaviour and cognition does not result in a description of intrinsic autistic features, but instead creates a concept of autism based entirely on criteria relative and relevant to the functioning of nonautistics. This knowledge in turn represents the scientific foundation for the project of 'curing', preventing, remediating, or otherwise eradicating autism, a project whose ethics remain unexamined and uncriticized.[3] Autistics and allied nonautistics have responded by promoting an approach of neurodiversity, in which humankind is heterogeneous, and in which autistics should receive the assistance, accommodation and respect they need in order to succeed as autistic people. The recognition and acceptance of human difference, and therefore the humanization of populations previously set aside from humanity, is at the core of neurodiversity, while its opposite, normocentrism, is the root and rationale for dehumanization. Whereas an unbiased, nonethnocentric approach is recommended for the description of non-dominant cultures, there is no scientific counterpart for the starting point of 'cultural diversity' that exists in social sciences.

'Describing a different life form' is an epistemological analogy. It is not an implicit judgement on the magnitude of the difference between autistics and nonautistics, and most of all, it is the opposite of a judgement that nonautistics should belong to humanity, but autistics should not.

Normocentrism: the unparsimonious three-step 'natural history'

The two main detrimental consequences of normocentrism are the experimental use of concepts tailored for nonautistics (mapping nonautistic cognitive loci to autistic processes), and the predominance of negative interpretations of autistic performance (deficit-oriented approach). These are the rule in cognitive neurosciences in autism. However, facts resist, and the birth, adolescence and maturity of models of cognitive functioning in autism follow a three-step course as the inadequacy of the normocentric approach slowly unravels.

Step one is 'X is impaired', where 'X' is a process (or collection of processes) characterizing typical functioning, supported or not by a dissociable brain component or network. This impaired 'X' is proposed as an explanation for a number of autistic behaviours and findings of atypical autistic performance. Examples of these proposed processes are numerous: theory of mind, executive function, central coherence, amygdala

---

[3] In some cases (e.g. Grossman, Carter & Volkmar, 1997) the dehumanization of autistics could be argued to be a generic consequence of the 'medical model'. However, abandoning this model does not alter the situation for autistics; dehumanization also marks the work of those who explicitly reject a medical approach to autism (e.g. Lovaas, 1993; Lovaas & Newsom, 1976; Lovaas & Smith, 1989). We also caution against the pervasive assumption that while some kinds of autistics may conditionally deserve human status, other kinds of autistics do not (e.g. see Baggs, 2006: 'You have equated differences in the way we function with differences in the amount of rights we deserve', from ballastexistenz. autistics.org/?cat = 222).

functions, deep processing, face/emotion recognition and, relevant for the current text, long-term memory. Were autistics actually missing the sum of the functions that they have been hypothesized to be missing, they would not be a form of life superior to cephalopod molluscs. Autistics have successively been supposed to be deprived of what makes humans human (theory of mind deficit, 'mindblindness'), what gives subjective life some constancy across time (amnesic model), what makes the brain organized (underconnectivity), what makes cognitive operations hierarchized (weak central coherence), what gives human behaviour its purposiveness (executive dysfunction model), what roots human relationships at the level of identity and emotion recognition (innate absence of social motivation), what prevents humans from being chained to their perception (absence of top-down control), and so on.

Conglomerating multiple individual normocentrisms into larger overarching concepts (like 'coherence' and 'complexity') to account for what individuals with autism are supposed to be missing does not make cognitive approaches less normocentric, while imposing on researchers the burden of demonstrating the neurological and empirical correlates of these large-scale constructs. However, the definition of these large, unifying statements is inherently circular. For example, if my definition of coherence is secondary to a preliminary conviction that it is something that is 'missing' in autistics, I am at risk of regarding anything found to characterize autism as 'missing coherence'. Without a priori definitions locating the interface dividing what coherent and complex are from what they are not, these large concepts are plagued by arbitrariness. They are inherently nonfalsifiable, even though they may orient research in a useful way.[4]

In all cases, as we see in step one ('X is impaired'), the validity of cognitive concepts used to understand the autistic difference is entirely dependent on autistics being nonautistics plus or minus something – the 'residual normality' issue (Thomas & Karmiloff-Smith, 2002).

Then, in step two, scientists who take a contrary view underline that each of these 'X is impaired' models is too powerful, and predicts impairments that appear intact under further scrutiny. It is the 'no, X is not impaired' stage. This second step consists mainly of repairing the 'noise' linked to the importing of nonautistic concepts into autism.

Lastly, in a third step, the purported defective process is reframed in a more detailed and task-oriented way. It is the 'X works differently' stage, where scientists reluctantly admit that autistics, although as human as

---

[4] The hypothesized unity of large constructs like 'coherence' also may be questioned (Pellicano, Maybery & Durkin, 2005).

nonautistic humans, are a different kind of human. Why not instead start at this point, and discard the two previous steps? We should not waste grant money in demonstrating that there are no nails at the end of tentacles. More importantly, we might consider the consequences for autistics of living in a society where the decisions made about how they should be regarded and treated are often founded on descriptions of autism at the 'X is impaired' stage.

Normocentrism: normocentric and deficit-oriented approaches in models of autistic memory

The history of memory models in autism follows the general three-step pattern of impaired/not impaired/different. The prototypical scheme in memory studies in autism is based on the use of normocentric concepts, usually presented in pairs (long-term vs working memory, surface vs deep properties, episodic vs semantic memory, cued vs free recall, recency vs primacy effects, face vs object memory). These concepts are isolated by the method of 'double dissociation' and/or by dissociating the effect of variables on nonautistic behaviour. This three-step course is particularly clear for the 'amnesic' model (step one; Boucher & Warrington, 1976). Under the pressure of numerous papers reporting typical levels of performance (Bennetto, Pennington & Rogers, 1996; Minshew & Goldstein, 1993; Rumsey & Hamburger, 1988; Summers & Craik, 1994), this model has generally been abandoned (step two; e.g. this volume, Williams, Minshew & Goldstein, Chapter 7; but see Boucher, Mayes & Bigham, Chapter 14). In the third step, most recent memory studies emphasize qualitative differences, in the presence of an identical level of performance for autistics and nonautistics (e.g. Bowler, Gardiner & Berthollier, 2004; Renner, Klinger & Klinger, 2000; Toichi & Kamio, 2002).

The effect of normocentrism on memory studies can be observed in the first stage of this three-step course, but also in problems linked to the generalization of empirical findings. Most findings related to atypical memory in autism are expressed as the superiority or inferiority of one memory subsystem compared to the equivalent subsystem in a matched comparison group. For example, the fine-grained conclusion of Bowler, Matthews and Gardiner (1997) is that episodic memory is intact in autism as long as cued recall is used, but that free recall shows impairment. When findings obtained through the use of a distinction coined for nonautistics (e.g. free vs cued recall) result in a principle (e.g. 'task support hypothesis'), this principle represents an elegant account of autistic performance in a certain task, 'A'. However, the validity of the generalization of this principle to another task, 'B', depends first on how

'A' and 'B' are similar, and second on the fact that *two tasks that are similar for nonautistics may not be similar for autistics*. The issue of generalization between tasks (or of external validity of a statement based on a task) depends on their similarity, which in turn depends on the *level* and *nature* of possible similarities. Difficulties in ecological situations may or may not be related to replicable deficits in cognitive tasks for the same reason. And there is some pernicious circularity at this point, as knowing when two items are similar for an autistic is not the starting point of the research, but the purpose of this research.

The finding of equivalent performance in autistics and TDIs does not eliminate the dogma of deficit. A study by Renner, Klinger and Klinger (2000) is especially instructive in this regard. Autistic children and TDIs of similar Chronological age (CA), but nonsignificantly superior Full-Scale IQ (FSIQ), were given a perceptual identification task, a recognition task and a free recall task. Both groups performed at the same level in the three tasks. However, *although overall recall was identical between groups*, there was a difference in the serial position effect. Serial position effect is indicative of primacy and recency effects, and is expressed as a proportion of words from the beginning, middle and end of the to-be-remembered list that are recalled. Autistics produced recall that was linearly dependent on serial position: the earlier an item was in the list, the less likely it was to be remembered (beginning: 16%; middle: 22%; end: 31%; average: 23%). In contrast, TDIs remembered more words presented at the beginning (28%) and the end of the list (21%) than those presented in the middle (16%; average 21.6%). The authors interpreted their finding as showing an *'impaired serial position effect'* attributed to 'a failure to effectively organise information in memory during encoding or retrieval, rather than memory impairment per se'. The authors conclude that autistics have 'an *impaired serial position effect* (i.e. an *impaired* primacy effect and *intact* recency effect) ... suggestive of possible hippocampal dysfunction'.

In fact recency is *superior in the autistic group and overall performance is equivalent*. The authors cannot conclude to a *performance deficit* in the presence of normal performance, but nevertheless *assert a deficit to explain a difference*. This indicates a bias towards interpreting findings as deficits. Differences as such are not an accepted result and have to be linked to a deficit to gain credibility. An alternative wording of the result is that autistics use different ways of remembering, characterized by a different balance of recall proportion at different points of the serial position.

Are anatomically based statements about memory (e.g. hippocampal hypothesis, Boucher *et al.*, 2005; DeLong, this volume, Chapter 8; frontal hypothesis, Bennetto, Pennington & Rogers, 1996) any improvement in this regard? They are probably worse. To the same extent that autism implicates an overall difference of cognitive functioning which prevents a direct mapping of typical constructs on autistic cognition, an overall difference in brain organization adds considerable 'noise' to the interpretation of localized differences in brain activation during a task. However, by definition, fMRI studies *combine* assumptions about functional isolation of a brain region of interest with that of cognitive operations, and with the residual normality of what could be termed 'regions of disinterest'. Identical level of performance and identical size or activation levels of a region of interest in an autistic and comparison group do not guarantee otherwise identical functioning. Conversely, differences in cognitive strategies or brain activation do not imply diminished efficiency. Differences in size or activation level indicate that two groups differ in the involvement of a certain brain-behaviour relationship, but should not be automatically considered as impairment.

Three examples of the normocentric interpretation of memory performance

Savant memory

Exceptional memory is implied in most savant abilities, in the form of a capacity to report – but also to manipulate – larger units of graphic, musical, linguistic or numerical material than nonautistics (see Pring, this volume, Chapter 11). Calendar calculation (CC) is an example of an autistic competence virtually not represented (at least as a spontaneous behaviour/performance occurring before adolescence) in nonautistic individuals. It has defied explanation for a century. The normocentric attitude involved postulating the over-functioning of a cognitive subsystem that could be associated to a similar performance in nonautistics, and to test if properties of CC correspond to those of this memory system. The deficit-oriented approach was manifested by the explanation given for this over-functioning, e.g. impaired coherence explaining orientation towards detailed material.

Mnesic retrieval interpretations for calendar calculation include eidetic, rote memory, combination of memory and computation, and semantic memory. The role of eidetic memory for calendar calculation (Duckett, 1977; Ho, Tsang & Ho, 1991) has been discarded since the publication of a report of a blind calculator (Rubin & Monagan, 1965), and in consideration of the short duration of this type of memory. Long-term 'rote memory' has also been proposed as an explanation for CC (Horwitz *et al.*, 1965; Horwitz, Denning & Winter, 1969). However, reliance on long-term memory retrieval procedures is not plausible for the entire range of CC: some individuals produce dates that cannot be directly memorized. This does not exclude the possibility that memory could play a role in calculations for a certain range of years. Episodic memory is also a candidate for explaining CC performance, due to the frequent ability of autistic calendar calculators to provide episodic information (e.g. weather forecast, menu of the day) for specific dates. However, nonautistic episodic memory is vulnerable to interference, whereas autistic memorization appears to be immune to interference, at least in some cases (Mottron *et al.*, 1998; Thioux *et al.*, 2006).

More recent models implicate mnesic/computation explanations. Basic calculation, like subtracting a certain number (e.g. 400 or 28 years) from a year in the distant future, may be used in order to bring the date requested closer to a more recent date possessing the same calendar structure. Within a one-year range, basic arithmetic may also be used in combination with 'anchor dates' (Hill, 1975). According to the 'anchor dates' hypothesis, calendar calculators would memorize canonical dates and use them to compute the day corresponding to the requested dates by a series of simple arithmetical operations. This hypothesis has been challenged by the finding of homogeneous response times for dates, no matter what criteria are used to classify these dates (Ho, Tsang & Ho, 1991) and by the considerable span for which correct dates may be given (e.g. 6,000 years). Lastly, resemblance between semantic memory and multidirectional access to calendar information has been underlined. Accordingly, the ability to give as rapidly as possible all months beginning by a certain day (reverse questions), as well as the day of the week corresponding to a given date (direct questions), closely resembles the nonautistic ability to provide all functions of a given object as rapidly as all objects corresponding to a certain function (Mottron *et al.*, 2006).

In the most sophisticated CC study to date, involving possibly the fastest known calendar calculator, Donny, Thioux *et al.* (2006) showed that Donny used a complex combination of memory for calendar templates and simple computations. However, memory and computation followed idiosyncratic restrictions. Memory and computation did not have the same role in past (no increase of reaction time according to distance) and future dates (distance effect for very distant dates). Simple computation presented unexplained asymmetries between addition and subtraction. The role of computation in retrieval was nonconventional: matching between two years in the future could be done without explicit computation. There were striking (and unexplained) differences among certain calendar templates. Even if the activation of templates was demonstrated through a priming effect of years governed by the same template, the nature of their memorization did not equate (in terms of level of consciousness or types of encoding) to a known memory system. In summary, the blend of devices used by Donny could not be reduced to the over-functioning of a sub-memory system with a corresponding equivalent in nonautistics.

Although explanations issued from nonautistic memory seem not to work, emphasizing the role of memory in CC seems the natural consequence of discarding the role of conscious use of algorithms. However, the heterogeneity of savant strategy in this regard was a source of surprise, and of ultimate modesty. In a study of a calendar calculator, DBC, with modest performances and rather long reaction times, we performed a series of experiments that aimed to test the possible use of a calendar algorithm by autistic calendar calculators. First, the systematic testing of all dates in a year revealed a homogeneous and random distribution of errors, whatever criteria of date classification and year of retrieval within DBC's range of knowledge are used. This was interpreted as an indication that storage and retrieval processes do not make use of these categories. Second, retesting DBC on the same dates one year later shows that his errors were not stable across time, which is not in favour of attributing errors to the misuse of an algorithm. Finally, DBC was able to answer three types of 'reversed' questions that cannot be solved by a classical algorithm. However, a brilliant autistic adult, Emmanuel Dubruille, recently published on the web the algorithm he uses for sophisticated CC, clearly in contradiction with our study on DBC.[5]

If there is not a clearly delimited memory subsystem that over-functions in CC, and if calculators may succeed with as well as without algorithms, how does it work? The disappointing results of attempts to understand savants to date suggest that explanations are premature, and that creation of ad-hoc concepts would be more fruitful, with the risk of having to keep to descriptions in the absence of emerging tools. In this vein, L. Selfe's descriptions of Nadia's drawing have been more influential on the understanding of autism than the numerous tentative explanations of her savant ability (Mottron, Limoges & Jelenic, 2003). To report that it exists and CC works, as behaviour and a performance, occurring in natural situations, and without external prompts, is more informative than explanations resulting from the 'wild' importation of cognitive modules from the nonautistic brain. From these descriptions, laws valid for autistics will emerge (e.g. implicit learning of structured material; cf. Pring, this volume, Chapter 11) even if they contradict those valid for nonautistics.

[5] membres.lycos.fr/theandroiddata/

Are autistics 'surface memorizers'?

In reaction to the over-fragmentation of memory systems, a so-called 'level-of-processing' (LOP) approach to memory has been developed. Whereas the classical cognitive approach multiplies the cognitive loci, each corresponding to a certain memory operation, the LOP approach (Gardiner, this volume, Chapter 1) proposes that the same representations, involving the same neuroanatomical substrata, are involved in most memory processes. This conceptualization of memory distinguishes shallow (e.g. phonological) and deep (e.g. semantic) processing of the same representations, a distinction that has been used to account for dissociation between autistic memory performances. In TDIs, a level-of-processing effect is established: the 'deeper' an item is encoded, the better this item is later recognized or recalled. Several variations of this effect have been studied in autism, with the replicated result that the level of encoding effect evident in TDIs is not observed to the same magnitude in autistics. The LOP framework is also relevant for the history of cognitive theories of autism as it supports the more extensive distinction between low-level and high-level processes, which grounds several attempts, including our own, to account for superior performance of autistics in most perceptual tasks, but also in some attention and memory tasks. As will follow, this framework has been allowed to characterize some aspects of autistic memory.

In our group (Mottron, Morasse & Belleville, 2001), we presented lists of unrelated words under three encoding conditions: phonological, semantic and no encoding orientation. Semantic orientation at encoding resulted in a better free recall than did orientation towards syllabic or absence of orientation. However, at retrieval, semantic cues led to better recall than phonological cues in TDIs, whereas both types of cues had the same effect in prompting recall for individuals with autism. The group by cueing condition interaction resulted from a more efficient phonological cueing and a less efficient semantic cueing than found in the comparison group. We concluded that executive, semantic or amnesic models were not supported by these data, and that autistics do not conform to the LOP principle to the same extent as nonautistics. In this task, autistic participants showed a normal free recall, and did not benefit more than the comparison group from orientation or recall cues (as an executive deficit would have predicted).

We interpreted our findings as showing a bias towards low-level processing and enhanced processing of superficial properties (here, phonological) in autism, possibly due to an 'imbalance' between low and high cognitive processes. Conforming to the Enhanced Perceptual Functioning (EPF) model (Mottron & Burack, 2001) we underlined that in pairs of operations like phonological vs semantic, local vs global, pitch vs contour, the higher order of the pair is not defective, but it contributes less to the operation invoked. Quoting the 'task support hypothesis' (Bowler, Gardiner & Berthollier, 2004; Bowler, Gardiner & Grice, 2000) we noted that the memory tasks in which autistic individuals perform at a normal or outstanding level use *related* test primes, whereas tasks in which they are usually impaired (as free recall) use *unrelated* test primes. Therefore, autistic memory performance appears to be more favoured by perceptual similarity between encoding and recall cues than nonautistic memory. However, in order not to fall under our own criticisms, this interpretation requires a definition of perception valid for multiple forms of life (e.g. 'subsystem of the brain that builds an analogical representation of the world') rather than a normocentric definition of perception.

Using a similar rationale, Toichi and Kamio (2002) presented Japanese written words to autistic participants and a comparison group, followed by three types of questions inducing three levels of encoding: superficial (questions about the type of character used), less superficial (questions about phonological properties of the word) and semantic. A recognition task administered consecutively resulted in similar overall performance in the two groups. However, autistics were *superior* to the comparison group in the two shallowest conditions of encoding (significantly only for graphic encoding), but nonsignificantly inferior in the deep encoding condition. In within-group comparisons, TDIs presented a clear LOP effect, in the form of superior encoding in the semantic condition: the deeper words had been encoded, the better they were recognized. In contrast, the three types of encoding conditions resulted in similar levels of recognition in the autistic group. The authors concluded that 'a lack of the levels-of-processing effect in spite of overall good performance suggests an abnormal relationship between episodic memory and semantic memory in individuals with autism'. If 'abnormal' means unconventional, we agree with this statement.

Another example of how atypical relations between 'surface' properties and so called 'deep encoding' modifies straightforward statements of impaired memory imported from nonautistic cognition is the effect of cue/material similarity on source memory. Source memory had been reported impaired in Bennetto, Pennington and Rogers (1996) to account for intrusions in free recall of lists of unrelated words. Bowler, Gardiner & Berthollier (2004) asked Asperger adolescents and adults to study lists of words in an active condition, where they had to perform actions related to the word, and in passive conditions. This was followed by a recognition task and by questions on the action performed at encoding of a recognized word (source memory). In the 'supported' condition participants had to select the appropriate source from activities listed, and as an uncued free recall task in the unsupported condition. Identification of source by Asperger participants was at a similar level to that of the comparison participants when support was provided, but their performance was poorer when support was absent. In place of a raw 'source memory deficit', Bowler and colleagnes therefore limited the deficit to memory tasks that require free recall of unrelated items, in the absence of specific instructions to learn that information, or without any support from the environment at test. However, we disagree with the conclusion that these findings show *an episodic memory deficit* implicating frontal *pathology*. If episodic memory is defined as the mere ability to recall episodic material whatever conditions are employed, rather than like the nonautistic way of performing this task, there is no more 'deficit'.

Similarly, not using categories during list recall, which is often invoked as the most consistent impairment reported in autism memory literature (Ben Shalom, 2003; Bowler, Matthews & Gardiner, 1997), is not impairment, at least when overall recall performance is identical. The 'failure' to use categorization during recall may be a difference between mandatory categorization and optional categorization for autistics (Mottron *et al.*, 2006b). Autistics may not use categorization when they are not explicitly told to. The fact that frontally injured patients also present with an absence of grouping at recall is not relevant for explaining autistic performance because these people also display impaired recall, which is not the case with autistic individuals. Possibly, *nonautistics need executive functions to reach a certain level of recall, whereas autistics do not*. Accordingly, 'unstructured' recall is generally not associated with an overall inferior recall performance (Bowler, Matthews & Gardiner, 1997; Hermelin & O'Connor, 1970; Minshew *et al.*, 1992) and is sometimes associated with a superior rote verbal memory (Fein *et al.*, 1996).

Notwithstanding these results, the low vs high (or surface/deep) distinctions may lose some validity when applied to autistics. Even if this distinction has anatomical counterparts, it does not inherently imply a hierarchy between 'low-level' and 'high-level' tasks. If perception does problem solving, and therefore is not limited to the construction of analogical representations but encompasses manipulation of these representations (e.g. mental rotation), the concept of 'perception' does not carry the same assumptions any more. Accordingly, there are now indications that 'low-level' processes, as they are delineated in nonautistics, contribute in autistics to what nonautistics describe as high-level processes. This may be true cross-sectionally in the form of participation of occipital areas in manipulation of information in working memory (Koshino *et al.*, 2005). This may also be true developmentally: 'surface' memory of verbal (echolalia) and written (hyperlexia) language is not a dead-end and may represent a way autistics enter language (Mottron *et al.*, 2006b).

Categorization, from 'memory of exemplars' to optionality

Categorization studies follow the same trend as other domains of memory investigation in autism. Category learning consists in building new concepts in semantic memory via experience with specific instances of these concepts. In autism, the study of category learning is very recent – although a few earlier studies investigated existing concepts, or already learned categories (Shulman, Yirmiya & Greenbaum, 1995; Tager-Flusberg 1985a, b; Ungerer & Sigman, 1987). In the first study of novel category learning (Klinger & Dawson, 1995, 2001), participants had to classify instances of imaginary animals to get familiarized with a category. Then they were asked to choose which of two animals was the best example of the category. CA-matched autistic and Down syndrome participants were not able to pick the right animal when the category was constructed around a prototype, whereas they were able to perform the task when there was a strict membership rule for the category. In contrast, TDIs matched for vocabulary comprehension were able to achieve both types of tasks. The authors concluded that 'both children with autism and children with Down syndrome have impaired prototype learning abilities' (p. 123). In contrast, a recent study by Molesworth, Bowler and Hampton (2005) explored category learning using a more extended familiarization with stimuli of varying prototypicality. This time, no differences were found between autistic and nonautistic participants. The authors concluded that categorization mechanisms were intact in autism.

However, when considering the time taken to learn the categories and the strategies employed, there seem to be differences in category learning between autistic and nonautistic individuals. For example, we investigated categorical perception, a phenomenon occurring when there is a qualitative difference in the perceived similarity between stimuli, depending on whether they are in the same category. The categories therefore have a top-down influence on discrimination of their members. Our study involved discrimination and classification tasks with a continuum of thin to wide ellipses. The representation of categories was similar in both groups, since classification curves were indistinguishable, but evidence of top-down influence from categories to discrimination abilities was found only in the nonautistic group. Autistic participants displayed no facilitation of discrimination near the boundary of the categories, which suggests a reduced top-down influence (Soulières *et al.*, 2007). Similarly, in another study, fine-grained individual analyses indicated that autistic participants take longer to adopt a definite strategy to categorize complex novel stimuli. Earlier in the training, they either try many different strategies or try to memorize specific stimuli (Soulières *et al.*, under revision).

Put together, results from these studies suggest that autistic individuals can achieve categorization at a similar level to nonautistic individuals. However, autistic individuals may, unlike nonautistics, try a variety of strategies when asked to categorize novel stimuli, which can result in slower category learning (see also Bott *et al.*, 2006). Also, discrimination and categorization may work more independently from each other: categorization may be 'optional' in autism, allowing a low-level or high-level treatment of information according to task demands.

Conclusion: promoting a 'form of life' attitude

Is there some positive research strategy that may come out these considerations? We described 'normocentrism' as the unrestricted use of concepts built for nonautistics. Some of these concepts are intrinsically linked to their nonautistic origin (e.g. semantic memory, episodic memory, perception, and low-level vs high-level operations). Some other umbrella concepts, like coherence and complexity, are especially at risk of exaggerating what autistics cannot actually do. However, there are a series of concepts like information processing or categorization that should be more neutral at times to describe the autistic world.

In this chapter, we also contend that the epistemological position of describing a different life form, *if associated with the ethical concern that autism is a contributing variant of humanity and not a defect or series of defects* (Dawson, 2004a), is paradoxically the one that permits the most ethical and accurate approach to autistic differences. What we propose has nothing to do with promoting a pre-theoretical, 'naïve empiricist' approach. When a scientist describes a different form of life, he/she employs pre-existing categories as basis for observation. However, the concepts he/she uses (e.g. limbs) *are not specific to one form of life, but are emerging abstractions resulting from the observation of phenomenal, functional or material regularities among life forms*. Although we may be more direct and comprehensive – possibly because, for some of us, autism is not only an object of study, but the form of life to which we belong – this position is in the neighbourhood of Bowler's (2001) affirmation, which

Rather than positing a distorted reflection of nature or a blindness to certain aspects of it ... aims to take account of how interactions among processes over time combine to produce adaptational end-points across a large range of domains of functioning. In this respect it can encompass the whole range of autistic symptomatology, not just those aspects relating to social impairment. (Bowler, 2001, p. 232)

Our thesis is that the deficit-oriented approach is inherent to a normo-centric attitude, and that this normocentric attitude disappears when the aim of scientific research descends from *delineating deficits* to *describing a different form of life* – of *human* life. The level of resemblance of the two forms of life will emerge at its own pace if cognitive research on autism is embedded in an *a priori decision that autism belongs to humanity*. Our position combines, following Dawson (2004a, 2004b), an ethical and epistemological concern: normocentrism is an approach which risks, deliberately or otherwise, autistics being dehumanized and rejected from humanity. At the same time, normocentrism is scientifically nonparsimo-nious: importing concepts from nonautistic cognition delays research by imposing noninformative steps. One may consider that this is the way science progresses, and that going against it is a Quixotic ambition. However, one may alternatively suggest that these steps, and their non-benign real-world consequences for autistics, might be avoided – by considering that autism is not a disease, and should instead be described and investigated as a different form of human life.

Summary

Studies on memory in autism are generally based on memory subsys-tems derived from, and therefore relevant to, research in nonautistic individuals. At the birth of each model of autistic memory, one aspect of memory is supposed to be underdeveloped. Then contradictory findings reveal that in more controlled conditions, or for certain indi-viduals, or for certain IQ or age ranges, this subsystem appears to work properly. Eventually, the scientific community concludes that this memory subsystem works, but differently. Three examples of this three-step 'natural history' of memory studies in autism are reviewed here: calendar calculation, surface memory and categorization. We find that, due to their normocentrism, cognitive studies in autism follow a nonparsimonious pathway. Numerous inaccurate predictions, and their real-life consequences, could be avoided by identifying and using con-cepts tailored for autism, and by using a 'difference' rather than a 'deficit' approach.

References

American Psychological Association (2001). *Publication manual of the American Psychological Association*, 5th edn. Washington, DC: APA.
Ben Shalom, D. (2003). Memory in autism: review and synthesis. *Cortex, 39*, 1129–1138.

Bennetto, L., Pennington, B. F. & Rogers, S. J. (1996). Intact and impaired memory functions in autism. *Child Development*, 67, 1816–1835.

Bloom, P. (2004). *Descartes' baby*. New York: Basic Books.

Bott, L., Brock, J., Brockdorff, N., Boucher, J. & Lamberts, K. (2006). Perceptual similarity in autism. *Quarterly Journal of Experimental Psychology*, 59, 1237–1254.

Boucher, J. & Warrington, E. K. (1976). Memory deficits in early infantile autism: some similarities to the amnesic syndrome. *British Journal of Psychology*, 67, 73–87.

Boucher, J., Cowell, P., Howard, M., Broks, P., Farrant, A., Roberts, N. & Mayes, A. (2005). A combined clinical neuropsychological and neuroanatomical study of adults with high-functioning autism. *Cognitive Neuropsychiatry*, 10, 165–214.

Bowler, D. M. (2001). Autism: specific cognitive deficit or emergent end-point of multiple interacting systems? In J. Burack, T. Charman, N. Yirmiya & P. R. Zelazo (eds.), *The development of autism: perspectives from theory and research*, pp. 219–235. Mahwah, NJ: Erlbaum.

Bowler, D. M., Gardiner, J. M. & Berthollier, N. (2004). Source memory in adolescents and adults with Asperger's syndrome. *Journal of Autism and Developmental Disorders*, 34, 533–542.

Bowler, D. M., Gardiner, J. M., & Grice, S. J. (2000). Episodic memory and remembering in adults with Asperger syndrome. *Journal of Autism and Developmental Disorders*, 30, 295–304.

Bowler, D. M., Matthews, N. J. & Gardiner, J. M. (1997). Asperger's syndrome and memory: similarity to autism but not amnesia. *Neuropsychologia*, 35, 65–70.

Dawson, M. (2004a). The misbehaviour of behaviourists. www.sentex.net/~nexus23/naa_aba.html

(2004b) Factum of the intervener, Michelle Dawson. In *Auton (Guardian ad litem of)* v. *British Columbia (Attorney General)*. www.sentex.net/~nexus23/naa_fac.html

Duckett, J. (1977). Adaptive and maladaptive behavior of idiots-savants. *American Journal of Mental Deficiency*, 82, 308–311.

Fein, D., Dunn, M. A., Allen, D. M., Aram, R. *et al*. (1996). Neuropsychological and language data. In I. Rapin (ed.), *Preschool children with inadequate communication: developmental language disorder, autism, low IQ*, pp. 123–154. London: McKeith Press.

Grossman, J. B., Carter, A. & Volkmar, F. R. (1997). Social behavior in autism. *Annals of the New York Academy of Sciences*, 807, 440–454.

Happé, F. G. (1999). Autism: cognitive deficit or cognitive style? *Trends in Cognitive Sciences*, 3, 216–222.

Hermelin, B. & O'Connor, N. (1970). *Psychological experiments with autistic children*. Oxford: Pergamon Press.

Hill, A. L. (1975). An investigation of calendar calculating by an idiot savant. *American Journal of Psychiatry*, 132, 557–560.

Ho, E. D., Tsang, A. K. & Ho, D. Y. (1991). An investigation of the calendar calculation ability of a Chinese calendar savant. *Journal of Autism and Developmental Disorders*, 21, 315–327.

Hobson, P. (2003). *The cradle of thought*. New York: Oxford University Press.

Horwitz, W. A., Deming, W. E. & Winter, R. F. (1969). A further account of the idiots savants, experts with the calendar. *American Journal of Psychiatry*, 126, 412–415.

Horwitz, W. A., Kestenbaum, C., Person, E. & Jarvik, L. (1965). Identical twin – 'idiot savants' – calendar calculators. *American Journal of Psychiatry*, *121*, 1075–1079.

Howard, M. A., Cowell, P. E., Boucher, J., Broks, P., Mayes, A., Farrant, A. & Roberts, N. (2000). Convergent neuroanatomical and behavioural evidence of an amygdala hypothesis of autism. *Neuroreport*, *11*, 2931–2935.

Klinger, L. G. & Dawson, G. (1995). A fresh look at categorization abilities in persons with autism. In E. Schopler & G. B. Mesibov (eds.), *Learning and cognition in autism*, pp. 119–136. New York: Plenum Press.

   (2001). Prototype formation in autism. *Development and Psychopathology*, *13*, 111–124.

Koshino, H., Carpenter, P. A., Minshew, N. J., Cherkassky, V. L., Keller, T. A. & Just, M. A. (2005). Functional connectivity in an fMRI working memory task in high-functioning autism. *Neuroimage*, *24*, 810–821.

Lovaas, O. I. (1993). The development of a treatment-research project for developmentally disabled and autistic children. *Journal of Applied Behavior Analysis*, *26*, 617–630.

Lovaas, O. I. & Newsom, C. D. (1976). Behavior modification with psychotic children. In H. Leiteberg (ed.), *Handbook of behavior modification and behavior therapy*. Englewood Cliffs, NJ: Prentice-Hall.

Lovaas, O. I. & Smith, T. (1989). A comprehensive behavioral theory of autistic children: paradigm for research and treatment. *Journal of Behavior Therapy and Experimental Psychiatry*, *20*, 17–29.

Minshew, N. J. & Goldstein, G. (1993). Is autism an amnesic disorder? Evidence from the California Verbal Learning Test. *Neuropsychology*, *7*, 209–216.

Minshew, N., Goldstein, G., Muenz, D. & Payton, F. (1992). Neuropsychological functioning in nonmentally retarded autistic individuals. *Journal of Clinical and Experimental Neuropsychology*, *14*, 749–761.

Molesworth, C. J., Bowler, D. M. & Hampton, J. A. (2005). The prototype effect in recognition memory: intact in autism? *Journal of Child Psychology and Psychiatry*, *46*, 661–672.

Mottron, L., Belleville, S., Stip, E. & Morasse, K. (1998). Atypical memory performances in an autistic savant. *Memory*, *6*, 593–607.

Mottron, L., Limoges, E. & Jelenic, P. (2003). Can a cognitive deficit elicit an exceptional ability? The case of Nadia. In C. Code, C. Wallesch, Y. Joanette & A. R. Lecours (eds.), *Classic cases in neuropsychology*, vol. II, pp. 323–340. New York: Psychology Press.

Mottron, L., Lemmens, K., Gagnon, L. & Seron, X. (2006a). Non-algorithmic access to calendar information in a calendar calculator with autism. *Journal of Autism and Developmental Disorders*, *36*, 239–247.

Mottron, L., Dawson, M., Soulières, I., Hubert, B., & Burack, J. A. (2006b). Enhanced perceptual functioning in autism: an update, and eight principles of autistic perception. *Journal of Autism and Developmental Disorders*, special issue: *Perception in autism*, *36*, 27–43.

Mottron, L. & Burack, J. (2001). Enhanced perceptual functioning in the development of autism. In J. A. Burack, T. Charman, N. Yirmiya & P. R. Zelazo (eds.), *The development of autism: perspectives from theory and research*, pp. 131–148. Mahwah, NJ: Erlbaum.

Mottron, L., Morasse, K. & Belleville, S. (2001). A study of memory functioning in individuals with autism. *Journal of Child Psychology and Psychiatry*, 42, 253–260.

Pellicano, E., Mayberry, M. & Durkin, K. (2005). Central coherence in typically developing preschoolers: does it cohere and does it relate to mindreading and executive control? *Journal of Child Psychology and Psychiatry*, 46, 533–547.

Pinker, S. (2002). *The blank slate: the modern denial of human nature*. New York: Viking Press.

Renner, P., Klinger, L. G. & Klinger, M. R. (2000). Implicit and explicit memory in autism: is autism an amnesic disorder? *Journal of Autism and Developmental Disorders*, 30, 3–14.

Rubin, E. J. & Monaghan, S. (1965). Calendar calculation in a multiple-handicapped blind person. *American Journal on Mental Deficiency*, 70, 478–485.

Rumsey, J. M. & Hamburger, S. D. (1988). Neuropsychological findings in high-functioning men with infantile autism, residual state. *Journal of Clinical and Experimental Neuropsychology*, 10, 201–221.

Shulman, C., Yirmiya, N. & Greenbaum, C. W. (1995). From categorization to classification: a comparison among individuals with autism, mental retardation, and normal development. *Journal of Abnormal Psychology*, 104, 601–609.

Soulières, I., Mottron, L., Giguère, G. & Larochelle, S. (under revision). Category induction in autism: slower, perhaps different, but certainly possible. *Neuropsychology*.

Soulières, I., Mottron, L., Saumier, D. & Larochelle, S. (2007). Atypical categorical perception in autism: autonomy of discrimination? *Journal of Autism and Developmental Disorders*, 37, 481–490.

Summers, J. A. & Craik, F. I. M. (1994). The effects of subject-performed tasks on the memory performance of verbal autistic children. *Journal of Autism and Developmental Disorders*, 24, 773–783.

Tager-Flusberg, H. (1985a). Basic level and superordinate level categorization by autistic, mentally retarded, and normal children. *Journal of Experimental Child Psychology*, 40, 450–469.

(1985b). The conceptual basis for referential word meaning in children with autism. *Child Development*, 56, 1167–1178.

Thioux, M., Stark, D. E., Klaiman, C. & Schultz, R. T. (2006). The day of the week when you were born in 700 ms: calendar computation in an autistic savant. *Journal of Experimental Psychology: Human Perception and Performance*, 32, 1155–1168.

Thomas, M. & Karmiloff-Smith, A. (2002). Are developmental disorders like cases of adult brain damage? Implications from connectionist modeling. *Behavioral and Brain Sciences*, 25, 727–50.

Toichi, M. & Kamio, Y. (2002). Long-term memory and levels-of-processing in autism. *Neuropsychologia*, 40, 964–9.

Tomasello, M., Carpenter, M., Call, J., Behne, T. & Moll, H. (2005). Understanding and sharing intentions: the origins of cultural cognition. *Behavioral and Brain Sciences*, 28, 675–735.

Ungerer, J. & Sigman, M. (1987). Categorization skills and receptive language development in autistic children. *Journal of Autism and Developmental Disorders*, 17, 3–16.

17 Memory in ASD: enduring themes and future prospects

Dermot M. Bowler and Sebastian B. Gaigg

Introduction

Memory difficulties are neither a prominent nor a defining feature of autism spectrum disorders (ASDs) yet these conditions are characterized by a consistent pattern of memory strengths and weaknesses. The earliest clinical reports of autistic memory often commented on good rote memory, and early experimental investigations mapped out a profile of spared and impaired areas of memory performance as well as highlighting the reduced role of structure and meaning in enhancing memory performance. The enlargement seen in the last two decades of our conception of autism to that of a spectrum of related conditions has been accompanied by research that has both confirmed many of these early findings in a wider diagnostic context and has also established distinct patterns of performance in other memory processes, such as an attenuated sense of self-awareness when recalling the personally experienced past and a diminished recall of incidentally encoded context. We now have sufficient understanding of memory in people with autism to enable some speculations about why in this group some memory processes should function typically and others not. Such speculations can also provide us with insights into how memory interacts with and depends on other psychological processes in ASD-specific ways, insights that in turn can illuminate a broader range of psychological functioning in this population.

Memory in ASDs: the early work

Although many of the other contributions to this book have summarized the early research on memory in ASDs, we want to present here an account that sets up some of the themes that will be developed later on. From the outset readers should bear in mind that this work covers a period of over forty years. During that time, our conception of ASDs has changed dramatically, from one that was limited to the kinds of children first described by Kanner (1943) to the notion of an autistic spectrum, first proposed by Wing and Gould (1979) and now enshrined in the two most widely used diagnostic systems, the *Diagnostic and Statistical Manual of Mental Disorders*, 4th edition, text revison (DSM-IV-TR; American Psychiatric Association, 2000) and the *International Classification of Diseases*, 10th edition (ICD-10; World Health Organization, 1993). Perhaps the most important distinction brought about by this change is that between autism accompanied by global intellectual disability ('low-functioning' autism – LFA) and that not accompanied by such disability ('high-functioning' autism – HFA), the latter including Asperger syndrome or disorder. This distinction sometimes impacts on memory function and sometimes does not (see Boucher, Mayes & Bingham, this volume, Chapter 14). Alongside changing conceptions of autism, our understanding of memory has also evolved. Gardiner (this volume, Chapter 1) provides more detail on current conceptualizations of memory, but for the purposes of the present chapter, readers should remain alert to distinctions in terms of memory *processes and systems* (such as encoding, retrieval, episodic memory, semantic memory), the *procedures* used to measure these systems (such as recognition, free recall, cued recall) and the *materials* utilized in these procedures, such as visual or verbal material.

Rote memory, span and free recall

Early clinical accounts of memory in LFA and HFA (Kanner, 1943; Wing, 1981) described good rote memory – memory for the material with little regard for its meaning or purpose – and gave rise to the widely held view that for individuals with ASDs, memory was not a particular problem. Experimental studies have operationalized rote memory in terms of memory span – the number of unrelated items an individual can repeat back in the correct order immediately after presentation and measures of span also form part of many psychometric tests such as the Wechsler scales of intelligence (e.g. the Wechsler Adult Intelligence Scale, Psychological Corporation). Empirical investigations have reported no differences either in psychometric digit span (Bartak, Rutter & Cox, 1975; Minshew *et al.*, 1992; Minshew, Goldstein & Siegel, 1997; Rumsey & Hamburger, 1988; Tubbs, 1966) or in experimental measures of span (Boucher, 1981; Hermelin & O'Connor, 1967, 1975; O'Connor & Hermelin, 1967; Ramondo & Milech, 1984; but see Boucher, 1978) between children with autism (usually LFA) and matched comparison children. However, as Poirier and Martin point out in Chapter 12, when problems with matching procedures and task sophistication are tackled, even adults with HFA can be shown to have diminished performance in comparison to typical participants matched on measures of verbal intelligence.

Free recall and serial position effects

Free recall procedures involve asking participants to recall supra-span lists of items, and here we typically see the serial position effects of primacy and recency. Recency effects are thought to reflect the operation of a short-term memory system that retains some of the physical characteristics of the stimulus (e.g. sensory modality) and primacy effects are thought to reflect the transformation of information into more abstract, modality-independent semantic representations characteristic of long-term memory (Atkinson & Shiffrin, 1968; Baddeley & Warrington, 1970). Although global impairments in the free recall by individuals with both LFA and HFA of supra-span lists of items have been reported for a variety of types of material including pictures (Boucher & Warrington, 1976), experimenter's actions and spoken descriptions of them (Boucher & Lewis, 1989; Summers & Craik, 1994), many studies report a difference only under conditions where semantic or associative features form part of the studied material (Ramondo & Milech, 1984; Tager-Flusberg, 1991; Bowler *et al.*, 2000) or on later trials of a multi-trial list-learning paradigm (Bennetto, Pennington & Rogers, 1996; Minshew & Goldstein, 1993, 2001). Some studies have shown no differences (Boucher, 1981; Minshew, Goldstein & Siegel, 1997).

Investigations of serial position effects often report superior recency and diminished primacy for individuals with LFA (Boucher, 1978, 1981; O'Connor & Hermelin, 1967; Renner, Klinger & Klinger, 2000), especially if they have low digit spans (Frith, 1970). Fyffe and Prior (1978) found that children with LFA also showed recency effects for sentences, which was not seen in comparison children matched on mental age and auditory memory span. Serial position effects of a similar level to those of matched comparison participants have been shown by several investigators (Bowler *et al.*, 2000; Toichi & Kamio, 2003). However, Bowler *et al.* (2000) found that overall free recall of adults with HFA at all serial positions was diminished. Renner, Klinger and Klinger also observed a diminished primacy on delayed recall and Toichi and Kamio found diminished primacy for concrete but not abstract words in adults with HFA. As recency effects are thought to reflect the contents of short-term store, such observations of enhanced or relatively undiminished recency effects confirm the findings on immediate and rote memory summarized earlier on. Moreover, the observation in some studies of undiminished primacy effects indicate that individuals with ASD can under some circumstances process and reorganize material in a way that goes beyond the physical properties of the stimuli.

Cued recall, recognition and implicit memory

Studies of *cued recall*, whether using rhyme (Tager-Flusberg, 1991), initial phonemes (Boucher & Warrington, 1976), word stems and fragments (Bowler, Matthews & Gardiner, 1997; Gardiner, Bowler & Grice, 2003), category labels (Mottron, Morasse & Belleville, 2001), learned associates (Gardiner, Bowler & Grice, 2003) or the cued recall components of tests such as the California Verbal Learning Test (CVLT; Bennetto, Pennington & Rogers, 1996) all show undiminished performance in people with ASDs, although Minshew and her colleagues (Minshew et al., 1992; Minshew & Goldstein, 2001) did report reduced delayed cued recall on the CVLT in high-functioning adolescents and adults with autism. By contrast with the findings on free recall, it seems that immediate cued recall is relatively intact in people from all parts of the autism spectrum.

Investigations of *recognition memory* in LFA participants have tended to report diminished recognition when either forced choice procedures (Summers & Craik, 1994), procedures that involve asking participants to identify an additional non-studied item (Ameli et al., 1988), or delayed matching to sample (Barth, Fein & Waterhouse, 1995) procedures are utilized. By contrast, recognition tends to be undiminished in HFA participants, whatever the procedure (Barth, Fein & Waterhouse, 1995; Bennetto, Pennington & Rogers, 1996; Bowler, Gardiner & Grice, 2000; Bowler et al., 2000; Bowler, Gardiner & Gaigg, 2007; Minshew et al., 1992). However, many of these studies had small sample sizes and low statistical power, and a recent study by Bowler, Gardiner and Berthollier (2004), with a larger sample of adolescents and adults with HFA, did report a small but significant diminution in yes/no recognition in their Asperger group (selected on present-state criteria, without reference to early language development) suggesting that there may be subtle impairments of recognition in the HFA population.

All the studies described above used explicit tests of memory, in which participants were told that their memory would be tested later on. The few studies that have used implicit tests of memory (Roediger & McDermott, 1993) in HFA participants have shown intact priming using both perceptual and conceptual primes (Bowler, Matthews & Gardiner, 1997; Gardiner, Bowler & Grice, 2003; Renner, Klinger & Klinger, 2000; see also Toichi, this volume, Chapter 8).

This brief overview of memory research in autism paints a picture that shows greater likelihood of diminished performance on tests involving free recall than on those involving cued recall, recognition or indirect tests such as priming. Performance on cued recall and on priming tasks is unremarkable both for perceptual and conceptual material. This pattern of diminished and undiminished performance has engendered considerable speculation about the way memory operates in people with ASDs. Three of these – the amnesia parallel, the role of executive processes and self-involvement in memory – are discussed in Chapters 3, 12 and 9 and will not be developed further here. It is to the others – task support, meaning and memory, and the ordering of events in time – that our discussion now turns.

Emerging and enduring themes

The Task Support Hypothesis (TSH): a heuristic analogy with ageing?

In a study of memory in children with LFA, Boucher and Warrington (1976) noted that whereas the cued recall performance of LFA children was similar to that of comparison children, their free recall performance was diminished. As the literature reviewed earlier shows, this discrepancy in relative performance between tasks where clues to the studied material are provided at test and those where such cues are absent is a robust finding in the literature on memory in autism. The discrepancy led Bowler and colleagues to articulate a *Task Support Hypothesis* (TSH), which postulates that the memory of people with ASDs will be better on any task where support for recall is provided at test (see Bowler, Matthews & Gardiner, 1997; Bowler, Gardiner & Berthollier, 2004).

Several recent investigations have both confirmed and nuanced the TSH. For example, in a pair of experiments designed to examine the effect of semantic relatedness on memory for incidentally encoded material, Bowler, Gaigg and Gardiner (in press b) adapted a procedure developed by Mayes *et al.* (1992) in which high-functioning adults with and without autism were asked to study a series of words presented on a screen inside a red box. Outside the box there was another word, which could be either an associate or a nonassociate of the studied word. Memory for all words (those inside and outside the box) was subsequently tested by means of a forced-choice recognition procedure. The results showed that both groups' recognition scores were similar, that they both recognized fewer context than target words and that they also recognized more words (whether target or context) that were accompanied by a related word than were accompanied by an unrelated word. When the experiment was repeated, this time asking participants to recall as many items as they could, although there was no significant group difference in overall free recall, the interaction between group and the presence or absence of a relation between the target and context words were significant. Recall by the participants with ASDs was not enhanced when the two words were related, suggesting that although some aspects of the relation between the two words had been encoded (otherwise the results of the first experiment would have been different), this was not done in a manner that was of potential benefit to free recall. Thus, task support appears to operate at the level of semantic relatedness of incidentally encoded material.

Recent experimental investigations have also shown that the question of task support is a more complex matter than simply providing participants with clues to correct responses. The findings of two investigations highlight particular circumstances under which provision of support enhances performance and those where it does not. Gaigg, Gardiner and Bowler (in press) adapted a procedure developed by Hunt and Seta (1984) in which typical adult participants had to recall lists of words containing varying numbers of items from different categories. Hunt and Seta found that asking participants to sort items into categories at study (i.e. to concentrate on the relational aspects of the material) enhanced participants' recall of items from categories that had only a small number of exemplars in the study list (imagine having to learn a list of 58 words among which were only 2 items of furniture; the link between them might easily be overlooked). By contrast, rating the pleasantness of words at study enhanced recall of items from categories with a large number of items in the study list (imagine there being 16 vegetables in the same list; the rating task would highlight the features of each individual vegetable thus making it more memorable). For adults with Asperger syndrome (selected on present-state criteria without reference to early language development), the TSH was confirmed: instructions in relational encoding enhanced recall in a similar way to that of typical comparison participants. By contrast, when Smith, Gardiner and Bowler (2007) instructed adults with Asperger syndrome in how to make use of semantic relations among items in studied lists that contained semantically or phonologically similar words, no enhancement in recall resulted for the Asperger participants. Thus it would appear that task support, if it is to be effective at a level that goes beyond individual items, needs to entail more than simple provision of instructions to the participant, but requires active involvement as well.

A final aspect of the TSH and the phenomena that gave rise to it relates to its resonance with the findings on memory functioning in normal ageing (Craik & Anderson, 1999; Craik *et al.*, 1990). When typical individuals age, their performance on tasks of executive function that are thought to be mediated by the frontal lobes (see Fuster, 1997) are seen to diminish, and this frontal decline is accompanied by decrements in performance on unsupported memory tasks. This analogy with the normal ageing process provides a fruitful heuristic for the development of further investigations of memory in people with ASDs. For example, when older people are asked to remember complex material, such as a set of objects presented in different colours at different locations in a grid, they are relatively unimpaired at remembering individual elements (object identity, colour or location) but not in remembering specific combinations of these (Chalfonte & Johnson, 1996). Because individuals with ASDs show similar patterns of memory to those seen in older people across supported and unsupported tasks, and because autism is accompanied by some degree of diminished performance on executive tasks (Hill, 2004a, b), we would expect them to show similar patterning of memory for elements and their combinations to those seen in normal ageing. The ageing analogy is useful, not because it purports to argue that people with ASDs are like older typical individuals (the latter group have had a lifetime of typical experiences that people with autism lack), but because it provides a useful heuristic device for the exploration of patterns of memory performance in the autistic population.

The ageing analogy, in conjunction with the TSH, also serves to highlight potential causal relations between memory difficulties and patterns of performance in other domains. One domain that characteristically poses problems for people with ASDs is that of mental state understanding. There is now some evidence that typical older individuals show diminished performance on tests of mental state understanding, even when the memory load of the test procedure is minimized through the provision of task support (Maylor *et al.*, 2002). Children with autism are characteristically delayed on their performance on unexpected transfer tests of false belief (Baron-Cohen, Leslie & Frith, 1985) yet continue to perform well on tests of subtractive reasoning, which are logically similar in structure (Peterson & Bowler, 2000). In both tasks, one protagonist hides an object in one location and leaves the scene whereupon a second protagonist moves the object to another location. The first protagonist then returns and in the false belief version, children are asked 'where will [protagonist] look for the object?' In the subtractive reasoning version the question is 'if the object had not been moved, where would [protagonist] look for it?' The second question, although linguistically more complex, provides task support by constraining the range of possible answers thereby increasing the likelihood that the child will respond correctly.

On this argument, failure on false belief tasks (and, by extension, difficulties in many of the kinds of real-life situations that require such reasoning) may be because they rely on the operation of those memory processes that are relatively difficult for people with ASDs.

The role of structure: semantics and syntax

If, as advocates of multi-store theories of memory maintain, material transferred to long-term memory is represented semantically, then the intact primacy effects described in some investigations imply that the memories of people with autism must be semantically organized to some extent, even if the good rote memory described in the early clinical accounts indicates enhanced memory for items without regard to their meaning. Numerous investigators (Aurnhammer-Frith, 1969; Fyffe & Prior, 1978; Hermelin & O'Connor, 1967; O'Connor & Hermelin, 1967; Wolff & Barlow, 1979) found that comparison participants were better than matched participants with ASDs at remembering sentences than unstructured lists with the same number of words as the sentences. Moreover, the comparison participants were also often more likely to cluster semantically related items that were randomly interspersed with other words at study. These observations, together with higher recency effects in their autistic participant groups, led O'Connor and Hermelin (1967) and Boucher (1978) to conclude that the memory of children with ASD consisted of a read-out from an 'echo-box', implying little processing of the material.

Although the majority of investigations have supported the notion of diminished use of syntactic structure to aid recall in people with ASDs, Fyffe and Prior (1978) picked up on and replicated an aspect of Aurnhammer-Frith's (1969) findings, namely that this phenomenon is seen only in individuals with low intelligence, whether with or without autism, and thus may have more to do with developmental delay than autism. Ramondo and Milech (1984) observed that the experiments on the role of structure in aiding recall confounded two aspects of meaning as expressed through language: the semantic and the syntactic. When they separated these factors experimentally, they found that the difficulties experienced by children with autism were not due to insensitivity to semantic relatedness but lay in their inability to use structural aspects of verbal material. However, Tager-Flusberg (1991) observed that Ramondo and Milech's procedures utilized semantic lists that contained only nouns and syntactic lists that contained nouns and other parts of speech. When she asked children with LFA, retardation and with typical development to recall two lists of 12 words, one consisting of animal names, the other of items from 12 different categories, whereas all three groups recalled similar numbers of items from the unrelated list, the children with LFA recalled significantly fewer items from the related list than did either comparison group. This suggests that the children with LFA experienced difficulty in using semantic relatedness among study list items to aid free recall. This finding has also been demonstrated in adults and adolescents with Asperger syndrome (Bowler, Matthews & Gardiner, 1997; Smith, Gardiner & Bowler, 2007; but see Lopez & Leekam, 2003), who are also less likely to use phonological similarities among studied items to aid recall (Smith, Gardiner & Bowler, 2007). Thus, it would appear that the early clinical and experimental findings that led Hermelin and O'Connor (1970) famously to characterize autism as a failure to encode stimuli meaningfully have been confirmed by later research. However, as we are about to see, the findings of other investigations call this conclusion into question.

Studies of semantic cued recall suggest that rather than being an encoding problem, the relative difficulty experienced by people with autism in using semantic information to aid recall may result from the stored information not being available in a way that can aid retrieval (Boucher & Lewis, 1989; Boucher & Warrington, 1976; Tager-Flusberg, 1991). Further evidence in favour of the retrieval impairment account comes from studies of illusory memories (Bowler *et al.*, 2000; Kamio & Toichi, 2007; but see Beversdorf *et al.*, 2000), using a paradigm developed by Deese (1959), and revived by Roediger and McDermott (1995), in which participants are asked to study lists of words all of which are strong associates of a nonpresented word (e.g. *bed, blanket, pillow, slumber, night*, all associates of *sleep*). In both free recall and in recognition, participants often falsely recognize or recall the nonstudied associate. Bowler *et al.* reported similar levels of false recall and false recognition in adults with Asperger syndrome as in typical comparison participants matched on verbal IQ, suggesting that the Asperger participants were sensitive to the associative structure of the lists. Other studies have also reported an absence of meaning-related memory difficulties in people with ASDs. For example, Ameli *et al.* (1988) found that the performance of high-functioning adults was higher for meaningful stimuli when asked to recall meaningful (drawings of objects) or meaningless (nonsense shapes) pictures in a delayed nonmatching-to-sample paradigm. But the term 'meaning' in this context refers to something different from that used in the studies that utilized verbal material. Here, there was no syntactic or semantic relationship among the items in either list; rather, one list was analogous to nonsense syllables, and the other to iconic representations of objects. Despite using the term 'meaning', Ameli *et al.* measured something very different from that tested by the studies reported earlier. In fact, their study shows that the availability of verbal labels has a facilitatory effect on the recall of adults with autism (see Poirier & Martin, this volume, Chapter 12 for more on the role of verbal mediation in memory). It is clear that the term 'meaning' covers a range of different phenomena, each of which is associated with a specific pattern of performance in individuals with ASDs.

Relational encoding: the key to understanding the role of meaning in memory?

The observation that semantic cued recall is usually intact in both LFA and HFA, whereas semantic relations are sometimes less efficiently recruited in aid of free recall, suggests that contrary to the conclusion of Hermelin and O'Connor (1970), semantic or associative relations *are* encoded in some way in this population. What sometimes poses difficulty is the use of such relations to aid recall. The difficulty therefore seems to be in the appropriate retrieval of meaningful information or in its application to the task in hand. If this is the case, then any task where performance entails using semantic or associative relations between studied elements should show diminished performance in an ASD sample. We have already discussed Bowler, Gaigg and Gardiner's (in press b) demonstration of how memory for related and unrelated context is differentially manifested under recognition and free recall, suggesting that although some aspects of the relation between target words and context words had been encoded at study this was not done in a manner that benefited free recall in that task. This differential effect of relatedness among encoded items between recall and recognition is reminiscent of the difference described earlier between the findings on free recall of categorized lists, where people with ASDs tend not to use categorical information to enhance recall, and those on illusory memories, where they tend to be subject to associatively generated illusions. A possible explanation for this difference, as well as for the findings of Gaigg and colleagues' study (in press), lies in a consideration of the structure of the task facing participants in the two experimental procedures. In a memory illusions experiment, the list of studied words is designed so that each item activates a set of associated words. The resultant illusory item represents the intersection of these different sets of activated items. The relations between studied and activated items can be termed what Halford (1993) calls *binary relations*, i.e. there is a many-to-one relation between studied item and its activation set. Contrast this with what happens when a participant learns a categorized list of items in a way that allows categorical information to be stored in a manner that might aid recall. Here, each word has to be related to each other word in a list, as well as to its stored category representation and that of the word with which it is being compared. This is a more complex task, arguably involving what Halford calls *ternary relations*, where not only inter-word relations have to be processed but also the relations between each word and its category label.

Thinking of tasks in terms of the number of elements that have to be processed to enable their successful resolution provides a testable theoretical framework within which to explore what Minshew and her colleagues have asserted as being the major characteristic of autism, namely that it is a disorder of complex information processing (Minshew, Goldstein & Siegel, 1997; Minshew & Goldstein, 1998; Williams, Goldstein & Minshew, 2006). The advantage of Halford's relational complexity framework over that proposed by Minshew and colleagues is that the latter is somewhat ad hoc. For example, Minshew and Goldstein (2001) report typical levels of performance for participants with autism on tasks such as short-term memory and paired-associate tasks, but less good performance on tasks such as list-learning and delayed recall of stories or complex geometric figures. Whilst the grouping of such tasks along a dimension of increasing complexity makes intuitive sense, it is difficult to see how complexity in this sense can be dissociated from increasing quantity of information. An analysis in terms of relational complexity provides some way out of this difficulty by providing a conceptualization that allows tasks to be classified *a priori* as simple or complex, and thus allows a more hypothesis-led approach to complexity and cognition in autism. Relational complexity has also been applied to the understanding of false belief in children with ASDs and typical development (Andrews *et al.*, 2003: Bowler *et al.*, 2005) showing that difficulties in this domain may be a specific facet of a more general difficulty in storing information in a way that enables it to be subjected to complex processing.

Episodic remembering: time travel and self-involvement

An influential theory of memory is that put forward by Tulving (1985) in which he posits several memory systems, two of which are the semantic system, consisting of our store of factual knowledge and the episodic system, which consists of memory for personally experienced events. The latter is accompanied by a feeling of the self travelling back in time and re-experiencing the event (see Lind & Bowler, this volume, Chapter 9 for further elaboration). There are several reasons for predicting that episodic memory might be diminished in autism: both lower performance on free recall tasks and frontal lobe pathology, as evidenced by impairments on some executive function tasks, are predictive of difficulties in this domain. Reduced episodic remembering on memory tasks has been demonstrated in high-functioning individuals with ASDs (Bowler, Gardiner & Grice, 2000; Bowler, Gardiner & Gaigg, 2007; Smith, Gardiner & Bowler, 2007). In addition, a series of experiments by Bowler, Gardiner and Gaigg (2007) showed that the residual remembering reported by people with an ASD appears to be qualitatively similar to that of typical individuals, supporting the view that episodic remembering is possible but not as common in this population as it is in typical individuals.

Episodic remembering has two components: a sense of self-involvement and an understanding of a temporal stream of events through which the self can travel in order to re-experience a past event. Diminished remembering can result from difficulties with either of these two processes. Here, we will deal only with the question of why memory for temporally distinct episodes might prove difficult for people with autism; the question of self-awareness and its continuity over time is dealt with in Chapter 9. There is some evidence that people with ASDs show diminished memory for the temporal ordering of events. Bennetto, Pennington & Rogers (1996) showed diminished performance on the Corsi block task in adolescents with HFA, and Martin *et al.* (2006) observed that in a short-term serial recall task, although the number of items recalled by adults with HFA was at a similar level to that of comparison participants, they made significantly more order errors, suggesting diminished sense of temporal sequence. Problems with temporal organization of memory is also evident in the characteristic difficulties seen in the organization of narrative accounts of events (Losh & Capps, 2003) as well as the diminished story recall (Williams, Goldstein & Minshew, 2006) seen in individuals with ASDs.

Although there is no direct evidence relating to why temporal sequencing and an episodic sense of time might be hard for people with ASD (see Boucher, 2001, and Poirier & Martin, this volume, Chapter 12 for further discussion), the themes explored in the previous paragraphs may help to illuminate the question. Separating out events in time involves a capacity to bind together *episodically defined* clusters of attributes – you must remember that it was your friend John that you met in the café on the high street on the day it was raining. This capacity to bind together distinct elements of an event is, as we have already seen, compromised in normally ageing individuals (Chalfonte & Johnson, 1996; Naveh-Benjamin, 2000), and on the basis of empirical evidence described earlier on as well as for theoretical reasons (Brock *et al.*, 2002), it is plausible that similar difficulties may be evident in people with autism. It is also possible that diminished binding of elements of an episode may be restricted to retrieval and not to encoding (but see Gardiner's observation on the complementarity of the concepts of encoding and retrieval in Chapter 1), thus opening the way to possible intervention strategies involving task support. In addition to helping to explain difficulties with episodic remembering in people with autism, the notion of binding may have more general explanatory power in relation to the patterning of memory in this population.

Different bindings, different memories

In controlled tests of memory, people with autism behave unremarkably when supported test procedures are utilized. When retrieval requires greater reliance on an individual's own resources, differences begin to appear. The common thread that underlies these differences appears to be a difficulty in establishing relations among disparate items of information in memory, either to establish semantic links or to make episodically defined clusters of attributes available for subsequent retrieval. It may also be the case that difficulty in accessing episodically defined clusters renders the processing of complex, ternary relations among items more difficult, thus compromising certain kinds of online problem solving such as that required in social situations.

It would be a mistake to see these difficulties as the result of an *inability* to establish links among disparate items of information. Much of the evidence reviewed here suggests that far from being incapable of encoding semantic relations or of retrieving episodic memories, people with ASDs are able to do these things. They just do them to a lesser extent than typical individuals. This observation makes the task of explaining the patterns of memory performance one of accounting for why performance on certain tasks may be quantitatively diminished yet remain qualitatively intact, rather than trying to document a set of impairments. A recent experimental study may provide the beginnings of an explanation for why binding might be intact yet diminished in people with ASDs. Bowler, Gaigg and Gardiner (in press a) carried out an experiment based on a procedure developed by Tulving (1962) in which participants with and without HFA were asked to free recall the same list of 16 words on 16 consecutive trials. The order of presentation of the words was different on each trial. Tulving (1962) found that despite the differing order of presentation on each trial, participants tended to organize their recall of the lists subjectively and that this subjective organization correlated with improvements in recall over trials. Bowler, Gaigg and Gardiner (in press a) found similar results for adults with HFA. But they also found that whereas the subjective organization of the members of the typical comparison group tended to converge to a common pattern over trials, that of the HFA participants did not. On the basis of these findings alone, it is not possible to determine why this should happen, but a consideration of this finding together with earlier research allows some speculations to be made.

Typical individuals tend to organize material conceptually. But it is possible that people with ASDs may, in addition, organize material according to other stimulus parameters – perhaps by initial letter, number of syllables, etc. This tendency not to limit the organization of verbal material simply on the basis of its conceptual attributes is borne out by findings such as those of Renner, Klinger and Klinger (2000) mentioned earlier. They found that although children with HFA had similar levels of free recall to typically developing children, their recency effect was higher and their primacy effect was lower, suggesting that they were recalling information on the basis of nonsemantic features. This greater reliance on nonsemantic features resonates with the enhanced perceptual functioning hypothesis put forward by Mottron *et al.* (2006), who argue that individuals with ASDs have an over-functioning perceptual system that more effectively competes with conceptual processing than is the case in typical individuals. This means that in any situation where typical individuals will process wholes rather than parts, or conceptual rather than perceptual features, a person with an ASD will be more likely than a typical individual to favour a perceptually oriented analysis. The further repercussions for this on memory are as yet largely untested in a hypothesis-driven manner, but many of the findings reviewed in this chapter are consistent with it. Diminished relational encoding, poor binding of episodically defined stimulus complexes, reduced encoding of context all suggest that the enduring representations of experience that are laid down by people with ASD are different from those of typical individuals. The repercussions of this on activities that rely on memory are considerable. Effective social interaction entails the establishment of a shared frame of reference, which in typical individuals seems to centre on semantic systems that are built up on the basis of abstract systems of meaning. If, however, each individual builds up their own slightly different set of representations based on an arbitrary subset of the available information, which is what people with ASD seem to do, then communication and interaction will tend to be compromised. Behaviour that is driven in a top-down fashion by knowledge that is built up differently may appear odd and stereotyped in the way that people with ASD sometimes seem to typical individuals.

Conclusion

In sum, much of what can be considered under the heading of 'memory' in people with ASD is not unduly different from what is found in typical individuals. But the patterning of what subtle differences there are can give us some clues to how the minds of people with ASD work. It seems that recollection is more under the control of the here and now, and when such recollection involves personally experienced events, these are remembered as one would a fact such as the boiling point of water. The narrative order of streams of events appear to be recalled with difficulty, and relations among events that are based on semantic links do not appear to figure in the remembering process to the same extent as in the recall of typical individuals. Precisely why memory in ASD should be patterned in this way is still a matter of conjecture, but there is a growing body of research that suggests that it may result from difficulties in binding disparate elements of experience in a way that transcends the perceptual aspects of stimuli. These difficulties have knock-on effects on the development of more abstract semantic representations of experience and on the recollection of personally experienced, temporally ordered events. Such difficulties repercuss on other areas of functioning such as executive control and social interaction, yielding the patterns of autistic symptomatology seen in everyday life.

Acknowledgement

The authors would like to thank the Wellcome Trust and the Medical Research Council for financial support in the preparation of this chapter.

References

Ameli, R., Courchesne, E., Lincoln, A., Kaufman, A. S. & Grillon, C. (1988). Visual memory processes in high-functioning individuals with autism. *Journal of Autism and Developmental Disorders, 18*, 601–615.

American Psychiatric Association (2000). *Diagnostic and statistical manual of mental disorders*, 4th edn, text revision. (DSM-IV-TR) Washington, DC: American Psychiatric Association.

Andrews, G., Halford, G. S., Bunch, K. M., Bowden, D. & Jones, T. (2003). Theory of mind and relational complexity. *Child Development, 74*, 1476–1499.

Atkinson, R. C. & Shiffrin, R. M. (1968). Human memory: a control system and its control processes. In K. W. Spence & J. T. Spence (eds.), *The Psychology of learning and motivation: advances in research and theory*, vol. 2, pp. 89–195. New York: Academic Press.

Aurnhammer-Frith, U. (1969). Emphasis and meaning in recall in normal and autistic children. *Language and Speech*, *12*, 29–38.

Baddeley, A. D. & Warrington, E. K. (1970). Amnesia and the distinction between long- and short-term memory. *Journal of Verbal Learning and Verbal Behavior*, *9*, 176–189.

Baron-Cohen, S., Leslie, A. & Frith, U. (1985). Does the autistic child have a 'theory of mind'? *Cognition*, *21*, 37–46.

Bartak, L., Rutter, M. & Cox, A. (1975). A comparative study of infantile autism and specific developmental receptive language disorder. I. The children. *British Journal of Psychiatry*, *126*, 127–145.

Barth, C., Fein, D. & Waterhouse, L. (1995). Delayed match-to-sample performance in autistic children. *Developmental Neuropsychology*, *11*, 53–69.

Bennetto, L., Pennington, B. F. & Rogers, S. J. (1996). Intact and impaired memory function in autism. *Child Development*, *67*, 1816–1835.

Beversdorf, D. Q., Smith, B. W., Crucian, G. P., Anderson, J. M., Keillor, J. M., Barrett, A. M., Hughes, J. D., Felopulos, G. J., Bauman, M. L., Nadeau, S. E. & Heilman, K. M. (2000). Increased discrimination of 'false memories' in autism spectrum disorder. *Proceedings of the National Academy of Sciences of the United States of America*, *97*, 8734–8737.

Boucher, J. (1978). Echoic memory capacity in autistic children. *Journal of Child Psychology and Psychiatry*, *19*, 161–166.

(1981). Immediate free recall in early childhood autism: another point of behavioural similarity with the amnesic syndrome. *British Journal of Psychology*, *72*, 211–215.

(2001). Lost in a sea of time: time parsing and autism. In C. Hoerl & T. McCormack (eds.), *Time and memory: issues in philosophy and psychology*, pp. 111–135. Oxford: Oxford University Press.

Boucher, J. & Lewis, V. (1989). Memory impairments and communication in relatively able autistic children. *Journal of Child Psychology and Psychiatry*, *30*, 99–122.

Boucher, J. & Warrington, E. K. (1976). Memory deficits in early infantile autism: some similarities to the amnesic syndrome. *British Journal of Psychology*, *67*, 73–87.

Bowler, D. M., Briskman, J. A., Gurvidi, N. & Fornells-Ambrojo, M. (2005). Autistic and nonautistic children's performance on a non-social analogue of the false belief task. *Journal of Cognition and Development*, *6*, 259–283.

Bowler, D. M., Gaigg, S. B. & Gardiner, J. M. (in press a). Subjective organisation in the free recall learning of adults with Asperger's syndrome. *Journal of Autism and Developmental Disorders*.

(in press b). Effects of related and unrelated context on recall and recognition by adults with high-functioning autism spectrum disorder. *Neuropsychologia*.

Bowler, D. M., Gardiner, J. M. & Berthollier, N. (2004). Source memory in Asperger's syndrome. *Journal of Autism and Developmental Disorders*, *34*, 533–542.

Bowler, D. M., Gardiner, J. M. & Gaigg, S. B. (2007). Factors affecting conscious awareness in the recollective experience of adults with Asperger's syndrome. *Consciousness and Cognition, 16*, 124–143.

Bowler, D. M., Gardiner, J. M. & Grice, S. (2000). Episodic memory and remembering in adults with Asperger's syndrome. *Journal of Autism and Developmental Disorders, 30*, 305–316.

Bowler, D. M., Gardiner, J. M., Grice, S. & Saavalainen, P. (2000). Memory illusions: false recall and recognition in high functioning adults with autism. *Journal of Abnormal Psychology, 109*, 663–672.

Bowler, D. M., Matthews, N. J. & Gardiner, J. M. (1997). Asperger's syndrome and memory: similarity to autism but not amnesia. *Neuropsychologia, 35*, 65–70.

Brock, J., Brown, C. C., Boucher, J. & Rippon, G. (2002). The temporal binding deficit hypothesis of autism. *Development and Psychopathology, 14*, 209–224.

Chalfonte, B. L. & Johnson, M. K. (1996). Feature memory and binding in young and older adults. *Memory and Cognition, 24*, 403–416.

Craik, F. I. M. & Anderson, N. D. (1999). Applying cognitive research to the problems of ageing. *Attention and Performance, 17*, 583–615.

Craik, F. I. M., Morris. L. W., Morris, R. G. & Loewen, E. R. (1990). Relations between source amnesia and frontal lobe functioning in older adults. *Psychology and Aging, 5*, 148–151.

Deese, J. (1959). On the prediction of occurrence of particular verbal intrusions in immediate recall. *Journal of Experimental Psychology, 58*, 17–22.

Frith, U. (1970). Studies in pattern detection in normal and autistic children. *Journal of Abnormal Psychology, 76*, 413–420.

   (1989). *Autism: explaining the enigma*. Oxford: Blackwell.

Fuster, J. M. (1997). *The pre-frontal cortex: anatomy, physiology and neuropsychology of the frontal lobe*. Philadelphia: Lippincott-Raven.

Fyffe, C. & Prior, M. (1978). Evidence for language recoding in autistic, retarded and normal children: a re-examination. *British Journal of Psychology, 69*, 393–402.

Gaigg, S. B., Gardiner, J. M. & Bowler, D. M. (in press). Free recall in Asperger syndrome: the role of relational and item-specific encoding. *Neuropsychologia.*

Gardiner, J. M., Bowler, D. M. & Grice, S. J. (2003). Further evidence of preserved priming and preserved recall in adults with Asperger syndrome. *Journal of Autism and Developmental Disorders, 33*, 259–269.

Halford, G. S. (1993). *Children's understanding: the development of mental models*. Hillsdale, NJ: Erlbaum.

Hermelin, B. & O'Connor, N. (1967). Remembering of words by psychotic and subnormal children. *British Journal of Psychology, 58*, 213–218.

   (1970). *Psychological experiments with autistic children*. Oxford: Pergamon Press.

   (1975). The recall of digits by normal, deaf and autistic children. *British Journal of Psychology, 66*, 203–209.

Hill, E. L. (2004a). Executive dysfunction in autism. *Trends in Cognitive Sciences, 8*, 26–32.

   (2004b). Evaluating the theory of executive dysfunction in autism. *Developmental Review, 24*, 189–233.

Hunt, R. R. & Seta, C. E. (1984). Category size effects in recall: the role of relational and item-specific information. *Journal of Experimental Psychology: Learning, Memory and Cognition, 10,* 454–464.

Joseph, R., Steele, S., Meyer, E. & Tager-Flusberg, H. (2005). Self-ordered pointing in children with autism: failure to use verbal mediation in the service of working memory? *Neuropsychologia, 43,* 1400–1411.

Kamio, Y. & Toichi, M. (2007). Memory illusion in high-functioning autism and Asperger disorder. *Journal of Autism and Developmental Disorders, 37,* 867–876.

Kanner, L. (1943). Autistic disturbances of affective contact. *Nervous Child, 2,* 217–250.

Losh, M. & Capps, L. (2003). Narrative ability in high-functioning children with autism or Asperger syndrome. *Journal of Autism and Developmental Disorders, 33,* 239–251.

López, B. & Leekam, S. (2003). The use of context in children with autism. *Journal of Child Psychology and Psychiatry, 44,* 285–300.

Martin, J. S., Poirier, M., Bowler, D. M. & Gaigg, S. B. (2006). Short-term serial recall in individuals with Asperger syndrome. Poster presented at the International Meeting For Autism Research, Montreal.

Mayes, A. R., MacDonald, C., Donlan, L., Pears, J. & Meudell, P. R. (1992). Amnesics have disproportionately severe memory deficit for interactive context. *Quarterly Journal of Experimental Psychology – Section A: Human Experimental Psychology, 45,* 265–297.

Maylor, E. A., Moulson, J. M., Muncer, A-M. & Taylor, L. A. (2002). Does performance on theory of mind tasks decline in old age? *British Journal of Psychology, 93,* 465–458.

Minshew, N. J. & Goldstein, G. (1993). Is autism an amnesic disorder? Evidence from the California Verbal Learning Test. *Neuropsychology, 7,* 209–216.

(1998). Autism as a disorder of complex information processing. *Mental Retardation and Developmental Disabilities Research Reviews, 4,* 129–136.

(2001). The pattern of intact and impaired memory functions in autism. *Journal of Child Psychology and Psychiatry, 7,* 1095–1101.

Minshew, N. J., Goldstein, G. & Siegel, D. J. (1995). Speech and language in high-functioning autistic individuals. *Neuropsychology, 9,* 255–261.

(1997). Neuropsychologic functioning in autism: profile of a complex information processing disorder. *Journal of the International Neuropsychological Society, 3,* 303–316.

Minshew, N., Goldstein, G., Muenz, L. R. & Payton, J. (1992). Neuropsychological functioning in nonmentally retarded autistic individuals. *Journal of Clinical and Experimental Neuropsychology, 14,* 749–761.

Mottron, L., Dawson, M., Soulières, I., Hubert, B. & Burack, J. (2006). Enhanced perceptual functioning in autism: an update and eight principles of autistic perception. *Journal of Autism and Developmental Disorders, 36,* 27–43.

Mottron, L., Morasse, K. & Belleville, S. (2001). A study of memory functioning in individuals with autism. *Journal of Child Psychology and Psychiatry, 42,* 253–260.

Naveh-Benjamin, M. (2000). Adult age differences in memory performance: tests of an associative deficit hypothesis. *Journal of Experimental Psychology: Learning, Memory and Cognition, 26,* 1170–1187.

O'Connor, N. & Hermelin, B. (1967). Auditory and visual memory in autistic and normal children. *Journal of Mental Deficiency Research, 11,* 126–131.

Peterson, D. & Bowler, D. M. (2000). Counterfactual reasoning and false belief understanding in children with autism, children with severe learning difficulties and children with typical development. *Autism, 4,* 391–405.

Ramondo, N. & Milech, D. (1984). The nature and specificity of the language coding deficit in autistic children. *British Journal of Psychology, 75,* 95–103.

Renner, P., Klinger, L. G. & Klinger, M. (2000). Implicit and explicit memory in autism: is autism an amnesic disorder? *Journal of Autism and Developmental Disorders, 30,* 3–14.

Roediger III, H. & McDermott, K. (1993). Implicit memory in normal human subjects. In M. Spinnler & F. Boller (eds.), *Handbook of neuropsychology,* vol. 8, pp. 63–131. Amsterdam: Elsevier.

  (1995). Creating false memories: remembering words not presented in lists. *Journal of Experimental Psychology: Learning, Memory and Cognition, 21,* 803–814.

Rumsey, J. M. & Hamburger, S. D. (1988). Neuropsychological findings in high-functioning men with infantile autism, residual state. *Journal of Clinical and Experimental Neuropsychology, 10,* 201–221.

Schwartz, S. (1981). Language disabilities in infantile autism: a review and comment. *Applied Psycholinguistics, 2,* 25–31.

Smith, B. J., Gardiner, J. M. & Bowler, D. M. (2007). Deficits in free recall persist in Asperger's syndrome despite training in the use of list-appropriate learning strategies. *Journal of Autism and Developmental Disorders, 37,* 445–454.

Summers, J. A. & Craik, F. I. M. (1994). The effects of subject-performed tasks on the memory performance of verbal autistic children. *Journal of Autism and Developmental Disorders, 24,* 773–783.

Tager-Flusberg, H. (1991). Semantic processing in the free recall of autistic children: further evidence for a cognitive deficit. *British Journal of Developmental Psychology, 9,* 417–430.

Toichi, M. & Kamio, Y. (2003). Long-term memory in high-functioning autism: controversy on episodic memory in autism reconsidered. *Journal of Autism and Developmental Disorders, 33,* 151–161.

Tubbs, V. K. (1966). Types of linguistic disability in psychotic children. *Journal of Mental Deficiency Research, 10,* 230–240.

Tulving, E. (1962). Subjective organisation in the free recall of 'unrelated' words. *Psychological Review, 69,* 344–354.

  (1985). Memory and consciousness. *Canadian Psychology, 26,* 1 12.

Whitehouse, A. J. O., Maybery, M. T. & Durkin, K. (2006). Inner speech impairments in autism. *Journal of Child Psychology and Psychiatry, 47,* 857–865.

Williams, D. L., Goldstein, G. & Minshew, N. J. (2006). The profile of memory function in autism. *Neuropsychology, 20,* 20–29.

Wing, L. (1981). Asperger's syndrome: a clinical account. *Psychological Medicine, 11,* 115–129.

Wing, L. & Gould, J. (1979). Severe impairments of social interaction and associated abnormalities in children: epidemiology and classification. *Journal of Autism and Developmental Disorders*, 9, 11–29.

Wolff, S. & Barlow, A. (1979). Schizoid personality in childhood: a comparative study of schizoid, autistic and normal children. *Journal of Child Psychology and Psychiatry*, 20, 29–46.

World Health Organization. (1993). *International classification of diseases*, 10th edn (ICD-10). Geneva: WHO.

Index